In the Shadow of Sectarianism

In the Shadow
of Sectarianism

LAW, SHIʿISM, AND THE
MAKING OF MODERN LEBANON

Max Weiss

HARVARD UNIVERSITY PRESS
Cambridge, Massachusetts, and London, England • 2010

Library of Congress Cataloging-in-Publication Data

Weiss, Max, 1977–
  In the shadow of sectarianism : law, Shi'ism, and the making of modern Lebanon /
Max Weiss.
    p. cm.
  Includes bibliographical references and index.
  ISBN 978-0-674-05298-7 (alk. paper)
 1. Shi'ah—Lebanon.   2. Status (Law)—Lebanon.   3. Lebanon—Ethnic relations.
4. Religion and state—Lebanon.   I. Title.
  DS80.55.S54W45 2010
  305.6'9782095692—dc22   2010008323

For Shirley

Contents

Preface

In the words of Marshall Sahlins, "the world is under no obligation to conform to the logic by which some people conceive it." Nothing could have driven home this point to me quite like the rich experience I have had as a foreign researcher in Lebanon, and, even more broadly, as an outsider writing about Lebanese history. To be sure, this adventure has proved to be a double-edged sword. On the one hand, my research and I were (and, no doubt, will continue to be) subject to scrutiny if not full-blown suspicion by some. I hope that this book clarifies the nature of my commitment to critically engaged scholarship in and on Lebanon and will open even more lines of communication within the field. Meanwhile, on the other hand, my outsider status afforded me certain opportunities to make use of primary sources housed in locations where few others had thought to look, which has meant, to some extent I hope, that I have been able to think beyond sedimented conventional wisdom about Lebanon and Lebanese history.

Ironically enough, I set out to write a story about Lebanon without talking about sectarianism. It is perhaps surprising in some ways, therefore, but unsurprising in others, that I ended up writing precisely a history of sectarianism, one that I hope succeeds in being both a detailed case study as well as a sufficiently nuanced and critical analysis. In contrast to the voluminous studies of Shi'ism in Lebanon already out there, this book is concerned in large part with the social, legal, and religious history of the Shi'i milieu in Lebanon under French Mandate rule. Moreover, it is also the first book to rely upon the records—*sijillat, mahadir,* and other documentary evidence— retained in the Ja'fari *shari'a* courts. These are rare documents kept in fragile institutions that have managed to survive for reasons of personal and collective care, to say nothing of historical accident and contingency. Over the course of the twentieth (and twenty-first) century, the "courts" in South Lebanon and Beirut where I did research have been bombed, burned, water-logged, transported on numerous occasions from one site to another, and even tangled up in the transient and shifting nets of political rivalry.

Many visitors to Lebanon—myself included—are struck by its natural splendor. Through the myriad twists and turns of my own research, I have also been inspired by the local built environment, and, in this respect, one improbable building had an exceptionally important role. The first Ja'fari *shari'a* court in Beirut—which later housed the Higher Ja'fari Court (*mahkamat al-tamyiz*)—was an old two-story villa in Ra's al-Naba'a, located just off al-Nuwayri Street, a beautiful ramshackle building that evoked in me fond but perhaps also impossibly nostalgic sentiments towards an "old Beirut" of villas, orchards, and open agricultural spaces. The bulk of my field research in Lebanon was bookended by two moments of tragedy in the recent history of modern Lebanon. Several weeks after I arrived in Beirut, Prime Minister Rafiq al-Hariri was assassinated in a car bombing that left over a score dead and initiated a slew of targeted killings that plagued the country throughout the period of my field research. Later on, toward the end of my research, I happened to leave Lebanon just weeks before the eruption of the 2006 war. By sheer coincidence, a trip that was meant to be a two-week vacation in California in order to attend the wedding of two dear friends stretched out into months of waiting, nail-biting, and often little more than impotent political outrage. On my first trip back to Lebanon the following winter, I was stunned to discover that the old court in Ra's al-Naba'a had been razed to the ground. Disoriented, my initial conclusion was that the building had been destroyed during the war. Later on I learned that the house had been demolished intentionally and that the Ja'fari court had been moved to the UNESCO building near Corniche al-Mazra'a. In this book I argue that the institutionalization of Shi'ism in Lebanon during the Mandate period represented the gradual process of Shi'i empowerment and publicization. Perhaps this more recent relocation of the court might also be said to symbolize the accelerated pace of institutionalization and empowerment experienced by the Shi'i community in Lebanon during the late twentieth century and early twenty-first century, a process that continues to unfold and to mystify.

In the Shadow of Sectarianism

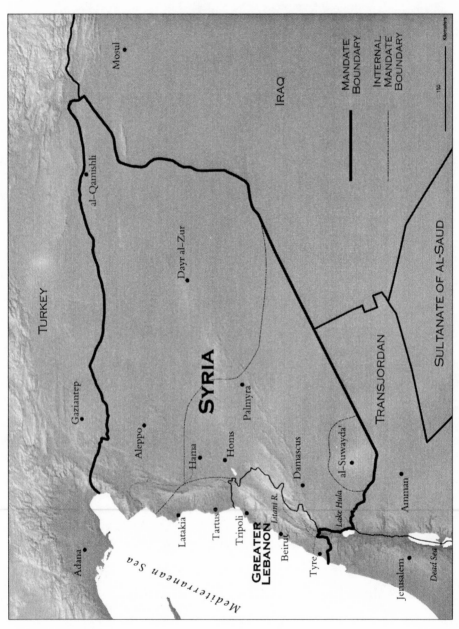

Map 1. The Eastern Mediterranean under Mandate Rule.

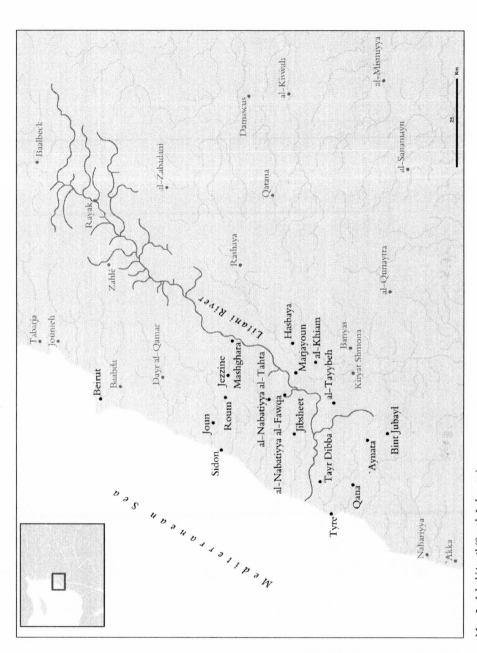

Map 2. Jabal 'Amil (South Lebanon).

Prologue—Shi'ism, Sectarianism, Modernity

In an interview with the Lebanese film critic Mohammad Soueid, acclaimed Syrian filmmaker Omar Amiralay (b. 1944) reflects on one of his earliest childhood visions, remembering "almost a fantastical image, not in its chronology, but in its location. I saw a touring bear trainer in Jounieh," the coastal city just north of Beirut. When pressed further on the incident, Amiralay hypothesizes, "I think he was a *Metwellite*. Or maybe he was a Gypsy." Asked how he had come to that conclusion, he replies, "We were told that *Metwellites* showcased animal acts and roped their goats with bells." The interviewer asks, "Did you insist on calling Shi'ites *Metwellites?*" "It was common practice then," Amiralay responds. "The referent *Metwellite* did not have a religious connotation in a sectarian mindset. In popular parlance, it referred to people who lived in misery. Before the emergence of Moussa el-Sadr, I did not know there were Shi'ites in Lebanon. In fact, for a long time, I did not even know there were Sunnis and Shi'ites in Islam."[1] By the early 1960s, the Shi'i milieu in Lebanon was in the process of gradually acquiring an ideological framework through which to launch social movements and to deploy political rhetoric that would articulate specific claims to sectarian rights and representation, whether or not neighboring Syrians were (or, more likely in this case, would openly claim to be) aware of these phenomena. Perhaps by mobilizing politically, by imbuing the term Métouali or Mitwali or Metwallite (or Matawila in the plural)—all various transliterations of what was then a more or less derogatory term referring to Shi'i Muslims—with new meaning, by casting off the dead weight of reductive and inaccurate narratives of their history, the Shi'i community could aspire to correct a whole host of social, cultural and religious misunderstandings, not least those that might involve animal husbandry.

Meanwhile, at about the same historical moment in the early 1960s, Shaykh Muhammad Jawad Mughniyya addressed the Lebanese Parliament. At this point Mughniyya was an independent religious intellectual but had formerly been president of the Ja'fari *shari'a* court, an institution that this book discusses in close detail. Railing against the continued marginalization of the Shi'i community in matters of political appointments in the government as well as the stubbornly scarce resources earmarked for Jabal 'Amil (South Lebanon) and the Biqa' Valley in the state budget, Mughniyya cogently argued that criticism of government policy or social issues from the position of "the sect" would always remain somewhat contradictory. Opposing positions taken by the South Lebanon Shi'i *za'im* Kamil al-As'ad, who was a powerful government minister with portfolio, Mughniyya affirmed, "the Shi'i sect doesn't believe in sectarianism, but if the Shi'a have a role in building this state then they must go out to play this role." Mughniyya went on to address the Shi'i minister directly, insisting, "this state is founded upon sectarianism, so how do you expect your sect, in the name of which you have been a member of parliament and a minister, to work at building the state while at the same time you expect [the sect] not to believe in the sectarianism that this state is founded upon"? Mughniyya concluded his circuitous remarks on the topic of national loyalty: "Yes, the Shi'a don't believe in sectarianism as an end in itself, but they believe in Lebanon and its constitution, so if they speak of sectarianism, and make demands in its name, they do so as a means of applying the constitution that stipulates it."[2]

Lebanese sectarianism could alternatively be portrayed and perceived, then, as both social malady and political remedy. One clever way around this apparent conundrum was proposed by Imam Musa al-Sadr, the larger-than-life figure who endeavored to lead the Lebanese Shi'i community out of obscurity, poverty, and marginality and into the limelight, catapulting the Lebanese Shi'a onto the world stage in the process. In an interview with *al-Hawadith* magazine in 1966, three years before the formal establishment of the Supreme Islamic Shi'i Council (SISC), al-Sadr suggested salvaging the utility of what was increasingly identified as an alarmingly divisive Lebanese sectarianism. The SISC has often been rightfully referred to as one of the most important institutions exemplifying Lebanese Shi'i empowerment. Here, al-Sadr explodes the conceptual apparatus of sectarianism into at least two distinct moral categories. What he called "positive sectarianism" would encompass the notion that "every sect be interested in reforming the affairs of their people (*abna'*), raising their moral, cultural and social level, and I don't believe this meaning of sectarianism is a matter to be condemned." On the other hand, al-Sadr proposed the notion of "negative sectarianism," namely, situations in which members of one particular sect "try to limit their lives to the people (*abna'*) of their sect, in isolation from the other sect, this meaning of sectarianism can be deemed social segregation and creates a barrier in the road of the development of society."[3] In taking this upbeat and positive perspective on the issue, Imam Musa al-Sadr effectively endorsed what the founding fathers of the Lebanese Republic—including the first president Beshara al-Khoury and the first prime minister Riad al-Solh—perceived to be the elemental social glue holding the country together, periodically referred to as, among other things, "sectarian affection" or "just sectarianism" (*al-ta'ifiyya al-'adila*).[4]

Without intentionally applying such rigorous standards of moral judgment to the description and interpretation of sectarianism, this book surveys some of the premises, practices, and historical processes of becoming sectarian in twentieth-century Lebanon, mainly through an account of some new ways in which the Lebanese Shi'i community became sectarian under French Mandate rule. Sectarianism is hardly the only meaningful category or theme for understanding Lebanese history, especially insofar as sectarian identity in Lebanon has historically proved malleable and fluid enough to function as a subnational, supranational, or even national signifier. And yet, long before the political mobilization of the Shi'i community under the charismatic influence of Imam Musa al-Sadr, decades before the radicalization of the Shi'i community and its adhesion to two dominant political currents, Amal and Hizballah, Shi'i sectarian identity was fundamentally, albeit gradually, being transformed and reimagined during this period. Narratives of Lebanese history and the Shi'i milieu informed by what I call the "mobilization" or "radicalization" thesis cling to what this book casts as both a partial narrative and a somewhat outmoded argument. Through administrative techniques reliant upon formal recognition—namely, the sanctioned public performance of hitherto forbidden religious practices as well as the establishment of new jurisdictions of Shi'i "personal status," which would subsequently be developed into the broader category and practice of family law—the French colonial state contributed to rendering the Shi'i community in Jabal ʿAmil and Beirut more visible, more empowered, but also *more sectarian,* in ways that it had never quite been before.[5]

Meanwhile, these gradual processes of transformation within the Shiʿi milieu in French Mandate Lebanon, which I refer to as sectarianization, paradoxically took place in the shadow of sectarianism, a point that may not be immediately obvious. Shiʿi communities in the Arab world have long been saddled with the obligation of crafting their religious, political, and cultural identities in the wake of a contested history of division, polemic, and, from time to time, heresiology. Historically, the shadow of sectarianism was cast upon Shiʿi Muslims through constructions and definitions of religious orthodoxy, at least in theory, and often enough in practice as well— one part of the legacy of early Islamic history. The institutional structure of the modern state in certain Middle Eastern contexts—Lebanon and Iraq, most notably—incorporated local communities in ways that were more or less determined by the demands of political sectarianism. Recent historical scholarship on Lebanon has more accurately located the emergence of modern sectarianism at some point in the nineteenth century. But the historical experience and processes of social and political development within the hitherto peripheral contexts of the Shiʿi community in Jabal ʿAmil and the Biqaʿ Valley remain obscured, in the shadow of what might be thought of as official or mainstream sectarianism in Beirut and Mount Lebanon. To be sure, the Shiʿi community was relatively quiescent politically speaking and culturally marginal during the French Mandate period, with occasional exceptions; as this book demonstrates, the transformation of Shiʿi sectarian identity in the Lebanese context was gradual, so subtle, in fact, as to appear unremarkable for most historians. But marginality or quiescence or even intentional quietism need not automatically be translated into historical irrelevance or historiographical invisibility. In this sense, therefore, and as opposed to more dramatic instances of sectarian discord—as in the 1840–1861 or 1975–1991 periods, most importantly—transformations in law, society, and religious culture within the Lebanese Shiʿi milieu under the French Mandate can also be located in the shadow of hegemonic interpretations of sectarianism, informed by taken-for-granted assumptions regarding the relationship between sectarianism and violence, or, at least, between sectarianism and states of political or cultural exception. My approach to everyday engagements with and creative appropriations of Shiʿi sectarianism in

French Mandate Lebanon, in contrast, aims to illustrate some other ways in which sectarianism has been imagined, experienced, and understood by various communities at different moments through time.

"As long as it is sectarian," Robert Fisk commented in the aftermath of the 2006 war, "Lebanon cannot become a modern state. The problem is that without being sectarian, Lebanon will no longer exist." In this seemingly commonsensical and widely influential formulation, sectarianism and modernity are fundamentally at odds, apparently irreconcilable, and yet sectarianism here is still equated with the conditions of possibility for being Lebanese. The subtle logic embedded in this pithy summation of Lebanese politics and political identities past and present points up the power of sectarianism as an overarching conceptual categorization in both scholarly and popular engagements with modern Lebanon. Linking sectarianism to existence in this way is more than rhetorical hyperbole, however, especially in the light of certain, but perhaps less well known, historical precedent. It is consonant with one tacit assumption held by French colonial authorities in Mandate Lebanon nearly seventy years ago. Reporting to his superiors in Beirut and Paris, one French official commented on how Shi'i Muslims in Lebanon "have been authorized to have their own courts of personal status [and] their *waqf* properties, institutions that in a country where everything is organized on confessional bases, give a community its legal existence."[6]

But is it reasonable to conclude, based on the historical evidence, that without being sectarian the modern state in Lebanon "will no longer exist"? What impact and effect has the so-called "weak state" in Lebanon had on the construction and conduct of various sectors within Lebanese society and culture? Are sect and sectarianism meaningful analytical categories for the study of Lebanon and, by the same token, the Middle East more generally? What is the relationship between sectarianism and modernity, and how has it changed over time? Why is sectarianism such an enduring phenomenon in the modern Middle East? Historians of the modern Middle East have tackled questions related to the uneven integration of the region into the world capitalist economy, the rise and fall of imperial polities, the emergence of nationalism and other ideologies, as well as the establishment of the Middle East state system and the construction of nation-states in the colonial and postcolonial periods. Within this broad and multiform narrative—which is understood here to encompass Orientalist, modernizationist, social scientific, and Marxist, but also culturalist, approaches to the history of the modern Middle East—the persistence or intrusion of stubborn sub-national ethnic or religious identities is often viewed as a direct challenge to the successful and ostensibly noble development of more coherently modern politics, cultures and identities.

Sectarianism and modernity can no longer be simplistically understood as inherently antagonistic; placing the terms side by side here may not nec-essarily be perceived as a radical move. Be that as it may, sectarianism and modernity remain slippery concepts, and historians and social scientists must offer richer, more satisfying explanations of both phenomena, as well as accounts of the historical transformation of each in relationship to the other. Unraveling the tenuous and untenable claims that purport to render sectarianism and modernity incompatible requires greater sensitivity to a broader palette of historical experience, which is precisely the work of this book. The remainder of this introduction maps out the conceptual and theo-retical terrain of the book, which lies at the interface of ongoing academic and political debates over the complicated correspondence between reli-gion and sectarianism, the practical and discursive dimensions of religious modernity, the impact of colonialism on the legal, political, and cultural construction of various kinds of difference—sectarianism, communalism, tribalism and so forth—as well as the role of the colonial and postcolonial state in promoting and authenticating sectarianism.[7]

How Did the Lebanese Shi'a Become Sectarian?

The fin-de-siècle Orientalist Israel Friedlaender wrote, "though figuring among the largest sects in the world," Shi'ism "is yet known but by name to the educated layman and not always grasped in its true character even by the student of the Orient." Despite the fact that sectarian polemic and heterodox movements were long the stock in trade among certain trends in the clas-sical Orientalist study of Islam, and despite the tumultuous circumstances that have moved Shi'ism onto the world stage in the late twentieth century, the social misunderstanding Friedlaender noted at the dawn of the twen-tieth century has only begun to change in the early twenty-first.[8] Even as scholarly, governmental, journalistic and popular discourses seem to burst at the seams with commentaries, discussions and predictions about Shi'isms both global and local, significant gaps remain in the historical record regarding the social, cultural, and intellectual development of Shi'i communities worldwide. The term sectarian is somehow always linked adjectivally in some of the following ways: sectarian violence, sectarian killing, sectarian tension, sectarian discord, sectarian hatred, etc. But whereas a cacophony of voices has identified the negative aspects of sectarianism, few probe deeply into the premises, practices, and historical processes that have maintained sectarianism as an overdetermined social, political, and cultural reality.

In an important essay on the genesis of historical Shi'ism written nearly half a century ago, Marshall Hodgson argues that the Shi'a became a sect through a gradual process of definition. Those who opposed the transfer of power and authority from the Prophet Muhammad to his companion Abu Bakr and instead supported the succession of the Prophet's nephew and son-in-law, 'Ali bin Abi Talib, only gradually acquired the trappings of what could be identified as a coherent sect. The partisans of 'Ali—*shi'at 'Ali,* those who eventually came to be known as "the Shi'a"—were no more and no less than a "minority party" during the phase immediately following the death of Muhammad. The Shi'a were transformed into a sect gradually over time, and in relation to doctrinal, political, juridical, and social change. According to Hodgson, there was no identifiable sect that we can accurately and responsibly call "the Shi'a" until, at the earliest, the time of the sixth Imam Ja'far al-Sadiq (d. 765). Moreover, such terms "probably did not come into full evidence even in Ja'far's lifetime." Hodgson was one of the first Islamicists to suggest that the making of sectarianism ought to be seen as historically overdetermined rather than doctrinally predetermined. Subsequent scholarship corroborated Hodgson's cogent assessment, showing how theological doctrine, legal traditions, and politics were pillars of an institutionalized sectarianism. The traditional equation of "schools of Islamic law" (*madhahib,* s. *madhhab*) with their eponymous founders might be a useful Orientalist heuristic but it is historically imprecise.[9]

In the context of nearly two centuries of a dynamic "sectarian milieu," the majority of what came to constitute the Imami Shi'i community supported the notion that authority had been invested in a succeeding string of twelve infallible Imams—the divinely inspired and chosen representatives of God on earth who would succeed the Prophet Muhammad and his blood relatives in leading the Muslim nation (*umma*). After the death of the eleventh

Imam Hasan al-'Askari, his infant son, the twelfth Imam, Muhammad al-Mahdi, is believed to have disappeared into occultation (*ghayba*) in 874 C.E, and Imami Shi'i messianic faith holds that the return of the *mahdi* (lit. the divinely-guided one) will coincide with the realization of peace on earth at the end of time. To the extent that Shi'ism—and throughout this book the term will always refer to the Imami or Twelver Shi'i community—often tends to stand in for the "sectarian condition" par excellence, case studies of the historical experience of particular Shi'i communities or specific Shi'i milieus may shed light on a broader array of issues pertaining to the problem of sectarianism. Just as the Shi'a—a heterodox Muslim sect—and the Ja'fari *madhhab*—a veritable legal school—emerged rather later than has conventionally been thought, Shi'i sectarianism in Lebanon has also evolved over time.

The intellectual, scholarly, and political center of gravity of the Shi'i community in Greater Syria is Jabal 'Amil, a mountainous region located in present-day South Lebanon. While the historiography of Shi'ism in the modern world has been predominantly concerned with political and intellectual history—and, not coincidentally, with Iran, however justifiable such a bias may be—a significant body of scholarship has also looked at the life and work of luminary religious figures hailing from Jabal 'Amil during the late medieval and early modern period.[10] In addition to making significant scholarly and philosophical contributions, 'Amili intellectuals played an indispensable role in helping to translate the arcane traditions of scholarly Twelver Shi'ism, with significant adjustments and modifications, into the state religion of the Persian Safavid Empire at the turn of the sixteenth century.[11] For the Ottoman period, however, the practice of Shi'ism and the history of Shi'i communities in Greater Syria remain partially veiled and relatively understudied.[12]

One potential avenue toward making better sense of the modern phenomenon of sectarianism in Lebanon might be to situate it within the context of social policies and institutional practices under the Ottomans. Nineteenth-century reforms and reorganizations, collectively labeled *Tanzimat*, entailed, among other things, the institutionalization of communal legal autonomy for non-Muslims living under Ottoman rule, what historians refer to in shorthand as the *millet* system. "Can we therefore trace political confessionalism in Lebanon," Maurus Reinkowski provocatively asks, "directly to

the *millet* system which should have existed in Ottoman times?" Refusing
the simple equation of the *millet* system with multiculturalist principles,
Reinkowski protests that this genealogy would be "very unlikely. For one
thing, the Ottoman state propagating Hanefite 'orthodoxy' did not easily
recognize a large number of religious groups such as the Shiites, the Druzes,
and the Alawites."[13] It might be even more worthwhile to consider the administration of law, religion and society under Ottoman rule in terms of what
Rudolph Peters calls "a plurality of jurisdictions under Hanafi hegemony,"
rather than orthodoxy.[14] Whatever the case, it is untenable to conclude that
there has been one and only one inexorable process of Lebanese sectarianization. Rather, there have been multiple histories of Lebanese sectarianism,
a plurality of Lebanese sectarianisms. As sectarianism evolves over time,
historians must consider how certain people, certain leaderships, and certain communities, indeed how certain sects have *become* sectarian.

A system of proportional confessional representation was formally put
into place in Mount Lebanon for the first time in the mid-nineteenth century. It has been argued that the establishment in 1843 of the so-called "dual
qa'immaqamiyya" by the *Règlement Shakib Effendi* marks the first occasion of sectarian representation being institutionalized in Beirut or Mount
Lebanon.[15] In the wake of punctuated sectarian fighting in Mount Lebanon
and the Chouf Mountains during the period between 1841 and 1858, the
Ottomans promulgated the *Règlement Organique* in 1861, establishing a
unique, separate administrative body known as the *Mutasarrifiyya* to govern the province of Mount Lebanon. This moment has also been identified
as an important watershed in the emergence of institutionalized sectarianism in Lebanon, and the *Règlement Organique* introduced proportional
confessional representation for the first time. Further reforms in 1888
reconfigured the Lebanese political system, allowing for Beirut to solidify
its increasingly independent and centralized power. To be sure, however,
none of these administrative developments should be taken as teleological
signs of the inexorable institutionalization of sectarianism in the emerging
space of Lebanon.[16]

The inhabitants of the provinces of present-day South Lebanon, the
majority of whom were Shiʿi Muslims, knew the region as Jabal ʿAmil, *bilad
al-shuqayf* or *bilad bishara*. With the collapse of the Ottoman Empire at the
close of World War I, Jabal ʿAmil and the Biqaʿ Valley were formally annexed

to the state of Greater Lebanon, declared by the French in September 1920 as part of their "sphere of influence" carved out of the lands of Greater Syria (*bilad al-sham*), and fashioned into the territories of what would become the Syrian Republic and the Lebanese Republic. The Mandate system was conceived by the Allied Powers in the post-World War I settlement as a "sacred trust of civilization" set up in order to safeguard the "well-being and development" of peoples who were deemed "incapable of governing themselves," effectively a quasi-colonial arrangement set up by the European powers and given formal sanction by the recently instituted League of Nations.[17] While the Shi'i community constituted a mere 15% of the national population according to a French census in 1921, they were a clear majority in Jabal 'Amil and the Biqa' Valley. In 1932, when the most recent official census was taken in Lebanon, the Shi'a still only made up around 20% of the national population. Paradoxically, the Shi'i community in Lebanon would continue to be perceived as a minority community well into the twentieth century, even in regions where they were a numerical majority. This has cut against the Shi'a in two ways: on the one hand, their Lebanese bona fides have been called into question due to the perception of their political attachment to Syrian and pan-Arab nationalism; on the other hand, their Shi'i-ness could also become a liability, as they were often accused of being Iranophiles, or, still worse, having ethnic Persian roots. Beneath this maelstrom of ideological contradiction and political rhetoric, the history of the Shi'i milieu in modern Lebanon is strikingly complex.

Perhaps the most significant and contentious dimension of the history of Shi'i communities in the Arab world during the modern period relates to their encounters and engagements with the state. Shi'i communities in the Arab world have been caught historically between the competing pulls of universalistic forms of identity and local historical contexts. The absence of the Imam has long raised difficult theological and ethical questions regarding the permissibility of collaborating with temporal authority. By association, Shi'i scholars, jurists, and intellectuals have held conflicted and conflicting attitudes towards the state; even more uncomfortable political questions about collaborating with bureaucratic and executive power were embodied by the question of engagements with the colonial state. The emergence of new kinds of political and cultural identification would require new ways of accommodating narrowly defined sectarian loyalties with broader commitments—be they local, regional, national, or universal—during both the colonial and postcolonial periods.[18] This played out in the Shiʻi milieu under French Mandate in particular ways. On the one hand, this includes what I call "sectarianization from below," which involved simultaneous Shiʻi demands for sectarian rights and religious recognition; on the other hand, this entailed colonial or elite strategies of divide and rule that I label "sectarianization from above." By no means should this argument be misconstrued as advancing the unsustainable claim that the French invented sectarianism or that colonialism is uniquely responsible for the creation of sectarian identities in the Middle East. Rather, an intricate and contingent constellation of forces collided at this historical moment, eventually coalescing into transformed constructions of Shiʻi sectarian identity. Since sectarianism in the Lebanese context is such a highly charged and overburdened term, it would be worthwhile to unpack it a bit more.

Explaining Sectarianism

Eugene Rogan recently noted how, among other things, what is "interesting in the new scholarship on sectarianism is how it demonstrates that both the European Powers and Ottoman Christians deployed sectarianism to political ends."[19] But sectarianism in Lebanon has not always or only been deployed to political, cultural, and ideological ends in an active or intentional sense. Moreover, European and local political aims often intersected and occasionally even fell into alignment; the local deployment of sectarianism was often inflected by a whole range of concerns that varied from community to community. Rather than breaking down the conceptual apparatus of sectarianism into "positive" and "negative" versions or "European" and "local" versions, therefore, I propose explaining sectarianism in terms of its political, its institutional, and its affective significance.

First of all, then, it must be affirmed that sectarianism can be political. From as early as the mid-nineteenth century the political system in what came to be known as Lebanon has been structured by a logic and practice of proportional confessional representation, which I will refer to as "political sectarianism." But historians must also remain attentive to other processes that transformed the institutions and practices of political sectarianism. The production and maintenance of sectarianism in Lebanon has been perpetuated, in large measure, by the administrative and parliamentary structures in which positions of power and political authority are allocated according to sectarian metrics.

Second, sectarianism can be understood as an institutional set of arrangements determining familial, local, regional, and even broader kinds of loyalty and affiliation. In Lebanon, as Mahdi 'Amil rightly points out, "the relationship of sects with the state is an institutional relationship."[20] Although the reading of the nature of the sectarian state and Lebanese sectarianism 'Amil proposes is not entirely satisfying, this book departs from that premise by placing the institutional bases of Lebanese sectarianism and Shi'i identity front and center. What role have political, legal, and religious institutions played in the sectarianization of the Lebanese Shi'a? How was the weight of those institutions brought to bear on the range of political possibilities and modes of cultural identification available to Lebanese Shi'is during the twentieth century? What effects did the establishment and maintenance of certain legal, religious, and political institutions have on the making of Lebanese sectarianism and the Lebanese nation? And, finally, what role has the modern state played in all of this? Is it fair to say that either the Mandate modernizing state, or the postcolonial independent Lebanese state, was a relatively weak and unwitting accomplice to the marginalization of certain regions and sects?

Both the political and the institutional registers of Lebanese sectarianism have had a complicated and conflicted correspondence with nationalism in Lebanon. The cultural, religious, and geographical diversity of Mount Lebanon and its surroundings has long confounded the successful gestation of Lebanese nationalism. Moreover, conventional narratives of a zero-sum battle between Arab nationalism and Lebanese nationalism foreground the unique character and questionable authenticity of the Lebanese national project as it struggles to instruct its diverse communities in the ways of citizenship and inter-sectarian harmony. "Confessional loyalties," Samir Khalaf writes, "have not only survived and retained their primacy, but also continue to serve as viable sources of communal solidarity. They inspire local and personal initiative, and account for much of the resourcefulness and cultural diversity and vitality of the Lebanese. But they also undermine civic consciousness and commitment to Lebanon as a nation-state."[21] Sectarianism and nationalism in Lebanon are often represented as separable concepts, each with its own genealogy and history. By contrast, Roshanack Shaery-Eisenlohr cogently points out, "the practice of what is labeled sectarianism and nationalism cannot be viewed as entirely separate from each other." Taking this insightful point seriously, however, would mean recognizing that sectarianism and nationalism are not necessarily or permanently linked; it might not be appropriate to assume that, in every period of Lebanese history and for every community, "sectarian struggles can be described as a set of competitions between different religious nationalist projects."[22] Historians may still ask penetrating questions regarding the conditions of possibility for the emergence and institutionalization of sectarian categories of practice and modes of identification both within and against the Lebanese national context.

Third, sectarianism can be an affective state, encompassing "identity" but also going beyond the limits of this analytic construct, as (sectarian) identity often functions as the marker of (sectarian) difference and may, therefore, not necessarily be such a useful concept.[23] Sectarianism in Lebanon is a way of being in the world that depends upon a set of cultural markers and social practices, a framework capable of holding familial, local, regional, and even international loyalties together in a variably defined and shifting communal bloc. Consider, for example, the following statements from some critical observers of the Lebanese political scene in the early 1950s:

> It is extremely difficult to measure the strength or weakness of the confessional spirit in Lebanon today. It has been formalized in several of the political institutions of the nation, and we may, somewhat loosely, characterize confessionalism as a comfortable, acceptable, and understandable way of doing things. There is virtually no sign that Lebanon is now willing to part with either confessionalism or regionalism in political life.

These words harbor deep resonance with the contemporary moment. Sectarianism is certainly not a static thing-in-itself, but rather a "way of doing things," and conceiving of it as "comfortable, acceptable, and understandable" might prove helpful in thinking through the everyday nature of Lebanese sectarianism. "Overt confessionalism," these analysts conclude, "is definitely frowned upon." This apparent contradiction between sectarianism as a "comfortable" and even taken-for-granted mode of existence, on the one hand, and as an "overt" act that is potentially objectionable, on the other hand, nicely sums up some of the tension inherent in both the theory and practice of modern Lebanese sectarianism.[24]

Methodological obstacles still remain in the way of more satisfying explanations of the phenomenon of historical and historicized sectarianism. Earlier approaches to the study of Lebanese sectarianism were grounded in the scholarly tradition of modernization theory. So, for example, Michael Hudson claims, the "reason that communal identities remain so strong, reinforced rather than obliterated by the communications explosion, is the result of historic doctrinal differences and memories of oppression, both antique and recent."[25] Another observer of Lebanese history finds that sectarianism

> had a long history in Middle Eastern political order. It was only recently, with the advent of nationalism, that the sectarian order began to be questioned. Questions of citizenship and nationality are recent in background and western in origin. Sectarian compartmentalization of political order seemed natural in the Middle East for many centuries and was accepted as the norm. With the advent of nationalist political thought in the late nineteenth century, that sectarian order came under attack. The rise of modern states in this century marked the earliest attempts at dismantling the sectarian order in most Middle Eastern societies.[26]

Such approaches present a polarized framework for understanding sectarianism and nationalism in Lebanon and other deeply divided societies, one analogous to the binary understanding of tradition and modernity; the transition from the former to the latter is made possible by the infusion of necessary components of modernization, institutions, enlightenment, civilization, and the like. As sectarianism has been linked to the administration of government in Lebanon from as early as the late Ottoman period, historians have attempted to pinpoint the historical originality of the phenomenon— asking which came first, sects or sectarianism, "the *zu'ama*'" or "the system." Although there certainly is some kind of fit between the sectarian state apparatus and pre-existing social conditions, conventional histories of Lebanon reify the perception that Lebanon's sects produced Lebanese sectarianism, or that the reverse is true, and not that sectarianism and sectarianization are dialectically intertwined. "Communal divergence," according to one such perspective, "thus led in time to a sectarian political, economic, and social system."[27] In this sense, earlier understandings of the nature of sectarianism in the Middle East mirror anti-colonial nationalist versions of South Asian history, which also posit the sectarian/communalist order as antithetical to the bourgeois project of state- and nation-building.[28]

A Sectarian Modernity?

A more nuanced understanding of sectarianism would view it as a malleable product, a historical effect, and not an impermeable condition. However malleable the product may be, though, presumably there must be minimal conditions for sectarian "membership." Without reifying the primordial nature of ethnic, subnational or communal differences, therefore, historians need to take seriously the claims of difference within deeply divided societies. Whereas primordialists, to provisionally make use of a somewhat crude schematization, might contend that sectarianism is an innate sensibility specific to certain societies that can be traced back to age-old loyalties, a more instrumentalist approach might conclude that sectarianism emerged purely in response to external forces such as modernization, social change, colonialism, foreign intervention, and so forth. However, sectarianism in the modern Middle East neither emerged out of whole cloth nor was it neatly imposed from without. Sectarianism, like other sociological categories and markers of affiliation, has depended and continues to depend upon routinized forms of cultural and social practice, and historians and social scientists should more carefully consider how sectarianism is produced, how it evolves, and how it spreads into the nooks and crannies of everyday life. This book affirms that sectarian politics, personal status law, and religious culture may simultaneously produce new modes of identification as well as restrict the prospects for national as well as non- or trans-sectarian political identities. Through its focus on the practical and institutional dimensions of Shi'i sectarianism in twentieth-century Lebanon, this book illustrates that there are multiple sectarianisms and that sectarianism needs to be understood as a plural phenomenon.

"What if the sect was," Mahdi 'Amil provocatively asks, "not a thing, but rather a political relationship defined in a historical form delimited by the movement of class struggle, with the restrictions of the colonial Lebanese social formation?" Here 'Amil rightly stresses placing focus on processes and effects rather than on sources and origins. This resonates with Ussama Makdisi's suggestion that, "we should spend less time trying to figure out who supposedly 'caused' sectarianism, as if indeed sectarianism is a self-evident phenomenon that requires no further investigation." Instead, historians should strive to answer different questions, namely, "what does sectarianism signify, what are its manifestations? And what is the context in which it first arose?" Fortunately, as one early twentieth-century scholar noted, sects "lend themselves to sociological explanation because in large part they were social products." As products or effects of history, sects are also open to historical explanation.[29]

States, societies, institutions, and communities become sectarian in unique ways, by diverse means, through processes that must be historically contextualized. The historian Ussama Makdisi shows how Maronite and Druze sectarian identity were produced in nineteenth-century Ottoman Mount Lebanon as a result of the reconfigured relationship between religion and politics. Ottoman reform and European intervention in Lebanese affairs recast the relationship between local "religion" and an emergent "modernity" by undermining local conventions that governed the politics of status and rank. Sectarianism in Mount Lebanon was the "expression of a new form of local politics and knowledge that arose in a climate of transition and reform": on the one hand, sectarianism was "a practice that developed out of, and must be understood in the context of, nineteenth-century Ottoman reform"; on the other hand, it was "a discourse that is scripted as the Other to various competing Ottoman, European, and Lebanese narratives of modernization." What might be called the "relational" aspect of Lebanese sectarianism also emerges through this narrative, as the Maronite community and the Druze community each found echoes of their own sectarianization in the historical transformations of the other. Makdisi accentuates the "shock of modernity," arguing that the "culture of sectarianism" in nineteenth-century Ottoman Mount Lebanon was historically constituted through the "rupture" of episodic intercommunal violence, which was itself predicated on a reconfigured relationship between religion and society.[30]

However, if Lebanese sectarianism was "born" in the nineteenth century, does this also mean that it can be "born again"? And if Maronite and

Druze sectarianisms were forged through episodic outbursts of violence in nineteenth-century Ottoman Mount Lebanon, why didn't other sectarianisms emerge in Lebanon at the same time, under similar social, cultural, or political conditions? Or, to put it slightly differently, how was it that other sectarianisms should develop elsewhere or at other times, in seemingly unremarkable, more quotidian, everyday forms? "The process of sectarianizing identity," Makdisi rightly asserts, "was immensely complex."[31] As mentioned, however, one of the most insidious dimensions of much writing on the problem of sectarianism in Lebanon is the problematic presumption that all politics and all sectarianisms are ultimately derivative of the Maronite experience so keenly analyzed by Makdisi and others. The specific "sectarian-ness" of each community in Lebanon—Maronite, Druze, Shi'i and Sunni Muslim—must also be historicized. If the modern history of Lebanon can be understood as a history of political sectarianism and intersectarian accommodation, it should also be perceived as a constellation of multiple histories of sectarianization.

Sectarian communities in Lebanon, insofar as they constitute semi-autonomous social and political formations, have forged negotiated and renegotiable relationships with modern and modernizing states. To the extent that modernity has by now been defined and debated in a dizzying number of ways, the category may no longer be of much apparent value. Among its notable elements identified and critically analyzed by Timothy Mitchell, for example, are: "the certainty of human reason freed from particular traditions"; "technological power freed from the constraints of the natural world; "universal history"; "modernization"; and "capitalist development."[32] Such categorical underpinnings of certain understandings of modernity in the age of nation-states have come under significant critical scrutiny. Another plank in the floorboards of modernity is the notion, based, presumably, on historical developments in nineteenth- and twentieth-century Europe, that a gradual yet thorough process of secularization would accompany the anticipated emergence of public spheres in liberal democratic societies. But the notion that economic development, intellectual progress, and political reform both reinforce and rely upon processes and practices of secularization, leading inexorably in turn towards the eventual elimination of religion from the public sphere, has been called into question as well. Studies of secularism and religiosity in the humanities and social sciences seem to constitute an intellectual growth industry.[33] In this light, however, another layer of confusion emerges in the absence of meaningful discussion regarding the question of sectarianism and the enduring misapprehension of religion and sectarianism as being inextricably linked in the Middle East and beyond. Historians need to distinguish "the religious" from "the sectarian," taking care not to conflate "the sectarian" with religious nationalism. In this connection, Ayesha Jalal makes a subtle yet helpful distinction in this regard, between "religiously informed cultural identity" and "the politics of cultural nationalism."[34] If religion is understood as the "kernel" or "essence" of sectarian expressions of identity, then sectarianism and modernity might conceivably be reduced to fundamentally opposing, perhaps even irreconcilable, categories. But if sectarianism and religion can be de-linked, as I affirm that they often actually have been and are, then historical narratives of religious modernity and sectarian modernity need to be viewed as distinct. Not only would this make religion and sectarianism more analytically comprehensible, but it could also, in turn, prove essential to understanding the historical foundations of sectarianism and other forms of political identity in the modern world.

Sectarian modernity, if such a term is to be of any practical value in the Lebanese context, must be situated in view of the ideological and practical sectarianization of Lebanese state and society, by which I refer to the institutional and discursive sets of practices and conventions that authorize, strengthen, and perpetuate the politics, culture, and affective ties of sectarian politics and modes of identification. Beginning in the early twentieth century, the conditions of possibility for the appearance of a new kind of Shi'i sectarian identity, of "Shi'i Lebanon" as such, were only beginning to emerge. Imami Shi'i communities dotting the landscape of Jabal 'Amil, the Biqa' Valley, and Beirut were gradually transformed into a more visible and more empowered community with a place for itself within the social and cultural milieu of Greater Lebanon. As the Shi'i community in Lebanon became sectarian in distinctly new ways during the period of French Mandate rule, a contested but durable bond was forged between the Shi'i community and the modern state. Even as "the Lebanese Shi'i community" haltingly became a legible and meaningful social and political category, vast differences in terms of class, status, politics, cultural orientation, religious affiliation, and even religiosity as such continued to characterize the Shi'i milieu in the state of Greater Lebanon. The experience of modernity in Lebanon has been fundamentally bound up with the problem of recognizing and managing sectarian difference. Even as the modern Lebanese nation-state was under construction, an ensemble of historical transformations gradually incorporated Shi'i society into the hegemonic national culture of sectarianism.

The Shi'i Milieu in Lebanon—Nation, State, and Society

Commonplace ideologies of sectarian-nationalism and national sectarianism continue to represent the Shi'i historical experience in Lebanon as fundamentally derivative of a more mainstream historical narrative. As the Shi'i milieu was gradually incorporated into the orbit of the modern state and the multisectarian national community, new contours and effects of a certain Shi'i sectarian modernity were haltingly coming into view. To be clear, the suggestion that sectarianisms in Lebanon are historical effects should not be mistaken for the untenable claim that Muslim or Christian sectarianism had no precedent in Greater Syria, as religious, cultural, and sectarian modes of identification were part of the historical landscape throughout the medieval and early modern periods. The point of this book is not to argue that there were no Shi'i modes of identification or forms of association or religious practice prior to the Mandate period, but that a new mode of identifying oneself, one's family, or one's "community" as Lebanese *and* Shi'i appeared under the French Mandate. Simply put, an institutionalized and widely shared Shi'i sectarian sense of belonging did not exist for Shi'i communities in Jabal 'Amil and the Biqa' Valley. This may partially be attributed to the fact that there was no such thing as a Lebanese national community prior to the late nineteenth century; but it is nonetheless also true that what it meant to be a Shi'i Muslim in Lebanon was dramatically transformed during the Mandate period. This transformation was mediated by the local dynamics and mechanics of sectarianization and state building.

The historiography of the French Mandate has been predominantly concerned with political history. On the one hand, studies of Mandate Lebanon have explored the key figures in the "communal leadership" who contributed to the making of the modern Lebanese state, tracking what Pierre Rondot called "the difficult passage of traditional communities into the modern state." On the other hand, studies of Mandate Lebanon have revolved around the rise of new local political ideologies, more specifically the apparently intractable dialectical tension between Lebanese nationalism and Arab nationalism. This approach also undervalues local and transnational forms of attachment, showcasing either sectarian communities (the "sectarian mosaic" thesis) or particular conceptions of the nation (Phoenician, Maronite, Lebanese) as natural categories of analysis. Arab nationalist narratives of history as well as certain strands of what might be termed "Shi'i nationalist" historiography demonstrate how many people within the Shi'i milieu strongly favored union with Faysal's Arab kingdom and its capital at Damascus, and never wavered throughout the Mandate period in their commitments to certain tenets of Greater Syrian pan-Arab nationalism. At the same time, some Shi'i Muslims in Greater Syria of different class, status, and regional backgrounds threw their lot in with the future of Greater Lebanon soon after the establishment of that polity. Whatever the case, by 1936, most Shi'i elites, political leaders and a significant proportion of the community at large had reconciled with the new status quo in the country brought about by the Franco-Lebanese Treaty, which recognized a modicum of autonomy for Lebanon in matters of trade and politics without requiring the French to evacuate the country or relinquish control over key levers of administration, security and military control.[35]

An increasing number of scholars sought to both move beyond traditional approaches to political history and to rewrite the multisectarian history of Lebanon in the late 1980s and early 1990s, in the context of the exceedingly destructive Lebanese civil wars and amidst ensuing ideological and political divisions. Still, Lebanese historiography continued to relegate the history of the Shi'i community and its regions to an inferior status. "Among the Lebanese people," Kamal Salibi writes, "the Christians were the first to begin adapting to the ways of the modern world, and the Shiites among the Muslims were the last."[36] Farid El-Khazen goes even further, contending, "communal disparities in Lebanon were not induced by state policies. Most of the disparities preceded the formation of the state in 1920. They were mainly a function of the uneven socio-political and economic development of Lebanese communities."[37] In other words, "communal" development is understood as being more strongly determined by pre-existing "socio-political and economic" features than the administration of government in post–World War I Lebanon. Even as such matter-of-fact descriptions of

Shi'i backwardness arise out of a matrix of cultural and political contention in Lebanon, such readings of economic and political development help
to reproduce and validate a nationalist narrative takes for granted the dis-
creteness of each sectarian community and then hierarchically orders them
according to certain standards of progress and modernity. Consider this
passage from Salibi's broad attempt at rethinking Lebanese history:

> Shiite religious learning, however, was only meaningful to Shiites; and
> while the achievements of the Jabal Amil scholars in the field were held
> in high esteem for a long time through the Shiite Muslim world, and
> most of all in Iran, they naturally had no impact on the Lebanese scene
> outside strictly Shiite circles. No effort of imagination could convinc-
> ingly depict them as part of a general Lebanese heritage.[38]

Such a categorical refusal of Shi'i presence within the historiographical
landscape is indicative of perduring assumptions in Lebanese national culture; it says more about the character of certain strains in nationalist historiography, which has consistently excluded the Shi'a, than it does about the
character of "Shiite religious learning" or the "Shiite Muslim world." Even
critical reappraisals of modern Lebanese history have maintained a distorted
representation of the Shi'i community as forever lagging one step behind,
their historical experience somehow derivative of other communities on
the Lebanese national stage. In his unparalleled and magisterial survey of
Lebanese historical writing, Ahmad Beydoun helpfully observes, "The history of Lebanon is, for a very large part, made up of a constellation of holy
histories." Beydoun presents a rich double entendre; such holy histories might
be imbued with holiness through forged connections to religious tradition,
but also through a process that might be termed historiographical sanctifica-
tion. Such persistence of holy histories in modern Lebanese historiography
cannot be attributed solely to the religious dimension of sectarian pasts.[39]

Lebanese historian Mounzer Jaber poetically sums up what might be
called the "lachrymose version" of 'Amili Shi'i history, in which "just as
the bird flies and the sun rises and sets, so does the executioner kill and
the martyr die"; there is always a morose "lesson and moral" embedded in
canonical accounts of Shi'i history. But if History in the 'Amili Shi'i milieu
had been equated for so long with "night and birth pangs and a string of

torments," what place could local historiography have amidst all of that "blind chaos and coal-black darkness"?[40] Nevertheless, from the early 1980s, academics, intellectuals, and journalists in the Shiʻi milieu began making a more concerted effort to "write the Shiʻa into Lebanese history," bridling against endemic historiographical neglect as well as political and cultural marginalization. Scholars such as ʻAli al-Zayn, ʻAli ʻAbd al-Munʻim Shuʻayb, and Nawal Fayyad affirmed the indispensability of the Lebanese Shiʻa in forging the course of history in *bilad al-sham* and, subsequently, within the Lebanese polity.[41] By placing Jabal ʻAmil and Shiʻi voices front and center, they posed a direct challenge to the historiographical tendencies that have silenced or sidelined the Shiʻi milieu, contributing to what might be thought of as a counter-hegemonic narrative. A profusion of theses and dissertations submitted to French and Lebanese universities helped to create a foundation for studying and writing early modern and modern Lebanese Shiʻi history. Meanwhile, deeper and more wide-ranging research into the history of particular towns, villages, intellectuals, poets, political leaders, and families supported the construction of metanarratives of economic development, political rivalries, scholarly life, and cultural production in Jabal ʻAmil, fostering a more expansive and historicized view of Jabal ʻAmil and Shiʻism in Greater Syria.[42] Viewed all together, these works comprise the lineaments of what might be called a Shiʻi nationalist historical narrative. On this issue, Sulayman Taqi al-Din writes:

> If Maronite sectarian history has made the history of Lebanon the history of sects . . . it made the other sects look at it through the eye of an *opposing sectarianism* such that we find ourselves up against complete sectarian narratives that bear approximately the same features and assumptions. Historians of the Shiʻa, like others, use the same language.[43]

The seemingly unshakeable conviction held by each sectarian community that they alone possess a monopoly over the history of their sect also plays a part in maintaining political and historiographical boundaries. In this sense, it appears that only "true" insiders are capable of writing a "true" history of the sect, the community, the nation, or whatever. But Shiʻi nationalist counter-narratives may also unwittingly legitimate the very master narrative of Lebanese sectarianism they had purportedly set out to challenge.

More recently, historians have employed innovative approaches and methodologies inspired by the comparative study of colonialism in order to illuminate how dynamic the Mandate system was in practice; on the ground it certainly was a "living institution."[44] In the wake of the First World War, the Mandate regime was set up by the recently created League of Nations under the legal guise of establishing a tutelary relationship administered by the European powers. As victors in the postwar settlement of the Middle East, France and Britain would help to shepherd "minor" peoples that were perceived as neither qualified enough for nor deserving of self-government. Ostensibly, this arrangement would lead toward eventual, but consistently deferred, conditions of independence and self-determination.

In the Lebanese case, further justification for French intervention came in the form of overtures toward the protection of minority groups such as the Maronites and the Shi'a, communities that were often perceived and portrayed as vulnerable. In October 1935, the influential Shi'i modernist monthly journal *al-'Irfan* published an article entitled, "Did the Shi'a Ask for Protection from the French?" Attributed to "a voice from the heartland (*ma'qal*) of the Shi'a" in South Lebanon, the author took umbrage at the notion that the Shi'i community would ever have invited the occupation of their country, or that they purposefully sought preferential treatment from the Mandate authorities. Insisting that the "Shi'a of Syria" were first and foremost "Arabs" and "Muslims" and then "Shi'is," a point regularly made in the journal, and that their future was bound up with that of the Sunni community in Lebanon and the region more broadly, this author stridently argued that there would have been no need for Shi'is to throw their lot in with the French, neither as a means for achieving formal recognition in the eyes of the state nor in order to be somehow "liberated" to engage in hitherto forbidden religious practices. Why would Sunnis, "moderate Christians," or the Shi'a ask for such "imaginary protection" from the French in the first place? Although Syrian Arab anti-colonial nationalism was capacious enough to integrate Shi'is articulating solidarity as Syrian Arabs, the right to cultural difference within the Arab nationalist milieu would eventually prove to be a bit more complicated.[45] At the other end of the spectrum, Muhammad Khalil al-Zayn, a Shi'i notable from the village of Jibsheet, made a public declaration in the southern market town of Nabatiyya in January 1946 that was recorded by colonial officials. "The Shi'is should not, in any case," al-Zayn argued, "suffer the presence of a foreigner in the country, with the exception of France which, alone, can guarantee the freedom of our religion and the sovereignty of Lebanon." Even once Lebanese independence from French rule had been achieved in 1946, Shi'i Muslims continued trying to make sense of their complicated and perilous historical circumstances, which had demanded some measure of collaboration and negotiation with or resistance to the colonial power. France could also serve as a model for emulation, occasionally perceived to be the only foreign power that took the interests of the Shi'i community to heart.[46]

Embedded within these conflicting arguments were some of the most divisive and difficult issues confronting the Shi'i community in Lebanon ever since the onset of French Mandate rule: the problem of collaboration with an unjust authority; the suspect loyalty and uncertain authenticity of Shi'is within Lebanon; inclusion in the "unity" of the nation versus "protection" as an independent "minority" constructed through difference; the articulation of communal demands for rights and justice; the shifting constructions of relations between Lebanese state and society; and the vexed relationship among colonialism, sectarianism, and nationalism in Mandate Lebanon. What mechanisms allowed for the expression of Shi'i sectarian identity within the context of Greater Lebanon and the postcolonial Lebanese Republic? How did sectarianism relate to French categories of citizenship, identity, and politics more generally? What was an appropriate response to foreign rule for a Shi'i Muslim in Lebanon during this period? What explains the tensions between universalistic categories (Islamist, pan-Arab, or Marxist), on the one hand, and particularistic identities (Shi'i, Lebanese, or 'Amili), on the other? To the extent that French rule structurally and ideologically influenced the transformation of the Shi'i community in Lebanon into an autonomous "sect among sects" (ta'ifa min al-tawa'if), or what Bernard Lewis called, albeit in a very different context, "one sectarian minority among many," this took place in paradoxical ways and had contradictory effects, and agency must not be attributed only to the French.[47] Throughout the period, the Shi'i milieu was buffeted by a variety of crosscutting political, religious, and ideological currents: transnational affiliations versus local concerns; the competing pull of Arab nationalism and Lebanese nationalism; loyalty to Jabal 'Amil as a cultural, political and religious Shi'i "heartland"; the reformation and modernization of Imami Shi'i religious and juridical traditions.

Whether overtly or tacitly, most Lebanese historiography accepts and authorizes the categorical imperatives underwriting sectarianism. Even the most critical historical narratives tend to explain key concepts such as equality, citizenship, rights and nationhood *with* sectarianism, without also simultaneously seeking to explain sectarianism itself. Social, economic, and political circumstances have allowed each community to develop strikingly similar narratives of sectarian independence, autonomy, and legitimacy. Less often remarked upon are the subtle institutional processes and practices that gave rise to stubborn and persistent forms of sectarian affiliation and community. The Janus-faced nature of communal identification—privileging both sameness and difference, or, perhaps, sameness in some sort of essential, naturalized difference—is one intractable contradiction at the heart of Lebanese sectarian-nationalism. Rather than accepting the apparent-ness or natural-ness of sectarian ways of being, institutions, and practices *prima facie,* historians should strive to understand the persistence of certain key themes in Lebanese history: recognition and erasure, inclusion and exclusion, sectarian difference and national unity. This book exposes some of the contradictions of Lebanese sectarianism by examining some institutional and discursive practices at the fluid and permeable boundary differentiating Lebanese society from the sectarian state.

Lebanese history in the twentieth century can be best conceived as a hodgepodge of mutually comprehensible and relational "cultures of sectarianism" operating within the framework of a broader national sectarianism or sectarian nationalism. "The molding of nationalist politics onto an Ottoman social order," Makdisi writes, "created a sectarian nationalism and the politics of nationalist elitism." Without entirely jettisoning the overarching concept of a sprawling and unitary "culture of sectarianism," then, historians may recognize how sectarianism becomes a badge of national affiliation even as particular sectarianisms are modulated according to the specific historical trajectory of a particular community. Within this framework for understanding Lebanese history, neither can there be one unitary model for the production of Lebanese sectarianisms, which I understand in the plural, nor is there a universal form of sectarian expression that is common to all sectarian communities at all historical moments. Each sectarian community in Lebanon has become sectarian in its own particular way as a result of specific sets of discursive, institutional and material

transformations. One of the enduring paradoxes of Lebanese political citizenship and cultural identity is that sectarian difference proved integral
to the making of the nation while national unity was forged through the
making of sectarian difference. If sectarian difference served as a sine qua
non for full participation in the national project, modernizationist assumptions about Lebanon may be challenged with an argument like that made by
Fuad I. Khuri, namely, "sectarian identity is not an 'obstacle to integration'"
but "a mechanism of integration."[48] Whatever the case, by the autumn of the
French Mandate an increasingly subjective identification with "Shi'i-ness"
had been cultivated in the context of a new kind of sectarian sensibility in
Lebanon. This was comparable to other kinds of sectarian belonging within
the boundaries of the Lebanese Republic, but distinguishable from being a
Shi'i Muslim within the context of the newly emergent nation-state of, say,
Syria or Iraq.

The history of Shi'ism in Iraq would make for an interesting comparison
to its analog in Lebanon, as both histories are marked by numerous shared
elements: the contested reconstruction of cultural identification in a multisectarian society; collective memory of oppression and martyrdom; internal
differentiation among various social groups ('ulama', peasants, elites and
others); and tensions between political and religious authority. However, a
satisfying comparison with the Iraqi case would have to attend to the ways
in which certain realities of sectarianism have been more or less important
and meant different things to specific individuals and communities in various moments. Exploring the relationships between the Shi'i community and
the Iraqi "national state" during the twentieth century, for example, Hasan
'Alawi argues that the Iraqi state and its attendant national institutions
underwent a process of "madhhab-ization" (tamadhdhhub). Skeptical that
there was any kind of popular sectarianism—what he calls "sectarianism
of the street"—'Alawi defines "madhhab-ization" as a political process that
reinforced vertical social cleavages "from above." In addition to the madhhab-ization of Iraqi society, 'Alawi perceives the madhhab-ization of the
national state to be among the most pernicious developments in twentieth-
century Iraq, particularly in that this process facilitated the formal exclusion
of the Shi'a and the impugning of their national loyalties. Consequently,
Iraqi state-Shi'i society relations were characterized by "constant tension,
misconceptions, lack of confidence and mutual mistrust." As in the case of

Lebanon, the construction of an inclusive national identity hinged on the erasure, or at least the suspension, of certain cultural and religious forms of attachment. In both the Iraqi and the Lebanese case, subnational loyalties were maintained even when they had to be concealed, at the level of the national state and among subnational communities themselves.[49]

Beyond some commonalities, the administration of the British Mandate in Iraq, to say nothing of Transjordan or Palestine, also differed from the administration of the French Mandates, at the very least in the matter of duration. By the same token, the administration of French Mandate Lebanon was unique from the administration of French Mandate Syria. For example, throughout the colonial period and after, the "weak state" in Lebanon is often said to have necessitated and legitimated the persistence of previously existing clientelist networks, even as the nascent state helped to foster new institutions of sectarianism. Broadly conceived, the state in Lebanon has been hindered by its multiple sectarian responsibilities and shackled to the logic of Lebanese sectarianism, often to the detriment of the public good or the welfare of the nation. The Lebanese state evolved quite differently in the capital than it did in the peripheries; Lebanon's regions and communities also developed in unique ways. To be sure, the fragmented composition of Lebanese national community has contributed to the state's failings and inadequacies, but the reverse has also been true. Yet, the implications of state weakness or even state failure cannot be undone simply by shifting the burden of social responsibility and economic development both rhetorically and historically onto the shoulders of particular individuals or communities. In French Mandate Lebanon, "there was an important distinction between the power to repress and the lack of the executive power characteristic of the modern state." Unlike other colonial contexts, however, as Roger Owen notes, "the French kept the number of government officials at a minimum, leaving the bulk of the educational, medical and other services to be provided on a communal basis."[50]

While guarantees of greater autonomy may have enticed some communal leaders into cooperating with the colonial authorities, the vicissitudes of the Lebanese nation-building project were historically bound up with the contradictions and inconsistencies of Lebanese state building in complicated ways. First, the fragmentation of the state apparatus and its attendant institutions was dialectically related to the divided state of Lebanese society. Second, the

absence of a powerful military—which was itself also restrained by competing sectarian commitments even at high levels of leadership—traditionally
led the state and "its communities" to rely on foreign powers, which had
far-reaching consequences with respect to questions of national sovereignty
and security. Third, the partition of institutional life into discrete sectarian spheres tended to reinforce a zero-sum mindset among institutionalized
sectarian communities and leaderships, which mitigated the prospects for
a collaborative ethos committed to national development.[51] In this regard,
we should be mindful of Paul Kingston's judicious assessment, that "institutional legacies of the mandate period in Lebanon may be numerous and
contradictory."[52] Viewing Lebanese "state-formation as an ongoing process
of structural change and not as a one-time event" may help to demonstrate
how the Lebanese state has both relied upon and fallen prey to certain politics and practices of sectarianism.[53]

Institutions of Personal Status

Some of the processes of juridical and religious institutionalization that
proved most significant for shaping the sectarianization of the Shi'i community become more comprehensible through reflection on other colonial
and imperial contexts.[54] In a comparative study of customary law in central
Africa, Martin Chanock urges historians of the colonial encounter to "consider the imposition of the law of the state onto the law of local communities
as a meeting of distinctive modes of social ordering."[55] Personal status legal
regimes imposed in French-administered colonial situations have operated
within a variety of different conceptual and structural frameworks and have
had diverse, historically contingent effects. In the Algerian case, for example, the French colonial state intervened in order to produce the hybrid legal
system that was one of the most notorious legacies of the colonial experience
in Algeria, where "assimilation was a threat to [Algerian Muslims'] cultural
heritage and identity, and hence to their very ability to act as a cohesive
social group."[56] In contrast, Dominique Sarr and Richard Roberts give some
perspective on the elaboration of Islamic law under French colonial rule
in West Africa: "In contrast to colonial Algeria, where French citizenship
extended to native Algerians conferred with it the jurisdiction of the French
civil code, in Senegal, the French citizens of Muslim persuasion retained

the rights to turn to Muslim courts for adjudication in cases concerning the Muslim personal status."[57]

The genesis of Shiʿi political and cultural identities in Lebanon must be understood in relation to the comparative historical experience of colonialism, sectarianism, nationalism, and law. Paradoxically, what little capacity Shiʿi Muslims living under French Mandate rule had for engaging in national life was predicated on their championing of sectarian unity and collective identity, as the very badge of their assimilation into the Lebanese national milieu. Unrecognized by the Ottoman state, Shiʿis in Jabal ʿAmil, the Biqaʿ Valley, and elsewhere in Greater Syria would have sought counsel for the adjudication of legal matters either in state-sanctioned Hanafi courts or in private homes, offices, or other spaces staffed by religious scholars. Alternatively, such issues could be adjudicated through requests for fatwas, non-binding legal opinions (*istifta'*). Such practices may have afforded Lebanese Shiʿis some measure of judicial autonomy during the Ottoman period; they remain difficult, if not impossible, however, for the historian of law and society to reconstruct.

In January 1926, the Jaʿfari *madhhab* was formally recognized as an "independent *madhhab*." This seminal event, which effectively resulted in the institutionalization of the Jaʿfari *madhhab* in the form of an integrated network of personal status courts with varying degrees of political and legal power, has had tremendous significance in the Lebanese Shiʿi community's gradual sectarianization. As a state creation with no substantial historical precedent in Lebanon or anywhere else, the Jaʿfari court represented an important innovation in the modern Shiʿi historical experience, marking a turning point in the trajectory of the Lebanese Shiʿa towards sectarian modernity, in which newly bureaucratized and standardized norms of legal procedure institutionally bound the Shiʿa to the state. "The process of colonization," as Emmanuelle Saada points out, "was continually traversed by law and legal structures. Far from being a pure exercise of force, colonization involved diverse levels of codification and, at the same time, was necessarily responsive to diverse judicial contingencies."[58] By contrast with the Algerian case, in which the legal system was fundamentally re-organized by the French over the course of the nineteenth century, the validation of the Jaʿfari court in Lebanon, which was made possible by the formal recognition of the Jaʿfari *madhhab*, was of a different quality altogether, one that was predicated less on a new kind of colonial knowledge, as in the Algerian case, than on a kind of organic, tentative and ad hoc process of institutionalization monitored and managed from above, but also shaped and defined from below. If Islamic courts had functioned in cities and in rural parts of Algeria prior to the colonial era,[59] and if Muslims in French West Africa retained the "right" to use Muslim personal status courts, Shi'i Muslims in Lebanon had less solid pre-existing structures to work with, and, perhaps most important, Lebanese citizens have had no other choice than to be attached to their sectarian community in such matters.

The formal recognition of Ja'fari personal status law points up the complicated and multivalent social and political relationships linking Shi'i society to the Lebanese sectarian state during the Mandate period. If the Ja'fari court—as one part of the broader reorganization of Shi'i society in Lebanon that might be thought of as a "millet-type structure," to borrow Elizabeth Thompson's felicitous phrasing[60]—became an indispensable tool for the reorganization and re-imagination of the relationship between Shi'i community and the state, the institutionalization of Shi'i law through the Ja'fari court was one of the most, if not the most, important innovations of this period, contributing to reconsiderations and redefinitions of collective Shi'i solidarity and identity. J. N. D. Anderson asserts that the *millet* system essentially "run[s] counter to modern ideas of national sovereignty and solidarity, but it also jeopardizes, in some respects, that religious liberty which it professes to safeguard."[61] Both symbolically and physically important, the Ja'fari court helped to put into place some of the groundwork for the crystallization and subsequent mobilization of a specifically sectarian Shi'i politics. This state-administered personal status court—its attendant functionaries, representatives, judges, lawyers, and clerks—gradually evolved into an institution more or less taken for granted, one that has aided the Shi'i community to preserve and also expand its communal autonomy within the parameters of the Lebanese nation-state. Despite the gradual nature of this transformation, and although Lebanese Shi'i 'ulama' had been theorizing and applying principles of Ja'fari law and jurisprudence for a long time, the institutionalization of the Ja'fari *madhhab* constituted a moment of historical discontinuity.

The Ja'fari court was empowered to adjudicate matters of personal status law—marriage, divorce, dower, maintenance payments (*nafaqa*), pious endowments (*awqaf,* s. *waqf*) and inheritance, as well as other cases dealing with property issues. But the court also played a unique role not just within the Lebanese Shi'i milieu, but also in shaping interactions among sectarian communities as well as the nascent relationship between the Shi'i community and the state. "The term *statut personnel,*" as J. G. Assaf noted in the mid-1930s,

> has two meanings, one strict, the other broad, commonly used in the Orient. In the strict or rational sense it comprises the state and the competence of persons. By contrast in its oriental, broad, sense, it encompasses all matters relating both to both the state and the competence of persons, the organization of privileged communities, of the family; the writing and validation of wills as well as the transmission of inheritance.

"In a word, everything falls under personal status, with the exception of contractual obligations."[62] There was nothing natural about personal status law in the Lebanese context; the legal category was a relatively recent innovation. Nevertheless, each community in Mandate Lebanon began carving out what increasingly resembled separate (if not always equal) sectarian legal regimes. The definition and administration of personal status law had crucial significance for shaping and reinforcing evolving Shi'i sectarian modes of identification in practice.

Uneven Lebanese state formation under the French Mandate both shaped and was shaped by institutions such as the Ja'fari court; meanwhile, the legalizing practices of institutions such as the Ja'fari court had contradictory effects. If *shari'a* courts in the Ottoman Arab provinces were "linked to the multifaceted nature of the modern Ottoman state," then the Ja'fari court in Lebanon—and, by association, its Shi'i constituencies—was now inextricably linked to the French Mandate (and, later, the postcolonial Lebanese) state.[63] Instead of viewing the recognition of personal status law as the authorization or recognition of tradition, then, consider the notion that

> when the shari'a is structured essentially as a set of legal rules defining personal status, it is radically transformed. This is not because the shari'a, by being confined to the private domain, is thereby deprived of

political authority, something that advocates of an Islamic state argue should be restored. On the contrary, what happens to the shariʿa is best described not as curtailment but as transmutation. It is rendered into a subdivision of legal norms (fiqh) that are authorized and maintained by the centralizing state.

This notion allows for an exploration of the significance of personal status law as a historically contested domain. But *shariʿa* law is not exactly "confined to the private domain" or "deprived of political authority" in the Lebanese context precisely because the French Mandate administration and the sectarian state contributed to the definition of religious jurisdictions. Consequently, the "weak state" in Lebanon has had to draw on different sources of legitimacy and has had quite a different history than other incarnations of the colonial or postcolonial "centralizing state."[64]

There has been no in-depth historical study of the Jaʿfari court and neither its court records nor related documents have ever been systematically analyzed.[65] Situated in conversation with French colonial archival material and other primary sources, these rare historical documents open a window onto the array of everyday social, economic, and familial relationships within the Shiʿi community during a time of gradual social change and political transformation. Reading records from the Jaʿfari *shariʿa* courts in relation to other contemporary sources facilitates the fragmentary rehabilitation of the historical experience of ordinary Lebanese Shiʿis. Islamic court records from the Jaʿfari courts are doubly important, moreover, when we consider how the written word has been monopolized by the *ʿulama'* and political elites; these documents are a rich source for social historians, empirical evidence from everyday life as well as the vehicle through which subalterns—peasants, women, workers, and minors— might speak. As with the voluminous literature on modern Middle East social history written since the "discovery" of Islamic court records, the Jaʿfari court records can help historians gain a richer understanding of the workings of this singular institution and its role in Shiʿi society and Lebanese culture.[66]

Ironically, sectarian institutions bonded Shiʿi society to the state but at the same time marginalized the Shiʿi community within the national body politic. The institutionalization of Shiʿi law and politics cultivated

Shi'i autonomy from the state, which could insulate the community from national political life in some ways even as the gradual popularization of Shi'ism as a marker of cultural and religious identity continued apace. In this sense, the Lebanese Shi'i community was transformed during the period of French Mandate rule, becoming sectarian in new ways that were defined by specific institutional relationships and cultural practices. The hegemonic culture of sectarianism cast a shadow over the conditions of possibility of civic participation in Lebanese political, legal, and cultural life, even as the Shi'i community became sectarian in new ways. Beyond recognizing the Shi'a as (often unequal) participants in the collaborative endeavors of Lebanese nationalism much earlier in the twentieth century than the historiography has previously recognized, this book explores some of the complex ways in which colonialism, religion and nationalism collided to produce new sectarianized modes of cultural and political identification. As such, this book may enable the construction of a different narrative of Lebanese Shi'i social history and the imagination of other trajectories for Lebanese society and culture.

The Plan of the Book

The incorporation of Jabal 'Amil and the Biqa' Valley into the state of Greater Lebanon initiated a process that both recognized and empowered Twelver Shi'i communities in an unprecedented manner. Chapter one, "The Incomplete Nationalization of Jabal 'Amil," traces the political, economic and social history of Jabal 'Amil from the early modern period up through the beginning of the twentieth century by looking at European travel writing, locally produced sources, French colonial archival material, and other documentary evidence. As the 'Amili Shi'a gradually acquired the trappings of a veritable political community, a call for the reinstatement of their "deprived rights" was one key component of what has been called the Shi'i "politics of demand," or *matlabiyya*. Mass political mobilization in the Shi'i milieu was rare during this period, with the exception of the 1936 Bint Jubayl Revolt, which I discuss in chapter six. Although the revolt has often been cherry-picked for ideological reasons, and fits into a particular political narrative of Shi'i history that essentializes "resistance" to state power, colonialism or foreign aggression, I discuss the exceptional nature of such an event in order to better throw into relief more subtle and subterranean practices of institutional and legal sectarianism. As the Shi'i community continued to grow in strength and numbers, and even as the politics of Shi'i rights and representation became increasingly affecting and articulate, the push and pull of Shi'i demands and state refusal became the template for evolving Lebanese state-Shi'i society relations. Attempts at political mobilization and institutional integration demonstrated both the promise and the limits of Shi'i activism under the Mandate.

The vexatious relationship between Shi'i religious culture and modernity also inflected the transformation of Shi'i identity during the first half of the twentieth century. Chapter two, "The Modernity of Shi'i Tradition," critically investigates the tentative advances of Shi'i modernism, delving into how the proposed reformation of 'Ashura' mourning ritual practices during the early twentieth century helped to bring about what I term "The 'Ashura' Debates." After Sayyid Muhsin al-Amin had put forward suggestions for a whole host of ways to reform the ritual practiced by Shi'i Muslims to mourn the martyrdom of Imam Husayn in the mid-1920s, heated arguments broke out among Shi'i religious scholars and intellectuals all over the world. A flurry of tracts and treatises published over the following decade wrestled with the most appropriate means and methods to update, modernize, or otherwise adapt Shi'i religious practices to new circumstances. Shi'i modernism addressed itself to ethical, theological and epistemological questions revolving around the struggle to reconcile "traditional" religion to "modern" forms of knowledge and social practice. This was further complicated by larger questions regarding such modern conditions as publicity, nation-states, and improved communications. In conversation with critical scholarship on religious practice, mourning, martyrdom and memory, this chapter charts some of the ways in which Shi'i religious culture, sectarianism, and modernity were fundamentally reshaped in the age of the sectarian nation-state.

To the extent that Shi'i religious modernism was one element of a burgeoning sectarian modernity, the advent of state-authorized personal status law was another. The book pivots in chapters three and four to examine categories and practices of personal status law. In the Mandate colonial context, legal institutions and legalizing institutional practices contributed to the making and remaking of political and juridical subjectivities in ways that did not always proceed in lockstep with colonial design. Chapter three, "Institutionalizing Personal Status," considers the intellectual roots and theoretical significance of personal status law, which is, categorically speaking, a modern innovation that represents a unique vehicle and instrument for the production of sectarian difference in Lebanon, similar to other colonial contexts such as Algeria and India, but also distinguishable by certain variations particular to the Lebanese context. Law makes up an important component of the scaffolding that gives shape to both political and institutional sectarianisms in Lebanon. Following the formal recognition of the Ja'fari *madhhab* in January 1926, the establishment of a state-administered network of personal status courts throughout Mandate Lebanon signaled a new phase in the development of sectarian Shi'i identity. Such new productions of sectarian law and difference both in and through legal institutions and court practices created the conditions that made possible the renovation of Shi'i institutional life in Lebanon. Despite its controversial position as part of the colonial state bureaucracy, the Ja'fari court was the most important Shi'i institution in Lebanon prior to the establishment of the Supreme Shi'i Islamic Council in 1969.

The formal authorization of Lebanese Shi'i personal status law by the Mandate state had implications for the exercise of Shi'i institutional power. Shi'i legal institutions were not only sites for the application of sacred law in matters of personal status. The Ja'fari court symbolized the extent to which Shi'is had managed to acquire a modicum of sectarian rights even as they increasingly came to identify with a kind of sectarian Shi'i-ness both under and through the Mandate; the court was a strong institution capable of both protecting sectarian rights and religious patrimony, on the one hand, and projecting Shi'i power outward, on the other. Chapter four, "Practicing Sectarianism," demonstrates how the Shi'i community began to practice sectarianism, to practice *being* sectarian, through contestations over the ownership and protection of sacred sectarian space, specifically through repeated demands for the validation of Shi'i claims to control religious patrimony—cemeteries, mosques, and other types of *waqf* property. Struggles to protect cemeteries and other kinds of religious patrimony are well documented in the French foreign ministry archive as well as in private papers I discovered in the archives of the Ja'fari courts in Beirut and Jabal 'Amil. What I call the "legalizing practices" of the Ja'fari court were emblematic of the contradictory ways in which inclusion within the Lebanese nation could be formalized through sectarian attachments.

To be sure, these legal institutions were first and foremost sites for the application of sacred law in matters of personal status. Chapter five, "Adjudicating Society at the Ja'fari Court," moves inside the court in order to illuminate some everyday aspects of adjudication through close readings of Islamic court records and other documentary evidence from the Ja'fari courts in Beirut and South Lebanon. Social historians have demonstrated how court records constitute a unique historical source, capable of capturing the texture and flavor of everyday life. Building on the insights of an entire generation of legal historians, this chapter expands the discussion of family law, Islamic law and society, and the politics of gender in Islamic law into undiscovered territory: cases drawn from early twentieth-century Lebanese Shi'i personal status law courts. As unmined historical sources, these documents detail the life experiences of ordinary people—women, peasants, workers and minors—who rarely left behind written records. Cases brought before the Ja'fari court and discussed in this chapter show not only how gender roles and boundaries were in flux in Shi'i Lebanon during the first half of the twentieth century, but also how the institutionalization of Ja'fari personal status law had contradictory effects for men and women. As a venue where it was possible for men and women alike to mobilize the power and authority of the community and the state towards individual or familial interests, the Ja'fari court was an indispensable site for the institutionalization of sectarianism in Shi'i Lebanon as well as the subtle reinforcement of everyday affective ties.

Legal and religious institutionalization under the Mandate also had implications for Shi'i politics. Bringing full circle the discussion of Shi'i attempts to mobilize politically, Chapter six, "'Amili Shi'is into Shi'i Lebanese?" underscores how sectarian claims were increasingly bound up with the institutionalization of Shi'i difference. Lebanese Shi'is were more and more inclined to consider themselves participants in Lebanon's fledgling sectarian democracy, even as the community had become more self-assured, more capable of articulating its political demands, and more fully integrated into the colonial religious sphere, but also more variegated and diverse. In the first part of this chapter, I discuss the 1936 Bint Jubayl Revolt, not, as it is often portrayed by historians, as evidence of unstinting anti-colonial or subaltern resistance within the Shi'i milieu, but rather in order to draw attention to the fact that concerted political action remained relatively rare during the Mandate period. Conventional narratives of Shi'i history in Lebanon tend to begin with the so-called Shi'a "awakening" or "mobilization" of the community under the charismatic influence of Imam Musa al-Sadr; from there, they may move on to discuss the rise of more militant political Shi'ism in the form of Harakat Amal or Hizballah, sectarian violence, or the politics and culture of "The Resistance." This book ends with an altogether different discussion of some of these themes. I conclude by reaffirming the importance of the period of French Mandate rule as an indispensable precursor to the political "mobilization" of the Shi'i community under the charismatic leadership of Imam Musa al-Sadr as well as the subsequent "radicalization" of the community amidst the escalation of the Arab–Israeli conflict, regional power politics and local repercussions of the Iranian Revolution. Historians and other social scientists have written much more on these topics, but they have failed to properly situate the latter-day stories of "mobilization" and "radicalization" against the historical context discussed throughout this book. The making of modern Lebanon has depended upon the sectarianization of Lebanon's communities as well as the institutionalization of sectarianism, a point I return to in greater detail in the epilogue. Therefore, the movement from Shi'i institutionalization to mobilization and radicalization must be set against a consideration of the genealogies, practices and effects of sectarian difference making more broadly. In that regard, this book should have suggestive implications for the study of sectarianism and the making of the modern world.

1

The Incomplete Nationalization
of Jabal 'Amil

Before the sixteenth century, the scholarly and cultural center of global Shi'ism was arguably neither Iraq nor Iran. Although generally considered to be an economic and political backwater, the region nestled in the gently sloping highlands of present-day South Lebanon known as Jabal 'Amil had been one of the most important centers for Shi'i learning and scholarship since the late medieval period. Located just south of the Lebanon and anti-Lebanon mountain ranges, Jabal 'Amil was part, albeit a peripheral part, of Greater Syria, an administrative unit that historically comprised present-day Syria, Lebanon, Jordan, and Palestine/Israel. But the peripheral regional status of Jabal 'Amil was belied by the significance of its intellectual, scholarly, and even political contributions. The valuable corpus of religious and philosophical writing produced by 'Amili *'ulama'* was internationally renowned. The knowledge, expertise, and physical persons of Shi'i scholars from Jabal 'Amil were all enlisted to help promote Twelver Shi'ism as state-supported orthodoxy in Safavid Iran from the beginning of the sixteenth century; whether intentionally or not, they also contributed to the centralization of state authority and the gradual consolidation of Safavid imperial power in the process. Indeed, the intellectual and symbolic formation of the Safavid Empire fundamentally depended on the importation of scholarly know-how from Jabal 'Amil, the heartland of Shi'i intellectual and religious life during the late medieval and early modern periods. Back in Jabal 'Amil, large clans and notable families played the role of political administrators and decision makers in matters of intra- as well as inter-communal relations from the sixteenth through the eighteenth century. Concentrated in South Lebanon and the Biqa' Valley, the Shi'a of Greater Syria remained relatively under-represented under Ottoman rule, although there were certainly exceptional cases of powerful Shiʿi families and clans that could occasionally challenge Ottoman power.[1]

This chapter traces what I call the "incomplete nationalization" of Jabal ʿAmil, by which I refer to the historical process that gradually but never fully incorporated Jabal ʿAmil into the national space of Greater Lebanon, in the transition from Ottoman rule to the post-Ottoman Middle East. From a place of utter marginality, the Shiʿi inhabitants of Jabal ʿAmil and Beirut would eventually emerge as discernible subjects on the Lebanese national stage, even if their intentions and aspirations were often unheard, misread, or misunderstood. Jabal ʿAmil was increasingly claimed as part and parcel of the Lebanese sphere over the course of the late nineteenth and early twentieth century, and drawn more and more into the orbit of Beirut. The coastal cities of Sidon, Tyre, and Haifa all went into various kinds of decline; this process was by no means uniform. However incomplete and tentative, though, the incomplete nationalization of Jabal ʿAmil was both a locally driven, bottom-up process that increasingly turned the loyalties of the predominantly Shiʿi region into one that supported inclusion within the Lebanese national community, while also inspiring new visions for participation in the Lebanese polity. Of course, around the turn of the twentieth century, local leaderships and ordinary people alike tended to support the continued affiliation of Jabal ʿAmil with the historic lands of Greater Syria (*bilad al-sham*). Over time, however, ʿAmili demands for recognition of Shiʿi cultural specificity, religious particularism, and legal autonomy would gradually orient the community towards approbating and even demanding continued inclusion within the state of Greater Lebanon. Yet, the establishment of a modern Lebanese state with attendant political institutions and political cultures—however ill conceived, however weak—was only a necessary and not a sufficient step toward producing sectarian politics, modes of identification, and categories of lived experience. Even as the rudimentary trappings of a modern Lebanese nation-state were coming into focus, there was also a concomitant process of "sectarianization"—an ensemble of historical transformations that eventually spread to incorporate Lebanese Shiʿi society under the hegemonic culture of sectarianism. The extension of French Mandate state power into peripheral regions like Jabal ʿAmil needs to be viewed in relation to larger problems of nationalism, Arab nationalism, Lebanese nationalism, and so on, but must also be understood in terms of these early encounters with the modern state. Before turning to discuss the relationship between the Shiʻi community and the state, however, we must briefly consider earlier historical, geographical, and descriptive representations of the Shiʻi milieu in Jabal ʻAmil.

Meeting the Métoualis, Representing Jabal ʻAmil

Twelver Shiʻi communities in Greater Syria suffered from a lack of formal recognition under Ottoman rule. Anti-Shiʻi policies and violence remained exceptional and the Shiʻi milieu was rendered more or less invisible even as the inhabitants of Jabal ʻAmil managed to eke out a relatively stable subsistence.[2] Writings by foreign travelers, colonial administrators, and Lebanese intellectuals that describe the daily life and mores of Shiʻi communities and individuals in Jabal ʻAmil and the Biqaʻ Valley constitute invaluable sources for the history of Shiʻi Lebanon. Shiʻi Muslims in Greater Syria during the Ottoman period were typically referred to in the plural as Matawila or Métoualis. Discursive constructions of "the Métoualis" as heterodox, esoteric, or even blasphemous could also be informed by deep-seated religious stereotyping, and would often be accompanied by the deployment of reductive understandings of civilization, status, rank, race, and nationalism. "Etymologically," according to the anti-historicist conclusion drawn by Fouad Ajami, "the origins of the word Matawalah or Metoualis were obscure. But the origins were not so important. It was the weight of the word and its history that made it a label of defeat and humiliation."[3] Be that as it may, there are etymological explanations of the term's origin. The most common elucidations noted that "Matawila" or "Mutawalli" was an abbreviation of the phrase "mata waliyyan li-ʻAli," or, "he died as a friend of (Imam) ʻAli (bin Abi Talib)." Ahmad Rida's seminal article in al-ʻIrfan, "al-Matawila, or, the Shiʻa in Jabal ʻAmil," provided a more detailed introduction to the genesis, development, and use of the term over time.[4] Muhsin al-Amin cited both Rida and Shaykh Muhammad ʻAbduh when he argued that the term could be traced back to an old battle cry used by Shiʻis in Jabal ʻAmil—"mut waliyyan li-ʻAli," or, die (imperative!) as a friend of ʻAli.[5] Lebanese historian Mounzer Jaber contends that the term did not come into widespread use until some point in the seventeenth century, and that even then it would be comprehensible only in terms of Shiʻi encounters with other communities—in other words, that the term has no intrinsic meaning and must be understood in a relational sense.[6] The historian Muhammad 'Ali Makki claims that the Shi'a in Jabal 'Amil applied the name to themselves in the spirit of self-empowerment, in order to escape the "reflections" of other Shi'i sects and communities upon them and to carve out their own "independence" for themselves, as well as to define themselves against other Shi'i communities elsewhere.[7] Both Jaber and Makki point up the relationality of the term and of Shi'i self-understandings more broadly. By contrast, Majed Halawi perceives endemic hostility, arguing that in order "to rationalize its neglect of the Shi'a masses, Lebanese society as a whole created an appropriately repulsive Mutawali 'character' which was easily scapegoated when necessary."[8]

Depictions of "Métoualis" in the writings of travelers, missionaries, and other foreign observers from the late eighteenth century through the mid-twentieth century were multilayered. Most emphasized the intractable insularity of the community. In the late eighteenth century, Volney painted a picture of the Shi'a of Greater Syria as set apart on account of their unique ritual practices:

> the Motouâlis [sic] add exterior practices that exhibit their mutual aversion. For example, they curse Omar and Moâouia [sic] as usurpers and rebels; they celebrate Ali and Hosain as saints and martyrs. They begin their ablutions with the elbow, in place of those that begin with the tip of the finger, like the Turks; they consider themselves soiled by contact with strangers; and, against general custom in the Levant, neither drink nor eat from the vase that was served to someone who is not of their sect, they will not even sit at the same table. These principles and customs, in isolating the Motouâlis [sic] from their neighbors, have made them a distinct society.[9]

Louis Lortet, another Frenchman to visit the region in the late nineteenth-century, echoes Volney's sentiment:

> The Metawalis profess Islam, but follow the sect of Ali: they are thus Shiites, like the Persians. They never take their meals with men of another religion, and always wash the glass from which a foreigner drank carefully. They are also obliged to purify over several days, so

as to erase the stain that they made by touching an infidel, even if this was with the side of their clothing. With this intolerant meticulousness one recognizes the practices of ancient Judaism. This tribe lives chiefly in the district of Bsharré, the valley of Leontès and the plain of Biqaʿ. Nearly independent, begrudgingly recognizing the authority [*pouvoir*] of the pashas, they are controlled by sheiks chosen from the principal families that constitute a veritable aristocracy. Métoualis, today fifty or sixty thousand, can, assure their leaders, put nearly twenty thousand men under their command. They venerate Ali and Hosein as saints and martyrs; they begin their ablutions with the elbow, and not with the end of the fingers like other Moslems. Religious hatred is so intense among these Orientals that, in the valleys of Lebanon, the inhabitants of different beliefs do not visit one another, do not even know one another, although the villages are often only of a few kilometers apart from each other.[10]

Nearing the end of the nineteenth century, Henri Lammens, the well-known Belgian Orientalist, writes:

> The Métoualis are Moslem Shiites or partisans of Ali, son-in-law and cousin of the Prophet. For this reason, they cordially detest the Sunnis or orthodox Moslems, who well return it to them. The Turkish government remembers them when it feels the need to fill the vacuums of its coffers or its military cadres.[11]

Spanning over a century and a half, these textual resemblances are uncanny and seem to support the proposition that the Matawila were isolated, aloof, and averse to social intercourse with "outsiders."

"In their bearing," writes the British Reverend John Wortabet while traveling through Greater Syria in the mid-nineteenth century, "the Metawileh are sanctimonious and pharisaical, proud of their religion and of their strict adherence to its ceremonial observances, and lay claim to superior learning."[12] In his mid-nineteenth-century account of manners and customs in Syria, Richard Robert Madden relies heavily upon the observations of one "Dr. Thompson" (who is actually William MacClure Thomson), a Protestant missionary who apparently had endless things to say about the "Matawila," claiming to "know by experience" that it would be "very unpleasant to reside in a Metâwely [*sic*] village" and that there would be barriers to

> forming any intimate relations with them. You never contract friendships with persons who will neither eat, drink with, nor visit you, and into whose houses you cannot enter without contracting or imparting defilement. The law must be broken down before people thus situated can either unite in religious ceremonies or contract family alliances. These Metawelies [*sic*] do thus live separated, both in fact and feeling, from their neighbours, hating all, hated by all. Of course, they refuse to eat with all classes except themselves; and so it was with the Jews."[13]

Although perhaps not dismissed here with exactly the same kind of derision withheld for "the chosen people," the Shi'a are described as being profoundly mistrustful in their dealings with outsiders, and yet somehow simultaneously self-satisfied and superior. As practitioners of a unique set of religious practices and customs, the Métoualis constituted, to return to Volney's words, "a distinct society." Perceptions of stringent practical measures implemented in order to maintain communal purity would persist well into the Mandate period. "Any person who is not métouali," Raymond O'Zoux writes in the early 1930s, "is unworthy to approach them; they have a great fear of being soiled and do not drink from a container that has been used by a man who doesn't belong to their community."[14] While it certainly may be "true that rural defenses remained high and the rural mentality a distinctly separate one," there is reason to consider that these perceptions of the Shi'a by foreign travelers may reflect less the objective truth of the situation than a "natural vexation at being unable to penetrate the closed world of the village society, and the kind of judgment this inevitably evoked from those condemned to watch it from the outside."[15]

Even more galling than insurmountable social obstacles, travelers were consistently beguiled by the question of where the Métoualis had originally come from. Insofar as founding narratives of origins are fundamental prerequisites for the establishment of modern national identity, the 'Amili Shi'i community found itself in a particularly uncomfortable position. Such an abiding interest in the question of origins and authenticity can be traced back to at least two competing arguments. First, foreign interlopers contributed to defining the Métoualis as a "people," a "race," "a distinct society" with obscure origins; this may have implicitly or even unwittingly drawn on and bolstered certain strands of Islamic heresiography. Second, a body of literature by Shi'i *'ulama'* as well as historians, geographers, and intellectuals sprang up in defense of Shi'i origins as authentically Arab and Islamic, tapping into the power of genealogy and cultural memory. These local renditions of 'Amili history trace the origins of Shi'ism in Greater Syria back to Abu Dharr al-Ghifari, a companion of the Prophet Muhammad from the Banu 'Amila tribe in the Arabian Peninsula, who migrated to the Eastern Mediterranean at some point in the seventh century.[16]

Under the influence of contemporary ethnological convention, Shi'i social and cultural difference became increasingly racialized during the late nineteenth century. Ruminating on the ethnology of the Matawila, Louis Lortet writes:

> From the anthropological point of view, the Metawalis are quite different from the Druses and the Maronites: the osseous frame is stronger, coarser; the frame taller, the shoulders broader; the high cheekbones and the width of the lower jaw place this race closer to the Mongols. But the shape of the eyes, the short neck, generally well formed, bring it back to the Persian type. The color of the skin is a rather dark brown, much more accentuated than among the neighboring populations, whose color is often as pale as that of the French of the south. The shape of the cranium and the face, dimensions of the various diameters of the head, draw up a strong relationship between this race and that of the Kurds of High Mesopotamia. I believe that one can boldly affirm that the Metawalis probably arrived in the thirteenth century. Many Kurds, just like Metawalis, are partisans of 'Ali, but without the exaggerated fanaticism which characterizes the Shiites of Syria. The costume of the Metawalis is about the same as that of the other Lebanese, only the head, always carefully shaven, is protected by a rather bulky turban. It is the only race in the area that preserved this old Turcoman hairstyle.

Lortet is supported in this reading of Métouali ethnogenesis by none other than the celebrated Orientalist Ernest Renan, who "also thinks that the Metawalis are men of the Iranian race, possibly the same Kurds of Iraq that moved to Syria during the era of Saladin."[17] Although he personally visited Greater Syria in 1881, the anthropologist Ernest Chantre turned to the raw data collected by travelers and scientific predecessors, such as Lortet, who had engaged in both descriptive observation and more in-depth techniques of assessment, such as cranial measurement. In his attempt to fully explain the ethnology and ethnogenesis of this "nearly independent nation" that was perceived as "quite different" than the other peoples of Greater Syria, Chantre concluded it was "likely" that they had originated in Mesopotamia and migrated westward at about the time of Saladin. Drawing on the field research conducted by two doctors who had resided in Syria for some time—Dr. Sénès and Dr. Sucquet—Chantre provides wide-ranging data regarding the anthropometry and morphology of this community.[18]

In their quest to pin down Lebanese origins, travel writers and some Orientalists concurred with contemporary anthropologists, classicists, and other scholars by making use of certain "scientific" methods of identifying difference among Lebanon's "peoples" and "races." Writing in the early twentieth century, Frederick Bliss employs similarly racialized rhetoric while also affirming another ethnic or national dimension. "Probably, on account of their distinct physiognomy," Bliss writes, "it is often assumed that they are of foreign origin. They certainly turn toward Persia as the stronghold of their faith, but this is because in that land the Shiʿah Moslems are in the overwhelming majority." Not content to simply point out "distinct" features or "Persian" affinity, however, Bliss goes further still: "The distinct physiognomy of its votaries is easily accounted for by an extraordinary exclusiveness enforcing through many centuries marriage within their own community."[19] To be sure, such a misapprehension of ethnic Persian identity behind all forms of Shiʿism was and remains a widespread belief. According to "Dr. Thompson," the "Protestant missionary" cited by Madden, "The Metâwelies appear to have immigrated from Persia,—[sic] they have a decided resemblance to the Jews."[20] Oddly enough, aloof and disdainful behavior that was again reminiscent of "Jewish" habit coincided here with Jewish "resemblance" as well. In a historical geography published in 1924, Yusuf Sufayr concluded about Shiʿi Muslims in Greater Syria that it was likely "that most of them are of Persian origin."[21]

That the Lebanese Shiʿi milieu had purportedly Persian origins was a widely held misconception, albeit one by no means accepted absolutely. The

Belgian Orientalist Henri Lammens (d. 1937) also became fascinated by the question of Lebanese origins and cultural diversity. Lammens played a key role in constructing the modern Lebanese university and taught Oriental Studies at the Jesuit Université Saint-Joseph in Beirut. In *La Syrie: précis historique,* Lammens laid out a theory of Lebanon as an island (*l'asile du Liban*), a refuge for persecuted and oppressed sects or minorities.[22] This so-called "island" thesis proved to be a tremendously powerful trope, one that would inform other approaches to explaining the particular experience of Lebanon, such as the "mosaic" thesis. Not incidentally, the "island" thesis presents one compelling alternative explanation to Phoenicianism, which presumed a coherent ancient ethnic provenance based in and around contemporary Lebanon that wound its way down through the ages, uninterruptedly, in order to run into the contemporary "Lebanese people."[23] In an essay he presented at an archaeological conference in 1928 and subsequently published in the journal of the Faculty of Oriental Studies at Beirut's Jesuit Université Saint-Joseph in 1929, Lammens takes up the controversial question of how best to locate the "origins of the Métoualis."[24] Some historians have fundamentally misread the significance of this essay. Kais Firro, for example, parroting the ideological history of 'Ali 'Abd al-Mun'im Shu'ayb, writes, "Not coincidentally, a debate erupted in 1926 [*sic*] on the 'racial origin' and the 'religious particularism' of the Shi'is, when Henri Lammens "discovered" that the Shi'i [*sic*] were of 'Persian racial origin.'"[25]

In fact, Lammens made precisely the opposite argument. Starting with a meticulous description of works by medieval Arab historians and geographers, such as al-Ya'qubi, who claimed that the cities of Baalbek as well as "Gobail [Jubayl], Beirout and Saida" had once been populated with Persians, Lammens chronologically summarizes some of the tendentious theses proposed by his Orientalist forerunners as well as Arab chroniclers in order to explain the existence of what they had called "the Persians of Lebanon" (23). Turning to etymology, Lammens suggests that the term Matawila either had to be derived from the root *alif-waw-lam* (*ta'wil*), connoting interpretation or exegesis, or the verb *waw-lam-alif* (*tawwala*), which could mean emulation or loyalty (29). Here Lammens gives some credit for inspiring his argument to Lortet, who had claimed that the Matawila bore "great resemblances" to the Kurds of Mesopotamia; he also cites the findings of other French Orientalists such as Christie and Renan, who had claimed to have met Matawila in regions of the Upper Galilee pronouncing Arabic words with a "Persian" or "Kurdish" accent, which, they concluded, was sufficient linguistic evidence to establish a firm genealogical connection to the Kurdish conqueror Saladin, for example (33–35). In his conclusion, however, Lammens comes to the preliminary "moderate judgment"—as novel among Orientalists at the time as it was common within the 'Amili Shi'i milieu—that the Shi'a in Jabal 'Amil, Baalbek, and across Greater Syria were for the most part *not* of Persian descent. Although their "physiognomy" might suggest otherwise, they were unmistakably and indisputably Arabs. To be sure, Lammens neither ruled out the possibility that the Shi'a of Lebanon could be "ethnologically" related to Persians, Kurds, or to the historical personage of Saladin, nor that there were certain "elements" that could be tied to Persian or Kurdish ethnogenesis:

> We can accept the conclusion of this brief summary, on the condition that we do not distinguish, as Renan seems to do, between Métoualis and Arabs. The name of Jabal 'Amila, present-day Jabal 'Amil, given to the mountainous region of Saida and Sour, a major center of the Métoualis, comes from the Banu 'Amila, sub-tribe of Banu Godam. So among the Bedouins of 'Amila—according to Ya'qoubi, in his time they populated the Galilee—that, after the 3rd century A. H. would have widespread theories of the Shi'a imamate. In other words, we should see, in the Banou 'Amila, the ancestors of the Métoualis of Lebanon.

Lammens effectively glazes an Orientalist patina of legitimacy over the top of a local theory of 'Amili Shi'i origins (38–39). Regardless of the conclusions, however, Orientalist and 'Amili Shi'i claims converged on the notion that the Matawila constitute a separate race or nation, whether their origins were considered to be found with the Kurds of Mesopotamia or among seventh-century Arabian tribes. French colonial knowledge likewise located Shi'i origins within racial hierarchies and ethnic blocs; Shi'i theories of origins were rooted in the "tradition" of genealogy.

However early twentieth-century writers elected to place them racially, geographically, or genealogically, many foreign interlocutors continued to find the Métouali lifestyle abhorrent or shocking somehow. The primitive character of rural life was opposed to the civilized urbanity found in cities like Damascus or Beirut, and the moral decay among the Matawila was contrasted to the common rectitude found among local Christians. "The Metoualis of Lebanon are heterodox Mohammedans," Richard Robert Madden discovers, "of a very loose character in faith and morals. They call themselves orthodox Osmanlis, but they are of the Schiite [sic] sect of Ali. Wild, uncivilised people, they are the least numerous of the inhabitants of the Lebanon. Their numbers now hardly exceed 20,000."[26] David Urquhart, the noted British evangelical, toured Greater Syria, and upon arriving in Jabal 'Amil, his narrative tone shifts profoundly:

> We were now approaching the southern extremity of the Lebanon. From the day before we had lost the horizontal masses; here the stratum was inclined, and when we got out of the valley as it were on the surface of the mountain, the strangest appearance was presented. The grey rocks stood up or lay all around, you could move in no direction without clambering over boulders or square fragments which sometimes looked like towers; or the rock was honeycombed and worked into holes and crevices. It was a wilderness of stones. This thorough contrast with the rectangular massive and smooth surfaces of rock, was produced by no difference of substance but solely by a slight change of position.[27]

Moving southward away from Beirut, changes in the landscape augured the appearance of an alien environment, one which seemed to exist outside of space and time: if Beirut is an outpost of civilization, does the geography of Jabal 'Amil stand in here for a certain kind of cultural alterity? Moreover, such perceptions would have been filtered through certain evangelical sensibilities expressed in religious terms; like other pilgrims, Urquhart understood much of what he saw through the lens of his Christian faith. Upon meeting a "Turkish gentleman, as I imagined him," who was "however a Metuali, and nephew to 'Hamed the Bey'," Urquhart was surprised to find that

> His appearance, address, costume, and attendance, was far above any thing I could have expected among the Metuali, and superior to any thing I had seen among the Druzes. There was no pretence . . . and I was glad that I had not been diverted from visiting this people by

the contemptuous discourses respecting them, to which my ears had become accustomed (315).

Although the reader is not told who was responsible for propagating those "contemptuous discourses respecting them," Urquhart

had been much dissuaded from venturing among the Metuali, or Kizzil-bash, as they were ferocious and fanatic; they would not eat with Christians or Mussulmans, nor use the dishes out of which they had eaten: that I risked being stoned as well as maltreated in a country where there was absolutely nothing of interest either in the way of scenery, antiquities, or people. I naturally apprehended that, being neither the guest of a chief nor within reach of any person of authority, I might fare ill as regards supper; but presently a stewed fowl and a dish of bourgoul made its appearance, which would not have disgraced any country (318–319).

Although the reader never learns by whom Urquhart was "dissuaded from venturing among the Metuali," nor who referred to the 'Amili Shi'i community as "Kizzil-bash," it was hardly uncommon for foreign travelers to hire guides in Beirut, potential sources for negative stereotypes about the Shi'i milieu in Greater Syria.

Aside from "racial" difference and a general aversion to social intercourse with "outsiders," visitors also identified religious practices that set the Matawila apart from other "races" in Lebanon. Henri Lammens, the Belgian Orientalist, exclaims,

How times have changed! Some Metawali kids come to contemplate us, but [with] nothing hostile in their attitude or in their words. We asked for water: we were led to the *gargoulette*. After our departure, it will be broken or more likely subjected to purification ceremonies: any object touched by an infidel being necessarily soiled. The case would have been differently serious if we had directly drunk from the *gargoulette*: not even destruction would be able to remove such a stain. Throughout our voyage we have never been able to accept a piece of bread or any other food, except from an old Metawali brigand.

Particularly fervent devotion to ritual purity is pointed out here even as the Matawila are criticized simultaneously for being uniquely *un*hygienic. "One can exaggerate everything," Lammens proceeds to bemoan, "except the state of degradation of the Métouali populations. In their place, one even forgets the great virtue of the Eastern people: hospitality."[28] The Reverend John Wortabet goes a step further, concluding, "the Metawileh, in their habits, dress, and mode of living, are by far the most filthy race in the country."[29] After a long day spent out in the countryside, David Urquhart "returned by moonlight to a merry supper in one of the most wretched hovels I ever entered." Urquhart meditates on the backwardness of the Shi'i milieu in greater detail:

> These houses might be supposed not the work of men's hands but of otters' tails, but for the claim of authorship, a human hand, (the left one) plentifully stamped upon the work. The clay is fashioned into all sorts of things, the purpose of some of which I could imagine, whilst that of others baffled my ingenuity, nor could I learn. In the one prepared for me, there was scarcely room under the raised platform for my horses to sleep. Above the horses roosted the cocks; both combined to make me pass what the French call a white, but what I should call a black, night. The people of the hut had no kind of vessel out of which I could get a drink of milk; their food is olives and cakes, the latter earthy as also the olives; ten olives is the rations for a full grown man, yet on this diet they live to an extraordinary age. They are in rags, except some of the Sheiks, and are all mendicants. They will come and stand round the cooking which goes on in the open air, and if one is asked to go and get some eggs, he will shrug his shoulders, and when told he will be paid for his trouble, he answers, "there is none." If another is asked to sell a sheep or a fowl, he answers, "it is not mine." The filth is revolting. It would seem as if they took a particular pride in exhibiting their rebellion against the law, originally proclaimed from Horeb and afterwards repeated from Mecca, both in regard to their persons and the cleanliness of their villages (232–234).

Encounters with the Matawila spurred some to differentiate the disorienting beauty of the natural environment from the primitiveness of the built environment, the material from the spiritual. These vivid depictions of the

Shi'i milieu are shot through with themes of pollution, as in the following comment from Frederick Jones Bliss:

> The exclusiveness of the Metawileh is enhanced by their own idea that ceremonial uncleanness is produced by contact, even at second hand, not only with members of other religions, but even with the Sunni Moslems, though fear of the power of the latter leads to a relaxation of the principle in Syria. . . . It may be emphasized that this insistence on cleanness is strictly ceremonial. In the Metawileh villages of the interior actual cleanliness is sadly wanting. Never shall I forget the night spent by my father and myself on the filthy floor of a khan, or stable of a squalid village in Naphtali, where shadowy cats, lean and grim, prowled around the saddle-bags that served us for pillows, nor the surprise I felt at two in the morning, when my father returned from a raid on the reluctant hospitality of the town, bearing some milk which an ancient dame had been persuaded to draw from a ghastly cow into our own vessel.[30]

The community was literally unclean; as a result, Shi'i ritual purity could hardly be perceived as anything but a farce. When considered together all at once, these examples contribute to a rather gloomy representation of the Shi'i social body, bound up with notions of sloth, laziness, and all-around passivity. The stubborn longevity of such notions is perceptible in the words of one French colonial administrator, who reported from South Lebanon in 1937: "Purity, moreover [,] does not mean hygiene."[31]

Travel writing can be retrofitted with political judgment, peppered with civilizational overtones after the fact. Bliss drew on biblical references, as if returning to antiquity upon venturing into the "kingdom of the Métoualis." "The race of Métoualis, or Metâouileh, Metaoâly in the singular," Lortet argued, "is less civilized, brutal at times and [they] profoundly resent the Christians."[32] "After fanaticism and an inveterate leaning for armed robbery," Lammens quips, "idleness is their capital sin. Though generally well-sized and strong, they prefer to let themselves die of hunger than pick up the shovel or touch a plough." Still, Lammens was willing to concede that among

> the causes of this general degradation appears me to be the secular oppression in which Metawalis lived. Since the death of Ali, the Shiites

were always persecuted by Sunnites. Obliged to hide, of shrouding themselves in secrecy and mystery, they drew from this insulation the feelings of savage hatred which burst in their relationship with their neighbors.

Waxing almost psychoanalytic, Lammens manages to find some positive attributes:

> There is after all a beautiful side to the character of these people: it is their attachment with prayer. They will not give it up for anything in the world. One had evidence of it in the last insurrection of Hawran. Opposite the Druses and under a hail of bullets, the Metawali contingents completed their ritual prayers with the same calm that one would find in their "mosque" of Bilâd Bésâra.[33]

Urquhart described this paradoxical quietist fanaticism in slightly different terms: "a troop of Metuali came up . . . [and] all spoke together, crying at the top of their voices, but were very submissive when it was signified to them that this was not the manner in which business could be done, and withdrew well satisfied, when told that if they appointed one of their number to make known their prayer it would be attended to" (253). The Matawila speak hysterically, en masse, in a united communal voice; still, on the other hand, they remain a "passive troop" that must be instructed in the ways of civilized social behavior. Whatever the case, Urquhart learned something quite different from his Christian hosts in Marjayoun:

> The varieties of the people are like those of the land or the landscape. Here they were Christians, characterised by the reverse of inferiority to their neighbours: curious as to the cause, I inquired if they had domestic industry. Just as a thrifty Highland housewife would have answered, they replied to me. The Sheik, comprehending the object of my question, added, 'We are not like the Metuali, who have to go far away to Sur, and pay three times the price of what they buy; we make at home everything we want.' 'And we dye it too', exclaimed a man sitting at his side, and holding up a pair of hands, the cerulean complexion of which, gave colour to his words (349–350).

Christians appear industrious and productive by comparison to the Matawila; their words, personalities, and character have "colour," their commentary purer, more authentic. An early twentieth-century New York Catholic missionary ministering among the Maronite community in Mount Lebanon recoiled upon the prospect of having come across a Métouali girl: "Her bristly hair, gaping mouth displaying rows of white teeth, haggard eyes, bronzed skin, coarse voice and boy-like ways were indeed sufficient to make her look the Mussulman." It turned out that, "though not a métouali in religion, [she] would indeed pass for one as far as ignorance and uncouthness were concerned. She did not even know how to make the sign of the cross and no one had paid any heed to her soul."[34] Identifying certain civilizational attributes was another way of discursively segmenting the Lebanese cultural landscape. At times, such descriptions of the Shi'i milieu in Greater Syria during the late Ottoman period seem almost completely detached from local lives.[35]

On the eve of World War I, two Ottoman officials were dispatched in order to provide the Sublime Porte with an overview of the conditions in the Syrian provinces. On that tour, Muhammad Rafiq al-Tamimi and Muhammad Bahjat also lamented the lack of culture and civilization that they found among the Matawila: "We must not forget the fact that among the Matawila there are no simple or small songs that represent the natural spirit in the Matawila as is the case with every people. When I asked one of their intellectuals about the reason for this, he answered by saying: 'The Matawila have no national solidarity ('*asabiyya qawmiyya*) but rather religious solidarity ('*asabiyya diniyya*).'"[36] In his 1918 geographical survey of Lebanon, Isma'il Haqqi Bey echoed those conclusions.[37] Around the turn-of-the-century, the Palestine Exploration Fund, a British group dedicated to forwarding the cause of Jewish colonization in Palestine, sought information about this curious group concentrated in southern Lebanon known as the Matawila. One surviving questionnaire used by those who canvassed the region presents a litany of questions about local mores, living conditions, and social taste. Among the questions put forward were: "Have the people always dark eyes and hair, or have some blue eyes and light hair? Are they of pure race, or mixed with Negro, Turkish, Circassian, Kurdish, Jewish, or other blood?" "Do the women wear veils? Are they allowed to talk to other men besides husbands or near relations?" "Give any native proverbs or common sayings, and their meaning. It is necessary to be very careful that these are not taken from European sources."[38] Colonial knowledge, Ottoman imperialism, nationalist discourse as well as Shiʻi historiography converged to produce strikingly similar objects of ʻAmili Shiʻi history, society, and culture, but all of this seemed to have little, if anything, to do with the historical experience of ʻAmili Shiʻis themselves.

Jabal ʻAmil and the Politics of Ottoman Reform

From as early as the sixteenth century, the eastern Mediterranean region was gradually incorporated into the world capitalist economy. Despite widespread advances and improvements in communications technology, transport, and trade over the course of the early modern period, economic integration in the Mediterranean basin was highly uneven, providing great benefit to some and working to the detriment of others. From the eighteenth century onward, port cities such as Beirut, Haifa, Jaffa, Salonica, Alexandria and others underwent rapid economic growth owing to increased trade even as other regions, including smaller port cities like Sidon and Tyre, were marginalized. Economic marginality and heightened economic marginalization in Jabal ʻAmil came with attendant political and cultural costs, as "the peripheral situation of South Lebanon was not only of a spatial order, but functioned equally in other dimensions. The marginal position in the geographical plan was associated with a historical, political, economic, and even cultural marginalization."[39]

Under pressure to modernize its bureaucracy and generate state revenue, the Ottoman state embarked upon ambitious projects of reform during the nineteenth century that were aimed at centralizing state power and reasserting control over provincial lands. Rather than viewing this course of action as the knee-jerk response of a moribund imperial state to Western military pressure or Ottoman anxieties over Western political and economic dominance, it would be more appropriate to conceive of mid-nineteenth-century Ottoman legal and administrative reforms as reasoned responses to local problems confronting the Sublime Porte on multiple fronts. Furthermore, there had been a constant ebb and flow of Ottoman state power and provincial autonomy. The advent of the *Tanzimat* era in the 1830s fundamentally transformed the social, political, administrative, and legal landscape of the Empire. Changes included granting additional rights to minority communities and modifying the legal codes governing commerce and land tenure, as well as redrawing administrative boundaries throughout the provinces. Shifts in Ottoman policies of taxation and military conscription pointed up changes in both the theory and practice of Ottoman state making and sovereignty. In addition to those laws that bestowed "rights" and citizenship upon new social groups in 1839, 1856, and 1869, the Land Code of 1858 "privatized" land by allowing it to be bought and sold on the open market. Meanwhile, the reassertion of state control over fallow and unclaimed land within Ottoman territory had contradictory effects, at once stimulating the rise of new landowners and facilitating the consolidation of traditional patterns in land tenure. Imperial decrees categorically redefined the form and content of Ottomanist citizenship and affiliation by extending that mark of distinction to residents within the boundaries of the Empire who had not previously enjoyed such status, namely Christians and Jews. This system effectively guaranteed basic levels of autonomy for non-Muslim "minorities" throughout the Empire, in the process creating conditions of possibility for concepts such as "tolerance" and "coexistence" to emerge, but also for concepts of religious "difference" to be transformed. The prize of citizenship was not formally extended to Twelver Shi'i Muslims or other heterodox Islamic minorities as such.[40]

These reforms emerged during a period of unrest and profound unease in some parts of the Eastern Mediterranean. Nationalist sentiment was beginning to stir across the length and breadth of Ottoman lands. In the wake of the Egyptian occupation of Greater Syria under the leadership of Ibrahim Pasha, the *Réglement Shakib Effendi* of 1843 established what is known as the dual governorate (*qa'immaqamiyya*), twinned Maronite and Druze polities that oversaw one of the most tumultuous periods in modern Lebanese history. From 1842 until 1860, horrific episodes of intercommunal violence rocked Mount Lebanon and the Chouf Mountains as well as Beirut and Damascus, precipitating full-blown Ottoman military intervention as well as the promulgation of an 1861 *Règlement Organique*. This decree established a new administrative body (a sui generis arrangement known as the *Mutasarrifiyya*) to govern the province of Mount Lebanon. After Beirut became an independent province in 1888, Ottoman administrative reforms had reshaped the political system in and around Mount Lebanon in a way that maintained the practice of apportioning positions of political representation according to sectarian affiliation.[41]

Within the late Ottoman administrative framework, Jabal 'Amil comprised two *sanjaks* of the province of Damascus—*bilad al-shuqayf* to the north and *bilad bishara* to the south. Geographically, Jabal 'Amil was bounded to the west by the Mediterranean, to the east by the anti-Lebanon mountains, to the north by the mouth of the 'Awwali River, and to the south by "Palestine." As Tripoli and Haifa acquired greater importance during the eighteenth and nineteenth centuries, and as the importance of Beirut grew still further during the nineteenth and twentieth centuries, Jabal 'Amil gradually devolved into the hinterland of second-tier port cities. Economic transformations that swept across the eastern Mediterranean in the late nineteenth century cascaded down from the imperial level to catapult a sliver of powerful landed families into new positions of political dominance and local fame. Amidst grinding poverty and diminishing economic horizons, the peasantry in Jabal 'Amil on the eve of Mandate rule scraped by through a combination of subsistence agriculture and sharecropping. Despite its "great originality," Roger Lescot wrote in 1936, "'Amili society still "remains in certain respects very primitive." Characterized by "a feudal and patriarchal organization that gives it its particular physio[g]nomy," Jabal 'Amil remained a place where "the family" still stood as "the essential cell" determining all social organization. The same report casually described the peasantry, the overwhelming majority of the population as "the ignorant masses."[42] A comparable report the following year noted that the "Métoualie agricultural population constitutes the most primitive grouping in the Levant."[43]

Meanwhile, Marxian approaches to class formation have tended to dominate the indigenous historiography of Jabal 'Amil. Khalil Ahmad Khalil analytically divides the population of South Lebanon into four broad categories. First are the large landowners, whom Khalil derisively refers to as the "Kulaks of the South." Second, Khalil identifies the merchant bourgeoisie who introduced capitalist relations of production and trade during the eighteenth century, who were centered on the southern cities of Sidon and Tyre. Historians might further differentiate this group between established families of some economic means due to their business or trade activities, on the one hand, and upwardly mobile notables-in-the-making, on the other, who came to be known as *wujaha'* (s. *wajih*). Third, Khalil identifies the "middling" and "small" peasantry, the largest demographic, who played an intermediary role not unlike that of the "petit-bourgeoisie." Finally, there is the "working class," divided between industrial workers in tobacco, fishing and craft production, on the one hand, and agricultural workers on the other.[44] In similar fashion, Ahmad Ba'albeki situates the process of rural development in South Lebanon in terms of what he calls "dependent capitalism," which resulted in the underdevelopment of the countryside and the effective marginalization of the agricultural economy in the south. Intriguingly, this dependency was not only conceived in global terms comprehensible to students of world-systems theory, but cast in relation to Beirut as well.[45]

By the turn of the twentieth century, the rise of nationalism and the spread of other ideologies would begin to transform what it meant to be a Shi'i Muslim in the Ottoman Arab provinces. A new class of upwardly mobile notables had begun to disrupt the "traditional" hierarchy of 'Amili society. This insurgent social class posed an estimable threat to landed elites (*a'yan*) and other large landholding families who had previously dominated politics and monopolized lucrative tax-farming grants (*iltizam*) during the Ottoman period. Over time, the rise of new social classes would contribute to reshaping the political landscape in Jabal 'Amil as well as the collective consciousness of its inhabitants. As part of a broader intellectual mobilization that contributed to and was dependent upon the spread of new ideologies and subjectivities, notable 'Amili Shi'i figures such as Ahmad 'Arif al-Zayn, Ahmad Rida, Sulayman Zahir, and others became key players in the turn-of-the-century stirrings of Arabism, local patriotism, and even defenses of Shi'i particularism. The relative liberalization of press restrictions and personal freedoms in the provinces afforded by the Young Turk Revolution of 1908 notwithstanding, the Ottomans continued struggling to tamp down on local nationalist activity before and during World War I. 'Amili Shi'is were among many activists arrested for clandestinely organizing "seditious" activity, specifically for participating in Arab clubs and other nascent political associations. During the period between the fin-de-siècle and World War I, Shi'i intellectuals, writers, and professionals contributed to expanding the Arabic public sphere in the Ottoman provinces. Ahmad 'Arif al-Zayn and other notable 'Amili figures became involved in local and regional political movements; al-Zayn, for example, joined a local branch of the Committee of Union and Progress (CUP). New journals were founded, including *al-Marj, Jabal 'Amil,* and the most important Sidon monthly, *al-'Irfan*. As part of the Ottoman backlash against local associational activity,

Cemal Pasha publicly hanged a number of political activists in Beirut and Damascus in 1915 and 1916—affecting scenes that continue to haunt the memory of both cities. Other responses to local organizing included the subsequent curtailment of press freedoms, as numerous periodicals, including *al-ʿIrfan,* were censored or even shut down altogether before and during World War I. Historians have shown how dire living conditions were for the residents of Greater Syria, including Jabal ʿAmil, who suffered through horrific conditions of famine, shortages of many basic goods, and a pervasive sense of uncertainty and chaos.[46]

After World War I, in the rubble of the Ottoman Empire, the administration, politics, and political culture of the Middle East were reorganized. Following the brief-lived experiment of Faysal's Arab Kingdom (1918–1920), the postwar settlement formally established French and British "spheres of influence" in the Levant in the form of the Mandate system, a tutelary arrangement by which the European powers were entrusted to help shepherd less developed peoples towards national independence. This "sacred trust of civilization" would promote the advancement of "mandated" countries and peoples toward eventual independence and self-rule. Consequently, the first French Mandate High Commissioner, Henri Gouraud, formally declared the creation of the state of *Le Grand Liban* (Greater Lebanon) in September 1920, an expansion of *Le Petit Liban—* essentially Beirut and Mount Lebanon province—through the annexation of the Syrian provinces of Tripoli and ʿAkkar, the Biqaʿ Valley, and Jabal ʿAmil. According to 1921 census statistics published in *al-ʿIrfan,* there were 62,796 Shiʿis in South Lebanon out of a total population of 130,361, or 48.2%. Out of some 710,562 people counted in all of Greater Lebanon, there were 104,947 Shiʿis, or a mere 14.8%; 3,274 Shiʿis lived in Beirut at the time. Although responses to the creation of Greater Lebanon were mixed, rurally based anti-French activism broke out in various parts of Jabal ʿAmil and the Biqaʿ Valley. In 1920 and 1921, armed bands of rebels led by Adham Khanjar and Sadiq Hamzeh attacked French positions in southern Lebanon, including an unsuccessful assassination attempt on French High Commissioner Henri Gouraud. Amidst the chaos that reigned over the region during 1920–1921, attacks were also launched on several predominantly Christian villages in south Lebanon, most notably ʿAyn Ibl. In the end, however, political amnesty was offered to Shiʿis who had participated as part of a bundle of enticements that were meant to help draw the 'Amili Shi'a deeper into the Lebanese national orbit.[47]

With the advent of the Mandate system and the creation of the state of Greater Lebanon in 1920, Shi'i leaders and ordinary people made public and private political demands on the local and national governments, to say nothing of requests sent to the French Mandate authorities and the League of Nations. In that sense, the community hardly differed from other communities placed under Mandate rule. Such tentative mobilization in Jabal 'Amil was aimed at convincing the state to invest in local infrastructure and to support the economic development of the south. The most common demands included: road construction, systems of water reclamation and delivery, electrification, a less onerous taxation scheme, and more equitable economic policies vis-à-vis Jabal 'Amil on the part of the state and commercial monopolies. Mounzer Jaber notes how *al-'Irfan* and other voices in the Shi'i milieu "called for the correction of the situation, in the name of equality among the Lebanese." "Equality," according to Shi'i intellectuals, politicians and activists during this period, was a specifically "French slogan."[48] The "deprived rights" (*al-huquq al-mahduma*) of the Shi'a was a rallying point for Shi'i activism throughout this period, part of a broader surge in activism referred to by historians as the Shi'i *matlabiyya,* or "politics of demand."[49] On January 18, 1928, South Lebanon MP Yusuf al-Zayn implored his fellow representatives to protect the "deprived rights" of the Shi'i South:

> My colleagues, I ask you, does it become us and satisfy our conscience to remain silent and not demand these rights [in the face of] the injustice associated with this sect. I don't think that any of my colleagues in this parliament feel the way that I do toward this unfortunate sect [that has been] denied its rights. . . . Believe, gentlemen, that one finds *Armenian* employees in this country, who are [even] more foreign than Shi'i employees: Is anyone pleased with this injustice? As I said, I am not a fanatic (*ghayr muta'asab*), but the amount of pressure is too great to bear [and] I want to know . . . who in this Parliament represents our identity (*shakhsiyya*) or that of our sect [?]

Even as he demanded greater representation within the government, al-Zayn wonders whether anyone truly "represents our identity," pointing up

the indeterminacy of Lebanese Shi'i identity at that moment. "We do not ask
for sectarianism, sectarian rights or a national constitution," al-Zayn affirms
in his rousing conclusion. "We ask for justice." Al-Zayn paradoxically calls
for "justice" for Shi'is in Lebanon without insisting that they be recognized
as such. The Shi'i community is "without anyone to hear us or to respond to
us we have begun to be ashamed of the government . . . and we have begun
to be ashamed of our sect itself and the lack of response to its demand for
even the simplest things."[50]

What I have called the incomplete nationalization of Jabal 'Amil contributed to the structural integration of 'Amili politics and society into
the purview of the Lebanese state and society, even as that integration was
incomplete, unequal, and uncertain. The institutionalization of Shi'i sectarianism in Lebanon was one significant component of more glacial transformations that were recasting Shi'i identity and politics. In fact, the outbreak
of violent unrest and "resistance" to colonialism or other forms of perceived
injustice remained somewhat exceptional throughout this period, as will be
seen in the case of "the events" of 1936 in Bint Jubayl (see chapter six). Shi'i
encounters with French Mandate colonialism are better understood in terms
of concepts like negotiation, bargain, and contract rather than through the
rigid notions of collaboration and resistance, which are woefully inadequate
and of limited analytic purchase. The Mandate period reinforced practices of
negotiation and congruence between Shi'is and the state even as entrenched
habits of neglect toward Jabal 'Amil and the Biqa' Valley continued apace;
all this in spite of the ebullience among some Arab nationalist figures during the heady days of the 1930s, and despite the logic of counterinsurgency
and tactics of fearmongering periodically employed by the French administration vis-à-vis the Shi'i milieu in Jabal 'Amil and elsewhere. The gradual
nationalization of Jabal 'Amil through colonial, nationalist and 'Amili Shi'i
rhetoric would not necessarily guarantee the seamless conversion of 'Amili
Shi'is into Shi'i Lebanese.

2

The Modernity of Shi'i Tradition

This plain, unvarnished tale is thrilling enough, but in the yielding of Hosein to an inevitable fate the Shi'ahs see a voluntary self-sacrifice, a vicarious offering for the sins of his people, foretold, they affirm, by the prophet himself . . . No wonder that for the descendents of those men, through whose malignant agency they believe that his atonement was accomplished, the Shi'ahs have nothing but fierce hatred!

FREDERICK JONES BLISS, *The Religions of Modern Syria and Palestine*

Streams of blood and, what is perhaps more important, streams of ink, representing the mental energy of the best and noblest in Islam, were shed to defend or to reject the claims of the Alids. But their claims are not yet settled, the minds by no means pacified, and the cry of revenge "Hasan! Husein!" sounds with undiminished violence through the lands of the Shi'a, arousing hatred and enmity in the hearts of its believers.

ISRAEL FRIEDLAENDER, *The Heterodoxies of the Shiites in the Presentation of Ibn Hazm*

The murder of Husayn is a fever in the hearts of believers that never cools.

'ABD AL-HUSAYN AL-HILLI, *al-Naqd al-nazih li-risalat al-tanzih*

The transformation of the Shi'i milieu during the first half of the twentieth century was strongly influenced by the complicated relationship between religious modernism and an emergent sectarian modernity. Just as the Shi'i community in Lebanon first acquired formal recognition as an "independent *madhhab*" by the French Mandate state, spirited debates erupted across the Shi'i Muslim world over reforms proposed to both the form and content of rituals held to commemorate the martyrdom of Imam Husayn on the occasion of 'Ashura'. This chapter attends to the specific texts and contexts of what I will call "The 'Ashura' Debates" of the 1920s and 1930s. These debates concerned the appropriate means by which to update, modernize, or adapt Shi'i religious practices and were exacerbated by quintessentially modern conditions of publicity, the nation-state, and improved communications technologies. As such, methods of commemorating the martyrdom of Imam Husayn—the modes and means of observing 'Ashura'—were challenged and refined in ways that were, simply put, unprecedented in the modern era. As Shiʻi mourning ritual practices were modified and expanded, the practice came into its own as an emergent institution in public life, one that proved crucial in defining the relationship between Shiʻism and nationalism, between Shiʻis and nation-states, over the course of the twentieth century. The public performance of 'Ashura' became unmistakably institutionalized by the 1930s. An adequate history of Shiʻi cultural modes of identification and sectarian categories of practice in Mandate Lebanon must consider the role those rituals played in defining the role of Shiʻi communities in local, regional, and global contexts.

This chapter explores some of the complicated ways in which religion and sectarianism have been intimately related but also proved capable of diverging to follow independent historical trajectories. The complex significance of religious practice can be situated within overlapping doctrinal, cultural, and political frames. Relationships between "public" and "private," the communal and the (trans)national, the religious and the secular were certainly overdetermined, but also fundamental to the transformation of sectarian and other sub-national forms of identity in early twentieth-century Lebanon. Certain dimensions of the relationship between religious culture and sectarianism in the experience of modernity were frictional, but tension and episodes of discord could also be smoothed out, and even prove clarifying, illuminating, and useful. The function and structure of Shiʻi mourning rituals proved to be dynamic during the first half of the twentieth century, and shifting political, doctrinal, and personal fault lines within and across the Shiʻi milieu were also brought into view on global, national, and local scales. Historians and other social scientists have consistently concurred that Shiʻi visibility dramatically increased during the 1960s and 1970s alongside the community's political mobilization under the tutelage of Imam Musa al-Sadr. Building upon some aspects of the narrative history introduced in the previous chapter, by contrast, this chapter demonstrates that the problematic of publicity influenced Shiʻi religious scholars, political leaders, and ordinary people much earlier in the twentieth century.[1]

A Brief History of Twelver Shi'ism

In order to properly comprehend the multilayered encounter between Shi'ism and modernity, one must return to certain foundations of Shi'i religious culture. Imami Shi'ism eventually emerged on account of a political dispute over the transmission of authority within the Muslim *umma*. Whereas the mainstream Muslim community (*ahl al-sunna wa-l-jama'a*) formally recognized the succession to Muhammad by his companion and father-in-law Abu Bakr, the "partisans of 'Ali" (*shi'at 'Ali*), as they would later come to be known, contended that 'Ali bin Abi Talib, the nephew and son-in-law of the Prophet, had unequivocally and repeatedly been designated by God to accede to power in the wake of the Prophet's demise. In addition to contesting the legitimacy of successive periods of rule by Abu Bakr, 'Umar, and 'Uthman—the first three so-called "rightly guided" Caliphs (*al-rashidun*)—the partisans of 'Ali also questioned the authority of the first Islamic dynasty, the Umayyads, who assumed power with their capital at Damascus following the assassination of 'Ali in 661 C.E. Be that as it may, it would be historically inaccurate to conceive of the partisans of 'Ali as constituting "the Shi'a" or "the Shi'i community" as the terms are casually bandied about today. In the seventh century, a constellation of disparate political blocs and associations challenging the legitimacy of what would later be called "Sunni orthodoxy" cropped up periodically in various locations. Although doctrinal and theological differences would only later be fashioned into political and institutional(ized) differences, many of these groupings held a common disaffection with the extant Islamic polity stemming from outstanding grievances regarding the selection of Muhammad's successor.

This generalized discontent within the early Shi'i milieu was radicalized into outright opposition during the reign of Yazid bin Mu'awiya. When 'Ali's younger son Husayn and a band of his companions moved to take up arms against the Umayyads, who were perceived as illegitimate rulers and held personally responsible for the assassination of 'Ali, Yazid dispatched his armies to put down what they considered a dangerous rebellion. After sending out his cousin Muslim bin 'Aqil to investigate the possibility of making camp at Kufa, in southern Iraq, Husayn received what turned out to be a false promise of security. The armies of Yazid apprehended Husayn and demanded that he declare a loyalty oath (*ba'ya*) to Yazid. When Husayn refused, he offered instead to turn around and head straight home, to return to the status quo ante just long enough to prepare and amass his troops for battle. But Yazid was persistent, instructing his emissary, Shimr, to vouchsafe passage for Husayn and his companions. On their return journey, however, near the desert outside Karbala, Husayn and his seventy-two companions were ambushed and slaughtered by Umayyad forces. Those women and children who survived were ignominiously force-marched back to Damascus, adding insult to injury after suffering their horrific misfortune.

In his classic essay on the formation of sectarian identity during the first century after the death of the Prophet Muhammad, Marshall Hodgson considers the making of Imami Shi'ism as a political and a historical process, rather than viewing the sect as a primordial creature. Turning away from the specific historical circumstances constituting the life of the Prophet, his companions and his successors, Hodgson is more interested in how sectarianism gets shaped over time, which casts such originary schisms within the Muslim *umma* in a wholly different light.[2] Legible theological and juridical divisions between Muslim sects only began to appear during the third and fourth Islamic centuries. Lines of theological division and political dissent were carved out through religious practice, theological disputation, and ritual, in addition to juridical and political institutionalization. Over time, Shi'i theology canonized a lineage of twelve divinely inspired Imams, understood to be God's agents (*wukala'*) on earth in the absence, or occultation, of the twelfth Imam, the long-awaited *mahdi*. Shi'i jurists compiled legal and jurisprudential manuals based on the Quran as well as the sayings of the Prophet Muhammad and those twelve Imams (*hadith* or *akhbar*)— the original authoritative sources of Islamic law. As scholars of the classical period have shown, however, the crystallization of Islamic "schools" of law (*madhahib*, s. *madhhab*) also took place long after their eponymous founders had passed away. The development of legal schools took time and the formation of sectarian identities and practices took place over the long term, through a process of judicial and political definition that varied from one historical context to another. Muslim jurists subsequently developed a corpus of literature elucidating principles of *usul al-fiqh*, including relevant Shi'i concepts such as *imama*, *walaya* and *ijtihad*.[3]

The martyrdom of Imam Husayn represents the central moment in Shi'i religious history and cultural memory, or what historian Sabrina Mervin calls its "founding myth."[4] Over time, techniques developed in order to commemorate those tragic events would come to symbolize important moral, political, and cultural ideals for Shi'i Muslims. Commemorations of the Karbala tragedy and the martyrdom of Imam Husayn are flashpoints of Shi'i communal identity and integral elements of Shi'i cultural memory. During the first nine days of Muharram, the first month of the Islamic year, Shi'i Muslims attend mourning congregations where the tragedy of Husayn and the seventy-two family members and companions who were killed along with him is related. The story is imbued with a highly evocative rhetorical style and emotional language in order to encourage the expression of communal solidarity with that suffering, including self-effacement for not having been by Husayn's side to fight alongside him.[5] This all culminates on the tenth of Muharram, technically known as 'Ashura' (although the entire ten-day period is often referred to as 'Ashura' as well), when public expressions of collective grief over the tragedy of Husayn are expressed.

From the formative period of Islamic history, Shi'i Muslim communities living in lands governed by non-Shi'i rulers have had to grapple with both mundane political decisions and more esoteric theological problems, including the question of how to preserve 'Ashura' commemorative practices. Juridical, institutional, and doctrinal forms of negotiation worked out between Twelver Shi'is and Islamic government, society, and culture, persisted into the modern period, but also adapted, changing over time and producing divergent relationships between Shi'i communities and the states within which they lived. In addition to specific regional or imperial variation, the persistent experience of minority dovetailed with prior discourses of exclusion and martyrdom. In turn, a more holistic Shi'i worldview emerged, one that was inspired by the symbolic resonance of the stoic and stalwart suffering of Husayn and his companions.[6] The ostensible exemplarity of what some historians call the "Karbala paradigm" has led students and scholars of Shi'i Islam in the medieval and modern period to focus on expressions of that suffering in diverse historical contexts.[7]

The character of 'Ashura' mourning rituals has changed over time. Over the course of the medieval and early modern periods, such ritual steadily became an increasingly institutionalized fixture of Shi'i life. The first formal public observance took place in tenth-century Iraq under Mu'izz al-Dawla al-Buwayhi, and included structured weeping in addition to ritualized cursing of Yazid and Mu'awiya.[8] With the exception of Buyid Iraq, however, Shi'i communities mostly practiced varying forms of *taqiyya* (precautionary secrecy) until the rise of the Safavids in Iran at the turn of the sixteenth century. Even if the "Karbala narrative," as Kamran Aghaie calls it, was a model for emulation in Shi'i politics, culture and everyday life, it has taken a number of forms at different times and in different places. "Symbolic understanding of events in the basic narrative" of Karbala, writes Aghaie, "have always enabled multiple, and not necessarily mutually exclusive, meanings for Shi'is."[9] With the establishment of a new kind of Shi'i orthodoxy in Safavid Iran, a qualitative shift took place in religious culture and ritual practice. The Safavid shahs who effectively institutionalized Shi'ism as state faith relied upon the advice and expertise of a cadre of 'Amili *'ulama'* in order to develop an "orthodox" court Shi'ism that could serve as a counterbalance against unruly folk practices inspired by Sufism and other esoteric belief systems.[10] Safavid orchestrations of public ritual not only promoted loyalty to the state, but also "constituted a sort of catalyst of emotive feelings of persecution, widely spread in popular Shi'ism, which could always be utilised in some way to fulfill political aims."[11] If Shi'i religious practice in Iran was consistently albeit differentially appropriated and mobilized by the state, Shi'i communities in Lebanon, Syria, Iraq, and South Asia, by contrast had to contend with their neighbors and the political structures within which they lived, confronting variable conditions of hostility and tolerance.

'Ashura' in Jabal 'Amil

Public commemorations of 'Ashura' and other types of Shi'i religious observance were infrequently recorded during the medieval and early modern periods in the Arab provinces of the Ottoman Empire. As more or less invisible minorities in Greater Syria, Imami Shi'is tended to practice one form or another of purposeful dissimulation (*taqiyya*) in order to protect the integrity of their community. Karen Kern points out that Ottoman population registers did not identify Shi'i Muslims "as a separate category since they were considered Muslims. Therefore, the census reports that existed did not include a separate category for the Shi'i population." But Kern also argues that the Sublime Porte "accepted the legitimacy of the Twelver Shi'ites, whom they called Caferiyye," and that Twelver Shi'is "were considered equal to Sunnis since they did not curse the first three Caliphs and followed the customs of the Seriat. They also had the right to visit the holy sites of Mecca and Medina."[12] To be sure, there were instances of Ottoman anti-Shiʿi action: when it came to combating any excessive power or influence wielded by Shiʿi clans in the Biqaʿ Valley, for example; or, when it was politically expedient as part of a broader defense against Safavid and subsequent Qajar meddling—whether imagined or in fact—in Ottoman lands. Be that as it may, Ilber Ortayli notes how Twelver Shiʿis were never subjected to anything as harsh as certain Ottoman policies that were directed against other heterodox Muslim communities, such as Yezidis, Druze, Nusayris, or ʿAlawis.[13] Marco Salati refers to the "moderate tolerance" that was shown toward Twelver Shiʿi communities in Greater Syria and Iraq during the early modern period: "The frequent hüküms sent from Istanbul forbidding the ʿashuraʾ ceremonies in the Shiite shrine cities of Iraq were out of sheer fear for pro-Safavid demonstrations and, in any case, were not intended to stop the pilgrimage altogether."[14]

Nevertheless, the observance of ʿAshuraʾ mourning rituals in Jabal ʿAmil remained relatively clandestine affairs during the Ottoman period, when they took place at all. Despite episodic Ottoman efforts to curtail Shiʿi empowerment, visitors to Jabal ʿAmil and Greater Syria during the Ottoman era still identified peculiar religious practices among the Shiʿa, almost universally referred to as "Métoualis" or "Matawila" (see chapter one). "The Metawileh spend the first ten days of the month Moharram in mourning and lamentation, as the anniversary of the death of El Hosain," the Reverend John Wortabet wrote in a descriptive account of his visit to Jabal ʿAmil during the mid-nineteenth century. "During those days they read a long and pathetic history of the occasion, and do no work in them. They call them 'The Ten Days'."[15] Almost half a century later, Frederick Jones Bliss wrote:

> Among the Shiʿahs the woes of the house of ʿAli are commemorated during the first ten days of Moharram, known as the ʿAshura. Only the tenth day is observed by the Sunnis, and for quite another reason: the creation of Adam and Eve, of heaven and hell, etc., etc. In some places this is kept as a fast, but I am told that in parts of Syria the Sunnis make of it a New Year's feast, wearing gay garments and going forth to picnics, thus widening the breach between them and

their Metawileh neighbors, whose grief and mourning culminate on this tenth day, the Good Friday of their passion season. The 'Ashura commemoration of the Syrian Metawileh is but a shadow of the Persian play. I am told that the local religious sheikhs forbid as sacrilege, or dishonor to the family of the prophet, even the publication of the history of the house of 'Ali in the form of a drama merely for private reading, any dramatic representation being considered out of the question. The reading of this history in undramatic form is, however, a sacred duty and privilege, pursued in all Metawali communities three times a day for the ten days. As the village mosques are small, the readings, usually conducted by a sayyid, or alleged descendant of 'Ali, may be given at the house of some comparatively well-to-do man, who acts as host, furnishing tea or coffee or cakes 'for the sake of Hosein'. The tenth day is kept with culminating solemnities. All shops are closed; all labor suspended. Shaving the head or face, wearing fine clothes, taking walks [:] these, with anything else that may give comfort or pleasure, are forbidden. The morning reading is lengthened out from sunrise to noon. Sighs and groans, beatings of the breast, cries of 'Ya Hasan! Ya Hosein!' increase in intensity. For while the Syrian form of recalling the woes of the house of 'Ali may be but a shadow of the Persian passion play, yet it stimulates the same emotions.[16]

Such travel narratives offer historians a glimpse of an insular community under intense pressure against openly mourning Husayn even as the subterranean practice of private observance was beginning to seep through the cracks into public view. According to Frederic Maatouk, the Ottoman governor in Nablus used to station soldiers in and around Nabatiyya in order to prevent the public observance of 'Ashura'; as late as 1918, armed guards were being posted outside local mosques. Consequently, Shi'is were compelled to hold observances in private homes or otherwise elude notice by the authorities when they dared to engage in public activities.[17]

From the end of the Ottoman Empire through the first decade of French Mandate rule, 'Ashura' mourning practices were observed in Jabal 'Amil in a limited fashion. The most substantial commemorations were held in Nabatiyya; there were smaller ceremonies in towns and villages throughout the South and the Biqa' Valley. The origins of public 'Ashura' commemorations in Greater Syria can be traced back to the migration of Iranian immigrants to Istanbul who subsequently settled elsewhere within the Ottoman Empire, particularly Beirut and Jabal 'Amil, towards the end of the nineteenth century. These itinerant Iranian merchants secured official permission from the Ottoman authorities to observe their unique religious rites however they wished for as long as they resided within the sovereign territories of the Sublime Porte. Maatouk credits one Iranian medical doctor in particular, Ibrahim Mirza, a graduate of the American University of Beirut, with bringing the public observance of 'Ashura' to Nabatiyya, what he calls the "capital of Jabal 'Amil," as late as 1917.[18]

Shi'is in Beirut didn't begin to engage in such practices publicly until the 1920s and 1930s. Rashid Baydoun, the Shi'i *za'im* and founder of the 'Amiliyya philanthropic society and school, endeavored to promote education and civic virtue among Shi'i Muslims in Beirut and throughout the South.[19] Mourning ceremonies were held annually at the 'Amiliyya primary school located in the central Beirut neighborhood of Ra's al-Naba'a from as early as 1929.[20] 'Amiliyya 'Ashura' functions were particularly important in order "to create a community consciousness and to serve secular, financial goals."[21] The situation was different in the villages of Ghobeiri and Shiyyah just outside of Beirut. 'Ashura' was purportedly first practiced in Ghobeiri in 1939, when one Haj Khansa made his home into a *husayniyya* after returning from an inspirational pilgrimage to Najaf. When that celebration ostensibly spilled out into the streets of Beirut, it augured a dramatic change for the public face of the community. Fuad I. Khuri noted that *Maqtal al-Husayn*, a text by the Iraqi *mujtahid* 'Abd al-Razzaq al-Musawi al-Muqarram, was used for recitations held in Ghobeiri. "Gradually," Khuri writes, "the ['Ashura'] ritual became the instrument the migrants used in order to display their solidarity, to absorb new migrants politically, and to shame the natives for their concern with petty family interests at the expense of Shi'ism at large." Defenders of these practices pointed out the socially beneficial effects of such ritual. "By using ritual as a frame of reference in politics and by championing the cause of the sect," Khuri continued, Shi'i notables and political leaders in Beirut were "able to mobilize new political forces and accordingly become reasonably influential."[22]

New public senses of Shi'i community congealed around shared experiences and common communal commitments. Shaykh 'Abd al-Husayn Sadiq built the first *husayniyya* in Nabatiyya in 1925; *husayniyya*s were soon built in many other places in Jabal 'Amil, including Tyre, Kafr Ruman, Bint Jubayl, Haruf, al-Khiam, Taybeh, and elsewhere, evidence of a kind of emergent religious infrastructure.[23] *Husayniyya*s are venues in which mourning sessions (*majalis 'aza'*, s. *majlis 'aza'*) are held, a space where the dramatic narrative of the calamities and misfortunes that befell Husayn, his companions and his family (*ahl al-bayt*) is related. These occasions are meant to bring the audience to tears, one vehicle by which those present personally empathize with the Karbala tragedy. During the first decades of the twentieth century, 'Amili Shi'a began engaging in what was and often continues to be (erroneously) portrayed as an Iranian tradition: self-flagellation (*latam*). The practice of cutting the skull with a blade (*tatbir*) probably reached Nabatiyya at some point around the turn-of-the-century. By 1921, the influential Shi'i modernist monthly *al-'Irfan* was admonishing the "Persians" (*a'jam*) in Jabal 'Amil for going too far for when they

> strike themselves with blades and swords [until] their blood flows as they perform the event of Karbala as it happened. This unlawful innovation has reached Nabatiyya due to the presence of some Persians there and it has created a scandal during 'Ashura' for most of the residents of Jabal 'Amil. Let us hope that the *'ulama'* and *a'yan* of Nabatiyya will verify the illegality of this rite which is not sanctioned by Islamic law.

Lest they jeopardize their religious credibility altogether, of course, the editors made clear that they were not seeking to prevent people from mourning Husayn, only to eliminate certain practices from their cultural repertoire. "We also condemn in the strongest possible terms," they concluded, "the taking of this day as holiday and as a blessed day for we are afflicted (may God cure us) with a scourge of immodesty and disregard (*ifrat wa-tafrit*)." This criticism in *al-'Irfan* illustrates how there was no unitary consensus on the specific manner in which these rituals ought to be observed. Moreover, if difference of opinion over how best to mourn Husayn continued to play an important role in the construction of and contestation over Shi'i cultural identities during the first half of the twentieth century, criticism in *al-'Irfan* evoked only some of the passion that would be inflamed in years to come during the 'Ashura' debates.[24]

Under the Colonial Gaze

Some historians argue that French Mandate policy in Lebanon "liberated" the Shiʻa to engage in religious rituals previously outlawed, or at least suppressed, under the Ottomans. The integration of steadily increasing numbers of Shiʻi political and religious figures into the colonial state apparatus—which is discussed in the context of legal bureaucracy in the coming chapters—might seem to lend support to such an impression.[25] Other historians have argued that the Shiʻa were victims of a nefarious colonial policy, at times privileged or even coddled as part of a more comprehensive attempt to divide and rule Greater Syrian society.[26] To be sure, the recognition of Shiʻi religious, cultural, and juridical rights, not to mention political and civil rights, was paradoxically embedded in a broad anti-democratic, anti-Lebanese nationalist, and anti-Arab nationalist streak through which the French sought to prevent the formation of broad-based anti-colonial alliances. The Shiʻi community in Greater Lebanon was not the only subnational group with which the French attempted to cut deals in order to undermine and avoid negotiating with Lebanese nationalist or Arab nationalist leaderships, parties, and social movements.[27] French Mandate rule certainly changed the conditions of possibility for the exercise of Shiʻi freedom and independence in matters of law and religious culture, but we need to recognize that it was a dialectical relationship between attempts at "divide and rule" from above, on the one hand, and clamorous demands from below for recognition and autonomy, on the other hand, that truly defined this transformation of Shiʻi sectarian identity in early twentieth-century Lebanon.

In May 1932, Sayyid ʻAbd al-Husayn Sharaf al-Din, one of the most important *marajiʻ* in Jabal ʻAmil, invited the *Conseiller Administratif* Zinovi Pechkoff to attend a mourning session (*majlis*) in Tyre on the occasion of ʻAshura'. Pechkoff recalls receiving a warm welcome from both the "Grand Sayed" as well as other *ʻulama'* in attendance, some of whom hailed from the region and others whom were visiting from Iraq. Vividly describing the atmosphere, Pechkoff estimates over four hundred people on hand, including "notables, peasants, merchants [, and] porters":

For ten days, the Shiites have been in mourning. These are the days of Achkhoura [*sic*]. Every night they congregate in ten houses of the

city to cry [over] the death of Hussein and Hassan, two children of Ali
Abou Ben Taleb [*sic*], cousin and son-in-law of the Prophet, murdered
at Coufa, in 1294 [*sic*] by Yazid, enemy of Ali and of his family.

Sharaf al-Din introduced his esteemed guest by "saying that the Shiites are
pleased to live under the banner of the great country that is France: country of Justice, Liberty and Equality." After Sharaf al-Din invited Pechkoff to
extend the "thanks" of the Shi'i community to the High Commissioner for
everything the Mandate had done for them, the ceremony was interrupted
by the arrival of additional mourners:

> Towards eleven o'clock P.M., cries, lamentations of doleful chants were
> heard coming from outside. This din approached. Someone knocked
> on the door. Men, some thirty of them, came in, nude to the waist,
> beating themselves with force on the chest, all red with blood. A rhyth-
> mic chant expressing the pain of a tortured love, then, exhausted, they
> walked up to sit on the stage, where they found seats.

Sharaf al-Din commences the mourning session by describing "the massacre of Shi'ites by the Sunnis." What followed is described with almost poetic
punctuatedness: "Everyone cried. Cries of despair. Then, with a signal from
the Grand Sayed, everything became tranquil. Profound sighs. A general
meditation." With real dramatic brio, the silence was then broken by "a single cry": "Vive la France." In the concluding prayer, "the Grand Sayed prayed
for France. 'May God give Victory to France.'" Pechkoff rejoiced in that this
was, to his mind, the "first time in which someone prayed for a Government
in this way . . . [and] mentioned something besides the martyrs Hassan and
Hussein, sons of Ali Abou Ben Talib."[28]

French Mandate officialdom regularly patrolled 'Ashura' mourning ceremonies in South Lebanon. "The great Shi'i celebration" took place "amidst
calm," reported one observer in 1933: "A number of delegations from villages of the region headed for Nabatyé, where demonstrations of the Persian
rite draw a number of believers and curious people every year."[29] "Like every
year," stated another weekly dispatch from Tyre in 1933, "the Shi'i *fetes* of
Achoura were celebrated in the company of a great number [that had] come
to Nabatyé from all regions of Djebel Amel." "For the first time," this report

continued, "the *fete* was also celebrated in Khiame (near Merdjayoun)."[30] A contemporary colonial report from South Lebanon also witnessed a public performance of the *shabih,* the mourning play re-enacting the tragedy of Husayn, in which "adolescents dressed in white, representing the partisans of Hossein, riding on a palanquin carried by a camel, were assailed by cavaliers dressed in black, representing the partisans of Moawiye [*sic*]."[31] During the 1920s and 1930s French monitoring of 'Ashura' ritual sometimes amounted to little more than brief notes filed in order to confirm that there was or was not activity to report. These records tracked such ceremonies as they gradually radiated outward beyond the traditional stomping grounds of Nabatiyya—one way in which the colonial administration could keep an eye on the Shi'i milieu.

In March 1935, Sharaf al-Din invited Pechkoff to attend another ceremony at the Great Mosque in Tyre, this time on the occasion of "Ghadir Day." This "exclusively Shi'i" event marks the day on which Muhammad is said to have designated 'Ali as his successor to lead the Muslim *umma.* Pechkoff understands that those events were "at the origin of the schism that existed until today between Shi'ism . . . and Sunni partisans." This is an interesting turn of phrase, particularly as "partisans" is typically a term reserved for referring to the "partisans of 'Ali," i.e. the Shi'a. After the story of Ghadir Day was recounted, Sharaf al-Din gave a speech extolling the virtues of "benevolent" French actions "ever since it became a presence in the Levant," affirming, "the Lebanese Republic will always be in the arms of the Mandatory Power." Subsequent speakers also expressed their acknowledgement of the "attention" that the Mandatory authorities had bestowed upon Jabal 'Amil over the previous years. However, the peaceful mood was quickly disrupted when "3 or 4 young firebrands (*énergumènes*)" from Tyre who were "reputed for their xenophobic sentiments, tried to tear away from the crowd a French flag that was carried at the head of the procession, saying: 'We are not Frenchmen, we are Arabs.'" For Pechkoff, such behavior was confirmation of "the mentality of certain young Shi'is from Jabal 'Amil" who, although often "in touch with Damascus, where most of them have done their studies," were also "influenced by agitators from Beirut." As they are "without employment or profession, they can find nothing better to do than to follow the *mot d'ordre* that is given to them, seeking to create a disturbance in the ideas of poor peasants in their milieu." Concluding his remarks in militaristic language that is reminiscent of his dispatches in the wake of the Bint Jubayl Revolt (see chapter six), Pechkoff declares that their "actions must meanwhile be closely monitored" and that "the inadequacy of the authorities in this remote region could on certain occasions have grave consequences."[32]

The 'Ashura' Debates

Although the *maqtal* (pl. *maqatil*) is technically a narrative recounting the demise of some historical or religious figure, a genre of Islamic litera-ture with wide-ranging significance, textual accounts of the martyrdom of Husayn and his companions have come to be recognized as the quintes-sential *maqtal*.[33] Sayyid Muhsin al-Amin wrote in his autobiography how one of his mentors, Musa Shararah, had begun holding modest mourning ceremonies in Jabal 'Amil during the late nineteenth century based on Iraqi traditions. Although critical of certain Iraqi *maqatil,* such as those attrib-uted to Abu Mikhnaf and Ibn Tawwus, which ostensibly propagated "lies" and "fabrications," al-Amin adduces further evidence that some version of 'Ashura' mourning ceremonies were indeed being held in Jabal 'Amil dur-ing the late nineteenth and early twentieth centuries.[34] Public renditions of the 'Ashura' mourning ceremony in Jabal 'Amil may have been initially limited to a spare dramatization, a dialogue between Husayn and Shimr, the Umayyad emissary blamed by Shi'is for betraying Husayn. Originally carried out in Persian, the play was later performed in both Persian and Arabic until, finally, it was performed only in Arabic. Those performances were based on an unwritten dialogue between Husayn and Shimr through 1936, when a text was introduced by 'Abd al-Husayn Sadiq, a pre-eminent religious figure in Nabatiyya.[35] The redaction of this text signified a notice-able shift from what had been a more limited performance rooted in a mood of enduring conflict and opposition—against the Ottomans—to a more self-conscious and performative discourse dedicated to morally educating the audience.[36] In 1927, *al-'Irfan* noted that 'Ashura' was being observed throughout the "Shi'i regions" of Lebanon, thanks especially to the guid-ance offered by *Nahdat al-Husayn,* by the Iraqi *mujtahid* Hibat al-Din al-Shahrastani, which the journal lauded as the "best work on the subject."[37]

The Shi'i milieu started to undergo an unprecedented degree of consoli-dation and, subsequently, what might be thought of as "publicization" under the French Mandate. Shi'i religious practices gradually progressed from quietist observation to visible public spectacle. 'Ashura' commemorations in twentieth-century Lebanon have been shaped by terms of contestation first clarified in what I will call "The 'Ashura' Debates"—a flurry of tracts published primarily during the 1920s and 1930s with diverse perspectives regarding proposed reformations of the mourning ritual practices. The 'Ashura' Debates occasioned a number of hard-hitting questions ranging from the permissibility of certain controversial practices, including head cutting or "cupping" (*al-hajjama*), self-flagellation (*al-latam*), and public weeping (*al-buka'*) to the ethical implications of gender mixing in such public assemblies. Comprehensible within a much longer tradition of Shi'i autocritique, the 'Ashura' debates were also indicators of certain transformations in Lebanese Shi'i public culture and self-understandings. Shi'i intellectuals across the Middle East participated in a set of debates about this growing problematic of "publicity," but also about the dynamic between modernity and tradition as it was filtered through questions of popular morality, competing ideologies such as nationalism and Shi'i particularism, and shifting gender norms. But as was the case in comparable disputations surrounding controversial practices such as wife burning (*sati*) in colonial India, the 'Ashura' debates were "underwritten and framed by a modern discourse on tradition," not one "in which preexisting traditions are challenged by an emergent modern consciousness, but one in which both tradition and modernity as we know them are contemporaneously produced."[38] The form, content, and historical legitimacy of 'Ashura' observances became an important point of contestation and discord during the late 1920s and early 1930s; in some respects, they may never be definitively resolved.

The fulcrum of these debates was a series of works by Sayyid Muhsin al-Amin (d. 1952) published over the first three decades of the twentieth century. Born in the southern Lebanese village of Shaqra, al-Amin was perhaps the most important 'Amili Shi'i religious figure of the era. He acquired the status of *marja'* from his studies in Najaf, after which he relocated to Damascus in order to act as spiritual leader of the small Imami Shi'i community there. Al-Amin's widely regarded scholarly erudition and voluminous publications garnered him a distinguished place in the annals of modern Shi'i history. In a five-volume work published over the course of the early 1920s, *al-Majalis al-saniyya* (The Prescribed Sessions), al-Amin set forward "proper" techniques for remembering and mourning the martyrdom of Husayn and his companions. This multivolume work recounts the history and biography of "Husayni" suffering and the epic tragedy of Karbala. As a result of its publication, al-Amin started a conversation among contemporary 'ulama' about taboo topics while advocating for his own vision of how Shi'i religious culture could be reformulated in a modern idiom. Proposing specific revisions to the ways in which Husayn's martyrdom was commemorated in contemporary Shi'i societies, al-Amin suggested streamlining and standardizing the texts used during 'Ashura' rituals, purging unsound sources or inaccurate accounts, proscribing certain practices as well as calling for a deeper awareness not only among Shi'i 'ulama', but also among lay believers, of the social and political ramifications of engaging in such cultural practices in the first place.[39]

Sayyid Muhammad al-Husayn Al Kashif al-Ghita' (d. 1954) was a prominent Iraqi Shi'i *mujtahid*, a kindred spirit of al-Amin in matters of both political and theological reformism. However, Al Kashif al-Ghita', for one, emphatically defended the practices al-Amin was calling into question, including self-flagellation and playing musical instruments in public.[40] Shaykh 'Abd al-Husayn Sadiq (d. 1948), a highly respected and somewhat conservative religious scholar from the southern town of Nabatiyya, which was (and still remains) one of the most important sites for mourning rituals in South Lebanon, penned a vitriolic response to al-Amin. As he was the most accomplished and well-known 'alim from Nabatiyya, some historians have read Sadiq's opposition to al-Amin's ideas as irrefutable evidence of his personal financial investment in the perpetuation of 'Ashura' celebrations in that town. But the 'Ashura' debates need not be viewed exclusively within the framework of power politics or economic self-interest. In *Sima' al-sulaha'* (Attributes of the Pious), Sadiq rebukes al-Amin by furnishing textual substantiation for mourning Husayn through controversial practices: weeping, mourning processions, *latam* and other forms of self-flagellation. Weeping (*al-buka'*) for Husayn, for example, according to Sadiq, brings people of all classes, backgrounds, and educational levels together for a common cause: strengthening Shi'i social and religious unity.[41] He cites several *akhbar* that portray public weeping as a widespread practice during the lifetime of Muhammad; the Prophet, his friends, family, and followers engaged in such activities on various occasions, while many of the latter were said to have wept upon his death. Sadiq claims that mourning ceremonies were held for Husayn from the time of the Imam Ja'far al-Sadiq if not even earlier (35–36). In his estimation, Shi'i religious gatherings could not be compared to other, more decadent events that might take place in the street, as when people get together and play musical instruments or revel in otherwise immoral ways. Furthermore, the implication here is that such practices should not be perceived as *bid'*, and that anyone who opposes *latam* might be compared to an "Umayyad waging war on *ahl al-bayt*" (66).

As for the contentious ritual practice of "cupping" (*al-hajjama*), cutting one's own head with a sharp blade, Sadiq affirmed that this was endorsed by both the conventions of modern medical science—the case of surgery is mentioned—as well as the dictates of a strong religious conviction, since both are dedicated to the protection and preservation of human life. Al Kashif al-Ghita' also pointed to "cupping" and "bloodletting" (*fasd*) as acceptable practices authorized by medical necessity.[42] Sadiq elevates self-flagellation, screaming, and weeping to the status of acts that accomplish the "rejection of evil" (*munkir li-l-munkar*) (71).[43] Mourning Husayn could be perceived and portrayed as one kind of opposition to worldly and cosmic oppression. Sadiq does not find any equivalence between "this life" and the "afterlife," considering the guarantee of one's "eternal" wellbeing to be even more vital than the fleeting affairs of this world (74, 79). But as Sadiq finds such practices to have been commanded—or, at least, tacitly tolerated—by the Imams and the Prophet Muhammad, they are considered as important as any other religious obligation.[44]

"The Most Important Thing is the Protection of the Self"

Muhsin al-Amin responded by publishing a slim tract entitled, *Risalat al-tanzih li-a'mal al-shabih* (The Message of Purification for the Works of the *Shabih*, or mourning ceremony; hereafter *al-Tanzih*), in 1928, in which he argues that certain practices commonly associated with 'Ashura' were actually recent incorporations into Shi'i commemorations and constituted, therefore, unlawful innovations (*bid'* s. *bid'a*).[45] Al-Amin takes an ironically conservative position on how 'Ashura' should be observed, which is somewhat counterintuitive in light of other innovative reformist ideas he promoted, such as the restructuring of Shi'i religious education along more

modern lines. In his strenuous objections to extant versions of 'Ashura'
mourning ritual practice, al-Amin explicitly calls for a "return to tradition."
Laying out a more programmatic agenda for religious reform than had been
articulated in earlier works such as *Iqna' al-la'im fi iqamat al-ma'atim* and
al-Majalis al-saniyya, *al-Tanzih* contains concrete recommendations: the
standardization of *maqtals*; the expunging of "fabricated *hadiths*" (*ahadith makdhuba*); the elimination of unacceptable expressions of grief and
mourning, such as self-flagellation; and the clarification of appropriate
boundaries of representation of Husayn, *ahl al-bayt,* and other characters in
the tragedy, with particular emphasis placed on the issue of gender roles. In
this regard, the work of *tanzih* (purification) al-Amin embarked upon can be
situated within a much longer history of Shi'i internal criticism and ongoing
attempts to purge esoteric or unsubstantiated stories from "authenticated"
religious traditions.[46]

Al-Amin broadly castigates those who knowingly take part in actions that
go beyond weeping over the injustice of Husayn's misfortune or mildly beating one's breast as part of the mourning processions (*al-mawakib al-husayniyya*). Here he oscillates between a theological argument based on sayings
attributed to the Prophet and the Imams (*akhbar*), who are all ostensibly
opposed to such practices, and a political intervention regarding the suitabil-
ity of public Shi'i observances in the multisectarian Lebanese (or Syrian, or
Iraqi) context. Al-Amin argues that the authenticity of the *akhbar* typically
cited to support the legitimacy of such practices is questionable, even going so
far as to claim that some were fabricated (*makdhub*) out of whole cloth. Such
a critique was premised, however implicitly, on the notion that ritual practice
is, at least partially, the outcome of human interpretations and actions that
may or may not have any firm basis in a particular religious tradition. Among
the primary themes around which this debate ultimately crystallized were
problems of the authenticity and authentication of *akhbar.*

In addition to making the simple point that cutting oneself was not the
"proper" way to mourn Husayn, al-Amin also expresses concern for the
public reputation of the community. Shame would be heaped upon the Shi'i
community with the repetition of those practices; negative impressions
would gradually accumulate as indisputable evidence of such disloyalty
towards proper observance called for in no uncertain terms by the Imams.
Reformed ritual practice, by contrast, could serve as a source of pride for

the community. Beyond theological reasoning, then, al-Amin delineates a vision of an appropriate public role for Shi'i Muslims in modern society. His use of the term modern (*hadith*) demonstrates how modernity was an intelligible category of practice that would have made sense to reformist *'ulama'* at the time, even if such a term were also subject to contestation and critique. The word *"hadith"* can literally mean both "tradition"—as in the oral traditions attributed to the Prophet Muhammad and the Shi'i Imams—and the adjective "modern." By opposing (blamable) innovation, al-Amin appears to making an essentially conservative argument. The introduction of practices such as *latam* was viewed as an affront to respectable Shi'i culture. More dangerous still, negative perceptions among "others" would become a liability as the Shi'i milieu struggled for recognition and respect in the eyes of their Sunni Muslim brethren as well as in the eyes of fellow citizens within newly created nation-states.

In this light, al-Amin's religious, intellectual and social intervention was indicative, on the one hand, of a shift in the relationship between Shi'i religious culture and modernity, and, on the other hand, of the difficulty in constructing a sectarian-national minority out of the diversity of what I have been calling the Shi'i milieu. Al-Amin was not simply protective of Shi'i tradition; rather, he was involved in the production of a particular version of Shi'i tradition. Nevertheless, this was less an instance of the wholesale "invention of tradition" than a wish on the part of al-Amin to find a more moderate middle ground for the gradual publicization of Shi'i difference. Indeed, al-Amin's impetus for intervening in the first place was bound up with a deeper anxiety over the perception of minority Shi'i communities by their neighbors as "un-modern" (i.e., barbaric, uncivilized, obscurantist). Despite the fact that al-Amin ascribed this ignorance to the behavior of "common people" who didn't know any better and to a number of misguided *'ulama'*, who were unable to rein them in, such actions would indubitably arouse the "distaste" of "others." Al-Amin issued a hortatory caution against the deleterious effects such practices would have in what might be described as Shi'i image management. This debate consistently revolved around an imagined relationship to "others" (*aghyar*), with al-Amin warning of looming communal embarrassment. He worried that those "others" would perceive the Shi'a as having been overtaken by "ignorance," "insanity" or "simplemindedness" (*sakhafat al-'uqul*) (2–12).

Through his reproof of the abhorrent physicality of 'Ashura' rituals, al-Amin also exhibits a specifically modernist anxiety about the sanctity of the individual body.[47] In contrast to Sadiq's interpretation of *al-hajjama*, al-Amin argues that "self-harm" (*al-idha' bi-l-nafs wa-l-darar*) was strictly forbidden. In fact, any activity causing bodily harm was, by al-Amin's lights, religiously unacceptable. Al-Amin does not come out as categorically opposed to cutting one's head open—when a doctor advises someone with an "intense fever" to let some blood flow as "treatment," for example, this would be morally defensible (14–15). Without a medical doctor's approval, however, al-Amin maintains that anyone who insists on engaging in such an activity is not only participating in an illicit act, but even angering Husayn in the process. Head cuttings as part of surgical procedures are deemed permissible as well, as long as they are done in the spirit of "self-preservation." In this stand against harmful or "unlawful" ritual practices, al-Amin makes an argument that stands in analogical alliance with modern medical science—both view the protection and preservation of an individual human life as among the greatest goods.[48]

Of course, the sanity or right(eous)ness of cracking one's head open on "scientific" grounds is as debatable as doing so for religious reasons. The potential benefit from draining blood from the head in order to treat a fever seems as unlikely (or as likely) as ritualistically shedding blood with the hope of achieving eternal salvation. The point here is neither to scoff at what people do and have done out of religious conviction or their faith in medical science nor is it to create an equivalence between the two for being similarly superstitious. Instead, the debate over proper techniques of mourning should be understood as indicative of an epistemic shift in Shi'i religious culture, a shift that was inflected by the experience and conceptualization of a certain kind of modernity, what might be termed a sectarian modernity.

The modernist epistemology underpinning al-Amin's intervention imbued the 'Ashura' debates with particular sets of meaning. "The most important thing is the protection of the self," writes al-Amin, elevating the individual above the community of believers and above the requirements of religious practice deemed unlawful (15). Al-Amin does not describe this ideal-type individual as a Shi'i, but as a human being. Although there were well-defined places for men and women in his modernist worldview, any "harm" done to him (and it is always a him) would have the same effect, regardless of the intentionality of the flagellant. In his words, "wounding is forbidden damage and harm and doesn't require one's conviction [in order to be a wound]. It results in damage, first of all, and in this the Shiʻi is no different than the non–Shiʻi: everyone is flesh and blood irrespective of *madhhab*" (21). Here is the universalistic impulse often found in al-Amin's oeuvre. Whether the practice of self-flagellation and self-mutilation is actually harmful or beneficial—in a physical, psychological, spiritual, or emotional sense—is not as important as understanding the cultural and intellectual contexts within which the ʻAshuraʼ debates took place. To pose a slightly different set of questions: What are the historiographical limitations of describing al-Amin and his supporters as critical of certain religious practices? From a theologico-political standpoint, might we not also read here the articulation of a kind of "cultural anxiety" about the anticipated repercussions of public religious ritual? If the Shiʻi reformist project of which Muhsin al-Amin was arguably one important figurehead cannot be simply be reduced to a reconciliation between "modern" science and "traditional" religion, as Islamic modernism often has been instrumentally defined, how else might historians understand the phenomenon? Here was an attempt to render "traditional" religion palatable to a newly envisioned Shiʻi public, to effectively modernize tradition in the process. The collective subject of such modernized tradition might be a constellation of *individuals* functioning as a (minority) community or as a globally linked set of networks. Whatever the case, al-Amin sought to protect the individual bodies and purify the spirits of human beings by proscribing behaviors that he deemed harmful and un-Islamic.

To be sure, those individual bodies were not all created equal. Al-Amin was troubled by certain challenges to traditional gender roles that were made possible by what comes through in his treatise as an almost carnivalesque atmosphere at ʻAshuraʼ commemorations. Al-Amin criticizes men dressing up as women (*tashabbuh al-rijal bi-l-nisaʼ*) in these mourning plays, citing what was ostensibly a fragment from a *fatwa* delivered by the venerable Shiʻi *mujtahid* al-Qommi (26–27).[49] In it, al-Qommi took up the question of how to portray female members of *ahl al-bayt* in the dramatized representation of the Karbala tragedy, the *shabih*, by arguing that a man need not fully dress up as a woman in order to indicate to the audience that he was meant to be one; the moral exemplarity of Fatima al-Zahraʼ or Sayyida Zaynab might also be demonstrated with a simple stage prop, such as a gown (*chador shap*).[50]

Gender roles as enacted in ritual were perceived by some to influence the reception and perception *by others* of Shiʿi "tradition," to say nothing of the effects such actions might have directly on those who participated. Al-Amin argues that women who participate in mourning ceremonies should not "scream" within earshot of "foreign men"; screaming is described as "ugly" and a woman's voice an "imperfection" (4). If the debate over the veil in the early twentieth-century Islamic world located communal honor on the face and upon the bodies of Muslim women in the modern Middle East, then Muhsin al-Amin relocated that honor within her subdued and modest behavior in religious ritual, if she was to participate at all. Women's voices, men dressing up as women, women and men playing music in public— all could be perceived as dishonorable and might lead to the shaming of the Shiʿi community. If al-Amin relied on a binary logic of shame-honor that was symbolically inscribed onto the bodies of women (and their male approximators), then women's participation in public performances was also a synecdoche for Imami communities in Lebanon, Syria, Iraq and else-where, in which the reputation of the latter turned on the proper behavior of the former. If "ideas about separating, purifying, demarcating and pun-ishing transgressions have as their main function to impose system on an inherently untidy experience," both the medicalized modernism and strict interpretations of appropriately gendered behavior advocated by al-Amin can be best understood in terms of an attempt to devise a new "system" as well as to maintain a kind of communal purity among the Shiʿa.[51] Just as al-Amin perceived and portrayed Husayn as having been martyred in order to "revive" the religion of the Prophet Muhammad, he also sought to "revive" appropriate techniques of mourning Husayn (15).

The Fallout from *al-Tanzih*

Al-Tanzih elicited a flurry of responses worldwide, from Shiʿi *ʿulamaʾ* to run-of-the-mill readers of *al-ʿIrfan*, which approvingly announced its publica-tion.[52] More critical rebuttals to *al-Tanzih* ranged in tone from the impassive to the vindictive. Almost incomparably more influential than *al-Majalis al-saniyya*, *al-Tanzih* polarized both elite and popular opinion from Lebanon to Lucknow. A number of influential *ʿulamaʾ* responded to the gauntlet thrown down by al-Amin. One unforeseen repercussion of the publication of *al-Tanzih* was the coalescence of an "anti-Amin" camp, what might be termed here an "anti-reformist" cadre. 'Abdallah al-Sbaiti wrote one of the first and nastiest of such tracts.[53] Finding little, if anything, to praise about al-Amin's reformist program, *Rannat al-asa* (The Sound of Sorrow) was more than the sum of its textual critique and theological disputation. Al-Sbaiti accused al-Amin of "consorting with the Devil," of representing a "missionary" line, and of contravening "the Imams, the *'ulama'* of the *umma* and all Muslims." (7–8). Rather than having the best interests of the community at heart, he accused al-Amin of seeking "victory for himself [and] not the rejection of evil" (*inkar al-munkir*) (9). Not only did al-Sbaiti consider the "reform" al-Amin called for unachievable, but speculated that it would launch him beyond the pale of the community, locating him in a hostile stance vis-à-vis the *umma* (21–22). Al-Sbaiti disputed the premise that "others" would ever make fun of Muslims for engaging in their religious practices, claiming that it shouldn't make a difference to a "true believer" even if "they" did. Conversely, he claimed that "others" would ridicule the community further still "if we are taken in by this theory" of reforming and modifying Shi'i ritual. By this logic, Muslims would have to give up other peculiar practices, like the *hajj,* for example (28–29).

　　In a similarly bitter rebuke, Hasan Muzaffar warned against the onslaught of an "Umayyad League," forces that prey on intracommunal dissension and pose a serious threat to the integrity of "the Ja'fari community."[54] Adducing textual evidence in order to authenticate the permissibility of weeping, holding mourning processions, and engaging in *latam*, Muzaffar recounts, for example, how Zayn al-'Abidin, the son of Imam Husayn, was unable to drink water due to his acute grief in the wake of his father's murder. Instead, he spontaneously cried blood, enough to fill a large vessel. Attributing this story to a "correct" (*sahih*) oral tradition, Muzaffar goes on to explicate the moral of his story: "a few drops of blood" spilled on one's clothes out of over-whelming "sorrow" elicited in the face of such tragedy pales in comparison to the horror of the unjustly wronged orphaned son who cried oceans of blood for his martyred father. At first Muzaffar explains how he thought that perhaps there was a mis-reading of tears (*dam'*) for blood (*dam*); the two words differ by just a single letter in Arabic. After consulting the "original" manuscript and finding it to read "blood," he concluded that Zayn al-'Abidin must have cried so much that his eyes grew irritated and dry, causing him to bleed. In other words, he concluded that the story was literally true as well as figuratively evocative (37–38).[55] Muzaffar also addressed the general concern about reception of Shi'i religious practice by "others," but instead of expressing concern over their "ridicule," he articulates a position in defense of cultural relativism. Whereas al-Amin forwarded ideas that bespeak a certain kind of universalism, Muzaffar claimed that every *umma* had its own specific habits. A congregation of grown men clad in black who are publicly weeping over someone who died centuries ago *should* strike a foreigner as strange, he conceded (16). In another use of analogical reasoning, Muzaffar argued that, during the early phases of Islamic history, some must have found the *hajj* strange or even unnecessary, without necessarily intervening to prevent them; cultural traditions would be endangered if they were always subjected to external criticism and required foreign authorization (15).

Even as Muzaffar insists that mourning Husayn through physical or even self-harmful activity is an appropriate means through which Shi'i "tradition" is transmitted from one generation to the next, like many other interlocutors in the 'Ashura' debates, he also articulated the exemplarity of Husayn and the moral imperative to emulate that spirit in the process of commemorating his martyrdom (14–18). The very public nature of mourning processionals, chest beating, or cutting could actually contribute to the transmission of Husayn's message. "This is a mourning procession, on the one hand," he writes, "and the representation of calamity [*raziyya*], on the other" (32). With respect to the issues of gender roles and the mingling of the sexes, Muzaffar wondered whether visitations (*ziyarat*) to sacred sites shouldn't be forbidden since there was often gender mixing in such circumstance as well as on the journey to get there (25). The problem of *tashabbuh al-rijal bi-l-nisa'* was also taken up by al-Sayyid 'Ali Naqi al-Lakhnawi, another critic of al-Amin who made the point that the Prophet Muhammad was certainly opposed to the practice of cross-dressing in general, but not in instances when men dressed up as women for a specific purpose and for a limited period of time.[56] Muzaffar also cited concurring positions held by al-Qommi and Murtada al-Ansari, both of which accepted the temporary "resemblance of a woman by a man" (*tashabbuh al-rajul bi-l-mar'a*), but deemed unacceptable the "feminization of man" (*ta'anuth al-rajul*) (19). In his inversion of al-Amin's reference to al-Qommi, then, Muzaffar makes a qualitative distinction between intention and action, an instructive example of the flexibility of *ijtihad* in Shiʿism, where the same intellectual genealogy or even the very same *fatwa* could be mobilized to support diametrically opposed claims.[57]

ʿAbd al-Husayn al-Hilli, an Iraqi Shiʿi *mujtahid,* was even more combative than Muzaffar and stridently argued that *al-Tanzih* was not a work of *"tanzih"* (purification) at all, but one of *"tashwih"* (distortion).[58] Conceding that certain practices (cutting, beating the chest, weeping) may have only become public events "in recent years," al-Hilli argued that weeping and beating the chest remained religious obligations (3–8). In one of the lengthiest and most systematic critiques of *al-Tanzih,* al-Hilli responded point-by-point to each practice rejected by al-Amin. He wished that al-Amin had not started this "war," complaining that the Shiʿi community at large stood to lose more than it would gain by letting such an internal communal dispute go public (10). Despite belittling al-Amin's anxiety about publicity, Muzaffar, like many critics of al-Amin's theological argumentation and political orientation, recognized, if only implicitly, the political, social and cultural significance of this new optic of publicity. It is in this sense that the 'Ashura' debates constituted a unique moment of deliberation over the proper techniques for practicing Shiʿi religious ritual captured in the public eye.[59]

In light of the outpouring of respect and support for al-Amin by many religious and political figures in the wake of his death in 1952, it is striking to come across so few published expressions of support for his work at the time of its publication.[60] This absence might partially be attributable to the fact that al-Amin's position quickly became hegemonic in mainstream Shiʿi circles. Although no mention is made of the influence of al-Amin's reformist bent, ʿAbd al-Husayn Sadiq redacted an updated script to be used as a basis for performing the *shabih* in 1936.[61] One of the few contemporary published works that praised al-Amin's intervention was a text by Muhammad al-Ganji, who asserted that *al-Tanzih* had been severely misunderstood and misrepresented by those religious scholars in Iraq, Syria, and Lebanon who criticized it.[62] *Al-'Irfan* consistently came out in favor of al-Amin and his reformist agenda. The didactic positions taken by the journal seemed intended to shape public opinion and transform popular consciousness. In January 1931, however, the debate over these reforms nearly broke out once again in its pages, when Muhammad ʿAli al-Haj Salman, writing from Bombay, published a piece entitled, "Muslims and Their Love for Al al-Bayt." The author extolled the virtues of love and affection that Imami Shi'is felt and visibly expressed for 'Ali and his family. Simultaneously, the author subtly sideswiped those who continued to oppose the reformation of the 'Ashura' mourning ritual and almost re-opened the festering wounds caused by the original *fitna*.[63] Nur al-Din Sharaf al-Din subsequently wrote a virulent response in which he cited no less than six eminent Shi'i writers in support of his position critical of al-Amin's proposed reforms.[64] The following month, Habib bin Muzahir published a shorter response that preceded a short note from the editorial staff, announcing that, as far as the journal was concerned, the debate was over, and the reformist stance identified with al-Amin was bound to become the practical law of the Shi'i land; there would be no need for further debate on the issue.[65] Despite this unequivocal language in support of the reformist position, *al-'Irfan* did not stop running articles on the subject. The "derision of others" continued to inform the positions taken by *al-'Irfan* as it weighed in against such practices. In April 1934, the editors reiterated their unflagging support for those "moderate Shi'a" (*al-shi'a al-mu'tadilun*) who participated in the "rejuvenation" of the "commemoration" of *ahl al-bayt*, without engaging in practices like "beating with swords and other unlawful innovations mixed up with it."[66] Shi'is and non-Shi'is alike could make use of similarly categorical terminology such as "moderate" and "extremist." For example, in one of his less well-known works comparing and contrasting Wahhabism and Shi'ism, Rashid Rida called upon "all reasonable Muslims, especially those moderate Shi'a (*al-shi'a al-mu'tadilun*) who are devout in their Islam, to rise up with us in a bold awakening in order to revive the creed of pure monotheism, to put an end to worshipping the dead, from the pure Imams of the family of the Prophet to all the pious ancestors."[67]

Regardless of whether mourning the martyrdom of Imam Husayn in its more extreme forms was equivalent to worshipping the dead, the controversy among Shi'i religious scholars regarding how best to commemorate the martyrdom of Husayn and his companions on 'Ashura' would not simply fade away. As the vehicle for a great deal of Shi'i political culture during the Mandate period but also a stakeholder in contemporary Shi'i cultural politics, the editors of *al-'Irfan* promoted a concordant position that aimed to cool the burning embers of the *fitna*. At the same time, the journal looked to shore up public support for both the goals and gains of al-Amin's reformist agenda, pointing out how new forms of public commemoration had become the norm by the 1930s. "Shi'a are accustomed to the mourning of Husayn in *majalis*," the editors noted. "They have started to reform these *majalis* and make them good from the perspective of proselytizing, moralizing and guidance." Such events were held at the Muhsiniyya School in Damascus, the 'Amiliyya School in Beirut and the Husayniyya Club in Sidon. The gradual regularization of these rituals notwithstanding, the editors of *al-'Irfan* inveighed against the fact that, "in some places there is still chaos, like what happens in Nabatiyya in Jabal 'Amil, and like what happens in more than one place in Iraq." In 1939, the journal acknowledged receipt of a letter from "the well-known nationalist" secondary school teacher, Sami Salim, who wrote from al-Diwaniyya (southern Iraq) to inform them about breast-beating (*darb*) and self-flagellation (*latam*). They called on the Iraqi government and the Iraqi people to work together towards banning that sort of action, which "harms the reputation of Islam." *Al-'Irfan* recommended once again that people read the Quran along with the *maqtal, Nahdat al-Husayn,* by Sayyid Hibat al-Din al-Shahrastani instead of engaging in such reprehensible activities.[68] Amidst the ongoing transformation of the Shi'i milieu, 'Ashura' practices gradually acquired increasingly popular, if not populist, qualities. "There are even Sunnis that attend now," as noted in one news item regarding Lebanese 'Ashura' ceremonies published in *al-'Irfan* in 1940. "But most who attend among both the Sunnis and the Shi'is come from the popular classes (*al-tabaqat al-'amma*)."[69] Critics of "traditional" mourning practices admonished believers not to bring shame on themselves or on their increasingly visible community and advised them to cleave to properly pious modes of identifying with their "tortured" love and collective cultural memory instead.

Shi'i Identity Between Religion and Sectarianism

Al-'Irfan categorically condemned any type of self-injurious behavior on 'Ashura', as it did not "fit with the spirit of the age."[70] This turn of phrase, with its implicit associations to the modernist fascination with the Zeitgeist, is particularly intriguing in trying to historically account for the articulation of a specifically Shi'i sectarian modernity. Al-Amin's discomfort with the flagellations of Muharram partially stemmed from his position vis-à-vis the concept of modern publicity. Such a phenomenon was contingent on the existence of a Shi'i "public"—as the community both constituted a public and was increasingly finding itself *in* public. The editors of *al-'Irfan* were saddened "that the government doesn't fulfill the demands of the Shi'a to make the day of 'Ashura' an official holiday." The rituals were now something of an "art" (*fann*) ever since they had undergone "a bold [and] appreciable development during the present era"; the editors insist that they are no longer characterized by "wailing and weeping" but have become occasions and opportunities for both "sermon and guidance."[71] A new sense of publicity as minorities within newly created nation-states among Shi'i Muslims required new ways of self-identifying and re-articulations of communal cultural intimacy.[72]

Most historical commentary on the 'Ashura' debates has depicted the Shi'i masses as passive emulators of religious elites. Historians conclude that opponents of al-Amin supported the continuation of mourning ceremonies, passion plays, and flagellations out of their own self-interest: either personally invested in these rituals—as in the case of Shaykh 'Abd al-Husayn Sadiq of Nabatiyya, for example; or steadfast rivals of al-Amin—as in the case of Sayyid 'Abd al-Husayn Sharaf al-Din. But it seems to me that reformists as well as their critics kept some distance from, and even harbored some distaste for, the world of common believers. In a classic essay, Werner Ende points out the "dilemma" faced by the Shi'i *'ulama'*, who, "out of fear of losing control over the uneducated masses of their community, endorsed the flagellations as a sign of piety, while at the same time refraining from joining these processions." The "Shi'ite fitna," Ende concludes, was a result of rival elite families seeking to maintain their political, economic, and symbolic authority.[73] According to Yitzhak Nakash, the debate "highlighted the importance of the Muharram observances in reinforcing the socioeconomic status of mujtahids, families, and religious functionaries within Shi'i society" and "also reflected the efforts of the mujtahids to protect Shi'i identity, and their own leverage over the lay population."[74] More recently, Ali J. Hussain argues:

> As with other unconventional and legally controversial innovated rituals, powerful members of the *ulama* class who saw the opportunity to reinforce the memory and symbolism of Husayn's blood and to gain popular support for the new Shi'ism legalized the innovated blood-

shedding rituals and encouraged them in the interests of their own religiopolitical agenda.[75]

Sabrina Mervin concurs that the 'Ashura' debates were, at some level, a contest for symbolic capital and political leverage among prominent scholars and *'ulama'*.[76]

All of these interpretations perceive cynical manipulation of religious practice by clerical elites. The flexible albeit hierarchical framework characteristic of Shi'i Islam calls on each individual to emulate a particular *mujtahid* of his or her own choosing in matters of *fiqh,* religious practice as well as mundane affairs pertaining to everyday life. The gradual abolition of self-flagellation turned out to be something of a commonsensical reform in most places that was hardly revolutionary, perhaps also on account of the fact that the habits under discussion, like most things in Shi'i Islam, are a matter of individual preference based on the practice of religious emulation (*taqlid*). Still, it is difficult to verify historically the claim that the 'Ashura' mourning ceremonies were nothing more than spectacles appropriated by religious elites to at once reinforce their symbolic authority and educate the Shi'i masses; it is equally implausible that historians will ever be able to determine with any degree of accuracy what role commitment played in the hearts and minds of ordinary people, or what role those sentiments may have played in motivating religious elites to promote or oppose such rituals. Moreover, these conceptions of the nature of the Shi'i "masses" ironically dovetail with colonial discourse. "The popular, illiterate masses," Roger Lescot reported from Jabal 'Amil in the wake of political ferment in Jabal 'Amil in the 1930s, "are sensitive only to the questions which affect them directly. Faithful to their chiefs who guide them in their own way, they only see in the current contentions the continuation of ancient rivalries."[77]

The debate over how one ought to engage in 'Ashura' practices remains contentious and has not been definitively resolved. In 1969, Nizar al-Zayn, who had taken over the editorial responsibilities of *al-'Irfan* from his father Shaykh Ahmad 'Arif al-Zayn in 1960, wrote that the lessons of 'Ashura' "are not just a special moral lesson for a particular sect (*ta'ifa*)." These are moral imperatives directed at the entire body social, and the intentional aim of holding public mourning ceremonies is not the explosion of pain or the stirring up of hatred and malice. Even more important, the point is not to "divide" one group from another or to "agitate" the feelings of one citizen against another. In a pithy formulation that more inclusively echoes the currently near-ubiquitous slogan, "Every day is 'Ashura', every land is Karbala," al-Zayn insists, "'Ashura' is for all." Al-Zayn records the public practice of 'Ashura' in Lebanon within the context of a social compact between the state and society. "Because the state is committed to safeguarding the freedom and creeds of its citizens, their practices of freedom and their creed must not contradict the entity of the state and the unity of society."[78] Here are the rough lineaments of an argument in defense of Shi'i citizenship within the context of Lebanese sectarian democracy.

Part of what being modern meant for Shi'i Muslim religious intellectuals and disciples in twentieth-century Lebanon was a critical engagement with the ethical and theological implications of reforming religious practice in light of how "traditional" Shi'i religious practices might be perceived, interpreted, and received by others. In the 'Ashura' debates, modernists opposed themselves to what they perceived as "barbaric" or "uncivilized" practices. This discourse on "unlawful innovations" (bid', s. bid'a) exposed one fundamental contradiction in their position: rooted in a commitment to making the community "modern," Shi'i reformers called for the preservation of "tradition," however the latter was defined. A stubborn adherence to modernization theory might explain the persistence of public Shi'i identities in Lebanon as follows: "The reason that communal identities remain so strong, reinforced rather than obliterated by the communications explosion, is the result of historic doctrinal differences and memories of oppression, both antique and recent."[79] Others might prefer to argue that, "tradition, involving as it does the sentiment of continuity, may be a more productive modality of change than modalities that depend on the sentiment of radical discontinuity."[80] Whatever the case, this durable and dialectical relationship between sectarianism and modernity on the one hand, and modernity and Shi'i tradition on the other, contributed to transforming what it meant to be a Shi'i Muslim in Lebanon during the period of French Mandate rule. Some Shi'i Muslims in Nabatiyya would continue to cut their heads despite certain theological proscriptions against "self-harm"; massive state-financed pageantry became the norm in many parts of Iran; in Najaf and Karbala, many people engage in public processions while they beat their chests and backs with their arms or with metal chains until their flesh turns scarlet; others in Beirut attend dignified mourning ceremonies in which they collectively weep for hours on end and march in highly regimented public processionals; a whole new generation engage in mourning through a reliance on diverse tele-technologies. A vibrant diversity of historical and religious interpretation remains a hallmark of Shi'i Islam, in its increasingly publicized forms.[81]

Debates over the reformation of 'Ashura' mourning practices were not exclusively internal to the Shi'i community or "only meaningful to Shiites." They took place in relation to other sects, to coreligionists elsewhere, and to the colonial state. The emergence of the Shi'a onto the national stage was neither a linear progression of inevitable emergence within Lebanese culture nor a seamless integration into state institutions. Rather, the contradictions inherent in Lebanese sectarian nationalism and public culture shaped the ground from which Shi'i cultural and political forms of self-understanding—malleable and shifting constructions—found favorable conditions of possibility for articulation. Whether individuals in the Lebanese Shi'i milieu were liberated or "liberated" to engage in rituals that previously had been suppressed, the increasing publicity of 'Ashura' mourning rituals coincided with dramatic transformations in Shi'i autonomy regarding the adjudication of personal status law. In the chapters that follow, I will link up these themes with sweeping changes that fundamentally reshaped the legal and institutional landscape of the Shi'i milieu under the Mandate.

3

Institutionalizing Personal Status

Legal status is not merely a juridical fiction . . . legal status is constitutive of lived communities, insofar as it organizes access to institutions.

EMANUELLE SAADA, "The Empire of Law"

One day while doing research at the Beirut Ja'fari *shari'a* court in the Ra's al-Naba'a neighborhood, I overheard a conversation in which someone loudly announced, "Enough, when the Caliphate ended, so did the conflict" between Sunni and Shi'i Muslims. Although I wasn't privy to the entire conversation, the comment intrigued me, as did imagining the types of discourse that would surround and authorize such a sentiment, and its opposite. To be sure, sectarian conflict has often been rendered invisible, or at least muted, by the hegemonic centralized power of Islamic empires and regnant religious institutions to define orthodoxy and, by the same token, to marginalize or invalidate heterodoxy. This chapter considers the practical, historical, and doctrinal significance of Shi'i recognition and empowerment in French Mandate Lebanon. Before that, however, this discussion would benefit from a brief and abbreviated overview of the political and ethical stakes of Shi'i participation and collaboration with temporal authorities within the broader context of Islamic history.[1]

The Problem of the State in Ja'fari Jurisprudence

During the period immediately following the lifetime of the Prophet Muhammad, sources of Islamic legal authority were initially restricted to the Quran and sayings directly attributable to the Prophet (*hadith*, pl. *ahadith*—also known in Shi'i discourse as *akhbar*, s. *khabar*). Shi'i jurists also asserted the indisputable and infallible (*ma'sum*) truth of the sayings and teachings of the Twelve Imams. Divinely inspired and selected representatives of God

who were to succeed the Prophet Muhammad and his blood relatives in leading the Muslim *umma,* the Imams were literally perceived to be representatives of God's justice on earth. After the son of the eleventh Imam was said to
have disappeared into a state of "occultation" (*ghayba*) in 874 C.E., Shi'i theologians developed the messianic principle that the return of the *mahdi* (lit.
the divinely-guided one)—this absent twelfth Imam—would coincide with
the end of time and the realization of world peace. Such Shi'i doctrine was
debated, reflected upon, and gradually codified into jurisprudential compendiums and manuals—legible, pedagogical and easily transmissible Islamic
legal traditions. But the legal principles and juridical practices of Imami
Shi'ism emerged gradually over time. Until some time during the 3rd and
4th centuries A.H./9th and 10th centuries C.E., there were no Islamic sects to
speak of as such, only competing blocs of political influence and intellectual
opinion. The institutionalization of the Imami Shi'i "school of law" (*madhhab*), like other Islamic schools of law, took place over the course of centuries.
In addition to the four eponymous "founders" of Sunni "schools of law"—
Abu Hanifa, Ahmad Ibn Hanbal, al-Shafi'i, Malik Ibn Anas—Imami Twelver
Shi'ism came to be known as the Ja'fari school (*al-madhhab al-Ja'fari*), an
attribution to the sixth Imam Ja'far al-Sadiq (d. 765), although the teaching
of the fifth Imam Muhammad al-Baqir is also generally credited with a number of important legal opinions and sayings in Shi'i *fiqh*.[2]

Sunni and Shi'i legal teachings reflect different sources of legislation
accepted by the jurists and religious scholars of each tradition but also
subsequent differences of interpretation vis-à-vis textual sources of political, scholarly, and religious authority. Whereas Sunni jurists recognize
the authoritative legitimacy of the Quran, the *hadith,* consensus (*ijma'*),
and analogical reasoning (*qiyas*), some Shi'i jurists recognize the right of
learned religious scholars (*mujtahids*) to practice their own interpretation
of the Islamic canon (*ijtihad*).[3] Likewise, Shi'i legal theory relies upon the
Quran and the sayings of the Prophet Muhammad and the Twelve Imams in
addition to interpretive strategies employed by *mujtahids,* the practitioners
of *ijtihad.* The earliest codifications of Ja'fari law consensually recognized by
Shi'i *mujtahids* were major compendiums of legal wisdom and moral guidance often referred to in shorthand as "the four books": *al-Kafi* by al-Kulayni,
Man la yahduruhu al-faqih by Shaykh al-Saduq, and *Tahdhib al-ahkam* and
al-Istibsar, both by Nasir al-Din al-Tusi.

Talal Jaber has proposed that the guiding principle of Shiʻi ethical and political discourse is "a refusal of central state power," because "Shiʻis imagine a form of society without a state."[4] To be sure, Shiʻi perspectives on the state have been defined, in part, by the notion that temporal state authority is axiomatically premature and, consequently, unjust in the absence of the *mahdi*.[5] Historians must take care, however, not to metonymically conflate certain revolutionary interpretations of Shiʻi Islam most often identified with Ruhollah Khomeini, for example, with the broad spectrum of voices and approaches across the length and breadth of Shiʻi history and legal culture. At times, Shiʻi scholars and communities have refused centralized state power, even while seeking other means by which to work toward a society where the weak (*al-mustadʻafin*) would no longer be subjected to the caprices of the powerful (*al-mustakbirin*).[6] Indeed, during the classical and medieval periods, Imami Shiʻi jurists vigorously debated whether the state—any existing state exercising temporal authority—by definition represented an usurpation of the power of the "infallible" just ruler that had received formal designation by God (*al-nass*). Any established authority—states, rulers, dynasties—claiming the mantle of political leadership in the absence of the *mahdi* would likely be perceived by some as unjust (*jaʼir*). Nevertheless, as Robert Gleave points out, "there was certainly a tendency over time for [Shiʻi] jurists to consider working as qadis for an illegitimate sultan permissible, providing the jurist considers himself to be working for the true Imam."[7] Gleave is on solid ground in making such a claim. In the eleventh century C.E., al-Sharif al-Murtada had elucidated some basic ground rules that would justify the "collaboration" of Shiʻi jurists with unjust rulers or states—the posts must be taken with the intention of doing good, either for the Imam or for the community at large. Nasir al-Din al-Tusi, the celebrated student of al-Murtada, took a slightly more refined yet similarly lenient approach toward the question.[8]

The first Safavid shahs in Iran imported Shiʻi religious experts and expertise—from Jabal ʻAmil no less—in their drive to canonize Shiʻism as the official faith of their emergent polity.[9] With the integration of Shiʻi legal culture into the state apparatus, a unique historical dialectic emerged, one in which the inflated power of the *ʻulamaʼ* was modulated by the ebb and flow of central state power.[10] According to Said Amir Arjomand, however, "the enforcement of the shariʻa through the state was never effectively institutionalized, as it was in the Ottoman empire in the same period, and Shiʿi law remained a 'jurist's law' with its typical pluralism that in fact became accentuated during the next two centuries."[11] The development of "jurist's law" in the Iranian context continued to evolve under the Qajars. As Abbas Amanat argues,

> the evolution of clerical leadership from the late eighteenth century to the middle of the nineteenth century could be best summed up as a vigorous move from the *madrasa* to the marketplace. In this process, academic seniority was transformed into a collective leadership, with no ultimate place reserved for a supreme authority. The *'ulama'* grew more autonomous, but serious perils from within compelled them to remain loyal to the state.[12]

The relationship between religious scholars and the state in Iran was dynamic, even volatile, and constantly changing.[13] Even as the Safavid and Qajar monarchs struggled to define Shiʿi "orthodoxy," attempts to absolutely standardize the practice of Jaʿfari law proved futile.

Meanwhile, the rise of the *marjaʿiyya*, an altogether new sort of scholarly organization emerging in the mid-nineteenth century, heralded a new phase in the institutionalization of Shiʿism in the modern world.[14] According to Ahmad Kazemi Moussavi, "the juridical process" of naming a source of religious emulation (*marjaʿ-i taqlid*) in mid-nineteenth-century Iran and southern Iraq was "an attempt to introduce a supreme religious authority during the absence of the Imam from the community."[15] But as Abbas Amanat cautions, the appearance of the pre-eminent *marjaʿ-i taqlid* and the emergence of what some have called the institutionalization of the *marjaʿiyya* "remained largely an informal practice. No set of objective standards for designating such a leadership ever developed, and no specific legal privileges were arrogated to this office. The marjaʿiyya was largely meant to address the need for a communal leadership rather than a supreme legal authority."[16] Just as such transnational Shiʿi religious institutions were increasingly being imbued with new significance, the transformation of the Middle East state system reintroduced difficult questions regarding the permissibility of collaborating with temporal authorities.[17]

Outside the Iranian context, the relationship between states and Shiʿi communities proved even trickier. From the turn of the nineteenth century, and possibly even earlier, the Sublime Porte was under varying amounts of pressure from the European powers to vouchsafe protections for minority communities living within the boundaries of the empire.[18] As Bruce Masters points out,

> Even if Westerners were not entirely responsible for the rise of sectarian animosities in the Middle East in the nineteenth century, Western observers penned much of the early literature on sectarian relations in the Ottoman Empire. They were typically biased against Muslims and their descriptions and analyses often distorted the reality of the complexity of the relationship that linked Muslims, Christians, and Jews in the twilight of the empire.[19]

Chapter one described how new iterations of Ottoman citizenship provided non-Muslim minority communities with enhanced powers of legal autonomy but also held out the possibility for increased cultural or civic inclusion, as yet an unattainable condition for Muslim minorities throughout the Ottoman lands. Rather than rushing to the defense of the Métoualis as unrepresented minorities worthy of recognition or protection, however, most Western travelers reinforced impressions of the Shi'i community as backward, insular, and not necessarily deserving of cultural recognition or political citizenship. As an unrecognized "minority" in the Ottoman world, the 'Amili Shi'i community was in an awkward position, compelled to oscillate between accommodation with and resistance to authority.[20] The power of the Ottoman state was nominally predicated upon notions of legitimacy and authority that were bound up with a religious doctrine excluding—if not negating—Shi'i identity. Under the Ottomans, some Shi'is chose or were intimidated into practicing precautionary secrecy (taqiyya). In the context of the collapse of the Ottoman Empire in 1918, and the dissolution of the Caliphate in 1924, the 'Amili Shi'i community was integrated into a new state structure nominally predicated on notions of representative—albeit sectarian—democracy. Both of these developments justified the reformulation of Shi'i positions vis-à-vis the question of how to engage with state authority.

Imami Shi'i (Ja'fari) law needs to be comprehended as a dynamic discursive system and an evolving set of juridical practices that changed over time through the interpretations of jurists and learned religious scholars. The adaptation of Ja'fari jurisprudence (*fiqh*) to state power and bureaucracy in the modern period was certainly controversial. Although initially restricted to personal status matters, the institutionalization of a new legal bureaucracy and religious hierarchy was one block in the edifice of what I have been calling sectarian modernity in Mandate Lebanon. Just as the Ja'fari *madhhab* was conceived, theorized and debated—assuming that the *madhahib* were formed over time and not within the lifetimes of their eponymous founders—over the course of the first few Islamic centuries, the Ja'fari *madhhab* was formally recognized in the context of a broader historical process that would redefine the Lebanese Shi'i community as a sect (*ta'ifa*) during the first part of the twentieth century.

Institutionalizing the Ja'fari *Madhhab* in Mandate Lebanon

Law plays a key role in the definition, maintenance, and remaking of colonial contexts. Colonial legal discourse and practice often entailed the delineation and specification of legal communities as such. Historical studies of the colonial encounter have illuminated various functions of the law and the legal sphere: the administration of justice; the formal management of legal institutions; the reconciliation of competing jurisdictional claims; and the development of juridical or political principles that legitimate the perpetuation of colonial rule. As Allan Christelow points out, "questions of law in the colonial setting were closely concerned with relationships between communities, and inequalities in power relationships between communities."[21] But the historiography of law in colonial contexts often reifies the work and effects of legal institutions, either by focusing solely on the discourse of the colonizer, or by positing too rigid a distinction between "the colonizer" and "the colonized." The field of law has functioned simultaneously as a site for contact and contention among state power, legal institutions, and various elements within colonial societies. Critical histories of law and other works across the sprawling landscape of colonial studies have now shown how "the law"—construed broadly enough to include the construction of various domains of jurisprudential reasoning and practice, legal institutions such as courts or more informal tribunals, and techniques of policing and control—effectively constitutes the ground upon which juridical and, often, political identities could be formed and negotiated.

Across the variegated landscape of the colonial and semi-colonial Middle East as well—from Levantine states under European "Mandates" and "protectorates" in North Africa and the Gulf to direct colonial "association" in Algeria—law was one focal point for determining relationships of power between colonizers and colonized populations. The institutionalization or, in some cases, wholesale invention of Muslim courts under colonialism was bound up with broader strategies of "divide and rule," which might both depend on and result in the creation of new juridical categories and practices. Legal institutions could marshal disciplinary power as well as produce disciplined effects. More than simply a value-neutral space for the adjudication of civil, criminal, or personal matters, "the law" and its attendant institutions often ideologically and physically structured the production of newfangled ethnic, tribal, or sectarian identities.[22]

In the case of Lebanon, juridical practices were tangled up with the production of sectarianism; law comprised an important element in the institutional scaffolding of sectarianism. Beyond the differential distribution of power and influence in political institutions along sectarian lines (political sectarianism), the theory and practice of personal status law were instrumental in delineating sectarian norms, boundaries, and modes of identification (sectarian affect); law could also function as a wedge between communities even as they developed relationships with the colonial state (institutional sectarianism). The administration of personal status law was one means by which each religious community carved out what increasingly resembled separate sectarian legal regimes and practices.[23] Be that as it may, in his classic study of Syria and Lebanon under the French Mandate, Stephen Hemsley Longrigg writes:

> The religious or community Courts, with their limited personal-status jurisdiction, were necessarily preserved intact as an inviolable legacy of Islam and the millet system; but they gave rise to widespread controversy, from which political motives were not absent, when repeated attempts were made by the High Commission to limit and modernize the range of community rights.[24]

Others have taken similarly reductive positions regarding the role of state power in the modernization of sectarian communities through the exercise of state-authorized personal status legal regimes. Pierre Rondot writes, "communities in Oriental society traditionally play a juridical role, in view of the guarantee and administration of individual rights and their members; they retain a certain domain of sovereign jurisdiction, the 'personal status' of their members." Here Rondot reinforces a notion of personal status as an essential component of local juridical practice that "the modern state" would have to confront. Rondot goes on to argue that the "modern state seeks to improve this system by modernizing it . . . practical developments that may enable a more harmonious integration of its communities."[25] In similar fashion, Sulayman Taqi al-Din claims, "Islamic *shariʻa* courts in Lebanon remained as they were during the Ottoman era, part of the juridical state structure," and not, like Christian, Druze, and Jewish communal courts, under the direct supervision of communal leaderships.[26] Such perspectives on the nature of personal status law jurisdiction in Lebanon are not quite as crude as those suggesting that the "continued existence of differing personal status law for various communities in one country is thus an example of the survival of an institution based on principles traceable from ancient times to the present." Nevertheless, most historians of Lebanon have failed to appreciate the extent to which legal categories, institutions, and practices were fundamentally transformed during the early twentieth century.[27]

If the legal framework in Mandate Lebanon was not neatly transposed from the *millet* system—to be sure, the institutions of Lebanese sectarianism appear to be derivative of the *millet* system in some ways—then neither was the post-Ottoman Lebanese legal structure equivalent to a set of invented institutions. The historical significance of the Jaʻfari court, therefore, is best viewed in the light of reconfigured relationships between the state and Shiʻi society. Moreover, the practical implications of the Jaʻfari court might be best understood in terms of the entrenchment of what Elizabeth Thompson called the "dual legal system" in Mandate Lebanon and Syria, wherein civil and criminal law would be distinguished from religious law, which was ultimately restricted to "family law."[28] Debates over the definition, administration, and effects of personal status law and legal institutions, therefore, might be considered in relation to the reinforcement of transformed Shiʻi sectarian modes of identification as well as the contentious historiography of the Shiʻi milieu.

The foundation of the Jaʻfari court has not been without controversy, be that political, legal, or even historiographical. In his indispensable survey of social, political, and cultural life in Jabal 'Amil, Sayyid Muhsin al-Amin remarks that Shi'i *mujtahids*, jurists, and judges were rarely hassled by the central government, that is, until 1864, when the Ottomans promulgated a provincial organization decree that reimposed their authority over the region, marking the end of an era misleadingly referred to in the Shi'i historiography as "tribal rule" (*hukm al-'asha'ir*). Up until this point, law had been practiced in a relatively unregulated, informal, and possibly invisible manner.[29] From the late eighteenth century, however, according to the Italian scholar Marco Salati, members of the al-Amin clan—ancestors of Sayyid Muhsin in Jabal 'Amil—"gained the virtual monopoly of the official position of "*mufti bilad Bišarah*," an obscure position that is attested in the literary sources and which entailed, among other things, "a pension for life, an *iqta*' [i.e., land concession] on villages and farmlands and other material benefits."[30] Describing his own experience of traveling through Jabal 'Amil during the mid-nineteenth century, Reverend John Wortabet noted that the "Métoualis" were

> governed by beys of their own sect, by whom they are treated with little regard to justice and righteousness, or even to the laws of the land. All cases of civil law among themselves are settled by the sufferance of the Turkish Government, according to the principles of She'ite [*sic*] jurisprudence, for which they have lawyers of their own, and a mufti appointed by the Pasha of Beyrout.[31]

Much more recently, Malek Abisaab has gone even further, arguing quite vehemently that Ja'fari law underwent no meaningful transformation during the Mandate period, primarily because having "civil status" and "elected deputies" as well as "qadis (judges)" and "muftis (those who issue legal rulings) according to the Ja'fari school of law for Shiites" were of relatively minor significance, and actually constituted nothing new at all. "In fact," according to Abisaab, "the Ottomans had already allowed such changes, and a number of Shiite scholars were appointed judges in late nineteenth-century Jabal 'Amil."[32]

Be that as it may, there is space to consider contradictory evidence on this point relating to the recognized status and function of Shi'i scholars and jurists in Jabal 'Amil during the Ottoman period. The Ja'fari *madhhab* remained formally unrecognized under the Ottomans, and, barring the introduction of any new empirical evidence that would help to resolve this apparently technical detail, any and all conclusions regarding this matter will have to remain sketchy at best. Ibrahim Al Sulayman contends that Shi'is from Jabal 'Amil were named to the position of deputy magistrate (*na'ib qadi*) during the early- to mid-nineteenth century, prior to the reassertion of direct Ottoman control over the region. "Yes," writes Al Sulayman, "the Ja'fari *madhhab* was official in ancient Lebanon, in which the Shi'a had a *madhhab* judge just like all the other sects. But before the tribal rule (*hukm al-'asha'ir*) under the rule of the Ottoman state, in order to overcome injustice and oppression the situation required, as was the case after the cessation of the tribal rule" that the Shi'i community not "dare to make public their *madhhab* and they would water down (*yaqtalun 'ala*) their Shi'ism." As if this wasn't confusing enough, Al Sulayman complicates things still further in the next breath, pointing out how "after the First World War and the attachment of Jabal 'Amil and other regions in Lebanon the Ja'fari *madhhab* was made official in Lebanon and judges from among them were appointed" all over the country, and, as with Sunni judges, their jurisdiction was "restricted" to matters pertaining to marriage, divorce, maintenance, inheritance, wills, minors and *waqf*.[33] Marco Salati concurs with one point, namely that, "in the course of the 19th century several *na'ib qadi* were operative in Ǧabal 'Amil: they were local *fuqaha'* vested with the power to represent, and act on behalf of, the Ottoman *qadi* of Sidon." Rather than making sweeping claims based on such thin evidence, though, perhaps historians would do well instead to consider the more judicious conclusion drawn by Salati, who identifies "a partial recognition by the [Ottoman] authorities of the confessional peculiarity of Ǧabal 'Amil." Whatever the case—and it is hoped that further research will only clarify this point—the "problem" remains, according to Salati, "that we know very little of the actual activities of these officials."[34]

Even if the Shi'i community had exercised some degree of legal autonomy during the eighteenth and early nineteenth centuries, this all started to change under the *Mutasarrifiyya* (1861–1920), at which point the Ottoman authorities began appointing Hanafi judges to administer courts of first resort in Sidon, Tyre, Nabatiyya, and Marjayoun. Some have argued that Shi'i *'ulama'* formally appointed to Ottoman judicial posts would have taken up such positions with the understanding that normative legal interpretation would require adherence to Hanafi convention.[35] So long as the Ja'fari *madhhab* remained unrecognized by the Ottoman state, however, Shi'is in Jabal 'Amil, the Biqa' Valley, and elsewhere in Greater Syria would continue to seek counsel for the adjudication of legal matters either in state-sanctioned Hanafi courts or in private homes, offices, or other spaces staffed by religious scholars. Alternatively, those issues that would come to be defined under the broad rubric of "personal status" or family law—marriage, divorce, maintenance, inheritance, and matters pertaining to *waqf* properties—could have been adjudicated informally through requests for fatwas (non-binding legal opinions) (*istifta'*). While such practices may have afforded Lebanese Shi'is some measure of judicial autonomy during the Ottoman period, they remain difficult, if not impossible, for the historian of law and society to reconstruct. Such secrecy surrounding the adjudication of Ja'fari law under the Ottomans remains an obstacle that prevents satisfying historical consensus.

From 1918, through the tumultuous years of 1920–21, and beyond the establishment of the Lebanese Republic in 1926, the French authorities deployed various strategies in their attempts to secure the loyalty of the Shi'i community. French forces fought to stamp out outbursts of armed rebellion among intellectuals, peasants, and others opposed to the imposition of Mandate rule and the inclusion of Jabal 'Amil and the Biqa' Valley within the state of Greater Lebanon. More benign expressions of this approach to control and co-opt the Shi'i milieu included the proclamation of a general amnesty in 1922 to all those who had taken up arms against the French. Even though the French had already established some contacts with Shi'i political leaders and religious personalities, overtures toward endowing the Shi'i milieu in Jabal 'Amil, the Biqa' Valley, and Beirut with greater degrees of recognition and autonomy remained sporadic and infrequent.[36]

Nevertheless, the establishment of Greater Lebanon in September 1920 potentially heralded a period of transformation in the relationship between centralized state power and Shi'i society. Meanwhile, Shi'i intellectuals began to call more and more and with increasing fervor for greater recognition of and representation for their community. By January 1924, *al-'Irfan* could run a piece entitled "The Ja'fari *madhhab*," in which the editors made the case for the Mandate state to recognize the force and legitimacy of Shi'i jurisprudence. The only member of parliament to stubbornly oppose the measure, according to the journal, was Dr. Halim Qaddura, a Sunni Muslim who, *al-'Irfan* asserted, "based his opposition upon regrettable chauvinism, particularly coming from an enlightened doctor such as himself." Appealing to what they perceived as a shared sense of "modernity" and "enlightenment," the editors asked why Hanafi judges were permitted to practice their craft, while Shi'i judges were not:

> Is that not detestable obstinacy? The government of Iraq has enacted a just law, appointing a Shi'i judge to rule according to his *madhhab* and to execute his law [*hukm*] everywhere the majority is Shi'a . . . So why are the Shi'is in Greater Lebanon not permitted a delegation of judges appointed for them in Sidon, Tyre, Marjayoun, Nabatiyya and Baalbek to rule according to their *madhhab*?

The editors viewed the Iraqi model as a legitimate template for the recognition of Shi'i rights and the satisfaction of sectarian demands, insisting that the implementation of such a measure would not lead to conflict in Lebanon. Rather, they made the argument that, just as Shafi'is, Malikis, and Hanbalis relied on their religious authorities and traditions without consequent sectarian troubles, neither would such conflict arise once Ja'fari law and jurisprudence received formal recognition. In closing, they declared, "there is no doubt" that the French High Commissioner will approve of this "justified hope" and "settle the issue by executing it."[37]

There are surviving court records from Nabatiyya and Tyre dating back to the second decade of the twentieth century, indicating that Shi'i Muslims may have gone to court *as Shi'i Muslims* during the late Ottoman period and may not have been utterly restricted to engaging in surreptitious or episodic legal activities. Records from the Ja'fari court in Sidon are illuminating in this regard. Rida al-Tamir brought a personal dispute before the Sidon court, arguing that the case should fall within the court's jurisdiction. The specifics of this case are not as relevant here as the practical consideration of how to resolve the matter of procedural jurisdiction. In an opinion written on September 5, 1923, Shaykh Munir 'Usayran, the presiding judge, concurred that the Sidon Ja'fari court was the most appropriate venue for the case. 'Usayran cited a decree from the state of Greater Lebanon issued on September 11, 1921, which stipulated that, "the Shi'a must seek counsel with the Shiʻi *qadi* in adjudicating all issues concerning personal matters."[38] This fragmentary scrap of evidence suggests that the term "personal status" may not yet have become the standard usage in Lebanon; and yet the practical institutionalization of Jaʻfari law was well under way, prior to its formal recognition by the Mandate authorities. According to Muhammad Taqi al-Faqih, in the early years following the French occupation of Lebanon, "there were Jaʻfari judges, but they used to give rulings (*yahkimun*) among the people according to the Hanafi *madhhab*, even if the disputants were both Shiʻis."[39] Muddying the waters still further on this conundrum of how to read institutionalized recognition, though, ʻUsayran would later claim that "Shiʻi jurisdictions in Lebanon reported, before the [First World] war, to the Mutessarrif of Mount Lebanon, a Christian functionary, and not to Constantinople, which was the capital of the Caliphate."[40]

As early as 1924, a formal French commission of inquiry was formed in order to resolve the matter and so that the French could "examine within what limits it would be possible to give satisfaction to the desire of the Shiʻi community." High Commissioner Maurice Sarrail received the following message from one colonial official in April 1925:

> On several occasions, the Shiʻi community of Greater Lebanon has requested that the local government entrust to it jurisdiction over cases that would currently be sent to Sunni shariʻa courts. It is worth noting the fact that their rite is clearly distinct from the Sunni rite and that the customs of Shiʻi Muslims present some significant differences from those of Sunnis; it is necessary, therefore, to set aside special [Shiʻi] courts of conflict.[41]

As an "identical question" confronted the Mandatory authorities with respect to the "Alawite State," the "creation" of "confessional tribunals" could also appear to be working "in favor of the Shiʻis."[42] Sarrail noted that investigations were ongoing:

> Under these conditions and before a decision is made, I estimate that it is inopportune to create new religious jurisdictions which would be likely to make opposition for us later when it would proceed to restrictions of jurisdiction (*compétence*). When it becomes possible for us to

enforce an *arrêté* that doesn't recognize anything but religious jurisdictions limited to matrimonial *statut*, it will be possible, without danger, to consider the creation of new religious jurisdictions which will be nothing but exceptional. Besides, it will be previewed in the intervening text that the Governor will have the qualifications to appraise the timeliness of creating these new jurisdictions.[43]

Although interested in "giving satisfaction" to the Shiʻis, the French were not yet ready to concede those rights. The High Commissioner was urged that it was still not "advisable to create a new jurisdiction" even after another "discussion took place regarding the current necessity of creating a Shiʻi jurisdiction."[44] The French had been toying with the idea of formally recognizing the Shiʻi community "by decision of the Governor" as early as spring 1925. By the end of that same year, *al-ʿIrfan* was aware that such legislation was in the works:

The matter of officially recognizing the Jaʻfari *madhhab* in Lebanon has dragged on and it seems to have been decided to publicize the order from the work regarding it in the near future. We do not know if it will come before the [promulgation of the national] constitution or with it.[45]

This correspondence among colonial officials indicated differences of opinion regarding just how legal jurisdiction—as it related to imagined sectarian communities—would be managed. In fact, for the most part, personal status legislation in Lebanon was originally envisaged as one means by which to *restrict* rather than augment the autonomy of religious leaderships. The colonial administration identified these jurisdictions as "exceptional," which would help to develop "autonomous" sectarian legal regimes without undermining the authority of the colonial state; in fact, the twinned aims of sectarian autonomy and colonial authority often worked together almost seamlessly.

In his capacity as High Commissioner of the French Republic in Lebanon, Henri de Jouvenel signed Arrêté N° 3503 into law on January 30, 1926, formally bestowing official recognition upon the Jaʻfari *madhhab*. Shiʻi law and jurisprudence became categories of practice legitimated by the colonial state. Article 1 proclaimed, "Shiʻi Muslims in Greater Lebanon comprise an independent religious sect (*ta'ifa*) and are to govern themselves in matters of personal status in accordance with the rulings of the *madhhab* known as the Ja'fari *madhhab*." According to Article 2, Shi'i Muslims were expected to turn to the Ja'fari *qadi* in districts that had a court; if there were no judge in their district, Shi'is would resort to the court nearest to their place of residence. Under the aegis of state-appointed Shi'i judges, the Ja'fari court system would be two-tiered: issues that could not be resolved in the courts of "first resort" (pl. *al-mahakim al-bada'iyya*) would be sent along to a higher appellate court (*mahkamat al-tamyiz*), based in Beirut. A two-story villa in the central Beirut neighborhood of Ra's al-Naba'a housed both a court of first resort and the appellate court. Courts initially operated in Burj al-Barajneh, Sidon, Tyre, Nabatiyya, and Baalbek; other courts were subsequently established in Bint Jubayl, Marjayoun, and elsewhere. According to Article 3, the higher court was to be administered by one "president" and two "advisors." The appointment of these officials would be carried out in consultation with Shi'i legal scholars and as many other legal assistants as the president and the Mandate authorities deemed necessary. Heavily credentialed Shi'i assistants, it seemed, were perceived as adequate to supply the necessary patina of legitimacy on this controversial institution.[46]

The formal recognition of the Ja'fari court echoes the late Samir Kassir's point that, in Lebanon, the "sociological reality" of sectarian communities "is accentuated by the maintenance of a juridical regime that preserves the separation of each one from the others."[47] An entirely new category of jurisdictional practice was instituted by the Mandate state through the formal recognition of the Ja'fari *madhhab*. This should be attributed to the work of colonial officials, planners, and bureaucrats within the administration and machinery of the colonial state—sectarianization from above; but Shi'i legal recognition also came about due to successful lobbying efforts by individuals and groupings within the Shi'i milieu in support of enhanced communal autonomy—sectarianization from below. As one of the first Shi'i courts to function within the context of a modern nation-state, the instantiation of the Ja'fari *madhhab* within the Lebanese state structure would imbue the tension between scholarly and political authority with new meaning, transforming Lebanese Shi'i life in ways that have had lasting repercussions well beyond the Mandate period. The Ja'fari court also contributed to the bifurcation of Shi'i identities along lines that have problematically been reduced to "collaboration with" and "resistance to" colonial sectarian-nationalism in Mandate Lebanon. However the Ja'fari court would end up being judged or historiographically portrayed, there was now an undeniable if not unchallenged state-approved judiciary participating in the bureaucratic transformation of legal life within the Shi'i milieu.

Staffing the Ja'fari Court

The colonial administration intended to install venerable religious figures at the helm of the Ja'fari court in order to infuse it with an aura of respectability and religious credibility. Their top three preferences, Shaykh Husayn Mughniyya, Sayyid Muhsin al-Amin, and Sayyid 'Abd al-Husayn Sharaf al-Din, all refused the nomination.[48] Muhammad Taqi al-Faqih, the son of Shaykh Yusuf al-Faqih, who would end up serving as second president of the Higher Ja'fari Court, claims that his father was initially offered the position but then elbowed out of contention for political reasons.[49] Three days before de Jouvenel put his imprimatur on Arrêté N° 3503, Sharaf al-Din met with him in order to express the "complete relief of his sect with the recognition of the Ja'fari *madhhab* and the establishment of the Shi'i court."[50] As with nearly simultaneous claims made by *al-'Irfan,* Sharaf al-Din cast the formal recognition of Shi'i legal autonomy as a progressive demand for sectarian justice. Be that as it may, some historians continue to assert that the court was a foreign invention implanted for nefarious purposes, namely, to carve up Lebanese society along sectarian lines. For example, it has become something of a commonplace to argue that anyone appointed by the state, from the "feudal period" up through the period of French occupation, was only able to judge and give jurisprudential rulings "in name if they were not upright mujtahids because the Ja'fari Imami Shi'a" believe, in accordance with the teachings of the Imams of *ahl al-bayt,* that the institutional positions of both *mufti* and *qadi* are reserved for *mujtahids* who are "capable of deriving legal rulings from the four sources: the Quran, the Sunna, consensus and rational evidence (*dalil al-'aql*)."[51]

In any event, after failing to convince Mughniyya, al-Amin, or Sharaf al-Din to accept the position, the French authorities appointed Munir 'Usayran, the scion of a notable family in Sidon as president of the Ja'fari court. The 'Usayrans had a storied past in Sidon, having served, for example, as consular representatives of Iran in Lebanon for generations. Munir 'Usayran would continue to serve as President of the Higher Ja'fari Court in Lebanon until his death in 1948. The editorial staff of al-'Irfan referred to him as "the well-known religious scholar."[52] But many opted to perceive Munir 'Usayran as a political appointee rather than a meritorious candidate. He certainly was a canny choice for the position on the part of the French, as he was particularly qualified to act as liaison between the colonial administration and the Shi'i religious classes in light of both his personal connections and linguistic faculties (he was fluent in French, Persian and Arabic). Although it may be the case that his appointment "reflected less his competency in matters of *fiqh* than his disposition towards diplomacy and his good relations with the French," there is no authoritative evidence that I am aware of (besides, how does one prove an absence?) confirming that he "was not a mujtahid at all."[53]

Munir 'Usayran was born in Sidon in 1877 and received an early education that was as common for children of the urban bourgeoisie as it was for the descendants of notable religious families. He attended the Marist Brothers Christian primary school in Sidon before pursuing his Islamic education in Nabatiyya. In fact, after completing his primary schooling in missionary institutions, 'Usayran studied under no other than Sayyid Muhsin al-Amin himself, later going on to receive religious training in Najaf.[54] 'Usayran eventually earned a religious diploma from Shaykh Husayn Mughniyya, which was formally recognized by Sayyid Abu al-Husn al-Isfahani, although there is no extant evidence that 'Usayran ever received an *ijaza*. One French communication reported that he had "practiced judicial functions since 1918, serving eight years as judge and 22 years as president of the court of cassation. Such training is worth a [religious] diploma."[55] Before his appointment to head the Ja'fari court, 'Usayran had worked as a *shari'a* court judge in Sidon. Ahmad 'Arif al-Zayn, the founding editor of al-'Irfan and nephew of Munir 'Usayran, mentions the latter in his seminal *History of Sidon* (1913), referring both to Munir and his brother Muhi al-Din 'Usayran as *the* two Shi'i *'ulama'* from Sidon to have "studied in the great school for Shi'is [in] Najaf al-Ashraf."[56] By comparison with his contemporaries and his colleagues, however, Munir 'Usayran published little.[57]

In October 1926, al-'Irfan announced the Ja'fari court appointments: Munir 'Usayran (president), Shaykh Yusuf al-Faqih and Sayyid 'Ali Zayn al-Husayni (advisors), Shaykh Mustafa al-Hurr (chief secretary), Hasan Hatoum (scribe), and Sayyid Jawad Ibrahim (court usher).[58] Many people, not least of which the first employees of the court (judges, scribes, translators, and lawyers), may have seen the institutionalization of Jaʿfari law as one means by which to defend the "deprived rights" (*al-huquq al-mahduma*) of the Shiʿi community against inequalities embedded within the Lebanese state and the colonial bureaucracy. Some Shiʿi Muslims saw juridical autonomy as a positive step forward for their community. It does not necessarily follow, however, as Hani Fahs suggests, that Shiʿi *ʿulamaʾ* in Lebanon universally considered participation in government institutions to be an appropriate form of engagement with the Lebanese state or an implicit recognition of "the other" in Lebanese society. Meanwhile, Fahs is correct to point out that the integration of the Shiʿi milieu into the Lebanese state is not necessarily the same thing as the development of institutions that can rival the state.[59] The institutionalization of Jaʿfari law in Mandate Lebanon can be read as both a moderate political victory for the Shiʿi community and a begrudging yet expedient tactic of cooperation with the colonial state. The significance of the Jaʿfari court may be better grasped through a more nuanced approach to what Julia Clancy-Smith calls "the in-between spaces of colonial encounters."[60] In the Lebanese context, these "in-between spaces" included sites of the struggle to define the sectarian-nationalist arena by defining the nature of Lebanese state–Shiʿi society relations. Although one current judge at the Beirut Jaʿfari court suggests the conceptualization of a "public system" (*nizam ʿamm*) beyond the sphere of state authority (*al-sulta*) is the best way to understand Shiʿi personal status legal institutions in Lebanon, the Jaʿfari court might also be situated in terms of what Ahmad Beydoun calls the "minimal public space" within which each sectarian community historically has been able to carve out its own niche while also enjoying "the exercise of the internal functions and the international privileges of the state."[61]

The Ebb and Flow of Personal Status Law Reform

In the case of the Lebanese Jaʿfari court, the French assumed that the power to define new juridical categories would be embedded within the institution itself. The Mandate authorities perceived the force of law in such a judicial institution to require little to no popular consent or charismatic religious pedigree, suggesting another example of what Sami Zubaida has termed the "etatization of law."[62] It hardly mattered whether the most respected Shi'i 'ulama' participated in staffing the court or opposed the institution on principle; legislating the practice of personal status law under the aegis of the Mandate state resulted in a fundamentally different relationship between the Shi'i community and the state. How Shi'i identity, politics, and society would be transformed as a consequence was difficult, if not impossible, to foresee.

If the May 1926 constitution protected the "guarantee of personal status" to all Lebanese sectarian communities, Arrêté N° 261 of April 28, 1926 limited the jurisdiction of personal status judges.[63] Over the next several months, Muslim and Christian clerics alike organized popular demonstrations to protest those more restrictive measures. Consequently, French policy on the issue descended into a tailspin. Maronites demanded a greater share of autonomy; some Muslims insisted that personal status jurisdiction should be extended to include property matters. On June 30, 1926, Mandate Decree No. 102 provisionally suspended Arrêté N° 261. It was not until February 3, 1930 that the "non-application" of Arrêté N° 261 was affirmed and a number of new laws reconsidered the jurisdiction of personal status courts in Lebanon.

The formal status of the relationship between the French Mandate and the states of Lebanon and Syria were renegotiated through the Franco-Syrian Treaty and the Franco-Lebanese Treaty of 1936. Arrêté N° 60/L.R. on March 13, 1936, formally recognized each "community" in matters of personal status, thereby assuring all of Lebanon's "religious sects" (al-tawa'if al-diniyya, s. al-ta'ifa al-diniyya) their right to sovereignty over personal status law. Among other things, the provisions of this measure included the compulsory nature of communal representation, mechanisms by which one could convert from one community to another, new laws governing property, and the contours of common law. Protests against the resolution immediately broke out all over the country, extending to almost all sectors of religious opinion. Due to overwhelming opposition, by June 1936 the Lebanese government was forced to reconsider the decree. On December 10, 1937, the Mandate authorities announced that Sunni and Shi'i judges would receive equal compensation and that the two legal jurisdictions would be placed on an equal footing in the eyes of the state. Finally, Arrêté

N° 146/L.R. of November 23, 1938, reformulated the 1936 laws in reasonably meaningful ways.

Religious intellectuals pushed back against this legislative move to limit
their power and authority. In March 1939, Sayyid Muhsin al-Amin sent
a letter to Gennardi, French Inspector-General of the *Contrôle du Wakfs,*
decrying the appropriation of religious authority by the state as well as the
attempts to legislate categorical distinctions between religious communities.
Al-Amin claimed that the outcome of "lively protests, and even a revolution
of spirit" among Muslims in the postwar lands of Greater Syria was perfectly
comprehensible insofar as these decrees were in "formal contradiction" with
"Islamic dogma and law." Shi'is and other people of faith protested this legislation, al-Amin argues, because they deemed it, "incompatible with the
prescriptions of heavenly religions; like them, he must also "profoundly
regret" the "distinction made between Muslims" in such legislation. In his
"capacity as Spiritual Leader of the Shi'i Islamic Community in Syria and
Lebanon," al-Amin called on the French to suspend the provisions: "I have
the honor of transmitting to your Excellency the energetic protests of Shi'i
Muslims against this *arrêté,* and against the fictitious distinction between
Muslims."[64] Another group of *'ulama'* urged the High Commissioner in
1939 not to fuse the jurisdiction of Sunni and Shi'i religious courts, making sure to first thank the High Commissioner for recognizing the "Jafferite
religion" in 1926, which had granted the same autonomy to the Lebanese
Shi'a that had already been extended to Shi'i communities in Iraq, Iran and
India.[65] Some Shi'i religious intellectuals declared that such objectionable
constitutional provisions were simply "not applicable for Muslims."[66]

Munir 'Usayran vociferously defended Shi'i juridical autonomy throughout this tumultuous period. In one statement, 'Usayran articulated a number of "apprehensions" about a rumor spreading throughout the Shi'i milieu
to the effect that the Lebanese Government was considering the administrative collapse of separate Sunni and Shi'i personal status jurisdictions into
one. He then goes on the tactical offensive, calling such a move a "Sunni
maneuver trying to make the Shi'i community in Lebanon lose its juridical
autonomy to the benefit of the Sunnis." 'Usayran claimed to be "expressing
the quasi-unanimous sentiment of the Community by demanding that the
current autonomous Shi'i jurisdictions be maintained." Shi'i interests must
be defended, both against the state and other sectarian communities; the

president of the Ja'fari court would have to fight in order to maintain as much power and autonomy as possible for Shi'i institutions.[67]

Judges Seeking Justice

The standing of religious elites in Jabal 'Amil was in relative decline during the first half of the twentieth century. Even so, some young seminary students—most notably those who comprised the ranks of organizations such as al-Shabiba al-'amiliyya (The 'Amili Youth) and 'Usbat al-adab al-'amili (The 'Amili Literature League)—hitched the interests of the religious classes to the broader communal struggles that have been discussed in this book and elsewhere in the context of the Shi'i *matlabiyya*, or, "politics of demand." Shi'i *'ulama'* were not the only segment of the Shi'i milieu demanding that the French Mandate authorities deal with enduring problems that plagued South Lebanon, the most important being dilapidated or nonexistent infrastructure—roads, water reclamation and distribution, and electricity provision. Shi'i *'ulama'* also advanced the causes of Shi'i reformism and religious modernism while also helping to carve out more space for the autonomy of Shi'i religious leaders and communal institutions, fundamentally altering and reshaping the nature of state-society relations in the process.[68]

To this end, some directly curried favor with the French. Sayyid Muhammad Yahya Safi al-Din, a judge at the Ja'fari *shari'a* court in Beirut, called on the French to fulfill their responsibilities toward the Shi'i community: "Must we lose our confidence and hope in the only Western nation that we had, until now, believed just and equitable?" Safi al-Din wondered. "Why is France liberal and the mother of justice only for its own population," he continued, taking "account of neither race nor religion? Why did France establish schools in Morocco and Algeria and assist in instructing the natives (*indigènes*) while . . . we are submitted to treatment that is as unequal and unjust as it is towards Muslims in general? The treatment that the Shi'ites are subjected to is equivalent to hostility." Safi al-Din complained that the bulk of the 20,000 liras allocated to religious institutions in Lebanon had been earmarked for Christians. "Muslims, Shi'is and Sunnis, form the majority of the population in Lebanon and they are not registered for more than 7,000 liras in this distribution. Is this just? Does this conform to the traditions of justice of France?" Although this set of demands was couched in a language of national equality and unity, Safi al-Din also zeroed in on the treatment of

> Shi'is of Jabal 'Amil in particular . . . [who] have been treated with absolutely inexplicable injustice and inequality. We must ask if we [Shi'is] are considered Lebanese or foreigners? If we are not considered Lebanese, why then must we pay taxes and why, after all, pay taxes to a government that mocks us? If we are considered Lebanese, [then] we are treated with flagrant injustice.

Meanwhile, Safi al-Din goes on enumerate some of the consequences in the region of the fact that Jabal 'Amil "pays heavy taxes [but] doesn't receive anything from the Lebanese government in return": "We lack roads, we lack schools, the ports of Tyre and Sidon are dilapidated and the entire fleet of these two small ports is in constant danger every winter." Safi al-Din makes demands akin to those of other 'Amili activists, but he also points out some of the personal and institutional connections between the Shi'i milieu in Lebanon and Iraq, noting,

> close to 100 young Shi'i men went to Iraq, to Najaf in order to receive their religious education and to become *ulama*. Each family spends approximately 50 gold liras per year per child [on this]. There, the young men acquire the habits that the English try to inculcate in them. Wouldn't it be more advantageous for the Lebanese government, and above all for the French government, that this money be spent in Lebanon . . . [to be] educated under the guidance of the French, to learn the French language and to learn to be respectful towards French traditions?

In hopes of stimulating the responsible paternal instincts within the colonial administration by highlighting the plight of Lebanese Shi'is, Safi al-Din contends that the mores and habits of Iraqi Shi'is had already been Anglicized to a certain degree. An analogous process of cultural transformation was possible among Lebanese Shi'i students, but the French would have to act even more boldly. As controversial as this may have sounded to some traditionalists, many would increasingly call for the establishment of local religious seminaries (*hawzat*, s. *hawza*) in Lebanon and elsewhere to

complement—not only to challenge—the scholarly significance of the seminary at Najaf. "Times have changed," Safi al-Din concludes. "You no longer
have an ignorant mass. In every village, in the most humble of homes, there
are people who know how to read and write: they are more or less up-to-
date with what is going on in the world. For example, this unjust division of
subsidies has brought about a very great discontentedness." He even makes
a sort of veiled ultimatum:

> If we do not obtain justice from France and if France continues to ignore
> us, we will be forced to achieve justice ourselves by making an appeal,
> like the Shi'is of Iraq, to the League of Nations and to the Ministry
> of Foreign Affairs in Paris. If Lebanon continues to treat us with this
> unjust inequality, we will be forced to refuse paying taxes.

To greater and lesser effect, mostly lesser, Shi'is from Lebanon already
had been petitioning the Society of the League of Nations and the French
Ministry of Foreign Affairs, so these were neither empty threats nor particularly radical demands. Embracing his sectarian affiliation as a badge of
colonial-national allegiance, Safi al-Din closed by assuring his French interlocutors that, in the end,

> I am a friend of France. From the beginning of the occupation, when
> others hesitated and spoke sometimes in favor of the English and some-
> times in favor of the French, I walked straight and declared clearly that I
> was a partisan of the French. I still have hope that the High Commission
> would very much like to repair the injustices and to establish the rights
> and responsibilities of every community that makes up Lebanon.

In conveying his response to those demands to his colonial superiors, one
French representative agreed with Safi al-Din, finding his demands "very
just" and calling upon the Mandate government to show support for the
Shi'i community, these "100,000 Lebanese": "Here [in Jabal 'Amil], nobody
knows the Lebanese government. All they know is France."[69] Even if colonial
discourse would like nothing better than to skillfully produce carbon cop-
ies of such an apparently earnest native informant, Safi al-Din augurs the
emergence of a new character, one that would acquire growing status and

stature as the twentieth century chugged along—the aggrieved Lebanese Shiʻi citizen.

In addition to demanding French support for Shiʻi rights, religious bureaucrats who served in the colonial state apparatus also called for the equalization of salaries among state-appointed judges.[70] According to Sami al-Khoury, the Lebanese Minister of Justice, the President of the Jaʻfari Court earned a monthly salary of 140.5 Lebanese Lira (L.L.) and his two legal advisors made 95 L.L. per month in 1935–36 even as the President of the Sunni *shariʻa* court earned 227 L.L. monthly and his advisors earned 140.5 L.L. per month. The Minister of Justice deemed such salaries appropriate, however, because Sunni judges heard more cases:

> There is no doubt that the objection of Jaʻfari judges is legitimate in the sense that they ought to benefit from a salary equivalent to those of Sunni judges, or that which will approach it more or less, considering the importance of the Shiʻi community; but this salary increase could never be justified . . . [because] the Jaaferite Court of Cassation judges 35 cases annually, [while] the Sunnite Court of Cassation judges 76 per year.

Another important consideration for al-Khoury was more generalized fiscal restraint: "The equalization of salaries for Sunni and Jaʻfari judges in the Court of Cassation will lead to an annual outlay on the order of 2130 Lebanese Lira (LL)." In the interests of financial prudence, a fair solution would be to pay judges at both courts 213 L.L. But as the Jaʻfari court bureaucracy continued to work without an established pay scale, and as the judges and "auxiliaries" of both the Sunni and Jaʻfari *shariʻa* courts had not been fixed into a "judicial hierarchy" yet, "giving satisfaction" to Shiʻi demands made neither fiscal nor ethical sense until the institutional landscape of personal status law in Lebanon could be further clarified.[71]

In April 1937, High Commissioner Damien de Martel was informed of "the disadvantages of the discrimination of which Shiʻi religious judges are victims in the matter of salaries." Khayr al-Din al-Ahdab, the new Minister of Justice, reported how 2,000 L.L. had been earmarked for "salary readjustment" among Shiʻi judges. The government took no action on the matter until May, when the salaries for Shiʻi judges were indeed raised, at which point Munir 'Usayran made an appearance before the Mandate *Cabinet Politique* in order to "thank the High Commission for its multiple interventions in this affair." However, he also took pains to declare that, "the allotted increase did not satisfy his colleagues or himself," and that the realm of Shi'i personal status law had still not been put "on an equal footing with analogous Sunni jurisdictions." 'Usayran telephoned the French High Commission once again on May 20 to restate his demands. Within several months, the Lebanese Parliament had approved the funding increase, but 'Usayran wished it would be implemented more quickly, reminding the French authorities of the persisting fact that Shi'i "judges receive lower salaries than their colleagues in Sunni *shari'a* courts." On December 10, 1937, the Mandate authorities reaffirmed their commitment to equalize salaries for all *shari'a* court judges.[72]

Equalization of state salaries for judges was a temporary fix for a symptom of more intractable problems of structural inequality. The Shi'i milieu was engaged with French Mandate rule through a variety of both combative and collaborative stances. In 1936, Hasan Sadiq, the Shi'i Mufti of Sidon, affirmed that the French could count on the Shi'a to stand alongside them, so long as the colonial government maintained salaries for judges and muftis at a level that was commensurate with their Sunni counterparts. "Among the different parts of the Lebanese population, there does not exist one that is more devoted to France than the Shi'i community. History attests to this." For reasons that are unclear, the bizarre historical narrative Sadiq is thinking of here includes what he strangely calls "the spontaneous support of Shi'is for Bonaparte before St. Jean d'Acre." In an unusual interpretation of the unrest roiling South Lebanon throughout the mid-1930s, Sadiq quickly turns to discuss more "recent events," in which "the services of Shi'i notabilities, at their head my father Cheikh Abdul Hussein Sadek, resident of Nabatiyya, prevented the Lebanese cause from being lost." Sadiq recasts the 1936 Bint Jubayl Revolt—discussed in much greater detail in chapter six—as an expression of Lebanese nationalist commitment, rather than evidence of separatist agitation or religious fanaticism. Sadiq positioned himself in line with a familial tradition of fealty to the French, using the tone of a snubbed friend or relative. "Unfortunately, the Shi'is have not until this day received the salary, more or less egalitarian, worthy of their indefectible attachment. They represent, after all, some 25% of the Lebanese population, and the taxes which they pay to the State are within that proportion." Although this figure was a bit on the high side, Sadiq made no criticism of what many other people at the time were describing as the unbearably onerous tax burden placed upon Shi'is in particular. Sadiq fancied himself a cultural ambassador, citing his recent "honor of being received by His Excellency the High Commissioner. Taking his hand, I recited several Arabic verses," of which he provided his own French translations:

> Oh, apostle of peace, History will protect you as an unforgettable
>   memory,
> My hand touches the generous hand that has given to my country,
> Jabal 'Amil will sing your name in all of its assemblies
> To you it is frankly devoted, having given anew the rights that by
>   others' hands were robbed.

Having established his allegiance to the French and his personal relationship with the colonial authorities, Sadiq divulged how Zinovi Pechkoff had indicated French intentions to offer him a salary bump: "At the start of 1935, my raise was decided, but since then no attention has been given to that decision." After subsequent requests to Pechkoff were ignored, Sadiq affirmed his faith in the French "egalitarian regime," even as Shi'i "inequality with my other Sunnis colleagues is flagrant." De Martel acknowledged that Sadiq earned two-thirds the salary of his Sunni counterpart and, several days letter, sent a letter to Munir 'Usayran, announcing that he was aware of the travails of his community and assuring him that he as not neglecting the issue.[73]

Personal Status Revisited

Amidst demands for salary equalization, there was also growing chatter about the possibility of dissolving the Ja'fari court into a unified *shari'a* court system. In the wake of their struggle for commensurate compensation as state judges, Shi'i religious bureaucrats rejected this proposal even as they sought to reorganize and reform the Ja'fari court system and protect the fragile autonomy of the Shi'i community. The process of judicial reorganization began in the late 1930s when Shi'i lawyers, judges, and other religious personalities were appointed to a commission that would present a comprehensive evaluation of the potential effects of such a change. The commission was "charged with studying the decree supporting the reorganization of the Sunni and Jaʿfari shariʿa courts," and the government expected the commission to pass along its "observations" to the secretary of State in less than one month. Shiʿi notables and intellectuals from all over the country, including Ahmad Rida, Sulayman Zahir, Muhammad Jabir Al Safa, and others supported the work of the commission, placing their "total confidence" in the representatives of "their community."[74]

The French found some unlikely allies for such an enterprise. *Al-ʿIrfan* had been a supporter of the recognition of the Jaʿfari *madhhab* and the establishment of independent *shariʿa* courts in the early 1920s. Subsequently the editorial board came out in favor of fusing the Sunni and Shiʿi religious courts, calling such a move the "best work that the authority and the government [could] do."[75] A number of other Shiʿi leaders wrote approvingly of reorganizing the *shariʿa* courts: "The Shiʿi community supports its representatives in the Commission charged with studying this reorganization . . . They have our confidence. We demand from you the immediate execution of this project."[76] Even as some figures in the community were gaining traction in defense of what effectively amounted to "separate but equal" personal status regimes, others continued to argue that special or differentiated treatment of the Shiʿi milieu would ultimately prove counterproductive for the national cause. Fault lines within the Shiʿi milieu under the Mandate developed not only between Lebanese nationalism and Arab nationalism but also between Shiʿi particularism and Islamic universalism.

To be sure, many were against the proposed reorganization. An anonymous group calling itself the "Delegation of the South" (*wafd al-janub*) sent a lengthy letter to the High Commissioner declaring in no uncertain terms that the fusion of Sunni and Shiʿi *shariʿa* courts was absolutely unacceptable. The authors acknowledged that both High Commissioners Gabriel Puaux and Maxime Weygand had informed them personally that this judicial reorganization was not a fait accompli so long as it still awaited further study by the government commission. But when some religious notables and ordinary people within the Shiʿi milieu "came to learn that the government had the intention of executing the project of the commission, even though [its report] had not been published yet and nobody knew anything about it," petitioners started to protest that any action taken prematurely would be "contrary to the

Ja'fari sect (*confession*)." Insofar as the project elaborated a plan for turning the Court of Cassation (*mahkamat al-tamyiz*) into a Court of Appeals (*mahkamat al-isti'naf*), the proposal was interpreted as contrary to Ja'fari law. "The Court of Cassation examines, in effect, the judgment to know whether or not [a ruling] is in conformity with the principles of *Chéréi* [*shari'a*] in order to approve of it in the first place, or asking in the second, the judge who gave [the opinion] to rectify it; for it is not permitted for a judge to invalidate a judgment rendered by another 'Moujtahed' judge." On the other hand, when a judge at the Court of Appeals "modifies a judgment according to his jurisprudence without taking into consideration the judgment rendered by the judge of 1st Instance, this is formally contrary to the provisions of the Chéréi." Also, the state appointment of a "Procureur-General" to such an envisioned Court of Appeals would amount to no less than "heresy," "because among the Shi'is, the judge must be a 'Moujtahed,' who has a deep understanding of the *shari'a* as well as precedents in the Quran and the *akhbar*. From an administrative point of view, these petitioners were outraged over the potential transfer of Shi'i jurisprudential authority. If the state were granted power over the "reclassification of judges," the Ja'fari court would be placed under even tighter control. Arguing that the executive branch ought only to "function on the order of politics," the expansion of powers in this way was seen as "contrary to the principles of good administration." Indexing some familiarity with the separation of powers concept, it was pointed out how "reformers in the West worked for dozens of years to remove every administrative jurisdiction from politicians" and "pursued their efforts until their full success in certain democratic states." It was only by the "grace of these efforts and the designation of permanent commissions chosen from among the competent administrative authorities" that "regulations and principles concerning nomination, classification, advancement and the fixing of salaries of functionaries" could be retained in the hands of communal or clerical authorities. In effect, these religious bureaucrats were calling for their own continued empowerment but implicitly endorsing the separation of mosque and state. Reversing the secularist's demand that religion be kept out of political life, these religious figures demanded that politics not be allowed to interfere in state-administered religious affairs, concluding that, "it is not permitted for us to imitate the West on this question and to copy its mistakes," which appear to have included the secularization of religious institutions, the restriction of the role of religion in public life, and the undue separation of religion from politics. The High Commissioner should only grant such juridical *compétence* to those for whom the function would be "purely political" and "to arrange the thing in a way preventing every present and future exploitation." Just as it would be "contrary to good administration to have Hanafi judges doing the same work as Jaafari judges, and to give them different salaries," religious administration was of "capital importance" and should be considered equally as important as political administration.[77]

Shaykh Husayn Mughniyya penned a trenchant letter in which he argued that the fusion of Sunni and Shi'i courts under the proposed judicial reorganization would "attack our independence in religious and confessional matters." Alluding to the principles of liberty and democracy he believed underwrote the protection of Shi'i legal jurisdiction, Mughniyya affirmed that "traditions of the community" and "freedom of belief" had been clearly protected ever since the Mandate government had recognized "our independence in religious and confessional matter[s]." Praying for "God to grant victory to France, this democratic nation that has drawn its sword to combat the National Socialist regime and to defend peaceful nations," Mughniyya reiterated his allegiance to "the noble principles" of France and affirmed that the Shi'i community "is prepared to give all of its assistance all of its support to France and its Allies." On the one hand, the Mandate is perceived to have "always sought to safeguard, before anything else, the traditions of the community and the freedom of belief"; the new legislation contravened that spirit. On the other hand, the proposed fusion "does not achieve, in effect, the principal goals envisaged by the projected reform, it does not economize the money of the Treasury, it does not ameliorate the course of affairs, it does not make the spirit of sectarianism disappear in Lebanon and it does not bring about its unification." Appealing to what must be thought of, therefore, as contradictory principles underwriting French Mandate rule in Lebanon, Mughniyya articulated how the unifying force of Lebanese sectarianism can be brought about through the recognition of particular spaces of sectarian autonomy. "You can not tolerate, in effect," he concluded, "that one community be favored to the detriment of another. Such discrimination will be fought, however, and profoundly resented by the members of the community."[78]

Upon learning that plans for this proposed fusion had been scrapped, Mughniyya wrote to reaffirm his "wishes for the prosperity of France and for the victory of its army." In the event that the matter of reorganizing *shari'a* courts should be raised again, he sets forth some differences between Sunni and Shi'i courts that ought to be kept in mind. First of all, from a "representative point of view," Mughniyya feared that such judicial reorganization would be hopelessly skewed in favor of the Sunni community at the expense of Shi'is. "Justice demands that the Shi'i community be represented by the President of the Association des Ulémas, or by its replacement, as the Sunni community is represented by the Mufti; thus, the rights of Shi'is will be conserved and the community will be treated like the Sunnis." The principles and practices of sectarian justice demand adherence to norms of equity and parity. Second, Mughniyya argues that any reform of Shi'i legal institutions that employed "civilians" would go "against *shari'a* law." Just as judges were typically expected to hold the rank of *mujtahid,* Mughniyya insisted that administrative positions should require similar qualifications. Third, Mughniyya referred to the need for salary equalization between comparable Shi'i and Sunni institution, "otherwise the Shi'i judges lose all their prestige *vis-à-vis* their Sunni colleagues." Mughniyya couched his avowed commitment to national unity and social peace in the language of sectarian rights and in defense of what I have called "separate but equal" legal status for the Shi'i community.[79]

On the Historical and Legal Significance of the Ja'fari Court

With the collapse of the Ottoman Empire, the Shi'i milieu in Greater Syria was unevenly transformed from an archipelago of families, clans, and communal "non-entities" into increasingly bounded "minority" sectarian communities with varying relationships to the national states within which they found themselves. By no means was the gradual emergence of sectarian solidarities, or modes of identification, or legal jurisdictions inevitable or a foregone conclusion. Rather, the institutionalization of personal status law courts during the period of French Mandate rule was part and parcel of the sectarianization of the Lebanese political, social, and cultural landscape. Alongside and against the colonial state, therefore, sectarian communities struggled—however recently empowered and made self-aware enough to do

so—to define the place of personal status law and the force of such jurisdictional categories in everyday life, a topic taken up in greater detail in
chapters four and five. Lebanese Shi'i sectarianization was the result of both
conscious intent on the part of the colonial authorities—sectarianization
from above—and demands from among Shi'i leaders and ordinary people—
sectarianization from below. Sectarian institutions such as the Ja'fari court
helped to define Shi'i society apart from the Lebanese state. In his discussion
of Muslim courts in colonial Algeria, Allan Christelow notes:

> under the colonial state, autonomy, or more accurately the institutional
> separation of the Muslim courts, became a means of imposing a sys-
> tematic basis for bolstering political inequality. In colonial Algeria,
> the Muslim court question was initially viewed from both angles,
> with Muslim leaders seeking to maintain or even broaden substantive
> autonomy, and the French seeking to impose a formal autonomy voided
> of its substance by virtue of the qadi's subordination to the French judi-
> cial system.[80]

To the extent that juridical "autonomy" means the "institutional separation of
the Muslim courts" from the state, there are limits to comparing the Lebanese
situation with the Algerian case, which was subjected to a much more inter-
ventionist approach by the French as they actually constructed a revamped
version of local Islamic law.[81] The instantiation of personal status law codes
for the autonomous administration of each community's sectarian affairs
became a colonial goal in Mandate Lebanon. In turn, protecting the "right
to difference" as a means of protecting communal autonomy or sovereignty
became a chief goal among certain local political and religious leaders.

At the same time, many Lebanese citizens-in-the-making perceived the
right to administer personal status matters in accordance with the precepts of
one's own community to be a fundamental expression of liberty in a sectarian
democracy. The congenital weakness of the Lebanese state only exacerbated
the fractious nature of emergent sectarian identities. "While the [1926] constitution provided for Western institutions," Meir Zamir writes in a political
history of Greater Lebanon, "Lebanese political culture was, in reality, largely
determined by traditional forces."[82] Such a perspective considers clan, family
or sectarian ties to be traditional, as opposed to other allegiances that can be

coded as modern.[83] But Lebanese political culture under the French Mandate consisted of social forces and political actors tenuously stitched together. To categorically view sectarianism as traditional and nationalism as modern is to ignore the ways in which the two have been, at times, mutually reinforcing. Nadine Méouchy puts the point slightly differently: "The sectarianization of the Lebanese social formation . . . was made possible by two concomitant processes: the consecration of the minority character of all the communities included within the 1920 boundaries . . . [and] the transformation of traditional communities into political communities."[84] Personal status law was one bulwark of Lebanon's emergent national sectarianism. Sectarianism became a hegemonic and durable organizing principle for politics and institution building in twentieth-century Lebanon. Its maintenance can be partially attributed to the historical dialectic between sectarianism-in-practice and sectarian forms of identification, all of which could pose challenge to the authority of the state and tended to, but did not necessarily or at all times impede the gestation of national unity.

Lebanese Shi'i responses to the codification of personal status legal codes were mixed. Though many viewed the recognition of sectarian sovereignty favorably, this did not automatically translate into separatist or secessionist demands. Sami Zubaida identifies the "impulse behind personal status legislation since the beginning of the twentieth century" in the following terms: "social reform, to provide security and some liberty to women and children under modern conditions; and the subsumption of family affairs under the legislative powers and controls of the modern state and its administration."[85] On the one hand, state recognition of the Shi'i community was perceived as a positive development, compared to previous refusals on the part of the Ottoman authorities to do so. On the other hand, some viewed such institutionalized distinctions between religious communities as inimical to those goals of crafting a unified national identity and promoting social harmony. Jamal J. Nasir points out that the category and the term "personal status" (*al-ahwal al-shakhsiyya*) only appeared in the late nineteenth century, a "recent legal term in Arabic, unknown to the classical Islamic jurists, and non-existent in all classical texts of Islamic jurisprudence."[86] More boldly still, Sofia Saadeh states, "the preservation of the personal status laws are [sic] part and parcel of the sectarian representation of the political system, and hence of the consociational system as a whole."[87]

The formal recognition of the Ja'fari *madhhab* and the establishment of a national system of Ja'fari *shari'a* courts constituted a watershed in modern Lebanese Shi'i history. In spite of the complicated history related in this chapter, the authenticity of the Ja'fari court and its staff and, by extension, the loyalty of the Shi'i community to the Lebanese state, would continue to be called into question and debated in both popular and scholarly historical narratives. Even if some might argue that "the highest Shi'i judge wielded little influence in the newly independent Lebanese state," the following two chapters elucidate some of the reasons why a less cynical take on the historical significance of the Ja'fari court is warranted.[88] "After the Mandate authorities created Jaafarite tribunals (which did not exist under the Ottomans)," writes Ahmad Beydoun, "the cadis [judges] swiftly acquired a certain importance, as their role and their prestige came to symbolize Shiite communal aspirations."[89] Not only did the Ja'fari exemplify the potential for sectarian institutionalization under the Mandate, but it also embodied the limits of Shi'i sectarian representation. The court played both a meaningful symbolic *and* institutional role, satisfying Shi'i demands for legal and cultural recognition, while also, in turn, demanding Shi'i rights. The relationship between ordinary Shi'is and the Lebanese state was increasingly mediated by a sectarian legal apparatus and by sectarian language. Shi'i society was reconfigured in such a manner as to bring to bear the power and authority of the state apparatus on personal status matters. Although a number of amendments and modifications were subsequently made to the original draft, the most recent version of the Lebanese personal status legal code, which applies to both Sunni and Shi'i *shari'a* courts in Lebanon and is still in force today, dates to July 16, 1962.[90]

Regardless of whether or not those engaged in the conversation I overheard at the Beirut Ja'fari court reflected on this point at the time, it is no small historical irony that in the aftermath of the dissolution of the Caliphate (*khilafa*), new conditions of possibility for different sorts of conflict (*khilaf*) emerged. When the French colonial state officially sanctioned the practical application of Ja'fari personal status law—an altogether new category of jurisdiction—through the formal recognition of the Ja'fari *madhhab*, Shi'i juridical, religious and cultural identities were reconfigured within the multisectarian environment of Greater Lebanon. Even if the jurisdiction of personal status courts was originally intended to regulate affairs of residency (*nufus*) and citizenship (*jinsiyya*) as well as all other dimensions of family law, religious courts in Lebanon soon started to behave as though their jurisdiction extended beyond "all matters concerning personal status."[91] The colonial state, religious bureaucrats, and Shi'i political leaders, as well as ordinary people engaged and clashed in ways that were productive of dynamic tension. This tension was crucial for defining the character of relationships between the Lebanese state and Shi'i society under French Mandate rule. The management of these sectarian institutions and religious patrimony was part of a broader French "Shi'a practice" that worked to carve out a specifically Shi'i space in Mandate Lebanon.[92] In Mandate Lebanon, personal status legislation was one bulwark of a budding institutionalized sectarianism. Concomitantly, what I call the "legalizing practices" of the Ja'fari court had far-reaching implications for the development of Lebanese sectarianism and Shi'i cultural self-understanding down until the present. Those evolving relationships among the Lebanese state, sectarianism-in-practice, and Shi'i society are the subject of the next chapter.

4

Practicing Sectarianism

The modern state appears here as a simple excuse legitimizing communitarian coexistence in modern times.

NADINE MÉOUCHY, "L'État et espaces communautaires dans le Liban sous Mandat français"

In concluding remarks on a dispute over a piece of *waqf* property in the southern Lebanese village of Mashghara that never reached satisfactory resolution in the colonial sources, one French administrator reported:

> Under the Ottoman regime, the Shi'i Community—like the [other] communities attached to Islam: Druze, Alaouite etc.—was not recognized and was legally treated as an integral part of the Sunni Muslim community. The Muslims of these communities were always subjected to the law of the Hanafi rite, the official rite of the Ottoman Empire.
>
> This is no longer the case in Lebanon, where the particular and independent existence of the Shi'i and Druze communities was consecrated by the creation of Chérieh courts for the Djafarite and Druze rite.
>
> As these communities [were] also separated from Sunni Islam, they obviously must exercise, vis-à-vis the latter, full independence in the management of their canonical interests and temporal patrimony.

Later that year, however, another Mandate official informed the French High Commissioner of the growing need to confirm that the "highest Shi'i religious judge" would indeed be "invested [with] the functions of supervision vis-à-vis the administrators of Shi'i *wakfs*." If the French were uncertain about precedent and protocol for resolving matters related to *awqaf* (s. *waqf*), Islamic charitable endowments, they were hardly alone in their confusion. "The President of the Higher Shi'i Court, whom the Lebanese government notified [regarding] the administrative autonomy of Shi'i *wakfs*, complained that, at the same time, they have not yet notified him of the powers with which he is invested."[1]

Such apparent ambiguity was not without cause. Notions of "autonomy" and "independence" within the Shi'i milieu vis-à-vis the Lebanese sectarian nation-state were newly emerging concepts during the period of French Mandate rule. Transformations in legal, social, intellectual, and cultural life tracked in the preceding chapters of this book had created the conditions of possibility for new struggles over Shi'i identity. The Ja'fari court had become a state-authorized venue for Lebanese Shi'i society to adjudicate matters pertaining to personal status—a topic that is examined in much sharper detail in the following chapter; in addition, the court was also becoming an influential actor in helping to carve out a greater degree of institutional autonomy for the Shi'i milieu in Mandate Lebanon—the topic of this chapter. On account of the fact that the Shi'i community had enjoyed no formal recognition during Ottoman times, there had been no reason to centralize documentation that could verify Shi'i legal ownership of cemeteries or other *waqf* properties. With the formal recognition of the Shi'i community, the need to validate Shi'i presence in Lebanon through empirically verifiable means became more and more pressing. This chapter demonstrates the challenges that confronted Shi'i political figures, *'ulama'*, and ordinary people as they attempted simultaneously to assert control over religious patrimony and to justify certain manifestations of Shi'i presence in Mandate Lebanon—in brief, to negotiate the proper management of Shi'i "canonical interests and temporal patrimony." The constellated exploits of these individual actors, collective aspirations, and institutional forces amounted to nothing short of the defense and definition of Shi'i communal cemeteries, *waqf* properties, and other examples of sacred space.

The dramatic transformation of Shi'i sectarian identity in Mandate Lebanon coincided with the creation of new kinds of sectarian infrastructure—embodied by the recently established Ja'fari court—as well as the adaptation of new means for communication among the state, communal leaderships, and ordinary people. But an institution such as the Ja'fari court was not exclusively the site for the application of sacred law in matters of personal status. As a quasi-colonial institution, founded, staffed, and supervised by a cadre of bureaucrats handpicked by the French authorities (see chapter three), the Ja'fari court exemplified how Shi'is managed to acquire a modicum of sectarian rights both under and through the Mandate. Sectarian claims became increasingly bound up with the institutionalization of Shi'i difference, which in turn helped to secure the place of the Lebanese Shi'a as a "sect among sects." This new juridical classification had an unmistakable impact on the transformation of Lebanese Shi'i subjectivity, such that rights and representation cast as specifically "Shi'i" would subsequently be claimable as entitlements of national sectarianism. In this respect, too, the sectarianization of Lebanon's communities may be better understood both in terms of what I have been calling "sectarianization from below"—demands for communal rights made by ordinary people, local communities, village councils and the like—and "sectarianization from above"—French colonial strategies and techniques of divide and rule. Sectarianism in Lebanon was hardly a unitary phenomenon; protean and adaptive, it both affected and emanated from each sectarian community in different ways, reflecting stubborn contradictions at the heart of the institutionalization of sectarian difference. Indeed, the cultural politics of difference in Lebanon is often refracted through the sectarian prism. Paradoxically, differences—religious, cultural, or sectarian—that might have been undermined by nationalism were modified in many cases into durable *national* institutions, inextricably bound up with the uneven process of Lebanese state formation.[2]

This book has been making the argument—in conversation with a broader body of critical historiographical literature—that the phenomenon of sectarianism must be understood, among other explanations, in relation to discourses of colonial modernity, indeed, to colonial forms of knowledge and power more generally. As Ayesha Jalal points out in the case of British India:

> The meshing of religion and culture with politics did not mean that all Indians were inherently bigoted in varying measures. Religiously informed cultural identities emphasized a sense of difference without foreclosing the possibility of Indians sharing common sentiments and coming together when circumstances were propitious for united action.[3]

Here Jalal opens up an alternative space for thinking through the problem of sectarianism in terms of cultural difference, which might help us avoid getting bogged down in the polarized argument between primordialists and instrumentalists. Whereas the former would argue that sectarianism is an innate, internal sensibility specific to certain societies dating back to age-old primitive loyalties, the latter might argue that sectarianism emerged mainly in response to external forces such as modernization, social change, colonialism, foreign intervention and the like.[4]

By contrast with both perspectives, this chapter highlights what I call the "legalizing practices" of the Ja'fari court, practical and institutional articulations of new forms of Shi'i sectarianism during the period of French Mandate rule. Looking at how "canonical interests and temporal patrimony" were defined and defended within the Shi'i community under the French Mandate, I locate the communal cemetery (*jabbana* or *maqbara*) as one key site for the production of sectarian Shi'i difference in Mandate Lebanon. Following the formal recognition of the Ja'fari *madhhab*, sectarian Shi'i modes of identification would become increasingly visible. Subsequent struggles to protect cemeteries and other kinds of religious patrimony illustrate some of the contradictory ways in which inclusion within the multisectarian Lebanese nation-state worked to "fix" certain forms of sectarian belonging and attachment. First of all, in order to set a backdrop for such a discussion of cemetery disputes, this chapter returns to consider some of the theoretical and legal justifications underwriting the rise of new sectarian modes of identification. Then, I turn to look at debates over the definition of Shi'i autonomy, as Shi'i leaders and ordinary people struggled both with and against each other to protect "their" *waqf*s and "temporal patrimony." Finally, I zero in on the cemetery as a flashpoint for the assertion of Shi'i presence. The trope of sectarian solidarity became a banner under which demands for Shi'i rights could be increasingly articulated in a specifically sectarian idiom. Responding to these new circumstances in complicated, often surprising ways, the Shi'i community began to practice sectarianism, to practice *being* sectarian through collective action as well as a host of institutional channels.

Recognizing Religious Patrimony

In a 1936 report on Shi'is in Lebanon written for the Centre des Hautes Études d'Administration Musulmane (renamed Centre des Hautes Études sur l'Afrique et l'Asie Modernes in 2000) (CHEAM), Roger Lescot notes how "curious" it is that, "in a Shiite country, the religious authorities" can

command such a strikingly low level of respect and power. This is attributed to the fact that *awqaf* "produce only thin incomes, hardly sufficient
for the maintenance of the mosques." Because only "rare civil servants, like
the Muftis, receive a state salary," therefore, "moral and intellectual primacy
tends to pass entirely to the lay *(laïque)* elite."[5] Under the Ottomans, Louis
Cardon (another French observer of the Mandate for Syria and Lebanon)
declared, the "surveillance of *wakfs* was neglected, revenues were squan-
dered and illegal operations multiplied." Channeling the spirit of benevolent colonialism, Cardon identifies a "new task" that France had set itself to
accomplish, namely, "to restore order in the administration of such property, to monitor the use of their income" and to ensure that those involved
could actually benefit from these properties.[6] Through Arrêté N° 3503
(January 27, 1926) the French Mandate authorities had formally recognized
the Ja'fari *madhhab,* redefining the Lebanese Shi'a as a state-recognized sectarian community. Citizenship and legal status in Greater Lebanon were to
be determined by a non-voluntarist form of political identity—confessional
affiliation. Because the exercise of Shi'i jurisprudence had remained a relatively clandestine enterprise under the Ottomans, the boundaries of "personal status" law—a new category of historical practice in Mandate Lebanon
for all of Lebanon's emergent sectarian communities—had to be delimited
as new relationships to the state were created and formalized within and
towards the Shi'i milieu. The institutionalization of Shi'ism rendered the
Ja'fari *madhhab* a legitimate source of legal authority in the eyes of the state,
and chapter five will explore how the Ja'fari court practically adjudicated
matters of personal status, which encompassed matters of marriage, divorce,
inheritance, maintenance *(nafaqa)* as well as *waqf* (charitable endowments)
and other property disputes.

Louis Rolland and Pierre Lampué, two French legal scholars, had a fairly
standard yet grandiose take on the legal implications of Mandate rule.
Insofar as the creation of the Mandates had resulted in the establishment
of a "special and new juridical regime," they argued that guarantees for the
protection of the "wellbeing and development of peoples who are unable to
govern themselves correspond to a 'sacred trust of civilization.'" Supporters
and administrators of the Mandate system must keep in mind the future of
"minor peoples. Major peoples have the obligation to make them progres-
sively leave this state of *minorité.*" Successfully converting those ideas into

practice would require certain procedural guidelines: "This legal construction of the international mandate is thus inspired by a general conception
of colonization, one which has the goal of developing (*mettre en valeur*) the
territories and raising up the individuals who live in them." Even if some
theoreticians of the Mandate system seemed to be aspiring to lofty goals,
however, those aspirations were strikingly similar to French colonial enter-
prises elsewhere: "The Mandatory also gives international protection to
states under Mandate resembling that which is applied to countries under
protectorate." Colony, protectorate, and mandate: less and less distinguishable versions of outright foreign domination. On the other hand, though,
legal exponents of French civilization also envisioned a sort of "statist autonomy" that would be unique to the Mandate system, in which the Mandatory
power (i.e., France) would be "responsible to advise and guide administrative action and to institute a judicial system in the States under Mandate."[7]

Some contemporary European observers of the Mandate system in Syria
and Lebanon explicitly supported the guarantee of legal protections for
Shi'i difference. For example, D.I. Murr and Ed. Bourbousson were relatively optimistic about the prospects for Shi'i sectarian modernity, arguing
that the recent recognition of the Ja'fari *madhhab* was "justified by the fact
that the prescriptions of the *djahférite* rite are much closer to modern laws
than Hanafi jurisprudence." Legal dispositions toward women were cited
as one bellwether of such modernity, as, "according to the *djahférite* rite (in
Lebanon), an only daughter inherits the totality of the goods of her father, to
the exclusion of her cousins, who do not have any successional right; whereas
according to the Hanafi rite, the same person (the daughter) only inherits
half of the succession, leaving the other half to the cousins." It was perceived
that the imagined benefits of legal modernity expressed in a Shi'i key should
be made available to everyone in the Shi'i milieu. But the official recognition of the Ja'fari *madhhab* in Lebanon had "created a bizarre anomaly":
"Whereas in Baalbeck (Lebanon) the Shiite daughter excludes (because she
is Shiite) her cousins and prevents the latter from inheriting with her from
her father, it is necessary to indicate that in Damascus, which is however
under French mandate, the girl shares with her cousins the succession in
question." In other words, if the Lebanese sectarian model could be standardized and even expanded beyond the borders of the Lebanese Republic,
more people would be able to reap both legal and financial benefits.[8]

Analyzing the legal apparatus of Mandate rule shortly after Lebanon had secured national independence, Pierre Rondot made a problematic yet pervasive argument that conceptually conjoins Islam and the state in Lebanon:

> One may find other examples of a similar inequality to the benefit of Muslims: Muslim personal status jurisdictions are in the charge of the state, as well as in the service of the fetwa (consultation for the application of Qur'anic law); cadis and muftis are named by the government. One might say, therefore, that in certain regards the Muslim religion seems like the only state religion in Lebanon.[9]

If the state were perceived as the ultimate guarantor and arbiter of nationally binding norms of justice, and if the state fulfilled its role by monopolizing the means of violence and lawmaking in Lebanese society, this would be a reasonable assessment. Rondot fails to notice (or fails to mention), however, that this relationship between "the Muslims" and the state was variable and contradictory, and, moreover, had disadvantages as well as advantages. For one thing, state supervision drastically reduced the scope of Muslim autonomy even as the Sunni and Shi'i Muslim communities struggled to gain greater representation in politics. Furthermore, "the Muslims" were not treated as a single group and rarely conceived of their interests as being shared vis-à-vis other sectarian groups. Rondot does not differentiate between Sunni and Shi'i Muslims in Lebanon, perhaps lacking the temporal distance necessary to historicize the institutions and practices he casually viewed as being bound up with the state and, therefore, as somehow consequently imbued with the powers *of* a state. The intrinsic contradiction at the heart of those Muslim religious institutions touted by Rondot was that, under the Mandate and through early independence, they were only moderately able to exercise any real legal autonomy. "For the Muslim communities, applicable laws and jurisdictions officially *seem to be* of a Statist character," argue Béchir Bilani and André Decocq, "but, in the reality of facts, are only relevant to the communal authorities."[10]

Despite marked differences between direct colonial rule and the Mandate system, the institutionalization of Shi'i law in Mandate Lebanon should be understood in quasi-colonial terms. Important as a site for the administration of Shi'i personal status law, the Ja'fari court also became a significant institutional and social actor in the Lebanese national context. The Ja'fari court mediated between various strata of Lebanese society, at times serving as the "official face" of the Shi'i sectarian community that otherwise would have had an infrequent audience with the authorities in Beirut; at other times, the court arrogated to itself and was imbued with both the duty and the right to take on roles and responsibilities hitherto delegated to the religious classes. In a mundane sense, the establishment of the Ja'fari court created an entirely new class of religious bureaucrats who worked in the legal hierarchy, helping to carve out a new institutional basis for the reformulation of Shi'i modes of identification and legal practice, one that could pose a challenge—both implicitly and explicitly—to other networks and institutions of power—political, social and otherwise—within the Shi'i community. This bureaucratization of personal status law had lasting implications for the administration of personal status law ("canonical interests") as well as the protection of Shi'i *waqf* properties (i.e., "temporal patrimony"). In fact, it was precisely such new kinds of centralization and bureaucratization that developed into institutional pillars of Shi'i autonomy and presence in Lebanon under the Mandate and beyond.

In Defense of Shi'i *Waqf*

One pillar of the expanding domain of Shi'i legal autonomy was increased oversight of *waqf* (pl. *awqaf*) property by the Ja'fari court. Although *waqf*s are administered at a local level, the power to oversee such properties has been invested in various institutions such as colonial property governorates or national ministries. If it is difficult now to trace the history of *waqf* in Jabal 'Amil for reasons of source dispersion and degradation, to say nothing of the historic decentralization of power and institutions in the region, it was even more difficult for Shi'i Muslims in Lebanon to adequately verify their property claims on account of the relative invisibility of the community under the Ottomans. Arrêté N° 753 of March 31, 1921, enshrined the right of the highest formally recognized Muslim authorities—without specifying sectarian difference—to take over responsibility for the administration of Islamic *waqf* properties. Following the formal recognition of the Shi'i community in January 1926, the Ja'fari court became the highest Shi'i religious authority in the country, subsequently entrusted to oversee *waqf*-related

matters among Lebanese Shi'is. Subsequent individual, collective, and institutional attempts to claim, define and control *waqf* property shed some light
on how the Lebanese Shi'i community was gradually transformed from a
"sect-in-itself" to a "sect-for-itself." Ja'fari court president Munir 'Usayran,
his two main legal counselors, and the employees and users of the Ja'fari
court were responsible—under the supervision of the French administration, to be sure—for managing Shi'i religious properties. Disputes over the
protection, preservation and maintenance of Shi'i *waqf*s started appearing
before administrators, judges and clerics in Ja'fari *shari'a* courts in Beirut
and Jabal 'Amil.[11]

In one notable case from the southern Lebanese market town of Nabatiyya,
the heartland of Jabal 'Amil, Dr. Bahjat Mirza Ibrahim and Tawfiq Amin
Shaheen presented a case asserting that the recently deceased Muhammad
Sabah of Nabatiyya had endowed as a *waqf* a large warehouse (*makhzan*)
in the market on the road leading to Marjayoun. The earnings from that
market were earmarked for uses that would benefit the local "poor and des-
titute." Notable scholar and political activist Ahmad Rida was appointed
as a legal guardian (*wasi*) for the charitable investment. One day, when the
roof of the *makhzan* collapsed, Rida dispatched one of the deceased's children, Sa'id Sabah, to repair it. Although Sa'id was hired for a fixed length
of time, he insisted on retaining the *makhzan* in his possession even after
that period had elapsed. Sa'id claimed to have arranged beforehand with
"Shaykh Ahmad" Rida to continue renting the *makhzan* for twenty years
at a fixed price—4,000 Turkish *ghurush,* that is, 200 *ghurush* per year—
under the condition that he would also spend twenty *ghurush* per year "in
the interest of the *waqf*," paying for any necessary repairs and renovations.
When that period came to an end on November 16, 1928, Rida asked Sa'id to
"take his hand off" (*raf' yadahu*) the property. Sa'id refused, continuing to
make excuses until the end of that year.

When Sa'id attempted to continue working on May 29, 1929, Rida took
legal action to prevent him from doing so, citing his prior irresponsibility
before the *shari'a* court judge. Rida testified in the Nabatiyya court that
Sa'id had spent earnings from the *waqf* on himself instead of on suitable
charitable endeavors. Ibrahim was among the first Shi'is to receive a medical degree from the American University of Beirut, as well as being the scion
of a well-known Iranian family that had settled in Nabatiyya around the

turn-of-the-century. He pointed out that Saʿid had failed in his duties as legal guardian and, consequently, "not a [suitable] *wasi* [at all]." Having "embezzled" from a pious endowment, Saʿid was accused of no less than ruthlessly stealing from the poor. Rida claimed to be looking out for the "public interest" (*maslaha*) of those whom the *waqf* was founded to benefit, for their protection from the negative impact of such an irresponsible administrator as Saʿid. The court ruled, "the *makhzan* was a *waqf* [ever] since the day on which the deceased, his [i.e., Saʿid Sabah's] father, bequeathed it . . . [and] this *makhzan* is registered with the *awqaf* of [the] Hayy al-Serail [neighborhood] in Nabatiyya." After concluding that "the *waqf* is legitimate," the judge ordered Saʿid to "cease and desist so that the guardians of the *waqf* can execute what is stipulated in the *wasiyya*." Despite claims made by Saʿid that this had been a *waqf dhurri*—that is a *waqf* endowed for the benefit of an individual benefactor—the court ensured that it remained a *waqf khayri*—a charitable endowment. In this case, the perpetuity of the *waqf* for the public interest was deemed a higher social good than the particular interests of a specific individual or family.[12]

The Jaʿfari court would hear numerous cases concerning the protection of religious patrimony. Consider this incident from Jezzine, a predominantly Christian village located in the mountains inland from Sidon. In a letter written to the *waqf* division of the High Commissioner on July 26, 1930, President Munir ʿUsayran alerted the French to a "point of great importance," which had inspired him to ask the administration to "give us assistance in case of attack or practical embezzlement to the detriment of Jaafari *Wakfs*." ʿUsayran asserted that the Sidon *shariʿa* judge had been "[i]nformed that an attack was [going to be] carried out against the Jezzine mosque," and consequently "asked the Qaimaqam to put a halt to [the attack], but they had not taken the appropriate action concerning his request."[13] A large group of concerned citizens wrote:

We addressed a letter to the Qaimaqam of Djezzine on 18 June 1930 demanding that he inform us about the encroachment upon the Jaʿfari Mosque by Farès Nemr, a resident of this place, as was reported to us. We sent another letter on the 30th of this month. Until now, we have not received any response. The aforementioned Farès confessed before Neematallah Hamdar to committing this aggression against the mosque, as was evident from an inquiry drawn up by the Sidon Court, according to which certain individuals encroached upon the properties of the Djezzine mosque. The informer did not wish, despite our demand, to specify if it concerned the mosque and the *Wakfs* of the Ja'fari Community.[14]

In response, an inquiry was launched under the supervision of the Jezzine district commissioner (*qa'immaqam*). The alleged attack: Faris Nimr Bou Sleiman had been accused of "encroaching" upon the boundaries of the "mosque property." When it ultimately came to light that the size of this reported violation amounted to approximately 30 cm., the owners of the encroaching building in question took responsibility, accepting the appointment of "experts" (*ahl al-khibra*) and engineers along with a committee appointed by the municipality in order to work together and rectify the situation. Bou Sleiman destroyed the entire section of the wall he had already begun building and started over at the recognized property line.[15] The municipality assured the Shi'i residents of Jezzine that no harm would come to the mosque. Four men who had worked with Bou Sleiman and other residents of Joun in the *Sahat al-Nuzul* village square wrote directly to the Jezzine *qa'immaqam*, claiming that, after investigating the building "with all precision and care," they had found no unjustified "addition at all" creeping onto the mosque property.[16] One month later, Munir 'Usayran wrote to Asadallah Safa, the Ja'fari *shari'a* judge in Sidon.

> It has reached me that Faris al-Qatrib [i.e., Faris Nimr] from Jezzine put a metal beam (*jassura*) across the space of the mosque and opened doors and windows. He must take the necessary precautions and write either to the governor of South Lebanon or to the *qa'immaqam* of Jezzine about this. We understand that the reparations will amount to something like two or three Ottoman lira.

Although the documentary record of the claim ends here, the Shi'i inhabitants of Jezzine found an ally in the Ja'fari court, even when the property violation was a minuscule 5–30 cm. The institutionalization of sectarianism in Lebanon could be accomplished through just such minute changes that gradually grew and developed over time.[17]

The Ja'fari court in Nabatiyya was also exercised to regulate the administration of religious patrimony. In 1931, Dr. Bahjat Mirza Ibrahim—already introduced above—and a number of local *wujuh* (notables) declared that the town's Great Mosque was in dire need of attention. Ever since the previous caretaker (*mutawalli*), Haj 'Aqil Fahd, had left his position, the mosque suffered grave "neglect," to the point that nobody in town knew the precise status of the *waqf* coffers: "how they go, how they come, or how they are spent." Even more galling for observant Muslims in Nabatiyya, the muezzin was consistently incompetent, failing to even standardize the timing of the call to prayer. Morning prayer was skipped over; sometimes the muezzin announced only afternoon or evening prayer; other days, he simply forgot altogether. Appearing at court in order to draw attention to the matter of the Great Mosque, Ibrahim and his supporters demanded that the Ja'fari court step in and ensure the orderly maintenance of religious life and to protect prayer regularity against the unreliable memory of this bumbling and irresponsible overseer. Tension between the wishes of the founder and the control of the *mutawalli* is "almost in the nature of things," as "in practice [the caretaker] has a great deal of independence in the management of the property, and the amount of institutionalised control over his actions is limited."[18] In this case, it might be argued, the moral authority of the court was marshaled from below in order to reshape the social and religious life of the Shi'i community.[19]

A similar predicament arose towards the end of 1934, when residents of the village of 'Aqrun (Sidon province) implored Munir 'Usayran to intervene in his capacity as sovereign Shi'i administrator. Some residents had intended to convert a piece of *waqf* property in the village into a site for the construction of a boys' school. When the man entrusted to execute the project failed to do so, a group of ten or fifteen involved community members requested Ja'fari court approval to assign one 'Ali Ibrahim responsibility for the *waqf* and to grant him "absolute jurisdiction" over the project. 'Usayran approved the request after a little over one month. The message must not have been delivered, however, because the same group of concerned villagers soon submitted a second petition making the same request. To this second petition, 'Usayran responded again in the affirmative—supporting the appointment of 'Ali Ibrahim—and requested that the judge of the Sidon court immediately attend to the matter.[20]

The defense and definition of Shi'i religious patrimony in Jabal 'Amil also had implications that transcended the Lebanese context. When Sayyid Muhsin al-Amin tried to register Shi'i *waqfs* in Damascus in accordance with "the principles of the Ja'fari *madhhab*," he was instructed to contact the pious endowments representative in Lebanon by way of the Ja'fari court in order to verify that those properties were indeed "philanthropic endowments" registered to the Shi'a. Although al-Amin had resided for some time in the al-Harab Quarter of the old city of Damascus, where he helped to lead the small Shi'i community, Ja'fari courts were not formally recognized in Syria under French Mandate. Having already informed the French authorities that he perceived this lack as a shortcoming, Munir 'Usayran sought to directly manage Shi'i religious patrimony under the aegis of the Lebanese Ja'fari court: "Given that no Ja'fari courts exist in Damascus to examine affairs relating to said *Wakfs*, I wish to ask you to stipulate to the *Direction des Wakfs* in Damascus not to occupy itself with Shi'i *Wakfs* until you have named an overseer for these *Wakfs*, like you have already done for Lebanon."[21] As Lebanon's Shi'is gained more of a voice and more visibility over the course of the Mandate period, some of the 10,000 Shi'is living in French Mandate Syria would have liked either to be integrated into Greater Lebanon or else be granted the same sectarian recognition that the Shi'i milieu in Lebanon had already been accorded. In this sense, al-Amin recognized the novelty and potential of the court as a specifically Shi'i institution. In his plea to the French representative and Munir 'Usayran, which is recorded in a folder kept at the Beirut Ja'fari court, al-Amin wrote how "since time immemorial, there has been no intervention in these affairs, neither practical nor theoretical." However, al-Amin also conceded that, since the court had become "the highest authority (*marja'*) over the Shi'i sect (*ta'ifa*) ... [and since] the Mandatory state has officially recognized the Ja'fari *madhhab*," he would like to behave as an "interlocutor" with the French representative in charge of *awqaf* as well as with the High Commissioner. In the end, al-Amin sought to register Shi'i *awqaf* with the relevant authorities in Lebanon, asking that the French "leave the issue of administering the *awqaf* of our sect to ourselves."[22]

Meanwhile, some other Syrian Shi'is also looked favorably upon getting integrated into the circuitry of the Lebanese Ja'fari court. Rida Murtada sought recognition from the court leadership upon taking over responsibility for the Sayyida Sukayna shrine in the al-Suyufi neighborhood of Damascus from his recently deceased father.[23] A similar request was made regarding the shrine of Sayyida Ruqayya when the overseer (*khadim*) went insane and had to be replaced.[24] Shi'i religious leaders and ordinary people alike—regardless of political orientation it appears—were increasingly recognizing the power and potential of Shi'i legal and religious institutionalization. For all his biases, Zinovi Pechkoff, the *Conseiller Administratif* in South Lebanon, doesn't seem too far off the mark when he argues that, at least as of 1936, Lebanese Shi'is "do not desire annexation to Syria for anything in the whole world. In Lebanon they play a certain role, they have their deputies, their cadis, their muftis, their personal status, etc . . . Incorporated into Syria, the Shiites, as a community, would cease to exist."[25]

Shi'i religious and political leaders worked to achieve communal aspirations during the 1920s and 1930s by demanding protection for Shi'i *waqfs*, which were often intentionally described as distinct from those of Sunni Muslims in Lebanon. In this regard, towering figures such as Sayyid Muhsin al-Amin and Sayyid 'Abd al-Husayn Sharaf al-Din, men who had both turned down offers to head up the Ja'fari court when it was first instituted, quickly recognized how the institution could be called upon to defend the particular interests of the Shi'i community. As for Muhsin al-Amin, he had generally attempted to maintain the separation of the Shi'i community's religious identity from state intervention by keeping political administration separate from clerical hierarchies. In the debates over the reform of the 'Ashura' ritual mourning practices, al-Amin had argued under the sign of modernist reformism that the Shi'i community should not engage in religious practices or any other habits that are physically harmful to individuals, but that could also be negatively perceived by "others" and therefore damage the image of the community (see chapter two). When al-Amin intervened in political life, his actions were consciously geared towards maintaining a morally upright image of the Shi'i community in the eyes of the colonial state and other sectarian communities.

Even though both men turned down the opportunity to become first president of the Ja'fari court, al-Amin is typically portrayed as principled and incorruptible, whereas Sayyid 'Abd al-Husayn Sharaf al-Din, his main rival during this period, is just as often cast as a "collaborator" with French colonial power. But binary categorizations of collaboration/resistance, betrayal/

loyalty, and treason/patriotism are not suitable analytical terms for making sense of the historical significance of these two men, or of the Shi'i milieu in general. For example, al-Amin and Munir 'Usayran, the first president of the Ja'fari court, had an ongoing personal relationship throughout their lives. Both al-Amin and Sharaf al-Din strove to steer the Shi'i milieu and its sectarian institutions toward safer shores even as struggles over the definition and preservation of the Shi'i community's "canonical interests and temporal patrimony" were capable of causing discord within the community as well as between the community and the state. Al-Amin and Sharaf al-Din may have differed in their style and personal behavior, as Sharaf al-Din was perhaps, in Sabrina Mervin's formulation, more "anxious to build a strong Shiite community," one capable of securing a place among the other communities in Lebanon, but both firmly acted to protect Shi'i religious patrimony.[26]

'Abd al-Husayn Sharaf al-Din oversaw a significant amount of *waqf* property in and around his hometown of Tyre. In 1932, when Tawfiq Khalil Halawa, a business associate, asked to be promoted to joint overseer of the city's cemetery and was rebuffed, he summoned Sharaf al-Din to appear before the Tyre Ja'fari court. Although Halawa claimed the cemetery had been endowed as a *waqf* in the name of the "Ja'fari sect"—that is, as a *waqf khayri* and not a *waqf dhurri*—Sharaf al-Din disagreed, claiming that he and his family were its sole custodians, with legal rights to monopolize the custodianship (*tawliyya*). Halawa made the case, however, that Sharaf al-Din had reneged on an earlier understanding of partnership between the two men, arrogating exclusive rights to managing the *waqf*—essentially making a *waqf dhurri* out of what should have remained a *waqf khayri*—but Sharaf al-Din held his ground. Most *waqf* properties in Tyre remained under the control of Sharaf al-Din or his family throughout the Mandate period; he had appropriated *khums* (Shi'i tithe) to initiate several of those *waqf*s, which allowed him to maintain a comfortable life for himself, his family and his political allies. For example, *al-'Irfan* reported that when his son Muhammad 'Ali returned to Tyre after completing his religious studies in Najaf, 'Abd al-Husayn Sharaf al-Din lodged him and his family (eight people in all) in various *waqf* properties around the city. In the end, the Ja'fari *shari'a* judge in Tyre, Shaykh Habib Mughniyya, thwarted Sharaf al-Din's efforts, affirming that the cemetery ought to remain endowed in the name of the Shi'i community as a whole, affirming the status of the cemetery as a *waqf khayri*. As with Sa'id Sabah's claim in Nabatiyya, which was ultimately rejected by the *shari'a* judge there, here was a case in which Mughniyya also elevated the interests of the common good of the community over those of a particular family, no matter how influential. In this, the family politics of *waqf* administration, the Ja'fari court was also capable of asserting its institutional muscle in disciplining and refashioning power relationships within the Shi'i milieu in a way that would have been downright impossible before its foundation.[27]

Institutionalizing Shi'ism

Other collective efforts were made to further institutionalize Shi'i presence by expanding the scope of Shi'i control over religious affairs. Towards the end of 1933, an alliance of doctors, *'ulama'*, teachers, politicians, notables, and other professionals spearheaded one such campaign to convince the French to establish a council that would "study and organize *waqf* affairs." Kazem Khalil, a well-respected lawyer from Sidon and one of the main architects of the project, informed an advisor to the French High Commission that he had received the unequivocal support of Shaykh Husayn Mughniyya, "the leader of the *Ulemas*."[28] Two weeks later, the French transmitted a copy of Kazem Khalil's correspondence to Munir 'Usayran and asked him for his perspective.[29]

'Usayran responded by enumerating the reasons why he believed the establishment of such an administrative body made good sense, although not exactly along the lines that the French had planned. In the course of making his argument, which was endorsed by more than a dozen notable Shi'i religious figures from all over Lebanon, 'Usayran explained what he perceived to be the differences between Shi'i and Sunni *waqf*. The letter supporting 'Usayran's position concluded, "all of the Shi'i *wakfs* should be seized, registered and the necessary steps should be taken in order to institute a Council and commissions for *wakfs*." The signatories to that endorsement reasoned as follows: "Under the Turkish regime, these *wakfs* had a special administration and agents who collected the incomes from the revenues of *wakfs* that were of great importance . . . [and] recorded in the special registers kept in the administrations and inscribed as well with the property services." Because those properties were mostly found "in the big cities," they continued, this made "easier the collection of revenues by the agents as well as the institution of commissions for the administration and organization of *wakfs*." 'Usayran proceeds to refer to *waqfs* whose custodianship (*tawliyya*) and administration (*idara*) are both overseen by the state *waqf* directorate—*madbuta*, which was not the case for Shi'is in pre-Mandate Lebanon—and those that are administered by virtue of a "*waqf* document"—*mulhaqa*, which was also not always the case for Shi'is in Ottoman Lebanon, at least not in any way that was regularly registered and centrally organized. 'Usayran made a case in defense of the Shi'i community departing from the premise that Shi'i *waqfs* had been

> neither Mazbouta nor Mulhaka, but for a long time certain philanthropists have established *wakf* buildings, on behalf of works of charity. Although our *wakfs* are much less numerous by comparison with those of the Sunni community, they are located in all of the territory of the Lebanese Republic from the border of Lattakia up to the Palestinian border. In every village, there is a mosque or a Maqam with a piece of land or a building that is set aside for such use. Certain ulama or residents on site have their hand on those *wakfs* and manage them in an illegal manner. These *wakfs* are registered neither in the special registers nor with the property services. The managers have never declared who will be responsible for the administration of these *wakfs*. If some authority were to ask them for [proof] of their administration accounting, the *wakf* would have no existence.

In light of this reality making the verification of Shi'i "temporary patrimony" difficult to pin down, 'Usayran posed the provocative question: "What kind of *wakfs* will those be that have no documents for demonstrating their nature?" Having worked in the bureaucracy of religious administration, 'Usayran certainly spoke with some experience in such matters: "For some time, I have worked to record *wakfs* of the community in the registers of the *shari'a* courts and then in the property registers. Now, I have encountered many difficulties in the course of this work. On the one hand, it was negligence of the judges and, on the other hand, in the villages where there are *wakfs*, it was the disavowal of the *mukhtars*." Such a dearth of documentation presented a real quandary when it came to speaking about and understanding the politics of presence and recognition under the Mandate—a difficulty no less vexing for contemporary historians of the Lebanese Shi'i community.[30]

Beyond gaining official recognition for the community in the eyes of the state, there were broader practical and institutional implications for such attempts to establish the identity of the Shi'i community. 'Usayran initially opposed the creation of any new Shi'i councils for *waqf* administration, perceiving that such a move might "risk creating a fuss and an uproar that would lead to the loss of certain *wakfs*." He pointed out one case in particular, "the affair of Tyre, which is still not registered and which is still left to languish in the *divers services* despite the fact that the *wakf* documents have a convincing force." Still, 'Usayran was eventually persuaded to accept the "advice" he had been given by the French vis-à-vis the creation of this new Shi'i organization. As there technically was "in all the district of the Lebanese Republic a Djafari Cadi entrusted with registering *wakfs*," 'Usayran came around to supporting the idea of a "Higher Ja'fari Council . . . with the seat at Beirut." This proposal would have entailed a number of provisions that more or less consolidated the power already vested in the Ja'fari courts. Firstly, "Shi'i judges currently working in the Lebanese Republic" would be tapped to staff the council. Those judges were to be "chosen from among the notables of the Community or a member of the *Conseil administrative* of the Caza," if not by the "President or a member of the Municipality. In the case where there are no delegates, the judge or the doctor of the location will be the delegate to the Council." Second, the "monitoring of these *wakfs* is the jurisdiction of the *shari'a* courts. It is the responsibility of these courts to name and to remove the *Mutewallis* of these *wakfs*." Third, in terms of logistical administration: "This Council must examine the means of registering the *wakfs*, to deliver the justifying documents for the *wakfs*, to manage the *wakfs* by the care of the Mutawallis in conformity with the clauses of the law and to work to increase the earnings." Fourth, the council would have to be authorized to "intervene with the local administrative authorities, in conformity with the law, with the aims of obliging the *mukhtars* to not hide what they know about the Shi'i *wakf* properties as well as about those registered by Cadis in the [other] districts." Finally, the "monitoring of judges is the jurisdiction of the Grand Cadi," who was "answerable to the High-Commissioner of the French Republic or is special delegate," pursuant to the terms stipulated in Articles 19 through 31 of Arrêté N° 753 from March 2, 1921.[31]

Although this "Higher Ja'fari Council" never came into being, broad sectors of the Shi'i community would seek to harness the growing institutional power of the Ja'fari court toward political ends. In 1933, Sami al-Khoury, the Lebanese Minister of Justice, learned that the Ja'fari *shari'a* court judge in Shiyyah was seeking to establish "his right to ownership of a piece of land" endangered by the expansion of the Ja'fari Benevolent Society. As in some of the mosque disputes examined earlier in this chapter, here was a charitable association growing beyond its territorial limits—the "development of buildings erected by said Society exceeded the land in question." After he

> denounced the maneuvers of collusion between the president of the benevolent society and the petitioner, the judge proceeded to nominate an administrator for the Ja'fari *wakfs* of Chiah [Shiyyah]. The latter referred the matter to the *Tribunal Chéri de Jaffarite* as a protest in the name of the *wakf* of the named piece [of land].

At this point the judge "ordered a stay until the execution of the judgment from the Commission of Delimitation while waiting for the unknown information of the suit before the Jaffarite Tribunal." Unfortunately, this is one of many cases to appear in the colonial archive or the records of the Ja'fari courts that fails to reach a clear resolution.[32]

Be that as it may, by the mid-1930s, the Ja'fari court was undoubtedly playing an important, perhaps even an inimitable intermediary role in Lebanese Shi'i public and private life. Even if there remained lingering questions about the authenticity and legitimacy of claims in defense of "temporal patrimony" made by individuals and institutions in the Shi'i milieu, the leadership of the Ja'fari court had no intention of allowing the institution to abdicate its growing power. In July 1936, Shaykh Habib Mughniyya, chief Shi'i judge in Tyre, informed Munir 'Usayran how the provincial governor had usurped his jurisdiction by intervening in the selection of court-appointed doctors. Mughniyya argued that those doctors, who were invited to offer testimony on health- and medical-related matters in the course of legal adjudication, were being chosen by the state according to unsatisfactory terms; even more, the new method of selection worked to "contravene Islamic law and the Ja'fari *madhhab*" as articulated in Arrêté N° 3503. 'Usayran marshaled the institutional strength of the Ja'fari court to pressure the Mandate government, contacting the Ministry of Health and the Ministry of Justice in order to confirm that there were standard practices regarding the apprehension and application of medical knowledge, and that these should conform to norms that were acceptable to the Shi'i community. Such a trend toward the centralization of Shi'i authority in the form of the Higher Court in Beirut was reconfiguring the landscape of power and influence within Shi'i Lebanon during the Mandate period. A new kind of religious infrastructure underlying the practice of Shi'i politics and political development was becoming apparent in Beirut and across the south.[33]

Defending Cemeteries, Defining Shi'i Difference

Historians of religion and society increasingly recognize the role of institutional practices in shaping the colonial religious sphere. In the case of Mandate Lebanon, the bureaucratization and centralization of Shi'ism—in the form of the Ja'fari court—created new institutional venues for demands to protect sectarian difference. In this connection, the cemetery became one important site where new forms of Shi'i identity crystallized, where new expressions of Shi'i difference could be perceived. In addition to shedding light on the mundane problems of *waqf* administration, struggles to defend and define Shi'i cemeteries also signify what was increasingly perceived as the inalienable right to demand protection for religious patrimony. "Cemetery related issues," Allan Christelow notes, "were a common means of focusing on issues of community autonomy and corporate identity in colonial Algeria."[34] And as Mushirul Hasan points out,

> Sunni and Shi'i Muslims in colonial Lucknow discovered new symbols of identification in the form of separate graveyards (qabristaan), separate mosques, separate schools, separate religious and charitable endowments. These institutions defined the boundaries within which Shias and Sunnis were required to stay apart. They were to live as separate entities in a world fashioned by the religio-political leadership.[35]

The contested historical process by which boundaries of Shi'i property and autonomy were shaped gained in importance during the Mandate period; the remainder of this section looks at a few such examples.

One case involved a woman from a Christian family in the village of Habil (Tyre province) that was accused by the Shi'i community—depicted in the sources as a collectivity—of illegally usurping their cemetery plot and an adjacent piece of agricultural land, known by the title, "al-Habbaq." The case was first raised in August 1929 at the Beirut court in Burj al-Barajneh, not in Tyre, and the Beirut-based Ja'fari *shari'a* judge Muhammad Ibrahim al-Husayni was persuaded to make a number of trips down to Habil both in order to investigate the site in question and to take the testimonies of a number of villagers, Shi'is and Christians alike. In claiming ownership over the property, this Christian family had formally disputed its status as an Islamic *waqf*. Despite their appeal for a change of venue, the court affirmed, citing the authority of Gennardi—French minister of *awqaf*—that it was empowered to hear the case in Beirut, and that such *waqf* disputes indubitably fell within the purview of the personal status courts.

The defendant claimed to have purchased a piece of property that was located adjacent to the cemetery from a Shi'i resident of the village. Toward the end of August, witnesses were brought to testify before the court or the court was sent to take the villagers testimonials; in all cases, Christians swore on the Bible (*injil*) and Muslims took their oath on the Quran. The forty-eight-year-old *mukhtar* of a neighboring village, a peasant who declared that he could both read and write, offered testimony that the cemetery had been used by the Shi'i villagers of Habil and its neighbors, even mentioning specific people he knew to have been buried there; when the court asked him if they had been brought there from somewhere else, he replied that they had died right there in the village. Another witness from the same neighboring village, a peasant of just over fifty who could neither read nor write, claimed that he had never known of graves there that were not Shi'i graves.[36]

On September 11, 1929, back up in the court at Burj al-Barajneh, a suburb of Beirut, the defendant appeared in court without any supporting witnesses, protesting that none could appear because they were all "at work." In lieu of their testimony, she produced a sale document that ostensibly confirmed her legal purchase of the piece of land in question on November 3, 1915, which had been verified by the state court in Kisrawan on February 11, 1927, from an absentee of the village who had emigrated to North America. However, the court ruled with little explanation that the document was "insufficient" to establish land ownership. Subsequent witnesses for the prosecution appeared and argued that the cemetery had been and continued to be used by the Shiʿi sect (*al-taʾifa al-shiʿiyya*), not by one particular family or another, as the defense had tried to establish, thereby validating their claim to ownership. Put simply, the alleged seller had no legal right to sell that land in the first place.[37] On October 30, the judge handed down a binding ruling in absentia (*hukm ghiyabi ka-l-wujahi*) in which the *waqf* status of the plot was confirmed: "Whereas the *waqf* status of the specifically Shiʿi cemetery present in the village of Habil has been verified to us," the court found, and whereas testimonies had been taken in court and in the village, "some of whom are trustworthy people," the sum total of adduced evidence had "established the truth" and the ruling was established upon "certain knowledge." The cemetery was confirmed as a *waqf* and the opposition of the defense was rejected.[38]

The power of the Jaʿfari court often resided in its ability to control the "rules of the game" inside the walls of the court, even as its power was also projected outwards. On other occasions, disputes emerged within the Shiʿi milieu. For example, the residents of the village of Shiyyah, which is now a part of the southern suburbs of Beirut, petitioned and pressured Munir ʿUsayran to protect their historic cemetery from being bulldozed as part of the expansion of the famous Beirut pine forest. From 1931 until 1933, ʿUsayran sought to work out a compromise among the colonial authorities, the Municipality of Beirut, and the Shiʿi community, which would allow for both the expansion of Beirut's most important public park and the protection of this sacred space. ʿUsayran delivered a *mazbata* (petition) in the name of the Shiʿi community requesting the revision of the current plan in such a way that "the cemetery of Chiah [Shiyyah] would not be affected by the alignment," or even that they be granted "another piece [of land] to allow us to bury our dead."[39] The French authorities repeatedly responded that "no response" was forthcoming from the High Commission and no further documentation concerning resolution of the case can be found in the colonial record.[40]

In another case, residents from the village of Roum (Sidon province) went over the head of their local court to directly petition the higher administration of the Jaʿfari court in Beirut to intervene on behalf of their historic cemetery. It appears that one Yusuf ʿAssaf had been planning to raze the village cemetery and build a private residence on that plot of land. According to Ahmad Sa'id Ahmad, an inhabitant of the village, 'Assaf had presented a summons to the mayor two months earlier requesting permission to tear down the Shi'i cemetery. Ahmad reported that a group of concerned citizens got together to bring the Jezzine *qa'immaqam* along with a village doctor to examine whether the cemetery was indeed "harmful to people's health," as 'Assaf and others were claiming. Ahmad countered that all religious *awqaf,* cemeteries, and other sacred sites must be fully respected and protected by the state. Nobody should ever be permitted to "violate them," no matter what the purported justification. Cemeteries are always near the villages that use them, Ahmad continued, arguing that the sensitivities of his community ought to be respected. Moreover, he went on, 'Assaf didn't even live near the cemetery in question; rather, he was said to live in a far off "Christian area," raising the specter of sectarian conflict here, arguing in an alarmist tone that once these usurpers had gained control of "their" cemetery, they weren't going to stop until the Shi'a gave up their homes as well.[41]

On March 11, 1931, Asadallah Safa wrote to remind Munir 'Usayran of the importance of this unresolved issue as well as the importance of lobbying the French in support of the Shi'i community in Roum.[42] A number of community members had also filed a petition with their local court in Sidon, claiming to speak for the "people of Roum." They insisted to the *qadi* that this cemetery had been used "continuously from ancient times until today without opposition or conflict." Until, that is, 'Assaf and other "Christians" (*nasara*) from the village began pressuring the town head to convert it into private housing. The petitions expressed outrage that those people would dare to overturn the established traditions of their sacred site, that they would contravene the "preservation of tradition." They sought to prevent this "aggression" as well as the subsequent "damage" that would ensue. 'Usayran wrote a personalized letter to the French High Commissioner in Lebanon three days later, beseeching him to "prevent" 'Assaf from "violating" the cemetery of the "people of Roum." He demanded the colonial state, "take this affair into consideration and intervene in order to prevent any violation against the cemetery in the village of Roum on the part of Youssef Assaf." Unfortunately, as in other cases discussed so far, there is no empirical means of discovering the outcome of this case, although it bears reiterating that these are significant archival traces of the piecemeal and gradual mobilizations of sectarian consciousness and popular sectarian loyalties.[43]

The village of Joun (Sidon province) was also embroiled in a similar cemetery dispute. A letter received at the Sidon Ja'fari court reads:

> The *mutawalli* of the sect's *waqf* Haj Husayn Ahmad Shams al-Din presented his resignation to your grace. We are without a *wali* (guardian) to arrange for the affairs of the mosque *waqf*. So, we got together and generally agreed to appoint Sayyid Ahmad Ibrahim 'Issa as *wali* of the *waqf* and *mudabbir* (administrator) of its properties, with overseers Mustafa Husayn Shams al-Din, Muhammad Husayn Barbar, Majid 'Ali Ghosn, Munir Husayn Salih and Tawfiq Isma'il 'Abed Mustafa. We still require support for the appointment so that they can begin their work.[44]

Ahmad Ibrahim 'Issa, *mutawalli* of those local *waqf*s, declared that Christian villagers had set fire to the Shi'i cemetery and that criminals had still not been brought to justice. 'Issa requested "the high intervention of the appropriate authorities, in order to safeguard the rights of the community."[45] "We are distressed to report that an attack was carried out today in Joune (South Lebanon) upon Muslim cemeteries in this village," others such as Mustafa Badr al-Din, Salman Zakir, Ahmad Rida, and Sa'id Sabbagh wrote to the High Commissioner in a supporting telegram. "We demand the punishment of the aggressors in order to safeguard the respect for the dead and sacred Muslim properties (*choses*)."[46] While some members of the Shi'i community directly appealed directly to the colonial authorities in their various tactics to defend and define religious patrimony, others tried to marshal the authority and force of the Ja'fari court to bolster the strength of their cases.[47]

The coastal city of Sidon also witnessed a heated dispute, in which the Shi'i community's claim to the al-Ansar cemetery pitted them against the Sunni community. The Sunni mufti of Sidon had made arrangements with the national corps of engineers, in collaboration with the national council for antiquities, to excavate on the site in the Dakerman neighborhood where the cemetery was located. In 1933, the religious leadership of both the Sunni and Shi'i communities claimed sole ownership of the property. Sayyid 'Ali Fahs wrote to enlist Munir 'Usayran's immediate intervention. On December 16, 1932, the Shi'i *mukhtar* of the Rijal al-Arba'in quarter presented a petition that affirmed the cemetery in question was a *waqf* belonging to the Shi'i community. Fahs transmitted the petition to the director of technical works in order to try and register the cemetery as a Shiʻi *waqf*. ʻUsayran regretfully reported that the cemetery had already been registered in the name of the Sunni community.[48]

Therefore, in November 1933, Munir ʻUsayran wrote to the inspector-general in charge of *Wakfs et Foncière Immobilière* to seek a clearer understanding of the cemetery in question. In that relatively lengthy letter, ʻUsayran informed the colonial authorities:

> the Shiʻi Muslim community possesses a cemetery in which they have buried their dead for a long time. Along the southern edge of the cemetery, there are deconsecrated graves called: "El Anssar cemetery." A public road separates the two parts. The graves are situated in the Rijal El Arbaine quarter where the *mukhtar* is a Shiʻi. This quarter includes the El Wastani quarter. The *mukhtar* of this quarter [El Wastani] is a Sunni.

Even though the leadership of the Shiʻi community requested their property to be registered in the name of the Shiʻi community, ʻUsayran explained how the Sunni leadership had beaten him to the punch.

> Some time earlier, I learned that the Mufti of Sidon, in his capacity as President of the Association of Muslim philanthropy, declared before the Cadastral Engineer that the affected cemeteries belong to the philanthropic association and that, in conformity with a decision taken before the occupation by the administrative council of the *caza*. With his demand, the *mukhtar* of the Dakermane quarter appeared before the Engineer and confirmed the declaration of the Mufti. When the [Shiʻi] *mukhtar* of the Rijal el Arbaine quarter learned of this, he made his opposition to the registration known and declared that the residents and all of the communities know quite well that the cemetery in question belongs to the Shiʻi community.

Although the engineers in question noted the Shiʻi opposition, the recently appointed property judge with jurisdiction over Sidon, Farid Amoune, brought no news to the Shiʻi leadership. ʻUsayran protested that Amoune had carried out the registration in the name of the Sunni community without contacting him or alerting any other Shiʻi officials. Furthermore, the Sunni Mufti of Sidon had disregarded the recommendations of the administrative council appointed to oversee the matter and deferred to Arrêté N° 3497 of the High-Commissioner from August 1, 1928, which had declared Shiʻi *waqf*s "independent." As a result, "there are no longer [external] authorities [watching] over the cemeteries of our community, [even as] it intervened to register the cemetery in question in the name of the Sunni community." Mobilizing his sense of tradition and convention to the defense of Shiʻi religious patrimony, ʻUsayran went on,

> before the [French] occupation, our cemeteries were registered in the title of cemeteries of the Muslim community, because under the Turkish regime, the Jaʻfari *rite* was not officially recognized. Still, we have evidence to prove our rights and our possession in fact of this cemetery.

Even though ʻUsayran did not adduce such evidence in defense of the community, here was another indication of some of the difficulties created by the ambiguous place of Shiʻi *waqf* holdings in Mandate Lebanon. ʻUsayran concluded his letter with an emphatic and emotional plea for help from the French colonial authorities, raising the specter of sectarian violence and intimidation by asking,

> Will the Sunni community not be satisfied until they have taken over every Muslim *waqf* and every mosque, without leaving us one in which to observe our prayers, and still they come to encroach upon our cemeteries?

ʻUsayran then requested that the French carry out an investigation to certify his claims and, having done so, to register the cemetery in the name of the Shiʻi community.[49]

ʻUsayran sought to reinforce communal solidarity by framing his communication to the colonial administration in the language of sectarian rights that might be verified and applied retroactively, even if the state was inclined not to grant such recognition. In July 1934, the High Commissioner concluded that, despite requests from Sidon and Beirut, the Financial Services of the Lebanese Government informed him that "according to the provisional delimitation," the cemetery was in fact registered by the Sunni *mukhtar* of the Dakerman quarter. Despite expressing its opposition, he continued, "the Shiʻi community has not presented any deed showing their ownership of the cemetery." However, even after Sunni ownership was confirmed, it was pointed out that, "Arrêté 186 of the High Commission stipulates a respite of two years for the Shiʻi community in order to raise a legal case to try and establish their ownership of the cemetery."[50] The response forthcoming from the inspector-general overseeing *waqf* affairs hardly differed from the prior assessment given by the Mandate government, reiterating the fact that "the Shiʻi community has not presented any deed verifying their ownership of this cemetery." Therefore, the judge "rejected the opposition and officially confirmed the *procès-verbal* N° 52 in the name of the Sunni community." Again, the Shiʻi leadership was informed that they would still be legally entitled to a two-year window within which to argue their "rights over the cemetery in question before the courts of common law."[51]

In a testament to the fact that the Jaʻfari court was regularly exercised by disputes over the protection and preservation of communal cemeteries, the same case was picked up again several years later, although still to no avail. In 1938, a group of people from Sidon wrote a petition to Sayyid ʻAli Fahs, the Jaʻfari *shariʻa* judge, complaining that the Shiʻi community "possesses a cemetery in the city where we have buried our dead for a long time. Ulemas, martyrs and great personalities are buried in this cemetery, the sort [of people] that, in our eyes, this cemetery is sacred." The petition explains how, "under the pretext that there are ancient monuments in our cemetery, the archeological service has the intention of acquiring to look into expropriation and to dig up our dead. We disapprove of this fact that is, among other things, contrary to *shariʻa* law and [other] laws in force." The petitioners articulated their belief that the French had a special obligation to respect and protect religious patrimony, by whatever means necessary, explaining that they

believe that the mandatory Authority, in conformity with the Mandate Charter, should safeguard religious establishments, including mosques and cemeteries. Is it possible, under these conditions, to authorize the archaeological service to dig up our dead in hopes of materially profiting from ancient monuments that might be found there? We publicly declare that we are prepared to place our bodies and our souls under the auspices of the Mandatory Power in order to prevent the undertaking of excavations in our cemetery.

They closed their letter with the stern warning that, "if the archeological service excavates, the consequences will be very grave."[52]

After receiving a note from Fahs, 'Usayran proceeded to petition the French Inspector-General directly, declaiming that the Shi'i community had never stopped "burying its dead in its cemetery in Sidon. Under these conditions, it is forbidden, according to the law, to expropriate this cemetery and to dig up the bodies." 'Usayran indefatigably demanded that the French authorities intervene to make "the archeological service give up its project. Also, you will safeguard Muslim religious law and you will have contributed to the respect of the dead buried in this cemetery and avoided offending the feelings of the living." Although there is no record of the decision taken by the Mandate authorities or the national archaeological service in this case, the Shi'i community in Sidon persevered in attempting to define and defend Shi'i religious patrimony. By mediating among numerous contests over the ownership and protection of sacred sites in South Lebanon, Beirut and elsewhere in Mandate-era Lebanon and Syria, the Ja'fari court effectively linked Shi'i society with the Lebanese state.[53]

The Practice of Sectarianism

The Lebanese Shi'i community awkwardly confronted new possibilities of sectarian citizenship emerging out of their newfound formal recognition under the French Mandate. As the constellation of individuals, families, and villages discussed in this chapter appealed to the "humanitarian principles" that the French Mandate state was simultaneously perceived to embody and rely upon, they mobilized particular conceptions of morality and justice. Lebanese Shi'is articulated a vision of the Ja'fari court—the most substantial and powerful Shi'i body in the country at the time—as a strong institution capable of both protecting sectarian rights and religious patrimony, on the one hand, and projecting Shi'i power outward, on the other. Of course, the use of petitions in order to demand "sectarian rights" and "colonial justice" was an ambiguous enterprise. Demands for justice made by the recently recognized Shi'i sect were framed so as to take advantage of a vague sense of formal solidarity the colonial state purported to be willing to bestow upon the benighted Shi'i community; petitioners carefully stressed how they sought protection through "the justice of the honorable French Republic." Indeed, many of the tactics utilized by Shi'is who made use of the Ja'fari court implicitly accepted the legitimacy of the legal institutions of colonial modernity. In this sense, "justice" could be deployed strategically—as one means of cynically positioning principles and practices of French colonialism as benevolent, but also in ways that could be appropriated and refigured by individuals within the Shi'i community.

Sectarianism is a practice, or a set of practices, hammered out over time through repeated social, cultural, political, and intellectual habits, the cultivation of a certain kind of group solidarity that is as dependent on subterranean practices of inclusion and exclusion as it can be on overt antagonism or spectacular acts of violence. If Shi'is began practicing sectarianism in Mandate Lebanon—as they defined and defended their "canonical interests and temporal patrimony"—the Lebanese Shi'i community could still see itself in terms of a "religiously informed cultural identity" rather than engaging in "the politics of cultural nationalism."[54] Shi'i Muslims in Lebanon practiced being sectarian by seeking state protections for religious patrimony. This process was contingent upon self-identification vis-à-vis Christian and Muslim neighbors—relational sectarianism—as well as upon institutional and political relationships structured by the sovereignty of a modernizing state—institutional sectarianism. Mounzer Jaber argues that "Shi'iness" was only discovered through "interaction" with Christians, Druze, and Sunnis in Jabal 'Amil and elsewhere.[55] Relationality, of course, can mean both cooperation and conflict. "Savage destruction and slaughter could take place between groups who continued to venerate the shrines and holy figures of each other's traditions" in nineteenth-century South Asia, but the Lebanese Shi'i community was more inclined to employ more pacific means as they "fought strenuously for immediate sovereignty over holy places."[56] Struggles over religious patrimony may be better understood as everyday forms of sectarianism.[57]

By attending to the internal diversity of the Shi'i community and trac-
ing what I have called the "legalizing practices" of the Ja'fari court vis-à-vis
mosques, cemeteries, and other sacred spaces, this chapter helps to make
sense of some of the contradictory processes and contested institutions that
were so emblematic of the making of sectarian Shi'i society in Lebanon during the first half of the twentieth century. If Shi'is started to perceive legal
action through sectarian institutions as one path towards empowerment
or emancipation, the institutionalization of Shi'i law and society concomitantly solidified the authority, the autonomy, and even the independence
of sectarian modes of identification—hallmarks of the sectarianization of
Shi'i Lebanon. The coordination of all these actors—among the bureaucratic administrators of the Ja'fari court, Lebanese Shi'i citizens, colonial
authorities, and the state—complicates the terms of what other historians of
Mandate Lebanon have called the Shi'i "politics of demand" (*matlabiyya*).
In the long run, this led to the increased visibility of the Shi'i community
and the reinforcement of claims to sectarian difference, as well as a subtle
shift towards greater Shi'i participation in public life. Even as Shi'i citizens-
in-the-making may have perceived political life to be stagnating in the midst
of corrupt "feudal" leaders and clientelist networks of patronage and power,
different strategies for political action were haltingly coming into view, even
as new legal infrastructure reinforced the institutionalization of sectarian
difference.[58]

Struggles for power, recognition, and the "right to difference" shaped Shi'i
politics and identity. "Difficulties encountered over the administration of the
Awqaf," Stephen Hemsley Longrigg writes in his classic study of Mandate
administration, "resembled those met in the field of personal-status jurisdiction: in effect, a clash between would-be increased efficiency and good sense
on the one hand, a politically-infused traditionalism on the other."[59] The
formal recognition and subsequent institutions of personal status jurisdiction helped to carve out new autonomous spaces for sectarian communities
without entirely subverting state oversight. "The objective of personal status reform," Nadine Méouchy writes, "was to unify, coordinate and centralize the organs where the action is supervised by the High Commissioner."[60]
Indeed, the formal incorporation of religious authority into the state apparatus constrained the exercise of clerical power even as it sanctioned religious
elites. In other words, the practice of personal status law was ambivalent,

pulling Shiʻis into the purview of the state but also helping to cement certain categories of sectarian difference.

While the Jaʻfari court proved moderately effective at making claims on the state and demanding Shiʻi political, cultural, and economic rights during the Mandate period, it was unable to translate all of that into the foundation for an effective politics. However, the Jaʻfari court also enabled certain practices of Shiʻi sectarianism—the practice of Shiʻi sectarianism as such—by providing an institutional framework through which the Shiʻi community could now directly communicate with the state, perhaps even structuring the extent to which it could appear in the eyes of the state. The actions and interactions discussed in this chapter point up the structural limitations of an institutionalized—and institutionalizing—sectarianism. Although recourse to a specifically sectarian vernacular was one increasingly common means by which the Shiʻi community asserted itself locally, institutional expressions of Shiʻi sectarianism in Lebanon could also be read as a badge of national affiliation.

5

Adjudicating Society at the Ja'fari Court

Each community is considered an independent State.

J. G. ASSAF, *La Compétence des Tribunaux du Statut Personnel au Liban et en Syrie*

The formal recognition of the Ja'fari *madhhab* in Lebanon in January 1926 and the subsequent development of a state-administered court system effectively transformed the ties between the French Mandate authorities and Shi'i society as well as the multiple relationships among the Shi'i community and other Lebanese sectarian communities. For the first time Shi'is in Jabal 'Amil (South Lebanon), the Biqa' Valley, and Beirut were brought into direct contact with the apparatus of the modern state. If the institutionalization of Shi'ism opens up new vistas for historians on the negotiation of juridical, social, and political issues within the Shi'i community, then the intervention of the state—by way of the court apparatus—into the lives of ordinary Shi'i individuals and families was an even more monumental, perhaps even revolutionary, innovation within the Lebanese Shi'i milieu.

The empirical backbone of this chapter consists of *mahadir* (court records), internal court staff correspondence, and missives between ordinary people and the court representatives from the 1920s and 1930s. These are sources that I managed to consult in the "archives" of the Ja'fari courts in Beirut, Nabatiyya, Sidon, and Tyre; they offer access to undiscovered worlds of ordinary Shi'i life, laying bare the everyday challenges and effects of personal status law in practice, which was one key component of the institutionalization of Shi'ism in Lebanon; and they have still never been systematically read or analyzed, effectively constituting an untapped source for historians of the French Mandate period and after. Apart from a corpus of works by notable religious scholars from Jabal 'Amil dealing with theology, *fiqh*, and philosophy, the Shi'i milieu in Greater Syria has left very few written traces for the historian. "To the extent that there is some kind of written record of

Shia life in Lebanon," Fouad Ajami tendentiously argued, "it is in the pages of Al Irfan."[1] Contrary to this questionable conclusion, however, it might be more accurately stated that, to the extent that there has been a perception of the absence of meaningful written records documenting the historical experience of ordinary Shi'i Muslims in Lebanon, historiographical neglect has been one of the primary outcomes. Even though court records can make a significant contribution to our historical understanding of the Shi'i milieu in Lebanon, they certainly do so in a very particular way. Court records capture moments of conflict and negotiation, which is obviously not the only way in which Shi'is—or anyone else—relate to one another, at present or in the past. Nevertheless, Islamic court records are unique historical sources that document the accumulation of small-scale changes in Shi'i identity, social relations, and juridical practice over time.[2]

According to the legal anthropologist Lawrence Rosen, "the world of formal courts offers a stage—as intense as ritual, as demonstrative as war—through which a society reveals itself to its own people as much as to the outside world."[3] A number of cases adjudicated before the Ja'fari court shed light on the ways in which the institutionalization of personal status law has had multiple and occasionally contradictory effects on men and women; has rendered public what might otherwise have remained private family matters; and has also created a semi-public venue within which it became possible for men and women alike to mobilize the power and authority of the community vis-à-vis the state in the service of their individual or familial interests. Gender roles and boundaries in Shi'i Lebanon were in flux during the first half of the twentieth century. Through a micro-historical view of some proceedings inside the Ja'fari *shari'a* courts in Beirut and South Lebanon, this chapter delves into the inner workings of the Ja'fari court in order to demonstrate that the evolution of Shi'i sectarianism was subtly inflected by the everyday administration of personal status law. After a brief recap of the history of the Ja'fari court through the 1930s, this chapter turns to an in-depth exploration of several cases that help to shed light on the political and historiographical significance of this quasi-colonial institution. By intervening in the everyday life of ordinary Shi'i Muslims, the state clearly contributed to the remaking of sectarianism in Lebanon. At the same time, however, ordinary people actively participated in shaping that process.[4]

The Establishment of the Ja'fari Court

Through Arrêté 3503 of January 27, 1926, the French Mandate authorities formally recognized the "Ja'fari *madhhab*" (legal school) as an "independent *madhhab*." This might briefly be called the birth moment of a visible Shi'i community in Lebanon. The colonial state initially sanctioned the operation of Ja'fari tribunals in Beirut, Sidon, Tyre, Nabatiyya, Marjayoun, Baalbek and Hirmil.[5] Some historians have viewed the separation of personal status matters from civil law and other jurisdictions as one means by which French colonial rule "preserved" local "custom" or "liberated" Shi'i "tradition." More judiciously put, such juridical reorganizations in Mandate Syria and Lebanon can be said to have given rise to what Elizabeth Thompson aptly terms a "dual legal system."[6] The extension of Shi'i autonomy over personal status matters strengthened the exercise of Shi'i agency but also gave rise to a struggle over communal sovereignty. Until the mid-1930s, the higher court in Beirut oversaw the district courts in a relatively informal manner. Subsequently, the French administration set about reforming the court system through an increase in state oversight and the imposition of a legal structure that was patterned after the institutions of French civil law.

The Ja'fari court system was two-tiered. When a case could not be resolved in a court of first resort (*al-mahkama al-bada'iyya,* equivalent to the French *cour de première instance*), it was sent up to the court of clarification (*mahkamat al-tamyiz*), also known as "the highest court" (*al-mahkama al-'ulya*). In clarifying the case, however, the president of the Ja'fari court and his advisers would rarely go beyond the confirmation or disconfirmation of a given ruling. During this early stage, the higher court could hardly affect the terms of legal adjudication. It was effectively licensed to send a thumbs-up or thumbs-down ruling to the lower courts. The earliest and only higher court records that I came across were in a folder dealing with the period from 1940–1943.[7]

Court workers—judges, clerks, scribes, experts, and assistants (but not lawyers, witnesses, or other legal representatives)—were state-appointed and salaried employees. From 1926 until he passed away in 1948, Munir 'Usayran served as court president and was joined by two legal "advisers," Shaykh Yusuf al-Faqih and Sayyid 'Ali al-Zayn. His salary was fixed at 140.5 Lebanese Liras (L.L.) per month and his two advisers earned 95

L.L. per month. These salaries were lower than the salary of the Sunni court president and his advisers, who earned 227 L.L. per month and 140.5 L.L per month, respectively.[8] The first judges appointed to the court in Beirut included Muhammad Ibrahim al-Husayni, Sayyid Muhammad Yahya Safi al-Din, and Sayyid ʿAli Fahs. When Munir ʿUsayran left his post as Jaʿfari court judge in Sidon to serve as president of the court system in Beirut, he was replaced by, successively, Asadallah Safa, Sayyid ʿAli Fahs (who was later transferred to Beirut), and Nur al-Din Sharaf al-Din. In Tyre, Shaykh Habib Mughniyya was chief judge at the Jaʿfari court throughout the Mandate period. In Nabatiyya, Muhammad Rida al-Zayn served as judge until the 1940s.[9] Court records attest to the fact that both Mughniyya and al-Zayn had been employed as Shiʿi judges in Tyre and Nabatiyya, respectively, since the late Ottoman period, even though the Jaʿfari *madhhab* was not formally recognized until January 1926. Although all of these men came from notable Shiʿi families in Jabal ʿAmil, they certainly did not all have the same scholarly credentials. Most did not have the *ijaza* (license) granted by the Shiʿi theological seminary at Najaf to students who had reached the scholarly rank of *mujtahid,* although having one might possibly have bolstered their claim to such positions of authority, at least, in the eyes of some.

The historical understanding of the everyday lives and experiences of ordinary Shiʿi Muslims in Lebanon can be greatly expanded through a reading of the Jaʿfari court records, a virtually untapped source for Shiʿi social history. The court records are handwritten texts maintained in modern, industrially produced folders and not on the oversized parchment typical of Ottoman and some other Islamic court documents. The *katib* (scribe) who wrote these documents kept separate folders for each type of case: inheritances in one, marriages, maintenance (*nafaqa*) payments, and divorces in another. Unfortunately, there is no complete or comprehensive collection or catalog of the Jaʿfari court records. Although the opinions of a specific judge were often grouped together, more than one judge might appear side by side in the same folder. This suggests that the folders were either passed around or that the judges rotated in and out of their posts. One of the major difficulties confronting any historian who uses *mahadir* (s. *mahdar*) as sources is the fact that cases were written down before they were fully resolved. This means that there are no summaries or digests but simply continuous reporting of what was going on in court and what was planned for the near future. Unfortunately, since there is not a complete collection of court records from the pre-independence period, the thread of some cases is not unbroken; in other words, if proceedings dragged on beyond the length of a single *daftar* (folder), and they often did, the case could be interrupted or even lost for good.

Be that as it may, the formal recognition of the Shi'i community in Lebanon effectively resulted in the veritable bureaucratization of Shi'i law. To the extent that there is a record of ordinary Shi'i life in Mandate-era Lebanon, it can be found in the records of the Ja'fari court. The incorporation of such broad sectors of society into the state apparatus fundamentally reconfigured Lebanese Shi'i self-understandings in new juridical terms. This collision between "traditional" jurisprudential authority and methods, on the one hand, and new legal institutions of colonial modernity, on the other, resulted in the transformation of Shi'i religious politics and cultural identities. The problematic of "collaborating" with temporal authority, here in the form of the Lebanese state, had become a practical matter and, therefore, was no longer simply a matter of theoretical controversy.

Defining Ja'fari Jurisdiction

In his illuminating ethnography of Islamic courts in Malaysia, Michael G. Peletz discusses the complicated terms of what he calls "the cultural logic of judicial process." Peletz deploys this concept in order to explain the "negotiation, compromise, and reconciliation" he witnessed first-hand during participant-observation fieldwork in Malaysian *shari'a* courts. He distinguishes this fluid environment from the reductive Weberian conception of Islamic law in practice as the uncomplicated application of an ideal-type, monolithic, and authoritarian *Kadijustiz,* imposed in a way that is "capricious, ad hoc and irrational." To be sure, the specific cultural logic of the judicial process in Malaysia is distinct from that found in Mandate Lebanon, or anywhere else for that matter, as Islamic legal culture has adapted over time and has illustrated a great deal of flexibility. It is in precisely this regard, therefore, that it is the task of the social historian to attend to the particularities of local contexts when analyzing the theory and practice of Islamic law without losing sight of larger, potentially comparative issues or themes.[10]

As with other Islamic family court systems, the jurisdictional framework of Ja'fari courts in Greater Lebanon was limited to matters of personal status—marriage (*nikah*), divorce (*talaq*), dower (*mahr*), maintenance payments (*nafaqa*), pious endowments (*awqaf*, s. *waqf*), and inheritance (*irth*). The vast majority of cases involved the court helping women recoup unpaid dowries or maintenance payments. Typically, a woman would take her intransigent husband to court for refusing to pay her *mahr* or to make obligatory *nafaqa* payments. Other common cases dealt with contested inheritances, the appointment of an overseer (*nazir*) for *waqf* property, land disputes, or the appointment of a legal guardian (*wasi*) to care for underage children.

The institutionalization of Ja'fari law raised numerous questions about the adjudication of everyday life disputes as well as the contested integration of the Shi'i milieu into the Lebanese state apparatus. Such unprecedented bureaucratization of Shi'i law and jurisprudence—the introduction of a state judiciary and its attendant cadres—raised new epistemological questions regarding the practical application of Shi'i law and theology within a modern nation-state context. When the Ja'fari *madhhab* was first recognized, lawyers and religious scholars like Rida al-Tamir, Munir 'Usayran, and others helped to delineate the theoretical jurisdiction of Lebanese Shi'i personal status law. Judges, lawyers, and ordinary people alike also helped to negotiate the practical boundaries of the court's jurisdiction during the first two decades of the court's operation.

In fact, the fluid boundaries of the court's jurisdiction point to the shifting categories of Shi'i personhood and citizenship during this period. In 1931, for example, a woman from South Lebanon tried to recoup *nafaqa* arrears owed by her ex-husband at the Beirut court.[11] Not only did the defendant wish to avoid paying her *nafaqa,* but he also sought to acquire exclusive custody of their daughter. On October 15, 1931, the husband's legal representative (*wakil*) asserted that the plaintiff had raised a *mahr* and *nafaqa* claim simultaneously, which was illegal, so both cases should be thrown out; he insisted that each claim should have been brought before the court separately. Moreover, the defense continued, the law (*sunan al-qanun*) required the case be tried in Tyre, where both parties had resided until recently, and not in Beirut, where this woman had recently moved. This woman's father appeared in court as her representative and argued that she had decided to live in Beirut and that it was her *right* to raise such claims wherever she resided. When she failed to appear again in court on January 9, 1932, the court ordered her to drop her *nafaqa* claims and convey custody over her daughter to her ex-husband.[12]

Although we cannot know with certainty the circumstances that prevented this woman from returning to appear in court, in his reflections on the case, Judge Muhammad Ibrahim al-Husayni makes some observations that bear upon the institutionalization of Ja'fari law in Lebanon. Husayni argued there is "no jurisdiction (*salahiyya*) except that of the *mujtahid*." Once the Ja'fari *madhhab* had been recognized by the French colonial state, Husayni continued, the Shi'i court enjoyed an institutional status equivalent to that of a *mujtahid mutlaq*—a Shi'i religious scholar with the requisite religious training and erudition to produce authoritative and binding interpretations of Islamic jurisprudence. According to this understanding of the relationship between law and society in Shi'i Lebanon, Ja'fari law (*al-qanun al-ja'fari*) located religio-legal authority (*marja'iyya*) in the Ja'fari court as it functioned in practice. In other words, "traditional" learning and theoretical jurisprudential questions would now be unable to avoid being modulated by the dictates of common legal practice.[13]

On the one hand, this argument was a means of authorizing the court, which was still a new and somewhat controversial institution. On the other hand, the implications of this argument are instructive for understanding the court as a key player in the gradual institutionalization of Shi'i presence in Lebanon. Ibrahim effectively argued that the court was institutionally invested with the power to adjudicate jurisprudential affairs of the Shi'i community, but with a difference. Shi'i jurists subsequently interpreted Arrêté 3503, which recognized the sovereign rights of Shi'i Muslims over their communal legal sphere, to accord judges certain privileges, including the ability to pass legal judgments that "only the *mujtahid*" would have been authorized to pass, even if the judges serving within the court's offices were not themselves technically *mujtahid*s. This perspective may shed some unusual light on the tension within the Shi'i milieu regarding the legitimacy of this national institution and the loyalties of its employees and users.

Of perhaps even greater consequence was the fact that such an understanding of the Ja'fari court moved beyond the recognition of precedent *within* the court by according its rulings and opinions a greater degree of authority within Lebanese Shi'i society more broadly. The practice of Ja'fari law in Mandate Lebanon gave rise to a new kind of institutional memory that would guide the application of personal status law in the future. The implications of such institution building extended beyond the walls of the courts, as chapter four demonstrated, institutionalizing a certain kind of Shi'ism that was rendered increasingly Lebanese. In lasting ways the Ja'fari court established precedents—in both the legal and institutional senses—that would become increasingly influential in determining the character of the Shi'i presence in Lebanon. The contradictions of Shi'i inclusion and exclusion were epitomized by the institutionalization of sectarian difference.

The ambiguities and controversies surrounding the formation of the Ja'fari court were addressed in piecemeal fashion even as Shi'i law was being re-defined and hammered out in practice. Articles 2 and 3 of Arrêté 3503 recognized the rights of Shi'i Muslims to seek counsel before the Shi'i *qadi* in their province (*muhafaza*) or in the nearest province with a Shi'i *qadi*, if theirs didn't have one. There were neither explicit legal stipulations determining whether a case had to be tried in the home province or place of residence of either the plaintiff or the defendant nor advising what to do in cases in which those two places did not match up. Consequently, mundane questions of administration and procedure came up regularly. As mentioned, Judge Muhammad Ibrahim al-Husayni ruled against the claim of a woman for her *nafaqa* arrears outside of her natal province. In that very same ruling, though, al-Husayni supported the right of a woman to raise a claim against her husband in court, even if she no longer lived in her home province and even if he was living somewhere else. Women's mobility and agency seems to have earned some measure of recognition, if only tacitly.

When a dispute was raised in both the Ja'fari and the Sunni *shari'a* courts, the court immediately endeavored to squelch any potential sectarian tension. For example, a man from Baalbek appeared in the Beirut court to verify that he had been married according to the precepts of the Ja'fari *madhhab*.[14] His wife denied this, claiming that they had been married "according to the traditions of Abu Hanifa" in the Sunni *shari'a* court before the marriage at the Ja'fari court ever took place—any legal disputes, therefore, should be adjudicated in the Sunni *shari'a* court. This woman decided that it was in her best interest to have the case moved to the Sunni court even as her husband argued that the case should be heard before the Ja'fari court. Her husband went so far as to claim that the marriage contract from the Sunni court was little more than a forgery concocted by the bride's father.[15]

Rather than interpreting the dispute as pitting one Islamic sect against another, the Ja'fari court ruled that there was "legally no difference" between establishing a marriage contract in a court that follows "any sect of the Muslim Imams." As presiding judge, Sayyid Muhammad Yahya Safi al-Din called for immediate reconciliation between the two parties. Without knowing whether this case was subsequently taken up at the *shari'a* court, it is likely here that either court would have ordered the wife to "follow" the tradition of her husband; the case most likely would have been returned to the Ja'fari court. Even more important, it seems to me, however, is how the judge attempted to downplay the sectarian claims of the litigants, insisting that there was no difference between Muslim sects as far as the application of *shari'a* law was concerned. The court downplayed its difference in some cases even as it would claim the right to that difference in other contexts.[16]

House Calls and "Extra-Judicial Interventions"

During the first two decades of its operation, the jurisdictional boundaries of the Lebanese Ja'fari court were fluid. One of the surprising things about the court is that it occasionally handled religious matters, e.g., it formally sanctioned and oversaw conversions to Shi'ism. Previously, conversion cer-emonies (*ibdal al-din,* or exchange of religion) took place in private—in the home of a learned religious scholar or within the walls of a mosque or *husayniyya.* The performance of such a ceremony in the communal court, within the purview of the state—rather than in the "autonomous" religious space of a mosque or the "private" home of a religious author-ity—demonstrates the increasing importance of the court and the com-plex process through which Shi'ism became institutionalized in Lebanon. Although rare, in such cases the prospective convert would appear before a judge or court assistant and publicly pronounce his or her fealty to "the Ja'fari *madhhab,*" both "by desire and by choice." The practice known as emulation (*taqlid*) in modern Shi'ism requires each individual to choose to follow, or emulate, the judicial and moral opinions of a highly educated and respected religious scholar, or "source" (*marja'*) of emulation, in mat-ters of religious practice and theology.[17] The prospective convert, then, pronounces aloud his or her intention to "emulate" Imam Ja'far al-Sadiq "by way of" a particular *marja',* such as *al-mujtahid al-akbar* Sayyid Abu al-Husn al-Isfahani, the Iraqi *mujtahid* of the age. As such, the convert thereby entered into a relationship not only with a religious representative of the Shi'i community in Lebanon, and, by association, the global Shi'i milieu, but also with the state.[18]

At the same time as such religious ceremonies were being brought into court, Ja'fari law was exported beyond the court walls. Let us consider a case in which Muhammad Rida al-Zayn, the erstwhile judge of Nabatiyya, intervened in an inheritance dispute in the village of 'Arabsalim. One group of heirs to a certain deceased man claimed that another group of heirs had misconstrued the will (wasiyya). Because the second group, which had been summoned to the Nabatiyya court by the first, failed to show up, al-Zayn made a personal "house call": he set up an adjudication session (majlis) in the village, divided the inheritance, and then sent the paperwork back to Beirut. The Higher Court argued that this was a legitimate course of action, notwithstanding the unorthodox methods and the fact that al-Zayn took a sizable commission for his services (250 Syrian Liras). Al-Zayn informed Munir 'Usayran and his advisors that this inheritance dispute might have led to "fighting and bloodshed" if he had not intervened. Indeed, Munir 'Usayran suggested that al-Zayn should be commended for his activities, which had prevented "vengeance and aggression." The higher court nevertheless recommended that if the situation required a return to the court at a later date, then the case would have to be heard in Marjayoun rather than Nabatiyya. Al-Zayn exercised a prerogative of legal mobility in order to help distribute an inheritance in the rural south, expanding the scope of state Shi'i institutions and personally profiting at the same time.[19]

Although massive rural-urban migration did not occur until the 1950s, Shi'is were increasingly moving to Beirut as early as the 1920s. Despite the enduring political connections between Shi'i migrants in Beirut and their home villages, many Shi'is noticed an increasing estrangement between their lives in Beirut and life back "at home" in their ancestral villages. Residents of Beirut often perceived "the South" as a place of lawlessness, chaos, and violence. Not long before his death in 1935, the notable 'Abd al-Latif al-As'ad scrawled a personal letter imploring 'Abd al-Husayn Muruwwa to intervene in another familial dispute in the south that was rapidly escalating out of control and that might result in unnecessary violence and bloodshed. Al-As'ad complained that such backward behavior was entirely inappropriate for a "sect of 200,000" that wished to be taken seriously by the rest of the country.[20] This sense of interconnectedness served as a background against which Shi'i politicians, judges and ordinary people had to make sense of their new reality under the Mandate. During the early 1940s, Eric Pruneaud, *Conseiller Administratif* of South Lebanon, sought to more effectively link the tactics of rule in Jabal 'Amil to the burgeoning Shi'i milieu in Beirut. He noted the increasingly visible Shi'i presence in and around Beirut, and pointed out how, "with the goal of obtaining their demands, the majority of Shi'is in Beirut are [now] registered [to vote] in the capital." Even as the relationship between the Lebanese center and its peripheries was being negotiated, al-As'ad's plea and Pruneaud's remark can be understood in terms of an arc of increasing Shi'i visibility in Lebanon.[21]

Legal practices outside the court did not necessarily entail travel over long distances. On one occasion, Beirut judge Sayyid Muhammad Yahya Safi al-Din was accompanied by the court scribe, Kadhim al-Husayni, to visit a man from Nabatiyya who had fallen ill and was convalescing at the French hospital in Khandaq al-Ghamiq. This man was unable to leave his hospital bed and appear in court in order to have his will notarized. The court literally "delivered" its opinion to this ailing man. Safi al-Din recalled,

> At 1 PM on Saturday, August 26, 1939, I showed up at the French hospital in Khandaq al-Ghamiq, accompanied by the scribe of this court, Sayyid Kadhim al-Husayni, at the request of Haj 'Abdallah Haydar Jabir from the people of (*ahali*) Nabatiyya, who [was] in fact present in the aforementioned hospital. I found Haj 'Abdallah in a sick condition [but] he had his wits about him. After I had spent a few moments with him, he requested that I record his will so that he might sign it with his [own] hand.

What followed was a verbatim transcription of Haj 'Abdallah's last will and testament: Haj 'Abdallah swore the *shahada;* witnessed that Muhammad was the servant of God, His Prophet, and that Muhammad was sent with "divine guidance" and "the religion of truth"; declared that 'Ali was the "Commander of the Faithful" and the "Imam of the Pious," and that the Imams were "truly" the "successors" to the Prophet; and proclaimed that "heaven is real," that "hell is real," and that "the Day of Judgment is coming, no doubt." He asked for his grave to be prayed over when he died and for certain prayers to be recited there for a set number of days; for his son and daughter to divide the remaining possessions in his house in Nabatiyya, but for only his son to inherit his collection of couches and rugs; and finally for his two brothers and nephew to be responsible for executing this will and testimony after he died. With the judge, the scribe and two additional witnesses present, the will was certified.[22]

The Ja'fari court was an active force in the management of everyday life in Shi'i Lebanon. Such legal house calls underwrote the emerging legal and religious infrastructure that structured the relationship between the Lebanese state and Shi'i society. The Ja'fari court increasingly intervened in the daily lives of ordinary Shi'is. In turn, ordinary Shi'is could marshal the institutional weight of the Lebanese state to their advantage in matters of personal status law, through the entry point of the Ja'fari court. The remainder of this chapter will be concerned with three cases heard at the Lebanese Ja'fari court. Each one provides a slightly different perspective on accounts of the politics and practices of everyday life among Lebanese Shi'is under the Mandate, for whom the Ja'fari court was an active and vital force. Even as these sources shed light on processes of legal institutionalization, they also provide the historian with some insight into the texture and flavor of everyday life in Shi'i Lebanon during a period of gradual social transformation. The Ja'fari court brought multiple sectors of Shi'i society in Lebanon together under the same roof. Consequently, this institution helped to recast the relationship between Ja'fari law and Shi'i society and to reconfigure the relationship between the Shi'i milieu and the state.

Adjudicating Shi'i Society (I):
The Squandered Inheritance of Nazih al-As'ad

Historians will often make the generalized claim that the primary historical function of Islamic courts has been to preserve the status quo in the social order. As such, *shari'a* courts are thought to represent an institutional means of maintaining tradition but also a means of cementing social peace. Be that as it may, such a reading can obscure the extent to which Islamic courts have also been engines for social change. The jurisdiction of the Ja'fari court in Mandate Lebanon extended into the realms of everyday life. On the one hand, such interventions were oriented toward protecting the "welfare" or the "interest" of the weak, the indigent, the mentally unfit, or underage and irresponsible individuals. On the other hand, some Shi'is in South Lebanon and Beirut perceived the Ja'fari court as poised to play a role in the protection of Shi'i patrimony and property, both of which were regarded as vulnerable to dangers posed by rival communities or the state. Struggles to protect religious patrimony often revolved around a communally and juridically defined notion of *maslaha*, often rendered into English as the "common good."

The concept of *maslaha* has a long and circuitous genealogy in the annals of Islamic law. Felicitas Opwis argues that "*maslaha* as a means for legal change has many facets and may be used for different purposes. To understand the potential of *maslaha* to expand and adapt the law, it is necessary for scholars of Islam and Islamic law to look closely at the way a jurist integrates this concept into the legal system as a whole."[23] Indeed, *maslaha* refers to a variety of principles and meanings; *maslaha* in theory does not always coincide with *maslaha* in practice. Therefore, historians must remain attentive to the ways in which jurisprudential opinions and juridical practices have been institutionalized into specific legal regimes.

During its first two decades, the Ja'fari court drew up on the concept of *maslaha* in several different ways. First, the court monitored, negotiated and regulated the burgeoning relationship between the Shi'i milieu and the state, arrogating exclusive rights to represent the Shi'i community and to determine its collective interests in the eyes of the colonial state. Second, the court was the highest formal arbiter of marriage, divorce, maintenance, property, and *waqf* disputes within the Shi'i milieu. Third, the court intervened in the daily lives of ordinary Shi'is by attempting to support the maintenance of proper family or social relations.

Property disputes, which surfaced less commonly in the court records than other types of cases during this period, fell within the jurisdiction of the Ja'fari court, which could be called upon, for example, to help preserve the inherited wealth of minors. In 1929, a young man named Nazih al-As'ad appeared before the Sidon Ja'fari court alongside the venerable *mujtahid* Shaykh Husayn Mughniyya, who at that time was still president of the Association of 'Amili 'Ulama', and arguably one of the most respected religious scholars in Jabal 'Amil. Hailing from the seaside city of Tyre, the As'ad family traced its lineage back to the Al al-Saghir clan, which retained a unique symbolic place in 'Amili cultural memory on account of its connections to Nassif Nassar, the valiant rebel leader who struggled against the late eighteenth-century Ottoman governor Ahmad Pasha al-Jazzar. During the Mandate, the al-As'ad clan was one of the most powerful in South Lebanon and its members held parliamentary office since the inception of Greater Lebanon.

With Mughniyya as his guarantor, Nazih sought to establish that he had reached the age of maturity and should therefore no longer remain subject to the guardianship (*wisaya*) of his elder brother, 'Ali Nusret Bey al-As'ad, a notable figure in their high-profile family.[24] The fact that Nazih was of age was sufficient justification for him to declare personal independence from his brother's supervision. In addition, Judge Asadallah Safa regarded Shaykh Husayn Mughniyya's presence and testimony in court as strong evidence of Nazih's independent status and ability to oversee his own affairs. He therefore ruled in favor of Nazih.[25]

The case did not end there, though. Once granted his majority, Nazih was accused by his older brother of behaving immaturely and of engaging in activities that called into question his ability to make responsible choices. Both the Sidon and Beirut Ja'fari courts were called upon to help monitor Nazih. The court learned, for example, that Nazih wanted to sell shares of property he had inherited from his father, the notable magnate Shabib Pasha al-As'ad, in his ancestral home of Zrariyeh, a predominantly Shi'i village in Sidon province. To that end, on March 1, 1932, one 'Ali Fakhri had dispatched his younger brother, Hasan Majid, to purchase on his behalf some of those pieces of land—known as "The Red Field with Wintry Eyes" and "The Fields." The state land registry office rejected Hasan Majid's request owing to the fact that he was underage. However, Judge Asadallah Safa furnished the Fakhri brothers with a written "legal permission" (*idhn shar'i*) that requested permission for the underage brother to complete the transaction, thereby effectively subverting the authority of a state agency.[26] The court had flexed its institutional muscle to help conclude this property transaction, opposing the decision of a state institution: the communal court trumped the state. In addition to calling Nazih to account for his financial transactions between 1929 and 1932, 'Ali Nusret Bey al-As'ad appeared before the Beirut court to request its assistance in ensuring that Nazih's finances and property were properly managed and maintained. He argued that Nazih's recklessness was endangering his family's wealth. On April 30, 1932, 'Ali Nusret complained that Nazih sold properties below their market value and spent an "excessive amount" of his savings. He therefore asked the court to put a stop to his brother's "transactions . . . pursuant to the jurisdiction of the *shari'a*"; to execute a comprehensive "accounting" of the value of the properties that had been sold by Nazih; and, finally, to place him under the court's "supervision." The court agreed to track the sale or purchase of land and other substantial holdings that passed through Nazih's hands.[27]

On May 10, 1932, Nazih declared to the judge that he remembered selling property whose estimated value was approximately 600 Ottoman liras. 'Ali Nusret countered that, in fact, Nazih had sold those properties for a mere 100 liras, accusing him of casually frittering away his inherited wealth. Nazih retorted that he had spent the money he earned from those transactions only on what he considered to be "reasonable, necessary things," including 60 Ottoman liras to pay for school supplies and some suits that he needed for a trip to Paris. The judge asked Nazih a barrage of questions regarding the financial benefit of his actions and whether he truly considered the decisions he had made defensible.[28]

As the court pored over these details of Nazih's lifestyle and spending habits in search of an appropriate mechanism to enforce greater fiscal responsibility, Nazih continued to defend his actions. Accused by his brother of other morally unacceptable behavior such as gambling, Nazih countered that he didn't have a gambling "problem," that he didn't sit around "the green table" or "gamble with the gamblers," although he may have played cards from time to time with his friends from school; he admitted to playing cards with some Frenchmen on occasion and losing fifty Syrian liras. After a period of study, the court reported that the properties sold by Nazih included: the property known as "The Red Field with Wintry Eyes," which was sold for 100 Ottoman gold liras to the Fakhri family on February 24, 1932; two other properties in Zrariyeh that were sold for 15 Ottoman gold liras to Mustafa b. Muhammad 'Abbas on April 20, 1932; and another piece of land on the same day to one 'Ali b. Ahmad Talib.[29] In the end, the court declared that he had spent his money in a way that was mildly inappropriate, although his behavior did not necessarily amount to carelessness that could be legally termed unreasonable spending (*safah*).[30] The court therefore ruled that Nazih's financial affairs henceforth would be monitored and that any financial transaction he wished to execute would have to be approved by the court before he would be allowed to proceed.[31]

The institutional weight and authority of the court was leveraged to intervene in intimate family matters of wealth and property. The court not only adjudicated personal status debates, but also actively participated in monitoring the private lives of Shiʻi individuals and families. Even an influential politico like ʻAli Nusret Bey al-Asʻad saw value in making use of the court. He sought formal legal assistance from the Jaʻfari court in managing his family's wealth. Although the court records do not give us clear answers to exactly why people like ʻAli Nusret chose this course of action over others, such questions point to some of the ways in which the activities of the court extended beyond anything like the rote application of personal status law.

Adjudicating Shiʻi Society (II): Can a Temporary Wife Inherit?

Social historians have shown how property relations are at heart social relations, that disputes over property should also be understood as social disputes.[32] The Jaʻfari court records shed light on some of the specific issues, social customs, and family relationships that characterized Shiʻi society under the Mandate. In this connection, for example, temporary marriage (*mutʻa*) is one of the most often cited yet misunderstood features of Shiʻi Islam. A *mutʻa* marriage, or temporary contract (*ʻaqd munqatiʻ*) is technically no different than a permanent contract marriage (*ʻaqd daʼim*), except that the contract is for a fixed period of time, after which the marriage is automatically dissolved. Although scholars have discussed its theoretical and jurisprudential dimensions, less attention has been paid to the question of *mutʻa* in practice.[33] If some cases adjudicated in the Jaʻfari court demonstrate the exercise of women's agency, other cases serve as a powerful reminder of how women's agency could also be circumscribed.

A woman—call her Jamila—concluded a marriage contract for a period of twenty years with a man—call him Hasan—whose first wife had given birth to twelve of his children. From Nabatiyya, Jamila later moved to Beirut, where she gave birth to one child with Hasan. After Hasan passed away, his large family appeared in court to divide the inheritance. The will was legally verified and read in the Sidon court on March 21, 1927. After the inheritance had been appropriately divided, a group of notables from Nabatiyya were

summoned to confirm that Jamila had been "released from [her second husband's] matrimonial authority upon his death." Jamila denied this, avowing
that the court's "declaration (*taqrir*) was untrue" because "in fact I . . . am
a legal wife of the deceased." Therefore, she continued, "I have the right to
the wife's share." She went on to declare—shocking those in attendance—
that one of the deceased's twelve children was actually hers and not born
to his first wife. On November 12, 1930, she cited a ruling from the higher
court confirming those assertions. Jamila requested that two of the children
appear in court so that the matter might be discussed further and the inheritance could be re-distributed in view of her rights as a second permanent
wife of the deceased.[34]

Jamila failed to attend the scheduled session because, as her son,
Muhammad said, she was injured after stepping on a nail, a strange tidbit of
descriptive detail. After the case was rescheduled, she again failed to attend,
but this time sent a doctor's note to the court on her behalf requesting a
postponement, which was granted. After this second absence, however, the
defendants requested that the charges be dropped since Jamila had failed
to provide a legitimate excuse for not attending and seemed to be wasting
the court's time.[35] On February 14, 1935, judge Sayyid Muhammad Yahya
Safi al-Din noted that the Higher Ja'fari Court (*mahkamat al-tamyiz*) had
already begun looking into the matter and opted to postpone the case until
the higher court came to a decision.[36]

The case resumed one week later, after the Higher Court ruled against a
change of venue or any further postponements.[37] The defense lawyer argued
that Jamila still had not verified her binding temporary marriage contract
with Hasan. In the absence of such a contract, hers would remain "just a ver-
bal claim" (*qawl mujarrad*), in the words of the defense lawyer. Jamila modified her story, arguing that the marriage was temporary at first but was made
permanent subsequently. One of the witnesses pointed out that if Jamila
produced a valid temporary marriage contract, she would be entitled, as a
second wife, to a larger share of the inheritance. Nevertheless, Jamila continued to insist that she had been legally married to the deceased under a permanent marriage contract although she never managed to deliver any proof
of such a claim. Her lawyer argued that the "evidence" (*bayyina*) supporting
Jamila's case was to be found somewhere in the home of the deceased, which
was also apparently where the contract had been executed. In a subsequent

court session, Jamila acknowledged that Hasan had been "insane and mentally impaired" at the time the contract was drawn up, a point confirmed by medical reports submitted to the court. Thus, even if a permanent marriage had in fact taken place and Jamila could verify it, it would not be valid due to the fact that the deceased was mentally unfit at the time to engage in such action. Jamila's lawyer claimed she had been married to Hasan for about a month before he died, which would place their marriage within the period after he fell ill. Hasan had been diagnosed with a terminal illness at around the same time that the will was drawn up. The case was eventually thrown out by Sayyid Muhammad Yahya Safi al-Din.[38]

According to a French survey of Shi'ism in Lebanon, "temporary marriages are a source of conflicts, in particular with regard to the children who are born from them and who the presumed father refuses to recognize. The shari'a courts of Tyre and Sidon are said to have to deal with such cases frequently." The French report expresses an implicit moral judgment of the social problems resulting from such a cultural practice, but as temporary marriages are often contracted without witnesses, the verification of their existence is difficult and attempts to make them public are quite rare. Moreover, in my reading, mut'a cases only appear in the records of the Ja'fari court occasionally. However salacious the idea of mut'a may have been to foreign observers, problems of paternity, social responsibility as well as the moral imperative for the court to intervene in such family matters were relatively common, but this more frequently concerned cases of permanent marriage contracts.[39]

Adjudicating Shi'i Society (III): A Problem of Zina

In the early 1930s, a man from the village of al-Qamatiyya (Baalbek province)—I'll call him Jawad—appeared in the Beirut court to accuse his wife Reem of illicit sexual activity (zina). In broad strokes, the story Jawad related is the following. Reem and Jawad had been married in late July 1932. Jawad claimed that he wrote a kambiyala (bill of exchange) for the portion of her mahr paid up-front and that he had bought her clothes and furniture ten days before the wedding was slated to take place. He had assumed she was a virgin, but after they were married and went home together, Jawad "discovered" that another man had impregnated her recently. Jawad was outraged. In court, Reem swore under oath that another man, and *not* Jawad, had impregnated her. Under the conditions of the *khul'* divorce that Jawad demanded, Reem would have to give up her rights to half of her *mahr,* any and all *nafaqa* payments, and there would be no provisional waiting period (*'idda*) during which the divorce could be annulled. Consequently, they were divorced, on August 12, 1932.[40]

Four days later, on August 16, Reem returned to court to argue that a mistake had been made in the execution of that divorce. According to Reem, Jawad forced her into having intercourse with him, impregnating her, and then divorced her shortly after they were married, without paying her *mahr, nafaqa* or child support. Furthermore, he had falsely accused her of being a woman who engaged in *zina* (*zaniya*). According to Reem's narrative, Jawad took her from the house of her father—who was in prison at the time—and held her against her will for four days before bringing her to court to get divorced. Reem claimed that he threatened her; witnesses who appeared in court in her defense also testified that he kicked her in front of a group of women while they were visiting Beirut.[41]

Reem returned to court on September 19 with her lawyer and a number of witnesses to continue pleading her case. When Jawad failed to show up, Reem requested that the case proceed in his absence, because her witnesses were present. Just as the testimony of witnesses was about to begin, Jawad barged into the courtroom an hour and a half late, without the formal proof required to authorize his lawyer as his legal representative. Reem scoffed that they had waited for a long time, that she and her witnesses had spent "large sums of money" to get there, and that they had all "got bored from waiting." The hearing continued. Some of her witnesses claimed to have heard firsthand that the couple had engaged in premarital sexual relations. Others had heard a rumor about Reem's fiancée getting her pregnant. One witness claimed that as she was on the way to get water from the village well, she passed by Reem's father's house; the door was shut but the windows were open and the witness claimed to have seen Jawad "stuck" (*mulaziman*) against Reem even as she tried to push him away. The witness went home for about a half hour and then returned to the well, where she ran into Reem, and asked her if her fiancée had the right to "fool around" with her like that. Reem replied that he had forced himself on her, tearing her clothes in the process. When this witness advised Reem to inform her mother of what had happened, Reem demurred, saying that Jawad would kill her if he ever found out that she had revealed what he had done. Within a week, word spread throughout the village, so Jawad and Reem went down to Beirut to buy supplies for a shotgun wedding. After Jawad had taken her to his house for three days, he tricked her into going to court and threatened to divorce her.[42]

Reem argued that her testimony at the time of the divorce had been made under "compulsion" and "threat" from Jawad. Another witness called into court on Reem's behalf claimed that Reem had confided in her on the day of her wedding, plainly informing her that Jawad had "married her by force" and that she had no say in the matter. Following the testimonies of six witnesses, all of whom confirmed Reem's version of the story, Reem's lawyer cited the following Quranic verse: "And for those who launch a charge against their spouses, and have (in support) no evidence but their own, their solitary evidence (can be received) if they bear witness four times (with an oath) by God that they are solemnly telling the truth" (al-Nur 24:6).[43] He also quoted a phrase that is attributed to 'Ali bin Abi Talib after a man who had engaged in zina (zani) sought 'Ali's counsel. The man pleaded:

> Oh, Commander of the Faithful, I committed zina, purify me. And he ['Ali] turned his head from the man and didn't hear him, so the man repeated it a second time, but [again] 'Ali didn't turn towards him. The man repeated [his confession] a third and a fourth time. Finally, 'Ali said there is no strength or power except in God, and recited the sha-hada four times.

The lawyer reflected on how 'Ali had dealt with such a man by asking how a pious person such as his client could commit such a heinous crime; he added that four repetitions of the confession would be required in order for it to be legally valid and binding. Reem's lawyer then recited another verse from the aforementioned sura: "Those who slander chaste women, indiscreet but believing, are cursed in this life and in the Hereafter: for them is a grievous Penalty" (al-Nur 24:23).[44]

From this perspective, because Reem had not confessed four times to committing zina, and because four witnesses had not confirmed that she had in fact done so, Jawad should be held to account for mistreating Reem in the first place and then falsely accusing her of committing zina. Reem's lawyer sought to turn the case on its head, arguing that it was Jawad's honor—and not Reem's—that was at stake. He described his client as a pious girl who had "not reached the age of mental maturity" (*ghayr baligha sinn al-rushd*, although we never learn how old Reem or Jawad actually were) and who had been "tempted" by her husband, an older man. In this narrative, the most significant piece of evidence testified to by Reem was that Jawad had already known she was pregnant on that Saturday afternoon in late July or even earlier, that is, before he married her and took her home with him.

Reem's lawyer argued that it was not legally permissible to hear the case after Jawad had already lived with her for three or four days (the testimonies vary), knowing full well that she was a *zaniya* who had been impregnated by another man. Moreover, once Reem publicly confessed to being pregnant, Jawad lost all his rights to raise the charge of *zina* against her because, at that point, there could be no way of knowing for certain who was, in fact, the father. Furthermore, the divorce should have been considered revocable (*raj'i*) rather than permanent (*khul'i*), which meant that Reem was still entitled to her dower (*sadaq*). After the child was born, it would have to undergo a blood test. Reem's lawyer closed his argument by saying, as "the unborn child . . . has not yet been born," the court must rule that, "the false accuser (*rami*) is this husband." If the child ended up being his, Jawad would be obligated to pay all of the child's expenses. On the other hand, if it was determined that the child was not his, Jawad would still have to pay child support, but he would be forbidden from including the child in his lineage (*nasab*). It was demanded that Jawad pay the remaining advance *mahr* of fifty Ottoman liras in addition to fifty Syrian liras per month as *nafaqa*. Finally, the unborn child should be legally attached to its legitimate father, no matter who he turned out to be. Sayyid 'Ali Fahs adjourned the case for two weeks in order to review all the relevant information.[45]

The court ruled in Reem's favor. On October 4, 1932, Judge Sayyid 'Ali Fahs explained why Reem could not have been guilty of *zina*. Once the marriage had been consummated, there would have been no logical reason for Reem to confess of her own free will that Jawad was not responsible for impregnating her. Therefore, the court concluded, her confession must have been made out of "fear related to a plot (*khadi'a*)" on his part. Reem's lawyer reminded the court that even if another man had impregnated her, Jawad would still be the child's legal guardian, in accordance with the Sunna of the Prophet,

"The child [belongs] to the bed (*al-walad li-l-firash*) and the fornicator gets the stone."[46] Under this interpretation, a child becomes the responsibility of the legal father even if there is only a possibility that the legal guardian is also the biological father.[47] Jawad had "agreed to a blood test for the child after the birth and if [the child's] blood matches his [father's] blood, he will be [legally] attached to him." Jawad was ordered to pay the full amount of Reem's dower, to take on guardianship of the child, to pay monthly maintenance support amounting to six Syrian liras until she gave birth, and, after the child was born, to renegotiate a fair payment schedule. Under the terms of their divorce, Jawad would have the right of invalidating the divorce—returning to Reem—up until the child was born.[48]

Jawad challenged the ruling by appeal. Still seeking to prove his version of events, Jawad's new lawyers opened with the argument that Reem had told Jawad that her pregnancy resulted from having intercourse with another man. When he heard this news, Jawad immediately sought a divorce, on August 2, 1932. As of that date, Reem had already confessed before the judge that Jawad had never had intercourse with her, at which time the judge confirmed the integrity of the divorce, without any provisional waiting period or *nafaqa* payments. It was only on August 16, 1932, Jawad's lawyers continued, that Reem returned to the court with a new story, claiming that it was Jawad who was father of the child; that her previous confession was made "under threat"; and that she was entitled to a retrial according to national law.[49]

Jawad's lawyers tried to portray Reem as sexually reckless and, therefore, untrustworthy. In response, Reem's lawyer repeated his earlier arguments, adding that Jawad had never legally demonstrated any illicit behavior on Reem's part. Refuting the claim that Reem had perjured herself, which technically would have entailed a stiff penalty, her lawyer repeated that Reem had been "compelled" into making her confession regarding Jawad's paternity. The only contradictory testimony in this case, according to his understanding of the events, was that given by Jawad. Reem's lawyer continued, "And Verily the Great Imams hath said that the [male responsibility that comes with] pregnancy extends from the seventh month until the third year." Jawad's claim that this other man had sex with Reem was also doubtful, Reem's lawyer argued, "because it is legally known [and] it appears in the glorious *Mecelle* that a confession outside the wise tribunal is invalid. This is with respect to the text, religiously [speaking]." The second point made by

Reem's lawyer was that, "the solid mind and consciousness do not concede that a bride being wed to her husband [would] be present in his [i.e., Jawad's] house" before their wedding had even taken place. Finally, Reem's lawyer reiterated that even if she had confessed one time to committing *zina,* her confession would have been insufficient "because [the] confession of *zina* must be [stated] four [times] according to Ja'fari law and according to Abu Hanifa (may God be pleased with him), [it] must be four [times] and in four [separate] tribunals."

In December 1932, the court heard additional testimony from more witnesses. The first, an ironer (*makwaji*) from Baalbek, claimed that two weeks before the wedding he spoke with Reem's father, who told him that Jawad had deflowered Reem in his house. Although this witness also heard some people in the village claim that it "is not appropriate" to go forward with the marriage under such circumstances, he participated in the wedding festivities anyway. He had also been present in court on the day of their divorce. Although he didn't tell anyone else about what Reem's father had told him, he didn't believe that Reem had been forced into testifying. Four more witnesses confirmed Jawad's version of the story; none believed that Reem had been forced into doing or saying anything, except perhaps getting pregnant. All of these testimonies were used by Jawad's legal representatives to demonstrate that Jawad had not falsely accused Reem but divorced her out of respect for her honor.[50]

On February 9, 1933, the sixth witness, who had been living in the Ghobeiri neighborhood of Beirut, appeared in court. He testified that he had also been present in court when Reem and Jawad were divorced. When Jawad's *wakil* asked him whether she had been threatened or forced or afraid, he said that he did not know, that she had not said anything to him about it, and that the only other person from her family present with her at the time was her maternal uncle. When Reem's *wakil* asked him whether he knew who was responsible for getting her pregnant, he said he had heard firsthand from some townspeople (*ahl al-balad*) that it was her husband who deflowered her and got her pregnant. Jawad's lawyer asked for clarification regarding this supposed first-hand information: how had he come by the news if he had been living in Ghobeiri? The witness answered that he returned to his village frequently. Jawad's lawyer asked the judge to make the witness swear on a number of issues: did he have any direct contact with Reem when she came to the court to get a divorce? Did he ask her how she could accept the divorce if she was pregnant? And did she herself tell him who impregnated her? The witness swore that he had not asked her at the time because there were so many people around.

In conclusion, Jawad's lawyer made two final points. First, Jawad had divorced Reem and she had accepted that divorce, acknowledging that he had never consummated the marriage with her. Second, only Reem's testimony and that of the person who ostensibly had intercourse with her was of any "value" (*'ibra*) because "matters such as this occur unseen without the involvement of a third person" and, therefore, "every firsthand knowledge and claim and estimation from someone else will be based on opinion (*zann*)." Essentially, Jawad's lawyer claimed that any other evidence Reem brought to support her own "personal testimony" was little more than "hearsay" (*aqawil*) of the type that "usually happens in small villages"; according to Jawad's counsel such evidence was inadmissible.

Reem's lawyer responded with a litany of specific issues about which he was still seeking clarification. First, had the supposed divorce been made "equivalent to a ruling"? Second, was there any "contradiction" in the original case, or was the contradiction to be found in the subsequent appeal? Third, was it true that Reem had been compelled to come to court? Fourth, if Reem in fact had been pressured into the divorce, could she still be formally accused of being a *zaniya*? And should the unborn child then be separated from its legal father? Fifth, according to the Ottoman *Mecelle* and the state *shari'a* code, did not Reem retain the right to appeal her divorce, even if it had been confirmed as a legal judgment (*hukm shar'i*)? Reem's lawyer claimed that there was no inconsistency in her claim of compulsion: she had made two statements, claiming in the second how she had been forced to give untruthful testimony in the first. Reem's lawyer insisted that it was Jawad who was inconsistent. On August 30, he claimed that he had been aware of her pregnancy on that Saturday in late July the day before their wedding, but nevertheless took her with him to his house the very next day. On November 12, he argued that he had not known she was not a virgin until he brought her home to consummate the marriage. His testimony must be thrown out, Reem's lawyer continued, because there was no way for him to resolve his two stories. Reem's counsel cited the Ottoman *Mecelle*, which stipulates that no statement made under compulsion is admissible as testimony, and that lying is grounds for an automatic dismissal of the case (*radd al-da'wa*). Reem's lawyer insisted that their evidence was neither opinion (*zann*) nor suspicion (*takhmin*) and that Jawad was at fault for knowing about Reem's pregnancy but not behaving accordingly. In short, "Why did he [Jawad] consent to bring her to his house" if he knew she was not a virgin at the time? Reem's lawyer went on to cite a story from unnamed "*fiqh* manuals," in which it is written that a jester (*hazzal*) came to the Prophet Muhammad and confessed that he had committed *zina*. The Prophet told him, "Perhaps you have not." The man persevered, "No, I committed *zina*." Then the Prophet said, "Perhaps you just kissed her." The jester repeated his confession and the Prophet continued asking him until he swore four times and the Prophet finally was persuaded that he had, in fact, committed *zina*. Reem's lawyer also cited Abu Hanifa again, who argued that a ruling of *zina* requires a formal statement before four tribunals on four separate occasions.[51]

Since she had confessed to being a *zaniya* on only one occasion and then claimed that the first confession had been pronounced under compulsion, Reem's case clearly did not satisfy those conditions. Therefore, in the eyes of the court and in the eyes of the state, the unborn child technically still belonged to Jawad. And because Jawad had testified that he had prior knowledge of her pregnancy when she moved in with him, he lost the right to claim that someone else had impregnated her. In conclusion, Reem's lawyer tried to sort out a number of unresolved issues. Why had Jawad behaved like this in the first place? Would he have behaved with such insolence if Reem's father had not been in prison at the time? And how could Reem have done what Jawad claimed she had done? He argued, "If she knew that her husband did not know of her *zina*, it does not stand to reason" that she willingly would have gone to his house, with full knowledge of her pregnancy and knowing that he was not the father. It was implausible, according to Reem's lawyer, that he would have welcomed her so easily if she had admitted to being pregnant by another man even if she had apologized for being a *zaniya* at that point.

By contrast, Jawad's lawyer wove the narrative of an honest man who had been jilted. When Reem told Jawad that she was pregnant, at first he thought it was a lie (*iftira'*). Even though he was "heartbroken," Jawad was so well meaning that he took her home with him anyway. After learning that another man had gotten her pregnant and that she was no longer a virgin, Jawad wanted a divorce; he was not planning to say anything publicly, "to protect her reputation." At this point, the judge asked for a recess in order to review all the details of the case.[52]

In early February 1933, Reem gave birth to a boy. On February 20, 1933, Judge Sayyid 'Ali Fahs rejected Jawad's appeal and upheld the original ruling. As for Jawad's claim that he was not the man who had impregnated Reem, the court ruled that the claim was "incorrect" (*ghayr sadid*). As for Jawad's claim that Reem's testimony was contradictory and unreliable, which would also invalidate her witnesses' testimony, the court also deemed that claim unconvincing. Jawad's request to have the case thrown out, moreover, was "illegal" (*ghayr qanuniyya*). The judge not only ruled in favor of Reem, but also added insult to Jawad's injury, pointing out that there had been no need to hear the argument in defense of Reem a second time, "even if it might have strengthened what we are saying in some respects."[53]

Institutionalizing Sectarianism

The practical application of personal status law involved the policing of moral boundaries and right conduct as well as the preservation of social peace. Norms of honor and responsibility defined and policed by the community were not only designed for women to obey, but also men, shaping the tenor and nature of gendered social relations. In the case of Reem and Jawad, a disputed case of contested paternity snowballed into a moral spectacle about honor, honest communication, and premarital sexual relations. Indeed, one of the most compelling legal arguments made in court was that Jawad was as obligated as Reem to shoulder responsibility in the maintenance of proper norms of moral conduct. How could it be, Reem's lawyer asked, that Jawad knew his betrothed had been impregnated by another man and then, the very next day, whisked her off to his house to live with her? The defense deftly shifted the burden of responsibility from this individual woman to a more broadly conceived sense of communal respect in which the enforcement of male responsibility and honesty was as important as the protection of a woman's honor. Considering the compromised position of this underage woman, whose father was in jail, and who apparently could not confide in her mother, it is remarkable—and a testament to the power of the social forces on her side—that Reem managed to win such a ruling.[54]

The success of the prosecution's argument may be partially attributed to its breadth and depth. Indeed, the subtle use of argumentation and evidence is one of the most fascinating aspects of this case. Sayings of the Prophet Muhammad (*hadith*, known in the Shi'i tradition as *akhbar*) and stories attributed to Imam 'Ali (also known as *akhbar*) intermingled with the opinion of Abu Hanifa, the Ottoman *Mecelle*, and the Lebanese state personal status law codes. The language employed in court was steeped in a religious vernacular and the Ja'fari court was a site in which the sayings of the Prophet and the Imams were taken seriously, considered admissible as evidence and convincing as part and parcel of sophisticated practical legal reasoning.

Of course, the power of religious discourse in legal disputes is limited. Beyond establishing the facts of a particular case, moral discourse in court (about *zina* or anything else, for that matter) is bound up with more general concerns about the need for transparency and social stability. Comments reputed to have been made "in front of people" (*amam al-nas*), or in the village, were accepted as legal testimony in court, despite the attempt by Jawad's counsel to dismiss such statements as "unmodern" or "traditional" and, by consequence, inappropriate. Such convention indicates the persistent value of public knowledge and social truth as well as the power of custom and local practices within the walls of the Ja'fari court.

According to Fuad I. Khuri, "while Sunni qadis approach problems of marriage and divorce contractually, the Shi'a add to it an element of morality, bringing to the forefront the weight of the immediate community." In other words, Khuri continues, "what is achieved 'informally' and 'intimately' at the court level in Shi'i communities is achieved at the family level in Sunni communities."[55] Although this distinction may be overstated, there clearly was more than a small hint of morality at work in the Ja'fari court during this period. As an institutional environment, the Ja'fari *shari'a* court facilitated a great deal of negotiation and dynamism. The language employed in the court varied among certain "modern" forms of legal argumentation and more "traditional" Islamic jurisprudential sources and methods even as law in practice at the Lebanese Ja'fari court transcended and contradicted such purported antinomies of "modernity" and "tradition." The jurisdiction of the Jaʿfari court was still being defined. As Muhammad Qasim Zaman has observed, "even in matters of personal status, the application of the shariʿa under colonial rule was in fact far from uniform."[56]

Social historians have amply shown how court records constitute a unique historical source, occasionally capturing the texture and flavor of everyday life in various Muslim societies. These records portray illiterate peasants, urban workers, and other historical actors in the context of the family and social networks that defined their lives; they also make possible the recuperation of women's voice and women's agency.[57] Shiʿi individuals, men and women alike, often appeared in the Jaʿfari court as shapers of their own destinies, as historical agents who brought autonomy and power to bear on the management of their daily life. Women not only raised cases before the *shariʿa* judge, but also held fast to their rights despite staunch opposition from their family, the court, or the state. Of course, the voices of Reem and Jamila and other women are filtered through their legal representatives, through the judges and through the legal machinery of the state: they are mediated subjects, mediated by what Sally Engle Merry aptly terms an "interpretive screen."[58] And, to be sure, "the problem entailed in weighing women's disabilities under the law concerns defining the role of law in the total array of social control forces that subordinate women in any given society."[59] Still, the appearance and activity of women at the Jaʿfari court alerts historians to more subtle transformations in gender roles and gendered boundaries taking place within families and communities throughout Shiʿi Lebanon during the first half of the twentieth century.

As incomplete and fragmentary as Shiʿi Islamic court records in Lebanon may be, they shed new light on what I have been calling the social and cultural history of the Lebanese Shiʿi milieu. This chapter is an introductory analysis of Jaʿfari court records from the Mandate period; there is still far more work to be done using these historical sources. Nevertheless, by attending to how Jawad's accusation of Reem engaging in *zina* could boomerang on him, I demonstrated how court records often shed light on moral issues as well as more narrowly defined legal questions. The case of Jamila and the ambiguities of *mutʿa* signals one way in which the Jaʿfari court dealt with specifically Shiʿi issues. Other historians may wish to consider how "anxiety about intercourse out of place was only a subset of a more general fear of moral and political disorder."[60] Here were stories recounting the lived experiences of ordinary people, stories that provide historical perspective on "what happens when ordinary, often subordinate people appeal to the state, specifically the legal system, to help them repair or reconfigure their relationships with others."[61] These sources, therefore, offer a fascinating look into the historical experiences of people who generally left behind few written records.[62]

The Ja'fari court played an increasingly central role in adjudicating Shi'i society, bringing elites and ordinary people under the same roof, institutionalizing Shi'ism, and helping to cement Shi'i presence in Lebanon. The administration of personal status law was one means by which the state attempted to manage Shi'i life during this formative period. Shi'i citizens-in-the-making took advantage of the court in their efforts to secure specific individual and communal rights. Throughout this foundational period, demands for access to state resources and arbitration within the Ja'fari court continued to bubble up "from below." The Ja'fari court played a unique institutional role, by making contact between Shi'i society and the Lebanese state possible and by reshaping the boundaries of the Shi'i milieu even as it was increasingly defined in new sectarian terms. These institutional transformations signal a broader process that would take place over the course of the twentieth century through which the Shi'i community would gradually evolve from a "sect-in-itself" into a "sect-for-itself."

6

'Amili Shi'is into Shi'i Lebanese?

With the formal recognition of the Ja'fari *madhhab* as an independent *madhhab* the Shi'i milieu in Lebanon would increasingly confront the perils and promise of newfound visibility but also would have to navigate a fraught relationship with the state. Chapter two tracked *mujtahid*s and other figures throughout the global Shi'i milieu who were exercised by heated debates during the 1920s over the most defensible manner in which to publicly mourn the martyrdom of Imam Husayn; as the preceding three chapters show, analogous dynamics were at play with respect to the institutionalization of Ja'fari law. Even if the formal recognition of the Ja'fari *madhhab* by the French colonial authorities effectively canonized Ja'fari law as an autonomous element of the Lebanese legal system and rendered the Shi'i community another legitimate participant in shaping Lebanese political and social life, initial responses to the halting institutionalization of the Shi'i milieu in Lebanon were mixed at best.

Enhanced legal autonomy and political entitlements didn't squelch Shi'i claims for increased parliamentary representation and greater attention from the state. Some Shi'i leaders would call for the expansion of Shi'i religious authority in the form of additional Shi'i corporate bodies attached to the machinery of the state, as others demanded expanded Shi'i participation in the appointment and regulation of judges and other representatives in state religious institutions. As with earlier phases of gradual Shi'i institutionalization and empowerment in which the Shi'i "politics of demand" was at work, colonial administrators, Shi'i leaderships, and ordinary people worked in tandem in order to, perhaps unwittingly, promote the further institutionalization of Shi'ism in Lebanon. Even as previous practices of negotiating Shi'i legal affairs directly with shaykhs or *'ulama'* in private homes or other designated spaces in Jabal 'Amil were supplanted, the institutionalization of Ja'fari personal status law and the reorganization of religious practices during the first half of the twentieth century helped to create the conditions of possibility for an incipient political mobilization of the Shi'i community. Over the course of the twentieth century, these subtle processes of institutionalization and empowerment would lead to expanded participation in grassroots politics of nationalist and internationalist as well as sectarian varieties. In the pithy formulation of Augustus Richard Norton, "not all of the Shi'a succumbed to recruitment along confessional lines, but over time large numbers did."[1]

As Lebanese citizens within the Shi'i milieu became more self-assured, more capable of articulating their political demands, and more fully integrated into the colonial religious sphere, the Shi'i community was increasingly inclined to consider itself a key player in Lebanon's fledgling sectarian democracy even as it was becoming more politically variegated and culturally diverse. If the Shi'i community in Lebanon was gradually transformed from a sect-in-itself into a sect-for-itself, the articulation of forces supporting what I have been calling "sectarianization from above" and "sectarianization from below" contributed to the crystallization of such revamped sectarian Shi'i modes of identification. Whereas the reformation of legal institutions took place within the crucible of gradual social change, an even more contested process of transformation structured the politics of Shi'i identity during the late Mandate and early independence periods.

The dialectic of inclusion and exclusion was one of the most consistently vexing problematics within the sectarian-national milieu in Lebanon under the French Mandate. Inclusion within the national community was predicated on an unswerving identification with an essential sectarian bloc in Lebanese society. At the same time, each sectarian community in Lebanon struggled to preserve its independence and autonomy vis-à-vis the state, in institutional terms, and vis-à-vis every other sectarian community, in cultural and political terms. Again, this configuration has been relatively unique for each sectarian community, but the ground upon which sectarian identities have been formed is common. By the same token, the triumph of sectarianism in the Shi'i milieu was far from a foregone conclusion. In order to demonstrate this point, which still may not be readily apparent, this chapter begins with a brief consideration of one rare instance of radical political activism in Jabal ʿAmil during the Mandate period, namely the 1936 Bint Jubayl Revolt. The second part of this chapter looks at certain dimensions and effects of Shiʿi institutionalization in the context of Lebanese national independence and the early years of the postcolonial Lebanese state.

The Political Economy of Tobacco

Many historians and commentators have noted how pan-Arab nationalist, Liberal, and left-wing voices were haltingly sounding off in Jabal ʿAmil with variable frequency throughout the late Mandate and early independence periods. Wealth inequality—particularly landed wealth—had been increasing in Jabal ʿAmil from the late Ottoman period, which contributed to the attractiveness of such political currents. In the context of the 1858 Ottoman land code, which set into motion lasting transformations in local patterns of land tenure, Lebanese historian Mustafa Bazzi notes how the process of social and economic transformation in Jabal ʿAmil was very different than what was experienced in Beirut and other provincial centers. Whereas Beirut witnessed tremendous economic expansion during the late Ottoman period, there was hardly any growth in landownership among peasants and "middling" classes in Jabal ʿAmil; the practical perpetuation of the *muqataʿji* system was effectively assured.[2] Be that as it may, a new class of upwardly mobile elites and political activists began posing a challenge to the entrenched power of large landowning families as well as the political authority of the established *zuʿama*ʾ. Meanwhile, the continuing hegemony of large landholding families increasingly put the squeeze on landless peasants, many of whom turned to sharecropping in tobacco, citrus, and grain agriculture.

The marginalization of primary agricultural production is an indispensable motif in the history of twentieth-century Lebanese political economy. To the extent that historians have discussed the question of agriculture, however, there has been much more interest in the political economy of silk in Mount Lebanon than in other commodities elsewhere. Masʿud Daher sheds some interesting light on this theme:

The history of the development of the Lebanese countrysides during the French Mandate period is nearly [coextensive with] the history of the struggle of tobacco farmers against the Régie monopoly throughout most of the cultivated Lebanese regions. Tobacco agriculture is considered the clear[est] model of the development of agricultural production directed toward both domestic and foreign markets, precisely like silk production was in earlier eras.[3]

Of course, the silk economy was one engine that fueled, at least in part, the spectacular growth enjoyed by Beirut and Mount Lebanon during the nineteenth century. Still, if silk cultivation and its economic benefits rendered other agricultural pursuits and their regions marginal or inactive, the history of silk has muted the historiography of other crops. Nevertheless, with the decline and eventual demise of silk production in Lebanon, tobacco acquired renewed importance.[4]

Alongside citrus fruits and basic food staples, tobacco was among the most important crops grown in southern Lebanon. In 1883, the Ottoman state granted a French tobacco company monopoly rights over trade and distribution of tobacco products originating in the Ottoman Empire. With the advent of the Mandate system under the auspices of the League of Nations at the end of World War One, the French tobacco monopoly (*Régie des Tabacs et Tombacs,* or Régie, for short) no longer had to bargain with the Ottoman state for special privileges, negotiating contracts directly with the French authorities instead. By the turn of the twentieth century, then, as demand grew for "Turkish" and "Syrian" tobacco, Jabal 'Amil was well positioned for deeper integration into regional and global trade networks.[5]

Farmers in Lebanon were required to secure permission from the Régie in order to grow tobacco at all, however, and although agriculture was the primary means of livelihood for many in the region, such requests were often denied. The Régie delimited where and how much tobacco farmers would be permitted to grow. According to the Régie's 1904 statement, peasants were to be permitted rights of usufruct (*tasarruf*) over no more than one half of one *dunam* (one *dunam* ≅ ¼ acre). Through such stringent policies, the monopoly regime squeezed the peasantry, forcing many to move abroad or relocate to Beirut. There was a consequent deterioration in the quality of local tobacco and a steep reduction in crop yields. As small-plot farmers were strong-armed into renting more and more land at even higher prices, the number of small landholders who were able to survive declined, simultaneously allowing for medium and large landholders to thrive, with attendant results for the further entrenchment of elite landed power across Jabal 'Amil. According to Osama Doumani, there were no more than 1,000 hectares of agricultural land dedicated to tobacco farming around 1914.[6]

Throughout the 1920s and 1930s, Shi'i representatives from Jabal 'Amil often struggled to draw attention to pressing local issues such as inadequate roads, insufficient water for drinking and irrigation, non-existent electricity, unpredictable job opportunities, and, perhaps most galling of all, onerous and unequally assessed taxes. Agricultural grievances were also cited as evidence of the disproportionate treatment of southern constituencies by the colonial state. During the parliamentary session of November 22, 1929, for example, Lebanese Minister of Justice Najib Abu Sawan assured his fellow representatives that the government would do everything in its power to ensure that the crisis in tobacco production in particular would be dealt with in such a way that ensured the "security of the country" while also protecting "the freedom to grow tobacco, the freedom to produce and sell it." Government policy, according to Abu Sawan, had to be reformed: "In organization, on behalf of labor and, in the economy, on behalf of production." Despite this lip service to "labor," however, by equating freedom with production Abu Sawan more or less seemed to be casting the lot of the local economy in with the Régie.[7]

The institution of the banderole ("wrapping") system in June 1930 imposed even tighter monopoly control over the production, sale, and distribution of locally grown tobacco. Some hoped this overhauled taxation system would alleviate the taxing conditions created by the Régie, including the editors of al-'Irfan, the Shi'i modernist monthly journal, who chirped, "The government will not extend the rights of the Régie beyond April 15, as the country has agreed to the 'banderole' system."[8] According to Meir Zamir, the collapse of prices in the 1930s negatively impacted growers and manufacturers alike, contributing to the loss of income for farmers and merchants while simultaneously squeezing monopoly revenue. In 1932, the banderole was modified and production caps were loosened. Renewing the monopoly, according to Zamir, was a means by which the government could "ensure regulation of the industry, help the growers and manufacturers and augment income from taxation on tobacco."[9] The new regime was quite restrictive, however. The monopoly system galled landowners and

agriculturalists alike by exacerbating a restrictive and inequitable arrangement, with even more dramatic effects on sharecroppers and the peasantry.
Waddah Shararah points out:

> The small peasant, above all one in peripheral villages where large fam-
> ilies were absent found himself in an increased dependency in regard
> to a large landholder who, practically unchallenged, was capable of dis-
> tributing the terrain that he had been allotted to whomever he wished.
> In response, they returned to [growing] more traditional crops: wheat,
> cereals, grapes, figs, olives . . . [which were] less profitable.[10]

Tobacco agriculture is highly labor-intensive, and pressure from the monopoly weighed heavily upon the minds and bodies of peasant farmers across the
south. As profits consistently flowed out of the region—either to Beirut or
to company investors abroad—economic growth in the south stagnated and
the 'Amili agricultural classes underwent a decades-long process of semi-
proletarianization. Many farmers began to work as sharecroppers or tenant
farmers on the lands of large landowners, zu'ama', or the Régie itself, even as
small peasant landowners struggled to secure a decent price for their crops.
Stringent Régie policies were exacerbated by the global economic depression in the 1930s, which dramatically reduced demand for commodities
such as tobacco, hitting peasants and subsistence farmers in south Lebanon
especially hard. Because demand for was relatively elastic, the plunge in
worldwide disposable incomes endangered revenue from cash crops such
as tobacco. The total territory of cultivated land in South Lebanon multiplied twenty times between 1918 and 1947; production efficiency jumped
nearly threefold over the same period; and total production peaked in the
early 1930s even as efficiency was gradually declining. The Régie and its
Mandate allies appeared to be on a collision course with the inhabitants of
Jabal 'Amil.[11]

A "Serious Effervescence" in Bint Jubayl

On January 30, 1935, the French High Commission promulgated a new law
(Arrêté 16/L.R.) regulating the production and sale of tobacco within the
territory of the Mandate state.[12] The colonial administration perennially

found itself unable to efficiently collect taxes; the state secured only 64% of the anticipated tax revenues from South Lebanon in 1935.[13] Meanwhile, additional restrictions that the Régie had placed on growers exacerbated local resentment and fostered building opposition to colonial rule and foreign economic domination. Writing under the pseudonym 'Abbas Bazzi, the Lebanese polymath Ahmad Beydoun has pointed out that the town Bint Jubayl was producing approximately 40,000 kilograms of tobacco per year at the time.[14] Meanwhile, other tensions were already running high across Lebanon, and Jabal 'Amil was hardly exceptional in this regard. When the notable 'Amili political leader 'Abd al-Latif al-As'ad died in March 1935, his funeral was an occasion for the expression of both grief and outrage over social and economic conditions in the south. 'Amili leaders and elected officials would only occasionally take public positions against the Régie. More surprising, however, was the extent to which anti-Régie activities spread to include such unlikely figures as the Maronite Patriarch Antoine 'Arida. Such opposition to Mandate policy and Régie practice often took the form of surreptitiously circulated flyers and petitions.

One such petition was at the heart of the 1936 Tobacco Revolt in Bint Jubayl, an exceptional moment of political activism that took place in Jabal 'Amil under French Mandate. The petition in question was found on the evening of March 31, 1936, in the possession of 'Ali Beydoun, a young man from one of Bint Jubayl's most powerful families, who was, in the Edenic language of French administration, "invited to present himself at the Caracol to be interrogated." After doing so without putting up much of a fight, Beydoun was subsequently detained at the police station, which was only 1.5 km from the town mosque, where congregants had been gathered in order to observe the ninth night of mourning sessions for 'Ashura'. As chapter two demonstrated, the significance of public 'Ashura' commemorations had dramatically increased from as early as the 1920s. Once news of the arrest started to spread, a group of people sped over to the police station to demand Beydoun's release. Mandate armed forces were placed on high alert and charged with looking out for any and all "seditious" petitions that might be circulating in South Lebanon, especially those that called for the incorporation of Jabal 'Amil into Greater Syria. Police reinforcements were dispatched from Beirut, but they would not arrive until later that night. At least one hundred people proceeded to storm the *caracol* (police station), and shortly thereafter "a crowd of 200 to 300 persons appeared in front of the station, demanding with force, insults and threats [Beydoun's] immediate release." Arguing that the sergeant's hands were tied and that anyone else in such a situation would have done the same thing, Zinovi Pechkoff, *Conseiller Administratif* for South Lebanon, noted how the Sergeant on duty took pains to explain to the demonstrators that Beydoun was not technically under arrest, and that as soon as he had been "questioned," he would be free to go. Pechkoff describes the crowd becoming "more and more threatening," and because there were only six officers on hand, the Sergeant felt pressured to release Beydoun before he could be "adequately" interrogated. At this point, the crowd, which was led by at least fifteen young men, proceeded to march through the town streets, "chanting insulting couplets with regard to the authorities and openly calling on the population to rise up against the established authority *(pouvoir)*." Around nine PM, 'Ali Bazzi, another young leader from an influential Bint Jubayl family, stepped forward to speak, exhorting the crowd to emulate demonstrators in Mandate Syria, which would never "recover its independence before having poured floods of the blood of its children." By approximately eleven PM, all available police forces had been assembled. At about the same time, an additional detachment of twenty or more police officers from Beirut arrived, bringing the total number of mobilized forces up to about forty. Eventually, the police arrested a number of demonstrators and held them in custody until the following morning. By the time a team of French investigators finally managed to travel by car from Beirut to the south, demonstrators had, "in the course of the night barred the road with 4 or 5 dry walls of large stones spread out on a course of 300 to 400 meters" and prevented them from entering the village. On April 1, which happened to be the tenth of Muharram, 'Ashura', the French security forces in Beirut received a *communiqué* from Jabal 'Amil, reporting that "a serious effervescence took place" in Bint Jubayl.[15]

The French police managed to hold the crowd at bay without releasing a single detainee, and, as of eight AM, the situation in Bint Jubayl was calm and it was thought that the "incidents can be considered finished." Two hours later, however, "the population" had reassembled with the intention of freeing seventeen detainees "by violent means," described in the French sources as "breaking the barricades of the *gendarmes,* throwing stones, baton blows." The colonial archive records increasing violence on the part of the demonstrators: "the assailants triggered a savage attack with stones and broken bottles, thrown like hail" against the *gendarmes* and officers on duty. The popular "pressure" was so great that the leadership ordered police to fire into the air, but to no avail. Amidst the chaos and "savagery" on display among the demonstrators, as "all kinds of projectiles" continued to be launched, a shooting order was given. Two 'Amili demonstrators were killed; several more were badly wounded, one of whom later died from his injuries. The detainees were subsequently whisked away to a military facility in Sidon. Although the situation was reported calm by four PM, when Pechkoff finally arrived on the scene, two more officers and 40 soldiers had been brought from Beirut and Mount Lebanon by two-thirty; by that evening, three more officers and 70 more soldiers (from North Lebanon and the Biqa') arrived; and, by the end of that day, the buildup had amassed seven officers and 150 soldiers under the leadership of Commandant Najjar. Protestors had lightly wounded six police officers, including a lieutenant who was hit in the face with a stone; his body and his eyes bruised, he was carted off to Sidon for medical treatment. By the end of the day, one young man from Bint Jubayl, Mustafa al-'Ashi, and two young men from the nearby village of 'Aynata, 'Aqil al-Daaboul and Muhammad al-Jamal, were dead, and two others had been critically wounded. The security forces remained stationed in Bint Jubayl for a few days even as the Ministry of Justice prepared to carry out an official inquiry.[16]

Colonial dispatches from the South most often depicted the events as the handiwork of a limited number of nationalist agents provocateurs. One report claims that "a group of young men in the region of the South" with "an interest in being separated from Lebanon by being attached to Syria" had been going village to village in order to raise awareness of the Arab nationalist cause. Other young men from Bint Jubayl who had been marching around their village chanting, "We want Syrian unity," happened by chance to pass by the police station where 'Ali Beydoun was being interrogated. Energized by that coincidence, the young men started to protest "louder and louder," at which point "some of them threw their shoes at the station." By the following morning, after supplementary forces arrived to carry out an inquiry, "the population gathered into a mob around the station." Despite attempts by the officers on duty to pacify the crowd, the people gathered there grew more and more indignant: "Excited by their women whom they

had put in front of them, the men started to launch stones, then they tried
to invade the *poste*. Shots were fired from the crowd, and the armed forces
were finally obliged to intervene more energetically." Although "the young
men who had been the cause of the events . . . tried to make believe that all
of the incidents had taken place because of the distribution of *cultures de
tabac* and they sent a series of dispatches to the newspapers to that effect,"
this colonial reportage affirms that the events had taken on a quality "apart
from the issue relating to the distribution of *cultures de tabac*."[17] Another
colonial representative stationed in Beirut wrote to the High Commissioner
about the "repression" by local police of "separatists" and "the most active
agents of Unitary propaganda," which were agitating in Lebanon under "the
inspiration of Damascene nationalists." According to this report, "the incident seems to have been tendentiously exploited by both unitary elements
and adversaries of the *Régie des tabacs* who, against every probability, claim
to give as the origin of the affair the failure experienced by the peasants in
their actions with a view to obtaining an increase of territories on which
to grow tobacco." He explained to de Martel that there was need for police
"reinforcements" in order to maintain order and stability.[18]

In one of the most substantial accounts of the events that had taken
place in South Lebanon, *Conseiller Administratif* for South Lebanon Zinovi
Pechkoff affirmed the "gravity" of the "incidents" while insisting that those
who participated did so out of, on the one hand, "religious conviction of
fanaticism," but were, on the other hand, troubled figures who were either
responding to "hidden instruction or on the take from abroad." Rumored
to be the illegitimate child of Maxim Gorky, Pechkoff was described by one
Lebanese commentator as the "stern strong frightening man of Russian origin" and, alternatively, "the dictator of the South."[19] Pechkoff dismisses the
incidents in Bint Jubayl as little more than the handiwork of Arab nationalists who supported the National Bloc in Damascus and demanded inclusion
with Syria. Although they were relatively few in number, even more dangerous were those "young men" who had recently returned from Damascus
"imbued with nationalist ideas" who had "the advantage of counting among
their ranks men, ambitious and without scruples, who, having no social
standing and consequently nothing to lose," were "always in search of remu-
nerative intrigues." As such, they brought to South Lebanon "propaganda,
active and underhanded, in favor of Syrian unity." As for the proclivities

of the general population, Pechkoff argues that those young and firebrand Arab nationalists had managed to convince the "ignorant masses" of the link between Greater Syrian "unity" and "the economic crisis." Moreover, Pechkoff claims that such nationalist rhetoric had

> reached the most attentive ears of the rural masses, already very affected by the general crisis which continues to prevail, as well as by the ceaseless fall in the prices of local products. These last days, they were strongly disappointed by the restriction that they claim was brought by the Société du Monopole to their tobacco plantations.

But certain tobacco growers were guilty of "misunderstanding" the situation and had been growing tobacco illegally, without explicit permission from the Régie. The proper political response from the ruling authorities would be to "take the administrative services of the State [as] separate from management of the business of the Régie. By ensuring the distribution of territories, the authority left itself open to criticisms and complaints and, in this way, lost much of its prestige." In this reading of the situation, the "secular fanaticism of the Muslim" goes a long way toward explaining how those agitators fed off the "dissatisfaction" of the masses in order to "unconscionably make them act for their own personal ends."

Finally, Pechkoff plays the religious card, explaining how proponents of "the achievement of Syrian unity" were participating in what was "at its foundation a Muslim movement." With rare exceptions from the Christian community, such as members of the Syrian Popular Party, including Selim Abou Jamra of Tyre, "all those who took part in the movement are either Sunnis who incontestably wish, in whatever way to pronounce their attachment to Syria, or Shiites deceived by the sectarian unity that the agitators do not cease shining in their eyes." Pechkoff also tries to write off the demonstrators by suggesting they represent little more than a "weak minority of the population." The "Shiite notables" have "strongly expressed their desire to remain within the framework of the Lebanese Republic." Twisting himself even more tightly into a knot, though, Pechkoff vacillates again, explaining how "the essential problem is not of a political nature, but rather of an economic and material nature." As "the mass of the people would have continued to ignore the political events if the elements of discontent were not so numerous," there are a number of other major concerns on the minds of local communities, including: "Educated but unemployed youth; inequality in the fiscal regime; lowering of prices of local products; limitation of tobacco growing; exceptional shortage of drinking water." All of this combined to "create an atmosphere of *malaise* that the troublemakers do not cease exploiting to their ends." At the heart of the matter were two primary concerns: the increasing sense among the *'ulama'* that they were losing control over the rebellious youth; and the general feeling that power-hungry political elites were manipulating the situation in order to garner more patronage and electoral support for their candidacy. Pechkoff then proposes a raft of economic solutions to the ongoing crisis in the south: "Extension of the lands intended to be planted with tobacco; agricultural credits to grant to small landholders; revision of the fiscal system; irrigation works and the adduction of water." On the other hand, however, Pechkoff strongly urges deeper political and military involvement on the part of the Mandate authorities in order to adequately pacify the region—enhanced surveillance and more sophisticated methods of control over the region and its entry points. Even as he dismisses the inhabitants of South Lebanon as "incapable of creating by themselves a serious movement of insurrection," Pechkoff recommends that in order to maintain "security in the interior of Jabal 'Amil," there must be "the permanent quartering of a troop detachment in the two localities of Beint Jbail and Nabatyé, center of every agitation and often the heart of rebellion."[20]

Competing Narratives

The findings of the investigator sent from the Beirut Mixed Court were reported in the French-language newspaper *L'Orient* on April 7. Although some "alleged" that the events were bound up with the problem of tobacco, Judge Timbal concluded: "It is not a question of tobacco, but of a separatist movement." The reputation of these young men who were committed to seceding from Lebanon and joining up with Syria was growing increasingly notorious. As of April 7, 200 gendarmes still occupied Bint Jubayl; 50 more were stationed in Nabatiyya, where there was an ongoing "souk strike." For their participation, 60 demonstrators were arrested and "transferred far away"; 20 more were detained at the Tibnine castle; still others were held in Sidon. Delegations from some 24 villages in the vicinity converged on

Nabatiyya on April 8, "to participate in a ceremony of forty days" that was, according to the colonial report, organized by the notables Ahmad Rida and 'Adil 'Usayran. In that ceremony, some 2,000–3,000 people had congregated at the Nabatiyya *husayniyya*, where eight speakers addressed the crowd, rue-fully recalling how "the innocent blood of those who claimed their rights had been cruelly and so arbitrarily spilled": "Although this public meeting where political speeches were made had not been authorized, the gendar-merie did not believe it necessary to oppose it. It was content to maintain order and record the events." On April 9, the markets in Tyre remained open and much of the south returned to a state of calm. Bint Jubayl, on the other hand, remained on strike and the "population of the town and of neighbor-ing villages" gathered at the town cemetery. French officials were alerted to an "important demonstration that was about to commence," although the conditions in town had been "calm for the moment." Nabatiyya was closed down, as the population of the city and its neighboring villages assembled in front of the Great Mosque. Popular demonstrations would continue throughout the month of April, to gradually diminishing effect. Meanwhile, the French Commandant had "assembled the notables and asked for calm." Pechkoff hammered away at one note, making specific tactical recommen-dations for crowd control and counter-insurgency, which would include the establishment of a "permanent detachment presence" in both Bint Jubayl and Nabatiyya. Their primary task would be "to ensure the security of the region and to obviate every inclination of uprising." In closing, he pointed out, "The same device is equally indispensable to envisage for Nabatiyya."[21]

Reading the colonial sources alone results in a skewed representation and ideologically biased version of "the events." Colonial discourse sought to appropriate the true voice of the Lebanese people by filtering those stakes that were economic (tobacco, global economic depression, infrastructural underdevelopment), religious ('Ashura' sensitivities), and personal (local deaths, factionalism) into the circumscribed realm of the political (Arab nationalism versus Lebanese particularism). Demonstrators and their allies were maligned for being little more than foreign implants. All unauthorized political activity in Jabal 'Amil was uncritically assimilated to a discourse of anti-colonial Arab nationalist "resistance." Historical interpretations of the Bint Jubayl events inspired by colonial perspectives might come to the conclusion that "it was hardly a spontaneous uprising by peasants, manufacturers and workers against a colonial company and an allegedly corrupt high commissioner. The crisis was a well-orchestrated event instigated by the National Bloc, Khuri's camp and certain businessmen who had vested interests in the existing system."[22] But colonial discourse was far from univocal. Roger Lescot, for example, recognized that, "the creation of the Régie and the limitation of lands dedicated to tobacco carried a perceptible blow to the local economy." Such "impoverishment," he argued, alongside "the social changes brought by the modern period . . . [were] at the origin of the recent troubles." Even more tellingly, he wrote, the "popular, illiterate masses" were untouched by "unitary and liberal ideology" and that they were only concerned with "the questions that affect them directly."[23]

Besides, however reductive colonial discourse may have been, certain Arab and Lebanese nationalist as well as Shi'i Islamist interpretations of the Bint Jubayl Revolt have exhibited similar limitations of their own, often reinforcing an impression of the incident as part and parcel of a unitary nationalist anti-colonial resistance struggle. Arab nationalist historiographers may continue to argue, along with Mustafa Bazzi, that the *intifada* ought to be seen as the paradigmatic clash between two perspectives on French intervention in the region: those who refused to cooperate with the French and fought for territorial connection to the sovereignty of the Arab interior, to Syria in particular, as against those who sided with the French and sought to help make their entrance into the region a success. If French colonial officials monitoring South Lebanon during the spring of 1936 timorously observed what they perceived as "nationalist agitation," Arab nationalist historians and ideologues have done little to disabuse the historiographical inheritors of colonial scholarship of such a perspective. In the Lebanese context, both colonial and anti-colonial discourse demands the strict separation of the national from the sectarian. In an essay written under the pseudonym of 'Abbas Bazzi, Ahmad Beydoun argued that the revolt must also be understood in terms of the resistance of a new generation against the authority of the clerical establishment as well as against the Mandate authorities and the Régie. Relatively unsuccessful in presenting a serious challenge the power of the "feudal system" (*iqta'iyya*), some of these young people ended up throwing their chips in with other elite families rather than seeking to undermine the exploitative system of social relations in Jabal 'Amil. However, Bazzi concludes that the uprising did little more than cause some "anxiety" for Pechkoff, and their "style of action" wasn't all that different from the politics of the religious and the political establishment.[24] More recently, Malek Abisaab attempts to draw some even bolder conclusions regarding the Bint Jubayl Revolt. "The historical record delineates clearly," Abisaab claims, "that ['Amili] peasants resisted the bourgeois-based conceptions of law, bureaucracy, and representation newly imported by the French." In consequence, he reads the uprising as evidence of "the precarious place of Jabal 'Amil (and the Bekaa) in Grand Liban, the peasant challenges to the prospective Lebanese state and its national discourse, and the tensions in peasant-notable alliances and intra-elite schisms during anticolonial struggles."[25]

But was the 1936 Bint Jubayl Revolt exclusively an episode of anti-colonial collective action and an unalloyed expression of explosive outrage over the unjust methods of producing and distributing tobacco in Lebanon? Historians can disagree on certain details, but what seems indisputable is that the events marked a milestone in the engagement of Jabal 'Amil with the Lebanese state. Even the staunchest critics of the colonial government, state agencies, and foreign power in Lebanon couched demands for economic justice, political equality, and infrastructural development in the language of the state. The 1936 Bint Jubayl Revolt was the largest instance of collective action and one of the only significant instances of popular protest in Jabal 'Amil during the Mandate period. Nationalist enthusiasm was aboil, especially as the French sought to renegotiate treaties that would legitimate the continuation of Mandate rule in Lebanon and Syria. Regional issues—the Palestinian cause and Syrian Arab nationalism being the two most salient—certainly played an important role, but the Tobacco Revolt was also fueled by the shifting dynamics of local politics as well as the particular sensitivities stirred up by the commemoration of the martyrdom of Imam Husayn on 'Ashura'. As Tamara Chalabi convincingly argues, the Bint Jubayl Revolt "demonstrated the limit of *matlabiyya* as it had been exercised. With the tobacco revolt, *matlabiyya* as an approach for soliciting the fulfillment of demands had reached the limits of its use, and the result was a confrontation." Moreover, repeated encounters with the "limitations of *matlabiyya*" over the course of the twentieth century eventually "promoted the development of a new politics of protest (as opposed to the politics of demand), which was predominantly expressed by ideological parties."[26]

Ahmad Beydoun cleverly refers to the uprising as a kind of "foundational myth" in the crystallization of 'Amili Shi'i collective memory.[27] In this sense, it bears repeating that such episodes of revolt or collective mobilization were rare within the Shi'i community, even if nationalist and Islamist narratives have subsequently valorized them ad infinitum in order to construct a narrative of unstinting resistance to foreign aggression and occupation in Greater Syria among Shi'i communities. On the contrary, the Bint Jubayl Revolt was a significant moment in the formation of Shi'i sectarian forms of identity, memory and historical consciousness, and yet the significance of the uprising has been overshadowed by the enduring legacy of more subtle mechanisms of sectarianization and religious identity formation. If analytical limitations of this nationalist reading of the French Mandate can be found in, among other things, the inadequacy of such reductive categories as collaboration and resistance, one might also argue that such flashpoints as the Tobacco Revolt embodied the ongoing yet unrealized desire on the part of 'Amili Shi'is to be more comprehensively integrated into the Lebanese national fold. The recognition of Shi'i presence in Mandate Lebanon would become increasingly important for processes of "sectarianization from above"—colonial or nationalist attempts at making Shi'i status separate but equal—as well as "sectarianization from below"—Shi'i demands for juridical and political autonomy and difference. It would be difficult to dispute that by 1936, the "Shi'i position"—as if there really had been just one and only one—was being more or less consistently voiced in favor of the continued if not increased integration of Jabal 'Amil *into Lebanon* and not reassignment as part of Greater Syria. Voluminous telegrams, petitions, and letters illustrate the extent to which Lebanese Shi'is also voiced support for inclusion within the Lebanese nation while simultaneously demanding fairer treatment by the Mandate state.[28]

The Succession to Munir 'Usayran

Although certain tendentious readings of Lebanese Shi'i experiences insist on an untrammeled and undifferentiated history of resistance, by the early 1940s, there was fading interest on the part of most sectors of the Shi'i community in undoing the sectarian institutionalization that had then been put into place. Sectarian institutions were perceived as proof of the community's legitimate presence in the country as well as of communal empowerment. "The Shi'i community prefers death," as two men from Bint Jubayl dramatically put it in a telegram to the High Commissioner, "to the execution of personal status law that opposes Muslim *Chéréi*."[29] Another letter from a number of prominent Shi'i figures articulated their gratitude to the "French nation" for officially recognizing the "Ja'fari religion" in 1926, which allowed the community to become "autonomous in its *Etat-Civil* and its courts, like those in Iraq, Iran and the Indies."[30] Another colonial report on the matter of personal status found that "the question of personal status represents a singularly complex political and social problem, because it must reconcile these differing aspirations and these irreducible antagonisms with formulas based upon freedom of conscience and the equality of sects, which, in the Oriental opinion, have a very different sense than the Western conception we had imposed. Therefore we were led to envisage a complete reform of the status of religious communities and of personal status in general," leading toward "a partial secularization *(laicization)* through the elaboration of an optional civil personal status of common law."[31]

To be sure, there had never been unanimous agreement in the Shi'i milieu regarding the intrinsic value of the Ja'fari court. In his survey of Jabal 'Amil published in 1938, Nizar al-Zayn lauded Sayyid Hasan Mahmoud of the village of Shaqra for turning down the *shari'a* court judge position he had been offered. Al-Zayn went on to discuss at length what he perceived to be some of the implications of the "men of religion" participating in politics.

> While it is the responsibility of the *'ulama'* to serve their *umma* and their country, it is also incumbent upon them to monitor the actions of the *zu'ama'* and if the latter are fulfilling their responsibilities toward their people, then the best thing is for the men of religion to turn to preaching and guidance, but if the *zu'ama'*, as in Jabal 'Amil, are serving their interests alone and mistreating their country, then the *'ulama'* must march at the head of the people and lead them toward what is in their best interest.

Even after the court had been formally recognized for over a decade, there remained disagreement regarding the ethical implications of "collaborating" with the French.[32]

In October 1941, Munir 'Usayran gave a speech in which he reaffirmed his individual commitment and the commitment of the Shi'i community gener- ally to the French agenda in the region. "You have in effect entered the country," he wrote, "holding in your two hands the torch of freedom and independence, towards which the Lebanese have always turned." Despite "certain obstacles," 'Usayran commended the French for the fact that their "courage and your concern have overcome them. We have never doubted that France would achieve our independence because France has always fought and continued to fight for freedom and democracy." Having heaped such effusive praise on the colonial project, 'Usayran attempted once again to parlay "the already old sense of loyalty among our community" into French attention to "the ques- tion of [Shi'i] demands." 'Usayran closed with the rallying cries: "Vive General Catroux and his Allies! Vive General de Gaulle! Vive Lebanon!"[33]

But this may have been equal part defensive strategy on 'Usayran's part as well as an attempt to exploit his connections with French government officials. 'Usayran paid a visit to Eric Pruneaud, *Conseiller Administratif* in South Lebanon, in December 1941 to discuss the matter of who would suc- ceed him as head of the Ja'fari court. By this point, Pruneaud already had people flooding into his office to discuss this matter. Pruneaud admonished 'Usayran to "be quite worried about his own situation" because many of those visitors were not his allies. As his age and failing health became more and more of an issue, the need to locate someone to take over for 'Usayran became even more imperative. In an update tacked on to 'Usayran's personal dossier the following year, Pruneaud noted, "Cheikh Munir has no influence in South Lebanon . . . The Shi'i *ulémas* speak aboutt him with contempt. But it will be quite difficult to replace his position."[34]

Although the Ja'fari court was the most important Shi'i institution in Lebanon during the Mandate and early independence periods, other attempts were made to institutionalize Shi'i presence further. For example, a Muslim 'Amili Higher Council (*Conseil Supérieur Amili Musulman*) was founded in 1942 with some fifty people. Ahmad al-As'ad was elected president by a com- mission of fourteen members. The stated goals of the council were "the social and moral rehabilitation of Jabal 'Amil in conformity with its past glory and to provide it with its most legitimate rights, rights that were illegitimately deprived," to ensure the "employment of all legal means for the spiritual and economic renewal of Jabal 'Amil," as well as to "regain the spirit of unity among all inhabitants, setting aside their religious and political differences *(couleurs)*." After a meeting at the home of Ahmad al-Asʿad in June 1942, which was attended by Rida al-Tamir, Yusuf al-Zayn, and others, the council decided "to present to the President of the Republic a proposal bringing his attention to the negligence that the Shiʿi community has suffered from the government on the subject of the distribution of government jobs."[35]

Certain figures in the Shiʿi milieu originally had been and remained skeptical of the appointment of ʿUsayran to his high-profile post. The ʿAmili politician Ahmad al-Asʿad made contact with the French authorities and attempted to cast suspicion upon ʿUsayran's scholarly and religious pedigree. In al-Asʿad's opinion, ʿUsayran "doesn't possess the degree of aptitude required by Shiʿi tradition to fulfill the functions of religious judge." Because the "only ones who have the qualifications to judge among Shiʿis" are the "shaykhs who, having completed their studies in the holy city of Néjef (Irak), have obtained the diploma of higher studies conferring the title of "moujtahed," any judgments produced by ʿUsayran "will be equivalent to nothing in the eyes of Shiʿis." Al-Asʿad spoke in no uncertain terms: "Mounir Osseiran is not a 'moujtahed'." However, in the absence of any candidate for the presidency of the Shiʿi court who was both a "true 'moujtahed'" and acceptable to the Mandate authorities, al-Asʿad makes it clear that it would be appropriate for the French to "designate" a "Shiʿi mufti of the Lebanese Republic" from among the most respected religious scholars in the country, much "like there exists a Sunni mufti. This high official would have the qualification to represent all Shiʿis from a religious point of view." In response to al-Asʿad's recommendations, the colonial office noted:

> The declarations of Ahmad Bey El Assad, concerning the qualifications required of a Shiʿi religious judge are in principle exact, in the sense that, according to customs established during a period when they still did not enjoy the autonomy of their community in matters of personal status, the Shiʿis preferred to address themselves, for the liquidation of their cases of this kind, with private judges belonging to their sect *(confession)* and whose authority was unanimously recognized.

The only figures that should be permitted to engage in these practices were "cheikhs or *ulemas* who had obtained the title of "moujtahed." However, it

was understood that "the definition of "moujtahed"" that the French intelligence relied on did "not confirm the personal opinion of Ahmed El Assad":
"Certain ulémas of Djebel Amel completed their studies without expatriat-
ing and hold, however, the diploma of 'moujtahed,'" a title that would have
been conferred "by another, older moujtahed." As proof of this claim, the
French cited the examples of Shaykh Habib Mughniyya and Shaykh Munir
'Usayran.[36] This tension between religious authority and state bureaucracy
would not simply disappear. Even Muhammad Jawad Mughniyya—who
would become president of the Higher Ja'fari Court during the 1950s, and,
later, something of an *eminence grise* within the Shi'i milieu—had some
unkind words to say about his predecessor. In a piece published in *al-
'Irfan* entitled "On *Shari'a* Law," Mughniyya criticized earlier incarnations
of the Ja'fari court in Lebanon, ridiculing the fact that Ja'fari judges were
appointed by Shi'i politicians without any sort of qualifying examination,
which "opened the door" to "ignoramuses and corrupt elements."[37]

If the French administration defended the selection of 'Usayran as an
intermediary between the Shi'i community and the colonial state, many of
his colleagues also considered him as an equal. The clerical elite in Shi'i
Lebanon continued to treat him with due deference until the end of his
tenure as court president. In 1940, Shaykh Husayn Mughniyya entrusted
'Usayran with the stewardship of the Association of 'Amili *'Ulama'*. when
his ailing health prevented him from remaining at the helm. Mughniyya
praised his "eminence" 'Usayran, informing the French High Commissioner
of the widespread support 'Usayran enjoyed from the community: "The
eminent qualities of his character and the great confidence which he enjoys
among the populations," Mughniyya wrote, "encouraged me to entrust in
him this delicate mission." A petition signed by over twenty Shi'i *'ulama'*
accompanied Mughniyya's letter, expressing how they "strongly support the
excellent choice" of Munir 'Usayran, perceiving him "as being the qualified
representative" of the 'Amili *'ulama'* who has the good judgment to decide
all affairs on their behalf.[38]

End of an Era

Regardless of the contested nature of the position and the person, the search
for a replacement to Munir 'Usayran in 1948 symbolized the conclusion of

the first phase of institutionalized Shi'i presence in Lebanon. By virtue of his privileged position at the apex of the Ja'fari court hierarchy, 'Usayran was one of the most visible symbols of Shi'i empowerment during the Mandate period. In the context of selecting the replacement for Munir 'Usayran as president of the Ja'fari court, 'Abd al-Husayn Sharaf al-Din articulated some potential criteria, arguing that there was no good reason why the French should not appoint a new "Controller-General" for Ja'fari religious courts. Whoever was to be named to such a position, however, "must be chosen from among people of good conduct, [the] pious, honest and upright *'ulama'.*" Such a figure "must be familiar with the letter of the law, the procedure of religious courts *(Chérié)*, the legislation regarding testimonies and the personal status of Ja'fari Muslims." It would not be necessary, however, for those appointed to these two positions to be licensed to practice *ijtihad*. Sharaf al-Din does not see anything wrong with the creation of a Shi'i appellate court to oversee the administration and operation of Shi'i religious courts, provided that it adhered to certain restrictions. Sharaf al-Din preferred to have a respected member of the Shi'i community, of whatever rank, in a position of power, rather than jeopardize communal control over the religious institution. The French already had a short list of replacements. "Quite educated, ambitious, devious *(intrigant)*, generally little-loved," was how the French described the *mufti* of Tyre and the "favorite son," 'Abd al-Husayn Sharaf al-Din, when he presented his candidacy for head of the Shi'i appellate court in November 1942. However, both Shaykh Habib Mughniyya and Sayyid 'Abd al-Husayn Sharaf al-Din supported the candidacy of Shaykh 'Abdallah al-Sbaiti of Kafra; the Khalil clan supported Shaykh Khalil Mughniyya.

After conferring with a broad range of people on Shi'i judicial appointments, including Shaykh Muhsin Shararah of Bint Jubayl, Pruneaud wrote a detailed brief on the conceptual background of the Shi'i religious hierarchy, supplying background information about the role of the judge in Shi'ism and providing typology of *mujtahids*. Pruneaud points out that, "one of the fundamental differences between Shi'is and Sunnis" is "the fact that Shi'is continue to give interpretations of Muslim religious law, whereas Sunni theologians consider the decisions of the four orthodox legal schools to be definitive." Those who had achieved the status of *mujtahid* had been "educated in Iraq at Najaf. In Iraq, they are divided into two groups according to the degree of education that they have received": *"moujtaheddin ordinaires"*

are "only qualified to give partial interpretations," whereas those who have
achieved the level of *"moujtaheddin moutlak"* are "qualified to give all
interpretations." "In Lebanon," Pruneaud notes, "the most celebrated from
among the Moujtaheddin Moutlak for their virtues, for their popular favor,
are called "Moujtahedin Akbar," that is to say, grand interpreters or grand
ulema." The only "Moujtaheddin Akbar" in Lebanon were 'Abd al-Husayn
Sharaf al-Din, 'Abd al-Husayn Sadiq—although he was derided as "old
and completely paralyzed, this shaykh once played a quite important role
that no longer amounts to anything"—and Muhsin al-Amin, a "militant
nationalist [and] intimate friend of the Solh family." In the second category,
"Moujtaheddin Moutlak," Pruneaud mentions Muhammad Taqi Sadiq, son
of 'Abd al-Husayn Sadiq, who had just "returned from Iraq around two
months ago" and "will probably not stay in Lebanon"; 'Abd al-Karim Sadiq,
from the village of al-Khiam, son-in-law of Shaykh 'Abd al-Husayn Sadiq;
Sayyid 'Abd al-Husayn Nur al-Din; Sayyid Mahdi Ibrahim; and Hasan al-
Amin, "considered by some as Moujtahed Akbar." "Moujtaheddine ordinaires" included Musa 'Izz al-Din, Muhammad 'Ali Miqdad, Muhammad
Jawad Mughniyya, Hasan Sadiq, Mufti of Sidon, and 'Ali Fahs.[39]

Pruneaud pointed out how legislation regarding Ja'fari *shari'a* courts
should require that "the judges of Shi'i courts must be holders of diplomas
from Najaf (Irak) or a certificate of a Moudjtahed el Akbar." This added
requirement may be attributed to the increasing awareness on the part of
the French about diminishing respect among Shi'is for the colonial religious
institutions and their local administrators. Pruneaud also speaks approvingly of the fact that "there was a question, a decade ago, of creating a Ja'fari
religious school near Sidon, an affiliate of Najaf." Such a project should be
viewed at the level of "an imperious political necessity, because all the grad-
uates of Najaf return to Lebanon impregnated with ideas of Arab nationalism." Moreover, "one searches in vain among those Moujtaheddin educated
in Najaf [for] a single real Lebanese." Narrowing this original pool from
his earlier report significantly, Pruneaud would later argue that the most
likely candidates for the post included Muhammad Taqi Sadiq, whom he
described as "the private secretary and *homme de confiance* of Sayed Aboul
Hassan el-Asfahani of Iraq, who is considered the greatest of all living Shi'i
'ulama'. Cheikh Mohamed Taki did not personally submit his candidacy,
but his merits are celebrated throughout the Shi'i community," even though

his "political sentiments are not known"; Sulayman Zahir, "member of the Arab Academy—a politician without religious titles—Arabophile and axophile supported by the Solh family and, under the table, by Youssef Zein"; Yusuf al-Harissi al-Faqih, who was "already a member of the Shiʻi Court of Appeal . . . and easy to corrupt." He was also the preferred candidate of Ahmad al-Asʻad and "certain milieus in Beirut"; finally, Hasan al-Amin "will be the candidate of the Osseyran-Khalil party. Possesses religious titles but with no social life experience. Personality without prominence and without education."[40]

In the end, Shaykh Munir ʻUsayran would be replaced as President of the Jaʻfari court by Shaykh Yusuf al-Faqih, one of his original two legal advisors. It is a remarkable testament to the contested historical legacy of the Jaʻfari court in Lebanon that there remain no published sources concerning ʻUsayran. Near the midpoint of the twentieth century, when other figures that had filled out the Jaʻfari court hierarchy began passing away, there was no hesitation to commemorate their lives and contributions to the Shiʻi milieu and to Shiʻi institutions, in print or in reality. The death of Sayyid ʻAli Fahs, to cite just one example, a Jaʻfari court judge in Sidon who went on to become an assistant to ʻUsayran in Beirut, was reported in the pages of al-ʻIrfan in May 1950.[41] His life was chronicled at greater length in the June 1950 edition.[42] Reporting Munir ʻUsayran's death in June 1948, by contrast, al-ʻIrfan summarily notes that "he played an important political role during the Ottoman and French eras and that he had a dignified high status among his sect and other sects and that he was well-known for his generosity and humility."[43] There was mention of a more detailed biography (tarjama) to come, but it never appeared. When ʻUsayran was replaced as president of the Jaʻfari court by Shaykh Yusuf al-Faqih in September 1948, Sayyid Muhammad Yahya Safi al-Din (previously a Jaʻfari shariʻa court judge in Beirut) and Hasan ʻAlawiyya became his two legal assistants.[44] Inasmuch as al-Faqih had served as ʻUsayran's advisor throughout the Mandate period, his selection to succeed ʻUsayran as Jaʻfari court president—a position he held for only a few years, until 1951—epitomized the court's institutional inertia. Al-Faqih was then replaced by an ambitious young mujtahid by the name of Shaykh Muhammad Jawad Mughniyya. Announcing that Shaykh Yusuf al-Faqih and Sayyid ʻAli al-Zayn (who was one of his assistants) were both retiring, al-ʻIrfan also noted that Mughniyya enjoyed the "approval (*istihsan*)" of all classes in the Shi'i milieu.[45] Mughniyya began building a name for himself during the 1930s by contributing regularly to *al-'Irfan* and criss-crossing Jabal 'Amil in order to preach and give political speeches. Mughniyya exemplified a broader challenge to the status and authority of traditional *'ulama'*, from religious and non-religious positions of critique that had begun to emerge under the Mandate, even as the sectarianization of Shi'i Lebanon was proceeding apace.[46]

The institution of the Ja'fari court represented the first opportunity for the Shi'i community to assert itself formally within the framework of the Lebanese state. To be sure, controversy surrounding the position of Ja'fari court president would persist into the early independence period and beyond.[47] Many Shi'i intellectuals and *'ulama'* corroborate the dominant historiographical narrative of Shi'i "mobilization" by arguing that the community was not capable of organizing itself in any significant institutional way until the creation of the Supreme Islamic Shi'i Council (SISC) in 1969. Without downplaying the significance of the SISC, from 1926–1969, the Ja'fari court was in many ways the official face of the Shi'i milieu.[48] Indeed, this argument was echoed by the third president of the court, Muhammad Jawad Mughniyya when he characterized the presidency of the Ja'fari court as "the highest official Shi'i religious post in Lebanon due to the absence of official Shi'i institutions at the time."[49]

National Independence, Communal Independence

As discussed in chapter one, World War I brought human dislocation, famine, and generalized uncertainty to Jabal 'Amil, to say nothing of substantial administrative reorganizations and political transformations. The effects of this historical moment on the region were unparalleled. By contrast, World War II proved somewhat less traumatic for both the lands of Syria and Lebanon, with the growing Anglo-French rivalry in the Levant proving a boon to nationalist aspirations across the region. There was a surge in nationalist activism against French Mandate rule in Syria and Lebanon during the 1940s. Despite endemic tensions between Lebanese nationalism and pan-Arab nationalism, such political differences were often put aside in order to protest the continuation of French rule in Lebanon. Although Lebanese independence was technically acquired in 1943, French forces didn't leave the country until November 22, 1946, an intermediary period that Nadine Méouchy describes as a state of exception.[50]

In spite of its steadily growing numbers and its historical significance, the Shi'i community has conventionally been left out of the narrative of Lebanese history under French Mandate. Absent any formal national census after 1932, French population estimates in December 1942 suggested a national population of approximately 1.06 million people, out of which there were some 197,423 Shi'i Muslims, or 18.6% of the national population. The official estimates from 1943 recorded some 200,698 Shi'is out of a total population of 1,046,421, or about 19% of the country. According to an unofficial census from 31 December 1944, the number of Shi'is in South Lebanon was still an overwhelming majority: 126,701 people out of a grand total of 211,963, or some 60% of the population, nearly three times their relative size in national terms.[51]

Nevertheless, historians continue to view the brokering of national independence in Lebanon as having been accomplished through the alliances made by "men of influence" from the Sunni community and the Maronite community. However, as this book has argued, the Shi'i community was actively seeking to find a way to integrate into the national leadership and the state structure. Shi'i Muslims in South Lebanon, the Biqa' Valley, and Beirut had begun calling for greater rights and representation early on in the Mandate period. The unwritten "gentleman's agreement" between Beshara al-Khoury and Riad al-Solh that institutionally regulated the balance of forces between Sunni Muslims and Maronite Christians in Lebanon—known as the National Pact—was an integral part of the founding mythology of Lebanese sectarian nationalism and national sectarianism. However, the National Pact gives no formal recognition to the Shi'i community, even though it was, most likely, the third largest sectarian community in the country at the time. In addition to reserving the position of president of the republic for a Maronite Christian and prime minister for a Sunni Muslim, the Lebanese Parliament would be required to maintain a ratio of six Christians to every five Muslims. Regardless of the fact that this quota system was based on a fundamentally flawed and outdated census, mainstream Lebanese historiography poses this agreement as a kind of formative moment, an exemplary case of tolerance and compromise among Lebanon's diverse population.

This political arrangement would ensure that in addition to always having a Sunni prime minister and a Maronite Christian president, there
would also be a Shi'i Speaker of the Parliament. With the exception of a
brief interregnum during the mid-1940s when a Greek Orthodox politician, Habib Abi Shahla, was Speaker of the Parliament, a Shi'i Muslim
would hold the position in perpetuity from 1947. Shi'i demands for protected formal political recognition within the Lebanese sectarian pantheon
intersected with the articulation of the new status quo in Lebanese national
politics. Despite stale platitudes about the National Pact as an articulation
of unflappable Lebanese national aspirations towards intersectarian harmony and untrammeled equality, certain groups were apparently more
equal than others. There was no formal political recognition of the rights
of Shi'i Muslims, not to mention the so-called "other minorities"—even
less well represented groups including Greek Orthodox, Greek Catholics,
Armenians of all denominations, Jews, and Druze—equivalent to the recognition afforded Maronite Christians and Sunni Muslims in this arrangement. The Maronite-Sunni "agreement" shadowed the unquestioned
dominance and centrality of Mount Lebanon in the imagined political
geography of Lebanon.

On the eve of World War II, Nizar al-Zayn wrote about the need for greater
rights and recognition for the Shi'i community, specifically with respect to
a high-level position in the executive or legislative branch. Although Shi'i
politicians had been making their voices heard, al-Zayn found that

> the rights of their region and their sect aren't only the appointment of
> three Shi'i judges instead of two but rather the earmarking of sufficient
> funds in the budget to establish schools in the villages that do not have
> places of learning, such as Habboush and 'Aynata and Markaba and
> Tayr Zina, etc., and to bring water from Shebaa or elsewhere to Tibnin-
> Bint Jubayl and the villages surrounding them, and to pave a portion of
> the roads of the South, and to demand the lowering of taxes.

These bread-and-butter issues would remain low priority. But al-Zayn also
introduces here the problem of greater Shi'i representation within the executive branch of government. In his words, "the presidency of the Parliament
is a position that deserves attention and it is the right of the Shi'i sect that

the Shi'i representatives themselves have lost with their weakness and their lack of agreement."[52]

Shi'i parliamentarians, intellectuals, political leaders and ordinary people had all been demanding greater representation in public positions, state hiring as well as a permanent position of Shi'i influence in the governmental structure, to say nothing of more in-depth state attention for pressing social and economic issues in Jabal 'Amil. The highest profile position held by a Shi'i Muslim in Lebanon at the time was the presidency of the Ja'fari court. Political horizons beyond sectarian legal institutions soon started to crystallize around the so-called "Third Presidency," the Speaker of the Parliament, a unique turn of phrase that purports to promote some kind of perceived equality among the Maronite, Sunni and Shi'i communities; the (first) President is always a Maronite and the Prime Minister (the second presidency) is by definition a Sunni Muslim. The Speaker of the Parliament would symbolize a new public face for the Shi'i milieu, signifying the arrival of the Lebanese Shi'a as a full-blown political community in Lebanon, the latest acme in a process of Shi'i institutionalization that had begun in 1926 and would continue through 1969 and beyond. The formal establishment of the Ja'fari Court, the Muslim 'Amili Higher Council, and the "third presidency" were part and parcel of this historical process of institutionalizing Shi'i sectarianism in Mandate Lebanon.

By the time of national independence, the Lebanese-ness of the Shi'i community in Jabal 'Amil, the Biqa' Valley, and Beirut was practically taken for granted. After a three-year hiatus imposed by French censorship and tumultuous circumstances, al-'Irfan returned to regular publication in the spring of 1945, two years after nominal independence, although still a year and a half before the evacuation of French troops from the region. In his opening editorial, Ahmad 'Arif al-Zayn reaffirmed the political commitments of the journal. "We are Arabs before Muslims," was his first point, and "the progress and unity and independence and freedom of the Arabs" remained the timeless goals of the journal. Secondly, "We are Muslims by religion and serving Islam is both our aim and our guiding principle." Finally, "We are Shi'is by *madhhab* and unifying the ranks of the Shi'a (*kalimat al-shi'a*) and guiding them toward the loftiest goal so that they may become a useful member at the heart of the Arab and Islamic world are among our most important aspirations and furthest objectives."[53] Still, neglect toward the political and economic development of the Shi'i milieu remained a burning issue, and it is in this sense that the cultural estrangement and structural inequalities endemic to the Shi'i community in Lebanon during the twentieth century articulated the most striking of ironies. Economic and cultural demands made for national equality under the Mandate increasingly turned into economic and cultural demands for sectarian parity. At the time of independence, the tension between national unity and burgeoning Shi'i autonomy remained unresolved, a tension that would not be satisfactorily resolved even in the course of the twentieth century.

Institutional and social transformations begun as early as the 1920s were accelerated during the 1940s and 1950s as the Shi'i community became more secure and more visible within the Lebanese national arena. Musa al-Sbaiti, a regular contributor to al-'Irfan, expressed some of the various ways in which national independence could be interpreted:

> Some people reckon that independence is an action, which, once completed, its men live forever after in comfort and calm. Independence is an ongoing action, a perpetual struggle, and ongoing variegated support for the fields of life requiring skillful capability that exerts all of its energy and effort, demanding confident souls who won't remain silent and who won't hesitate to come to its aid; eager pliant minds, and steadfast, patient hearts that won't submit and won't give up.[54]

Shi'i struggles for equality and justice would transcend the formal acquisition of national independence. Indeed, the structural developments that contributed to the recognition and reinforcement of Shi'i autonomy under the Mandate would have effects that made the integration of Shi'i regions such as Jabal 'Amil into the national fold even more difficult. Sbaiti praised the "'Amili nation" while recognizing the incomplete integration, or, as I have put it, the incomplete nationalization, of Jabal 'Amil. Among other things, the Shi'i "politics of demand" was oriented towards protecting and promoting sectarian Shi'i interests and the interests of Shi'i employees of state-led sectarian institutions as part and parcel of their incorporation into the national community.

The Shi'i community had acquired a place in the Lebanese political landscape as well as within the cultural consciousness of the nation. But neither declared independence in 1943 nor full independence in 1946 did much to accomplish significant change regarding impressions by others of Jabal 'Amil or of Shi'is in Lebanon. For example, Michel Chiha, one of the founding fathers of modern Lebanon, who subscribed to a kind of "geographical determinism," a strain of Lebanese nationalism emphasizing the physical coherence of the Lebanese polity, wrote in the well-established tradition of belittling and marginalizing the Shi'i community and its regions.[55] "History in this country," Chiha writes of Jabal 'Amil, "is incorporated into the landscape. Each rock is a memory, each village a kingdom. The inhabitant of today admittedly appears indifferent to this size. The site is more alive than him. It is not but a little further that one finds, on the mountain, in covered white stone residences of red tiles, in the medium of some greenery, moving faces." Having sufficiently established the Lebanese "nature" of the South, however, Chiha goes on to argue that Lebanese society must work to actively incorporate the region into the national fold:

> South Lebanon is not known enough, not liked enough. It suffered a kind of disgrace for a long time. Perhaps tired of a resounding past, it thought of itself as withdrawn from the world. Gradually, after a thousand years, it had been forgotten. This country that is Lebanon eternal, this prolongation of *our mountain* which leads to the pleasant slopes of Galilee, these borders of Tyre and Sidon which still resound of the crowned steps, it is necessary for many reasons that we return there with our heart.

"Lebanon has obligations toward the South," Chiha concluded. "For the future of Lebanon, it is appropriate that each one here knows it and remembers it."[56] Using language of "our mountain"—Mount Lebanon—as opposed to theirs—Jabal 'Amil—and talk of "settlement" of the country, Chiha clearly articulated the perceived separateness of Beirut and Mount Lebanon from the peripheries of Greater Lebanon. Echoing much earlier dismissals of the Shi'i community in Lebanon, Pierre Rondot noted that "the Shiites form a vigorous race; totally rural, this population is dominated by an aristocracy of landowners, less advanced but more debonair than their Sunni counterparts. The community, with 83 per cent illiterate, is by far the least educated in Lebanon; it still has no more than the smallest intellectual elite." Reinforcing notions of 'Amili separateness that would continue to stymie relationships between the Lebanese state and Shi'i society throughout the twentieth century, Rondot claims that Shi'i "representatives complain freely of [their] insufficient place in the state and sometimes toy with the idea, in imitation of the Sunnis, of dissociating from it."[57]

Between Institution Building and Social Mobilization

Social and economic conditions in Jabal 'Amil continued to roil Shi'i intellectuals all over Lebanon during the early independence period. Muhammad Husayn Nasrallah complained that Jabal 'Amil remained in a state of decline. "There is no doubt that the representatives of the people are the ones who are responsible," Nasrallah argued, because they "forgot the villages where they lived for a time to get lost among the clubs of Beirut" and became "uninterested in the message thrown on their shoulders." This problem transcended local examples of specific duties shirked:

> The situation is so bad in Jabal 'Amil that it threatens to collapse on every side. The feudalism (iqta'iyya) that the government fuels anew by facilitating the degradation among the ranks of the 'Amili people after the intellectuals thought that it had been done away with in the independence period. Where are we? The middle of Africa? And in what epoch? The Middle Ages."

Paradoxically, this ironic language of protest that rhetorically characterizes Jabal 'Amil as both asynchronous and noncontiguous with Lebanon dovetails with some of the foreign depictions of the region discussed elsewhere in this book. "We are in Lebanon," Nasrallah continues,

> the civilized country that almost overtakes the West in its lavish spending and its wastefulness and with its places of leisure and its dance clubs and its cars and its skyscrapers, and a chunk of the heart of the nation (watan) still complains of poverty and disease and ignorance, and there is nobody to hear it. Wretched are the people whose life isn't in their own hands but rather in the hands of feudalists.[58]

The implications of political engagement on the part of Shiʿi religious scholars in Lebanon were historically determined and conditional on the mood
of the moment.

During the 1930s and 1940s, amidst a decline in the status and influence
of religious careerism in the context of Jabal ʿAmil and Shiʿi Lebanese life
more generally, two other religious scholars began to make waves in the Shiʿi
milieu through their activism and their writing. ʿAbdallah Niʿmeh went so
far as to argue that Muhammad Jawad Mughniyya and Muhammad Jawad
al-Chirri were the only two religious figures in late Mandate and early independence Jabal ʿAmil who had any interest in popular preaching, promoting positive change, and supporting the improvement of the Shiʿi milieu.[59]
During the 1940s, al-ʿIrfan was packed with essays written by these two,
as well as updates regarding their activities in Jabal ʿAmil and elsewhere
in Lebanon. Decades later, al-Chirri recalls going with Muhammad Jawad
Mughniyya to travel on "speaking tours in South Lebanon aiming to awaken
southern society and to urge it to demand its rights."[60] When they attempted
at one point to form a new society called the Social Reform Corps (hayʾat
al-tahdhib al-ijtimaʿi), Ahmad ʿArif al-Zayn, the editor of al-ʿIrfan, was sufficiently inspired to compare the two of them to another luminary duo from
ʿAmili Shiʿi intellectual history: Muhammad Ibn Makki al-ʿAmili (d. 786),
the so-called First Martyr (al-shahid al-awwal), and Zayn al-Din al-ʿAmili
(d. 1558), the Second Martyr (al-shahid al-thani).[61]

Muhammad Jawad al-Chirri was born in Jabal ʿAmil in 1905. He received
his religious education in Najaf and, like other ʿAmili religious students
of his generation, which was a much smaller cohort than the generation
that preceded them, al-Chirri returned to Lebanon in order to preach and
teach. During the 1930s and 1940s, al-Chirri began regularly traveling
around South Lebanon and Beirut, giving lectures and preaching to what
he construed as a moribund Shiʿi community.[62] In 1949, he immigrated to
Dearborn, Michigan, where he became the Imam of the fledgling Lebanese
Shiʿi community; in 1963, al-Chirri helped to found the Islamic Center of
Detroit, which remains a thriving cultural and religious center.

Al-Chirri published his first work, al-Khilafa fi al-dustur al-islami, in 1946,
ostensibly upon the request of Sayyid ʿAbd al-Husayn Sharaf al-Din. An earnest analysis of the problem of the Caliphate in Islamic history, al-Chirri
distinguishes between three kinds of political rule: popular democracy;

"minority rule," which he defines as domination by one class, tribe or any social group; and divine appointment. In a remarkably prescient commentary on problems faced by Muslim minorities in the U.S. and Europe in the late twentieth century, al-Chirri insists that Muslims participate to "elect a government insofar as they are a people, not insofar as they are a Muslim people," pointing out the possibility that such a government might rule according to the "criminal laws of Italy" and still remain a "legitimate government" (hukuma shar'iyya).[63] This dovetails with some of his other published writings, including an essay in which al-Chirri traces the long arc of freedom traversed throughout the history of "humanity" (al-insaniyya). "Political freedom," writes al-Chirri, somewhat naively, "is guaranteed under correct Islamic governments because among the greatest obligations upon a Muslim is to tell the truth as well as to hear the voice of truth and to obey even if the hearer is a ruler."[64] Once resident in the United States, al-Chirri published a number of works in both Arabic and English, striving, among other things, to publicize in the United States a positive image of Islam, in general, and of Shi'ism, in particular. In an introduction to a subsequent reprinting of al-Khilafa fi al-dustur al-islami, Muhammad Baqir al-Chirri, Muhammad Jawad al-Chirri's brother, notes that, in the period just before his father's death, Imam Musa al-Sadr had corresponded with al-Chirri about the possibility of visiting the U.S. Al-Chirri had responded that there would be great "value" in his coming to meet Lebanese- and Arab-Americans as well as to explain the "conditions of the South" in Lebanon both to them and to political representatives in the United States government.[65]

Muhammad Jawad Mughniyya was born in 1904 into a poor family in Tir Dibba, a village near Tyre. Both his mother and his father died before he reached the age of fifteen. After moving to Beirut, where he lived on his own for several years, selling books and other goods on the street, he left Lebanon to pursue his religious studies in Najaf. He returned to Lebanon in 1936 and secured a religious post in the village of Ma'rakeh before moving to the town of Tir Hirfa. Mughniyya struggled financially throughout this period. In fact, he was even taken to court for failing to pay his abandoned wife and daughter their due maintenance.[66] The case eventually made its way up to the Higher Ja'fari Court (mahkamat al-tamyiz). In an opinion rendered by Munir 'Usayran on October 8, 1937, the case should be resolved by having Mughniyya transfer a modest piece of land he owned to his abandoned wife along with the remaining money he still owed her.[67] Mughniyya studied under the supervision of notable scholar and Chief Mufti of Tyre 'Abd al-Husayn Sharaf al-Din. From the late 1930s and 1940s, Mughniyya and al-Chirri began contributing regularly to al-'Irfan, among other publications, participating in religious and theological debates, and also advocating increasingly on behalf of the politically marginalized Shi'a in South Lebanon.[68]

In his first published work, al-Wad' al-hadir fi Jabal 'Amil: bidayat al-qahr wa-l-hirman (1947), Mughniyya bemoans the underdevelopment of Jabal 'Amil, valorizes downtrodden 'Amili workers and peasants, denounces corrupt zu'ama' who claim to speak in the name of the people but who do nothing for them in practice, and criticizes the clerical classes, whom he lambastes for pious hypocrisy and inadequate responses to local political and economic problems. Real liberation and national independence are more complex and ambiguous than nominal political emancipation. To the workers of Jabal 'Amil: "Look at yourself O Worker, how you spend your day in a stupor! And pass the night hungry! You do not find work to earn yourself a loaf of bread, and if you fled from hunger to Palestine, they would throw you in the pits of jails . . . as though you were a war criminal!" And to the peasants of the South: "And you, O peasant from whom the government fills its coffers while you and your kin work night and day, only to live the life of insects! Disease afflicts you and you can neither treat it nor get medicine . . . You drink water mixed with mud and garbage! Your children play with cats and dogs!" Here is a clarion call for greater participation within the Lebanese state, neither a retreat into community nor an unbridled assault on the flawed, sectarian logic of the state, an unambiguous call for revolt. "Be resentful of your representatives," he declaims, turning his attention to corrupt political leaders, "as they were resentful of the government when it did not obey their party and self-interested demands."[69] In line with opinions of Musa al-Sbaiti and others, Mughniyya recognizes that the road to communal self-empowerment is long: "We are colonized and subjugated so long as we are ignorant, even if we have liberated ourselves from the Turk and the French" (21). Mughniyya continues to hack away at "The French and their followers [who] wanted to name this mountain The South [,] camouflaging that it is a part of Lebanon." In the end, "Lebanon became a state and Jabal 'Amil [was] among its colonies" (25).[70] Echoing the situation introduced in the opening pages of this book, Mughniyya awkwardly confronts the difficult truth that, in Lebanon, even universal claims for rights must be couched in the hegemonic language of sectarianism in order to be intelligible within the system. "We do not want the representatives of the South to lobby [on behalf of] one sect over another or one element over another or one region over another," Mughniyya argues. Instead, "what we want is for Jabal 'Amil to be a true part of Lebanon," and "until history measures all the parts of the Lebanese Republic by a single standard, without privileging or discriminating between one or another, and without Mount Lebanon as France and The South as Jabal 'Amil!!" (30–31).

Working his way up through the official channels of state-recognized religious hierarchy, Mughniyya was appointed Ja'fari *shari'a* court judge in Beirut in 1948; became an assistant (*mustashar*) to the President upon the departure of Munir 'Usayran and the appointment of Shaykh Yusuf al-Faqih to the presidency of the Higher Ja'fari Court; and served as court president from 1951 until 1956. As with others of his generation, one of Mughniyya's most consistent grievances was his frustration at the lack of Shi'i representation in government institutions. Mughniyya imagined the Shi'i community ought to respond to such an oppressive political environment through tactics other than brute resistance. As Chibli Mallat writes, "the tone of Mughniyya's writings and discourse rang more of revolt than pity," that is, "of revolt against the State and the deputies who (mis)represent it."[71] In *al-Shi'a wa-l-hakimun*, one of his best known works, Mughniyya addresses the thorny ethics of political violence. Sandwiched between Shi'i quietists or fin-de-siècle modernist reformers on the one side, and the more fiery and radical approaches emanating out of Shi'i circles from the 1960s onwards on the other side, Mughniyya occupies a position somewhere between patience and action, between institution building and revolt. He argued that those protesting against the abuse of power "should not enter into an overt struggle over sovereignty and power . . . but rather they should connect their struggle to the guise of reform and ensure the rights of the people."[72] The rights of the people must be secured and the institutions of power and the state need to be reworked. Although he had not yet developed any coherent critique of the ideological or political bases of Lebanese sectarianism, here is an implicit nod in that general direction.

But reform in and of itself is an insufficient political goal; the simple transfer of power from one leadership to another is likely to be inadequate. For

Mughniyya, the subject of history is not the jurist, the expert, or the political boss; it is the people, and his political theology imagines the active participation of subaltern classes, which cannot always be expected to submit to the guidance or conventional wisdom of an elite cadre of learned men. Though Mughniyya identifies social justice as the highest good, he does not argue that it should be pursued by any means necessary, nor does he believe that one particular social class is destined to secure and administer it. In contradistinction to arguments generally attributed to Imam Ruhollah Khomeini, Mughniyya finds that "sovereignty during the infallible Imam's absence belongs to the people in general and not to the jurists only."[73] In fact, Mughniyya published a succinct rebuttal of the Khomeinist perspective on the jurist and the Islamic state. To be sure, Mughniyya didn't diverge much from Khomeini in determining that religion is the source from which all politics flows, and that any attempt to separate them, whether analytically or practically, is futile. For Mughniyya, "society" needs the state to represent its interests in the same way that people need water, air, and other basic elements of life. Mughniyya's critique of Khomeini broadly falls on two points: the problem of *wilayat al-faqih* and the problem of *al-dara'ib al-maliyya*. As for the former, Mughniyya poses the question whether this concept can be generalized to the point of *wilayat al-ma'sum*, the sovereignty of an infallible interpreter of sacred law. Mughniyya takes exception with this notion and accuses Khomeini of conflating the right to rule (*hukm*) with a more expansive conception of juristic authority (*sulta*). As for the latter, Mughniyya highlights the questionable ethicality of tax revenues going to the coffers of the state versus being spent to help the poor and the needy. Mughniyya equates coming up with just assessments of these issues with the thorny question of modernity (*al-'asriyya*) as such: a state is modern if it is governed by the sovereignty of law and justice and not the arbitrary rule of political or elite bosses. Unlike the infallible ruler, however, the humble jurist is affected by historical contingency, by his context and environment, by shifting social, geographical, and economic circumstances, by all that is apparent; in other words, he is capable of producing unjust rulings. Bringing this discussion even closer to the mundane minutiae of everyday life, Mughniyya points out that "the functions of the State are not all religious and mosque-related. There are also administrative and social functions that texts do not address and we leave [these] to the

learned and scholarly in defining the interest, even if it is an emulation of
the West, as long as the interpretation does not sanction something that is
religiously forbidden or forbid something that is religiously sanctioned."[74]
For Mughniyya, one of the fundamental questions challenging the virtue of
establishing an Islamic state almost certainly emerges from his class background as well as his experience of a multicultural and multiconfessional
Lebanon—Will the state be one for all of its citizens or will it end up granting special rights and privileges to the religious elite?

Both Mughniyya and al-Chirri contributed to the propagation of a discourse of social justice and equality within the Shi'i milieu, in the context
of the postcolonial Lebanese nation-state. Both appeared at a transitional
moment, between previous reformist impulses and more radicalized struggles for sectarian rights yet to come. The processes of Shi'i definition and
politicization in Lebanon were gradual ones, shaped at this moment by and
between reformism and revolution. Historians must remain attentive to the
multiplicity of perspectives and positions that exist among and across disparate Shi'i communities. Both Mughniyya and al-Chirri reject the premises
of *wilayat al-faqih,* albeit from differing perspectives. Both were, like many
Shi'i intellectuals of the twentieth century, concerned with sorting out some
of the difficult ethical and political implications of engagement with the state.
In some ways, these two religious scholars represented two potential futures
for the Shi'i community in Lebanon. If Muhammad Jawad Mughniyya represents the integration of poor, religious Shi'is from Jabal 'Amil into the
apparatus of the Lebanese state, Muhammad Jawad al-Chirri represents the
uprooting and dispersal of 'Amili Shi'is to all points on the map. Although he
was a contemporary of Imam Musa al-Sadr and Imam Ruhollah Khomeini,
Mughniyya never fully embraced the tactics of armed struggle or supported
the theory of *wilayat al-faqih.* Neither Mughniyya nor al-Chirri was drawn
to the revolutionary fervor of those two better-known figures.

The Romance of the Shi'i "Awakening"

Even if ideas about social justice and equity made by and for the Shi'i community were gaining currency as early as the 1930s and 1940s, and despite
the exceptional examples of social unrest described at the beginning of this
chapter, there was neither sufficient impetus nor institutional resources to

successfully rally the Shiʻi community to its own defense in ways that were politically meaningful or lasting during the Mandate period. This is perhaps the main reason why histories of the Shiʻi community in Lebanon tend to start in or around 1959, when Imam Musa al-Sadr arrived in Tyre in order to begin taking on a leadership role within the Shiʻi milieu. The conventional historiography of Shiʻi empowerment and mobilization under the influence of Imam Musa al-Sadr follows the pattern of a romantic narrative. On the one hand, the Shiʻi "awakening" is, much like national "awakenings," the inevitable unfolding of a long dormant sensibility within a community that is perceived to be both bounded and natural. Once liberated from external oppression and internal malaise, the true essence of this social and political unit may finally emerge in order to thrive. On the other hand, such an awakening is a process characterized by struggle, the struggle to break out and simultaneously negate all experience that has come before. The historical narrative of Shiʻi awakening and mobilization depends on a near-total disavowal of those earlier processes of gradual transformation and subtle sectarianization discussed throughout this book, which are generally subsumed within a reductive conceptualization of the Shiʻi milieu as essentially passive, oppressed, or quietist. To the extent that the Shiʻi community in Greater Syria remained relatively disorganized, however, such a discourse of empowerment and mobilization creates an even more negative impression of its past.

Majed Halawi has critically analyzed the mobilization of those Shiʻi masses inspired and guided by Imam Musa al-Sadr.[75] On the one hand, Halawi points out how a diversity of repressive forces within Lebanese Shiʻi society—clannish mentalities, patriarchal family structures, entrenched political and religious leaderships—articulated with currents in Lebanese political culture in order to militate against the broader interests of the Shiʻi masses. The historiographical effects of those forces have been that "the Shiʻa zuʻama (pl. of zaʻim) are designated as the agents of change in Shiʻa history. Very little, if anything, is said of the involvement of the Shiʻa masses in promulgating that change" (25). He goes on,

Ignoring the politics of the people, such as the political will and role of the Shiʻa masses in initiating the protest against the French mandate

in Lebanon and for the Arab nationalist cause, Lebanese Shi'a historiography provides only a narrow and partial formulation of key movements in Shi'a history. More importantly, it invalidates and obscures
much of the determining sources of that history (26).

In this light, then, the task of the historian would be to illuminate the ways
in which power has produced certain representations of the "Shi'i subaltern" and to recuperate the authentic experience of the marginal sectors of
that most marginalized subnational community. But this reading of 'Amili
Shi'i history intimates little more than a circumscribed space for legitimate
popular protest, mediated by Arab nationalism. On the other hand, Halawi
presumes timeless Arab nationalist sympathies within the Shi'i milieu,
oversimplifying the Shi'i historical experience during this period, caught as
it was among Lebanese sectarian-nationalism, Arabism, internationalism,
and broader networks of Shi'i belonging; again, the Shi'i milieu has been
as polarized by the tension between Islamic universalism and Shi'i particularism as by the tension between Lebanese and Arab nationalism. Halawi
exposes another weakness inherent to this "literature of awakening" in writing that an "oppressive bond between leaders and followers was symptom-
atic of the stagnation that characterized Shi'a society as a whole on the eve
of Lebanese independence" (213).

Historians and social scientists have been disproportionately concerned
with the awakening or mobilization and, subsequently, the radicalization
and militarization of the Shi'i milieu in the second half of the twentieth
century. However, preceding the rise of political Shi'ism and sectarian Shi'i
political parties in Lebanon, prior to the emergence of Imam Musa al-Sadr,
the Movement of the Deprived (*harakat al-mahrumin*) and Harakat Amal,
well before the birth of Hizballah and its affiliated social and legal institutions, there have been multiple forms of political engagement, social inter-
connection, and diverse expressions of cultural identity within the Shi'i
milieu. Such preponderant scholarly and popular focus on the mobilization,
awakening, radicalization or militarization of the community misreads the
multiple meanings of sectarianism in Lebanon and throws another kind of
shadow over the diversity of Lebanese Shi'i historical experiences throughout the twentieth century.[76]

The romance of the Shiʻi awakening rejects passivity and quietism, rendering earlier instances of "collaboration" with the state unacceptable or else invisible. In terms that seem to play with the contradiction identified by Muhammad Jawad Mughniyya at the start of this book, one late twentieth-century contributor to al-ʻIrfan conceptually engaged with the "game of sectarianism" while attempting to approach the comparative history of the Maronite and Shiʻi communities in Lebanon. "If we thumbed through the political history of the Shiʻa of Jabal ʻAmil" compiled by "ancient and modern historians," he wrote, "we would find that this mountain [i.e., Jabal ʻAmil] . . . never tried to be an ally to the point of dependency with any foreign powers, be they distant or neighboring. The history of the ʻAmilis is almost empty of reliance upon external alliances or dependency or domination." With an astonishing level of communal self-aggrandizement, the author contends that the alliance between the ʻAmili Shiʻi community and the eighteenth-century Ottoman governor Zahir al-ʻUmar was "an alliance of equals."[77] Comparing the Shiʻi historical experience to the Maronite, the author concludes that the latter cynically wrapped their "sect" in the "robe of a minority," while the ʻAmili Shiʻi community had always taken care to hold onto the "independence of its decisionmaking and its freedom to move toward self-defense in the face of internal rivals and foreign enemies."[78]

Once the doubled narratives of quietism/mobilization and collaboration/resistance are cemented into place as defining the history of Shiʻism in Lebanon, it makes no sense, ideologically speaking, to imagine an institutional history of Shiʻi gradual publicization and empowerment during the Mandate period. In other words, what was once a diverse social environment that could accommodate various and contested attempts at integration into the state structure and national body politic would come to seem unimaginable if not ludicrous in retrospect. As in other colonial contexts, therefore, "perhaps the most important act in de-fetishizing resistance is the acknowledgment that resistance tends to be exceptional."[79] Hopefully the account presented in this book can help to demonstrate how interrelated processes of gradual awakening and consciousness-raising buffeted the Shiʻi milieu in Lebanon throughout the twentieth century. This was a story of gradations, of incremental steps towards political recognition, communal empowerment, and national engagement. Much like the complex tableau Lara Deeb assembles in her ethnography of the late twentieth-century Shi'i milieu, this book shows how "the institutionaliza-tion of sectarianism in Lebanon was accompanied by a more subtle process by which the category of sect became increasingly necessary to the groups themselves," but also makes plain that this process was already well under way much earlier than previously thought.[80]

Epilogue: Making Lebanon Sectarian

In the spring of 2005, a modest alliance of Shi'i intellectuals, politicians, and citizens staged a press conference at the 'Amiliyya Society in the Beirut neighborhood of Ra's al-Naba'a—the educational and civic nucleus of Shi'i modernism in Beirut and the former home of the Ja'fari court—in order to declare their independence from the hegemony of Hizballah and Amal, the two dominant Shi'i parties in Lebanon. Even though they were initially met with little more than shrugs and ridicule, the group briefly declared what might have amounted to a political Shi'i "third way." As the trend gradually passed away, the ideological vise grip of Shi'i unity was soon tightened. In December 2005, the head of the corps of 'Amili *'ulama'*, 'Afif al-Nabulsi, issued a fatwa effectively interdicting any "Shi'i political body" from replacing Hizballah and Amal MPs who had walked out of Parliament in protest over the ongoing political deadlock. In response, a number of intellectuals, including a number of "secular Shi'is," published a trenchant response to al-Nabulsi, claiming that this sort of brazen religious intervention in Lebanese political life was unjustifiable.[1] Furthermore, they announced their intention to formally raise a legal challenge against al-Nabulsi, claiming that "no one has the right" to threaten the constitutional rights of Lebanese citizens who wish to participate in the political process, and that their "resorting to the law" was a completely legitimate response.[2]

Nothing less than the age-old question of authority and political representation within the Shi'i milieu was at stake in the case of this controversial fatwa. These iconoclastic individuals described a broader struggle within the Lebanese Shi'i milieu over the character and limits of "republican values." They decried not only the language and tone employed by Shaykh al-Nabulsi, but also by his main supporters on this issue—Sayyid Hasan Nasrallah, the

Secretary-General of Hizballah, his deputy Naʿim Qasim, and Shaykh ʿAbd al-Amir Qabalan, the vice president of the Supreme Islamic Shiʿi Council (SISC)—demanding that they cease making such threats "out of sensitivity to the danger" that had "descended upon the republic." To be sure, this was a relatively minor incident, one that would constitute little more than a blip on the radar screen of Shiʿi politics in Lebanon. However, the extent to which such a challenge was effectively silenced without much work illustrates, in some small measure, the ideological and cultural hegemony of "The Resistance" and its all-encompassing "Resistance Society."[3]

The perception of absolute Shiʿi unity and political homogeneity in Lebanon remains powerfully stubborn. But the polarized concepts of unity and diversity or loyalty and betrayal remain crucial sites of contestation and struggle within the Shiʿi milieu. Meanwhile, regional geopolitical developments and local intrasectarian squabbling continue to shape the landscape of Lebanese politics. In the wake of the Syrian withdrawal from Lebanon—to say nothing of the dramatic destabilization and massive human casualties caused by the 2006 war—persistent uncertainties continued to cast a pall over the country. While the Shiʿi community closed ranks still further, cracks in the façade of Hizballah's renewed dominance were discernible even during that summer.[4] Although historians are by no means in the business of predicting which direction a community or a country is likely to turn, nor should it be their responsibility to do so, at least one thing is clear: Lebanese Shiʿi political culture has historically been characterized by diversity and dynamism, and there is no reason to believe that this will not continue to be the case. Shiʿism in Lebanon cannot be reduced to unitary definitions—Islamist, revolutionary, iconoclastic, quietist, or Resistant—especially in light of the extent to which Lebanese Shiʿi identity, politics, and culture were transformed and have evolved throughout the twentieth century.[5]

Shiʿi political culture has adapted in tandem with broader changes in Lebanon. In February 2009, Lebanese Minister of the Interior Ziad Baroud issued a memorandum permitting Lebanese citizens to have their religious affiliation—their formal sectarian identity—removed from their civil registry records, on the heels of similar decisions that had already been implemented regarding passports and national ID cards. One painful historical irony of such a decision resides in the fact that the so-called "war of identities" of 1975–1976, to take just one dark example, would have been practically impossible and nearly unthinkable had such decisions been taken earlier, or if sectarian affiliation hadn't been institutionalized as a social fact in Lebanese identity cards and elsewhere in the first place. Implausibly, one spearheader of this recent campaign against sectarian identification was Husayn al-Husayni, one of the earliest supporters and allies of Imam Musa al-Sadr in calling for the empowerment of the Shi'i community in Lebanon, and among the earliest elected officials within the institutional structure of the SISC. From 1984 until 1991, that is, during the tumultuous later years of the Lebanese civil war and even after the conclusion of the Ta'if Agreement, al-Husayni was Speaker of the Lebanese Parliament, the so-called "third presidency" and the most powerful position designated for a Shi'i Muslim within the government. More recently, al-Husayni has turned his attention to the matter of reforming the Lebanese national civil code, with the support of an NGO called the Civil Center for National Initiative.[6]

"A sect must dominate or be dominated, or withdraw from the game," is an all too common way of interpreting how sectarianism functioned in the context of the bloody Lebanese civil wars.[7] Sectarianism is often also interpreted in this manner in the context of contemporary Lebanese politics, which might be understood as the continuation of the civil wars by other means. But what if every Lebanese sect concurrently acted to "withdraw from the game"? The scenario is far-fetched, but perhaps useful as a thought experiment, especially insofar as it allows for meditation on the meanings of sect and sectarianism as well as hinting at the utter futility of "the game." Over the course of the twentieth century, the stakes of sectarianism could be better defined by less dire, less violent metaphor than that of bloody "game" or communal "domination." The fields of law, religious culture, and community institutionalization were brought to bear upon questions of existence, empowerment, and effectiveness in the Lebanese Shi'i milieu during the first half of the twentieth century. This book has demonstrated that Shi'i sectarian identity in Lebanon was fundamentally transformed during the periods of French Mandate rule and early independence through interlocking processes of gradual change.

Collaboration and contract, therefore, and not unstinting "resistance," have distinguished a broad spectrum of Lebanese Shi'i encounters with the state and state power. The 1950s and 1960s witnessed the earliest signs of what is now called Lebanese Shi'i mobilization, a phenomenon that would help to create the conditions of possibility for the subsequent radicalization of the community during the Lebanese civil wars. To be sure, the Lebanese civil wars and successive instances of Israeli aggression and occupation—to say nothing of other forms of external intervention—also influenced the process of Shi'i radicalization in Lebanon. But neither the "mobilization" nor the "radicalization" of the Shi'i community is comprehensible without some understanding of the processes and practices that contributed to the transformation of Shi'i sectarianism during the Mandate period.

An adequate understanding of the historical evolution of sectarianism in Lebanon demands and deserves more thoughtful, more nuanced approaches to the history of Shi'i Lebanon than have been proffered up to now. Sectarian sentiment within the Shi'i milieu—which all too easily seems to discursively metastasize into full-blown sectarian rancor, discord, or violence—continues to be misdiagnosed as a "new" Lebanese malady.[8] The romance of the Shi'i awakening endures. Perhaps even more problematic than the notion that Shi'i presence in Lebanon only became legible and visible following the rise of Imam Musa al-Sadr and his Movement of the Deprived, however, is the insinuation that the history of the Shi'i community in Lebanon is only discernible through the lens of contemporary political Shi'ism, global political trends, or the influence of the Iranian Revolution. The flip side of this argument, namely, that quiescence and passivity characterized the community in the "pre-Musa al-Sadr" period, has also had its allure. Pierre Rondot, the mid-century French legal scholar, wrote that the Shi'i community in Lebanon, "long disorganized, has only found legal existence and autonomous religious organization under the Lebanese Republic." Not coincidentally, Rondot linked this institutionalized "legal existence" to questions of social organization and population counts. Even if the Shi'i community in Lebanon could claim to constitute "a vigorous race" in his opinion, Rondot also pointed how, as of 1947, Shi'i "religious leaders play no more than a modest role in public life. The great majority of Shiites live outside Lebanon, in Iran and Iraq, where their religious and cultural centers are found."[9]

The mainspring of Lebanese history may well remain the problem of sectarianism, but the making of sectarian Lebanon has been and will remain historically contingent. The adjudication of personal status law and the public practice of religious ritual in a multisectarian environment such as Lebanon generate certain points of tension and contention, both within a particular community and in relation to other sectarian communities. Therefore, the dialectical dilemma of Lebanese history—continuity and change, sameness and difference, intolerance and broadmindedness— would not be eliminated by the stroke of a pen redistricting sectarian political apportionment, nor could it be lastingly resolved through a war of all against all in which sectarianism were mapped crudely onto space, place, territory, or identity. The social and cultural history of Shi'i Lebanon during the Mandate period illustrates the extent to which sectarianism in Lebanon requires maintenance and work, accomplished through both practical and discursive means.

Lebanese sectarianism, or, more appropriately, the sectarianisms of Lebanon's diverse communities and milieus, is neither a naturally occurring phenomenon nor a packaged product nefariously foisted upon the Lebanese people. Lebanese sectarianism is neither the epiphenomenal root of all evil nor the inevitable outcome of colonial, nationalist, or irredentist recapitulations of religion. Rather, local and ground-level aspirations for recognition, autonomy, and power on the part of political strivers, religious leaders, and ordinary people were articulated even as the modernizing Mandate state attempted to implement tactics of divide and rule that would fix Lebanese society in sectarian blocs and create a newfangled sectarian political geography in the process. The fact that the construction of sectarian institutions and the formation of political identities in Lebanon have been so productive and destructive at the same time is one of the tragic ironies of the making of Lebanese sectarianism. On the one hand, the generation of sectarian solidarity reinforces social and cultural connection, strengthening the foundation of sectarian society. On the other hand, the reproduction of sectarian institutions, boundaries, and practices reinforces social and cultural division, weakening the foundations of national unity without necessarily disrupting the pull of nationalism altogether. While the renovation of sectarian forms of identification in Lebanon need not be misconstrued as the invention or innovation of sectarianism as such, there is some value in attending to the ways in which sectarianism in twentieth-century Lebanon has been transformed and rearticulated over time. The tension between subtle and overt expressions of sectarianism represents one of the fundamental paradoxes of Lebanese sectarianism that started to become apparent during the period of French Mandate rule.

This book explains the making of Shiʻi sectarianism in Lebanon in terms of a gradual historical process of transformation, one that has gone on for much longer than was previously recognized. Lebanese Shiʻi sectarianization needs to be attributed, for one thing, to French colonial privileging of sectarian and subnational modes of identification, which could serve as political wedges against anti-colonial resistance bridging sectarian or national divides. I have called this tendency—including both attempts at "divide and rule" as well as certain deployments of the French *politique des races*—"sectarianization from above." Writing shortly after Lebanese independence, Joseph Abouchedid proudly argued that the reason for the "failure" of the Mandate system was a misunderstanding by the French of the "evolved and civilized" nature of the Lebanese and Syrian "elite." Hence, the French Mandate authorities dealt with local elites as inappropriately "as if they were dealing with the Atlas Tribes or the Blacks of the Sudan."[10] On the other hand, Shiʻis from South Lebanon and Beirut exercised historical agency in articulating demands for greater rights and representation for their community even as they were becoming more conscious of that marker of affiliation through juridical and religious practice. I have termed such popular and parliamentary pressures "sectarianization from below." In this regard, Susan Pedersen somewhat overstates the global dimension of the Mandate system at the expense of local events, arguing, "the mandates system had some impact on the inhabitants of the mandates as well . . . [but] this impact was less on the manner in which inhabitants were governed or on the timetable to self-government than on their appropriation (or "learning") of transnational political practices."[11]

One paradox of Lebanese Shiʻi society during the Mandate period—insofar as this historical moment offers insights into Lebanese sectarianism in practice and the administration of Mandate rule in general—is that inclusion within the Lebanese sectarian-national milieu was in some ways more restrictive and in other ways more empowering than remaining on the margins. Shiʻi marginality was built into the sectarian-national framework developed under French Mandate; some structural impediments to Shiʻi national integration were cemented during this period. That their more intimate participation in the multisectarian regime tended to result in the erasure of cultural, religious, or political singularity is one of the great ironies of modern Lebanese history. The historical evolution of communal institutions, such as the Ja'fari court, pointed up the process of Shi'i institutionalization that only gradually became visible. The contested process of staffing and administering the Lebanese Ja'fari court illustrated how fraught the process of communal institutionalization was with respect to issues of power, access, and status. Concomitantly, entrenched cultural and political representations of "the Shi'a" and "Shi'i" parts of the country acquired increasingly fixed connotations in the national vernacular. Some historians have argued that the Ja'fari court was a relatively unimportant institution because it didn't play a consistently large public role in Lebanese politics or political culture. Even a judge at the Ja'fari court in Beirut claimed that the court had a "minimal influence" on the course of Lebanese Shi'i life during the Mandate period, arguing that the SISC represented the first Shi'i institution to play a significant role in the life of the community.[12]

Indeed, the establishment of the SISC in 1969 is often perceived as the most important episode in the crystallization of Lebanese Shi'i society, on the one hand, and the irrevocable integration of the realm of Shi'i autonomy into the apparatus of the state, on the other hand. But Hani Fahs reminds us that the Shi'i milieu underwent institutional integration into the Lebanese state much earlier. "And so it was," Fahs writes, "that the Shi'a found themselves, with the beginning of the modern state in Lebanon, up against a perplexing choice." On the one hand, "they had to demonstrate additional acceptance of the state, exemplified by their early entrance into its institutions, [both] political and administrative (the *shari'a* courts are an example of a realm more sensitive than others)." But, on the other hand, the Shi'i community also "had to prove their worthiness of that entrance in terms of loyalty and qualifications, so they lined up in defense of the state and the nation." Meanwhile, they also "lined up" in "the process of building [the state]." Somehow, amidst all of this, the Shi'i community remained integrated within "their Arab and Islamic and Shi'i context," connected to Arab nationalist interests but also committed to the national state, the homeland and political participation, linked to universalist faith but bound by sectarian obligation. Fahs argues that Shi'i "minoritarian feeling" (*shu'ur aqlawi*) trailed into retreat, regulated by the extent to which the state attended to the community, accepted them, and, finally, opened the doors to civic and national participation. "Those doors opened wider ever since independence, [but] very slowly, which has only recently turned over into incredible speed and leaps forward *(indifa'at)* that must be considered with precision and realism and long-term vision."[13]

The SISC was formally established over the summer of 1969, after at least two years of political wrangling and what *al-'Irfan* termed "difficult birth pangs." The journal called for immediate elections to be held in order to form an executive council under the oversight of the Speaker of the Lebanese Parliament, the "Third President" Sabri Hamadeh. Although Imam Musa al-Sadr was praised for "his intelligence, brilliance, learning, grace and activism," the journal also insisted that members of this council be drawn from the ranks of the most reputable religious scholars, including Shaykh Muhammad Taqi al-Faqih, Shaykh Musa 'Izz al-Din, Shaykh Muhammad Jawad Mughniyya, Shaykh Muhammad Mahdi Shams al-Din, and one Sayyid Muhammad Husayn Fadlallah.[14] Indeed, not everyone was optimistic that Imam Musa al-Sadr could singlehandedly bundle together and push forward the interests of the entire community.[15] Nevertheless, once these administrative loose ends had been sewn up, President Charles Helou and Imam Musa al-Sadr held a joint press conference certifying the national credentials of this new organization—referred to at one point as the "Ja'fari Dar al-Ifta'"—and of the Shi'i community more broadly. Al-Sadr spoke on behalf of

all children of the Shi'i Islamic sect in Lebanon who have never differed in their national and patriotic obligation. With absolute pride and confidence and hope I say that we are now more prepared [than ever] to bear all of our national responsibilities in order to safeguard the independence and freedom of Lebanon and the security of its territory, whatever sacrifices that requires and however expensive the cost.

"Whoever thinks," al-Sadr continued, "that the existence of different sects in Lebanon and the administration of the matters of these sects are causes of weakness in nationalist and patriotic feelings looks at this matter from a narrow view."[16] President Charles Helou affirmed the satisfaction that he and the entire Lebanese Republic found with the fact that "your sect" has adequately demonstrated its "loyalty" and "honesty": "What is this homeland *(watan)* but a single family united by its belief in the one God, the Lord who has neither description nor limit . . . united also by its faith in the spiritual values that are the best foundation for this homeland *(watan)* in particular."[17]

The institutionalization of the SISC signified both another logical advance in the development of Shi'i institutions in Lebanon as well as the stirrings of a new phase of transnational Shi'i cooperation and collaboration. Social and political relationships within the Shi'i milieu during the Mandate and early independence periods were far from stagnant. In brief, by the time the Shi'i community had been displaced, reorganized, and mobilized under the leadership of the charismatic Imam Musa al-Sadr, there were already institutional foundations in place for the communal leadership to rely upon. Within the Shi'i milieu, the Ja'fari court had once been *primus inter pares*. Mounzer Jaber convincingly argues that historians can consider 1926 as the moment of "the fashioning of the contract of the Shi'a with Lebanon."[18] But if 1926 was a turning point in the development of autonomous Shi'i institutions within the purview of the colonial state that heralded the emergence of a new phase in the social, religious and political history of the Lebanese Shi'a, the institutionalization of the SISC in 1969 constituted its high water mark. It is difficult, though by no means impossible, to imagine the foundation of an institution such as the SISC without the fundamental transformations in Lebanese Shi'i life brought about by the organizing and speechifying of al-Imam Musa al-Sadr. It is similarly disingenuous to presume that such a popular mobilization could have taken root without the sweeping institutional and social transformations traced throughout this book.

Rather than viewing the establishment of the SISC as the most radical innovation in the administration of Lebanese Shi'i communal affairs during the twentieth century, therefore, it would be more historically accurate to think of the institution as emblematic of the longer-term transformation of the Shi'i community from an unrecognized heterodox community into a formally recognized sectarian minority. The template for conflicted relations between the Lebanese state and Shi'i society was created under French Mandate rule. The construction of a specific kind of Shi'i sectarianism during this period was contingent on the development of institutions and cultural practices that were both productive of and restrictive concerning the possibilities for Shi'i empowerment, identification, and promotion. A hodgepodge of social, political, and cultural forces shaped the formation of Shi'i self-understanding and cultural and political identities over the first several decades of the twentieth century. All of this took place well before the arrival of Musa al-Sadr and the emergence of his Movement of the Deprived onto the scene, well before the explosion of the "belt of misery" surrounding Beirut, well before the outbreak of bloody civil conflict in Lebanon, and well before the unfolding of an increasingly tragic and hyper-militarized Arab–Israeli conflict. The contention that "Lebanese Shi'i expression took on a sectarian character from the mid-1970s—a development consonant with the increasing militancy of Lebanon's other major communities at a time when the country was disintegrating" is only partially true, in fact, insofar as late twentieth-century Shi'i political mobilization and subsequent radicalization represented a great leap forward for Lebanese Shi'i sectarian expression, but this shift is better understood as one of multitude, magnitude or intensity than of kind.[19]

The discursive and institutional practices contributing to the making of sectarian Shi'i Lebanon—viewed in this book through the lens of religious practice and personal status law—may also shed light on the problem of sectarianism in other world-historical contexts. The complicated historical relationships among the sovereignty of the state, the nation, and the sect are just beginning to be explored. The subsumption of sectarian autonomy under the umbrella of personal status jurisdiction was not perceived to threaten, but rather to bolster, the legitimacy of the sectarian-national state. Among the difficulties resulting from this institutional landscape was the absence of effective mechanisms for ensuring the preeminence of the state over the communities, or at least a more equitable balance of power among these actors. The maintenance and management of state and para-state institutions in Lebanon would have required a level of vigilance and enforcement on the part of the central state authorities that proved unattainable, as well as a rationalized understanding of overlapping regimes of power—juridical, religious, familial, and political—that could not be simultaneously enforced. It is in this sense, moreover, that the "triumph" of sectarianism over nationalism or internationalism later in the twentieth century appears less strange. It need not be understood as inevitable or irreversible, however.

Certain forms of modernity in Lebanon are sectarian; by the same token, sectarianism in Lebanon is a thoroughly modern phenomenon. But a corollary set of principles needs to be derived in order to establish some of the ways in which Lebanese nationalism, citizenship, and democracy are correspondingly sectarian. Moreover, if modern Lebanese sectarianism has been made, it can certainly also be unmade. Like the making of Lebanese sectarianism, though, the unmaking would inevitably hinge on complex institutional and discursive transformations as well as profound reconceptualizations and reformulations of deeply entrenched systems of law, ideology, and culture. This most difficult task of imagining and building an alternative, non- or trans-sectarian social and political framework would work against many of the inertial forces now hegemonic in Lebanese political, cultural, and civic life. Such an agenda, moreover, would have to be addressed to restructuring educational, media, political, and legal institutions, all the while showing respect for alternative modes of identification and associational life—besides and beyond the sectarian. This would demand no less than thoughtful creativity, sustained engagement, and collective action, to say nothing of unprecedented vision and courage, on the part of individuals and institutions scattered across the landscape of Lebanese society and culture.

ABBREVIATIONS

NOTES

BIBLIOGRAPHY

ACKNOWLEDGMENTS

INDEX

Abbreviations

AUB	American University of Beirut
BIH	Bulletin d'Information Hebdomaire
BSOAS	*Bulletin of the School of Oriental and African Studies*
CHEAM	Centre des Hautes Études sur l'Afrique et l'Asie Modernes
CSSAAME	*Comparative Studies of South Asia, Africa and the Middle East*
CSSH	*Comparative Studies in Society and History*
IJMES	*International Journal of Middle East Studies*
MAE-Nantes	Ministère Français des Affaires Étrangères, Centre des Archives Diplomatiques de Nantes
MJB	Al-Mahkama al-shar'iyya al-ja'fariyya fi Bayrut (Ja'fari *shari'a* court, Beirut)
MJN	Al-Mahkama al-shar'iyya al-ja'fariyya fi Nabatiyya (Ja'fari *shari'a* court, Nabatiyya)
MJS	Al-Mahkama al-shar'iyya al-ja'fariyya fi Sayda (Ja'fari *shari'a* court, Sidon)
MJT	Al-Mahkama al-shar'iyya al-ja'fariyya fi Sur (Ja'fari *shari'a* court, Tyre)
MT	Mahkamat al-tamyiz (Higher Ja'fari Court)
SISC	Supreme Islamic Shi'i Council

Notes

Note on Transliteration and Translation

Throughout this book Arabic has been transliterated according to a simplified version of the system employed by the *International Journal of Middle East Studies*. For the benefit of non-specialists, all diacritics have been omitted, with the exception of 'ayn (') and hamza ('). Common English forms of places, names and terms are used instead of the Arabic or the French when appropriate (i.e. Beirut not Bayrut or Beyrouth; Munir 'Usayran not Mounir Osseiran; and Shi'ism not *al-tashayyu'*). Adherents of the faith called Shi'ism are alternatively referred to in the plural as Shi'a or as belonging to the Shi'i community whereas individuals are Shi'i Muslims or Shi'is. All translations from Arabic and French, unless otherwise noted, are my own.

Prologue—Shi'ism, Sectarianism, Modernity

1. Mohammad Soueid, "Omar Amiralay, the Circassian, Syrian, Lebanese," in Rasha Salti, ed., *Insights into Syrian Cinema: Essays and Conversations with Contemporary Filmmakers* (New York: Rattapallax Press, 2006), 100. The interview was originally published in Arabic in *Mulhaq al-Nahar,* April 10, 1993. To be sure, such ignorance was far from unique or uncommon around the world, even decades later. See, for example, Jeff Stein, "Can You Tell A Sunni from a Shiite?" *The New York Times,* October 17, 2006.

2. Muhammad Jawad Mughniyya, "Munaqashat al-majlis fi al-huquq al-ta'ifiyya," *al-'Irfan* Vol. 49, No. 10 (June 1962), 1015.

3. *Al-Hawadith,* 7 October 1966, reprinted in Ya'qub Dahir, *Masirat al-Imam al-Sayyid Musa al-Sadr: yawmiyyat wa-watha'iq Vol. 1: 1960–1968* (Beirut: Harakat Amal, Hay'at al-Ri'asa, 2000), 233.

4. Mas'ud Dahir, *Lubnan: al-istiqlal, al-mithaq wa-l-sigha* (Beirut: Ma'ahad al-Inma' al-'Arabi, 1977), esp. 221–223 and 363–368. For another positive assessment of "constructive" Lebanese sectarianism from a different angle, see Kamal Yusuf

Hajj, *al-Ta'ifiyya al-banna'a aw falsafat al-mithaq al-watani* (Beirut: Matba'at al-Rahbaniyya, 1961).

5. For a variety of reasons, this book does not deal extensively with the Shi'i milieu in the Biqa' Valley (Baalbek and Hirmil). But see, for example, 'Aida Zayn al-Din, *al-Tatawwur al-iqtisadi wa-l-ijtima'i wa-l-siyasi li-madinat Ba'labakk fi 'ahd al-intidab al-faransi 1920–1943* (Beirut: Dar al-Farabi, 2005).

6. Robert Fisk, "Who's Running Lebanon?" *The Independent* online, December 15, 2006, http://www.independent.co.uk/opinion/commentators/fisk/robert-fisk-whos-running-lebanon-428530.html (first accessed 12/16/06; last accessed 12/6/09); and J. Darché, *Les chiites du Liban,* Rapport N° 108 du CHEAM (1937), 8.

7. A list of notable exceptions might include: Muhammad Qasim Zaman, "Sectarianism in Pakistan: The Radicalization of Shi'i and Sunni Identities," *Modern Asian Studies* Vol. 32, No. 3 (1998): 689–716; Ussama Makdisi, *The Culture of Sectarianism: Community, History and Violence in Nineteenth-Century Ottoman Lebanon* (Berkeley and Los Angeles: University of California Press, 2000); and Eugene L. Rogan, "Sectarianism and Social Conflict in Damascus: The 1860 Events Reconsidered," *Arabica: Revue d'études arabes* Vol. 51, No. 4 (2004): 493–511.

8. Israel Friedlaender, "Jewish-Arabic Studies I. Shiitic Elements in Jewish Sectarianism," *The Jewish Quarterly Review* Vol. 1, No. 2 (1910), 189. See also Friedlaender, *The Heterodoxies of the Shiites in the Presentation of Ibn Hazm* (New Haven: [s.n.], 1909); Marshall G. S. Hodgson, *The Order of Assassins: The Struggle of the Early Nizârî Ismâ'îlis Against the Islamic World* (The Hague: Mouton, 1955); Bernard Lewis, *The Assassins: A Radical Sect in Islam* (London: Weidenfeld and Nicolson, 1972 [1967]); and John E. Wansbrough, *The Sectarian Milieu: Content and Composition of Islamic Salvation History* (New York: Oxford University Press, 1978).

9. Marshall Hodgson, "How Did the Early Shi'a Become Sectarian?" *Journal of the American Oriental Society* 75 (1) (1955), 12. See also Devin J. Stewart, *Islamic Legal Orthodoxy: Twelver Shiite Responses to the Sunni Legal System* (Salt Lake City: University of Utah Press, 1998); and Peri Bearman, Rudolph Peters and Frank E. Vogel, eds., *The Islamic School of Law: Evolution, Devolution, and Progress* (Cambridge, Mass.: Islamic Legal Studies Program, Harvard Law School: Distributed by Harvard University Press, 2005).

10. Mounzer Jaber, "Pouvoir et société au Jabal 'Amil de 1749 à 1920 dans la conscience des chroniques chiites et dans un essai d'interpretation" (Thèse de 3ᵉ Cycle, Université de Paris IV, 1978); Jaber, "al-Kiyan al-siyasi li-Jabal 'Amil qabla 1920," in Ibrahim Beydoun, ed., *Safahat min tarikh Jabal 'Amil* (Beirut: al-Majlis al-Thaqafi li-Lubnan al-Janubi, 1979); 'Ali Ibrahim Darwish, *Jabal 'Amil bayna 1516–1697: al-hayat al-siyasiyya wa-l-thaqafiyya* (Beirut: Dar al-Hadi, 1993); Haydar Rida al-Rakini, *Jabal 'Amil fi qarn (1163–1247 H/1749–1832 M)* (Beirut: Dar al-Fikr al-Lubnani, 1997); and Ja'far Muhajir, *Jabal 'Amil bayna al-shahidayn:*

al-haraka al-fikriyya fi Jabal ʿAmil fi qarnayn (min awasit al-qarn al-thamin li-l-hijra/al-rabʿ ʿashr li-l-milad hatta awasit al-qarn al-ʿashr/al-sadis ʿashr) (Damascus: IFPO, 2005).

11. Albert Hourani, "From Jabal ʿAmil to Persia," *BSOAS* Vol. 49, No. 1 (1986): 133–140; Jaʿfar Muhajir, *al-Hijra al-ʿamiliyya ila Iran fi al-ʿasr al-safawi: asbabuha al-tarikhiyya wa-nataʾijuha al-thaqafiyya wa-l-siyasiyya* (Beirut: Dar al-Rawda, 1989); and Rula Jurdi Abisaab, *Converting Persia: Religion and Power in the Safavid Empire* (London: I. B. Tauris, 2004). But also cf. Andrew J. Newman, "The Myth of the Clerical Migration to Safawid Iran: Arab Shiite Opposition to ʿAli al-Karaki and Safawid Shiism," *Die Welt des Islams* Vol. 33, No. 1 (Apr. 1993): 66–112.

12. But see the following essays in *La Shiʾa nell'impero ottomano* (Rome: Accademia nazionale dei Lincei; Fondazione Leone Caetani, 1993): Abdul-Rahim Abu Husayn, "The Shiites in Lebanon and the Ottomans in the 16th and 17th Centuries," 107–119; C. Edmund Bosworth, "Bahaʾ al-Din al-ʿAmili in the Two Worlds of the Ottomans and the Safavids," 85–105; and Marco Salati, "Toleration, Persecution and Local Realities: Observations on Shiism in the Holy Places and the *Bilad Al-Sham* (16th–17th Centuries)," 121–148. See also Stefan H. Winter, "Shiite Emirs and Ottoman Authorities: The Campaign Against the Hamadas of Mt Lebanon, 1693–1694," *Archivum Ottomanicum* 18 (2000): 209–245; and Winter, ""Un lys dans des épines": Maronites et Chiites au Mont Liban, 1698–1763," *Arabica: Revue d'études arabes* Vol. 51, No. 4 (2004): 478–492.

13. Maurus Reinkowski, *Ottoman 'Multiculturalism'? The Example of the Confessional System in Lebanon* (Beirut, 1999), 13. Among the voluminous literature on the *millet* system, see, for example, Benjamin Braude, "Founding Myths of the Millet System," in Benjamin Braude and Bernard Lewis, eds., *Christians and Jews in the Ottoman Empire: The Functioning of a Plural Society* (New York: Holmes & Meier Publishers, 1982), 69–88; and Aron Rodrigue, "From *Millet* to Minority: Turkish Jewry," in Pierre Birnbaum and Ira Katznelson, eds., *Paths of Emancipation: Jews, States, and Citizenship* (Princeton, N.J.: Princeton University Press, 1995), 238–61.

14. Rudolph Peters, "What Does It Mean to Be an Offical Madhhab? Hanafism and the Ottoman Empire," in Peri Bearman, Rudolph Peters, and Frank E. Vogel, eds., *The Islamic School of Law: Evolution, Devolution, and Progress* (Cambridge, Mass.: Islamic Legal Studies Program, Harvard Law School; Distributed by Harvard University Press, 2005), 157.

15. Carol Hakim-Dowek, "The Origins of the Lebanese National Idea, 1840–1914" (D. Phil., University of Oxford, 1997). I would like to thank Carol Hakim for clarifying this point for me. See also Samir Khalaf, *Civil and Uncivil Violence in Lebanon: A History of the Internationalization of Communal Conflict* (New York: Columbia University Press, 2002), 275–277.

16. Leila Fawaz, *Merchants and Migrants in Nineteenth-century Beirut* (Cambridge, Mass.: Harvard University Press, 1983); Engin Akarlı, *The Long Peace: Ottoman Lebanon, 1861–1920* (Berkeley and Los Angeles: University of California Press, 1993); and Jens Hanssen, *Fin-de-Siècle Beirut: The Making of an Ottoman Provincial Capital* (Oxford: Oxford University Press, 2005). Thanks to Jens Hanssen for pointing out how even as "Beirut became administratively independent from Damascus" the city and its leaderships "'self-centralized' their domain," and for reminding me that "no matter where and when you locate 'the origins of the confessional system'," historians need to be careful not to conclude that such designation works to "overdetermine its subsequent adoption." Personal communication, November 30, 2009.

17. The historical literature on the Mandate system is vast. See, for example, Philip S. Khoury, *Syria and the French Mandate: The Politics of Arab Nationalism, 1920–1945* (Princeton, N.J.: Princeton University Press, 1987); Elizabeth Thompson, *Colonial Citizens: Republican Rights, Paternal Privilege and Gender in French Syria and Lebanon* (New York: Columbia University Press, 2000); Nadine Méouchy, ed., *France, Syrie et Liban 1918–1946: les ambiguïtés et les dynamiques de la relation mandataire* (Damascus: IFEAD, 2002); Jean-David Mizrahi, *Genèse de l'état mandataire: service des renseignements et bandes armées en Syrie et au Liban dans les années 1920.* (Paris: Publications de la Sorbonne, 2003); Nadine Méouchy and Peter Sluglett, eds., *The British and French Mandates in Comparative Perspectives* (Leiden: Brill, 2004); and Susan Pedersen, "The Meaning of the Mandates System: An Argument," *Geschichte und Gesellschaft* 32 (2006): 560–582.

18. Yitzhak Nakash, *The Shi'is of Iraq* (Princeton, N.J.: Princeton University Press, 1994); Madawi al-Rasheed, "The Shia of Saudi Arabia: A Minority in Search of Cultural Authenticity," *British Journal of Middle Eastern Studies* 25, No. 1 (1998): 121–138; Rainer Brunner and Werner Ende, eds., *The Twelver Shia in Modern Times: Religious Culture and Political History* (Leiden: Brill, 2002); Juan Cole, *Sacred Space and Holy War: The Politics, Culture and History of Shi'ite Islam* (London: I. B. Tauris, 2002); Nakash, *Reaching for Power: The Shi'a in the Modern Arab World* (Princeton, N.J.: Princeton University Press, 2006); Vali Nasr, *The Shia Revival: How Conflicts Within Islam Will Shape the Future* (New York: Norton, 2006); Liyakat N. Takim, *The Heirs of the Prophet: Charisma and Religious Authority in Shi'ite Islam* (Albany, NY: State University of New York Press, 2006); Maria Massi Dakake, *The Charismatic Community: Shi'ite Identity in Early Islam* (Albany, NY: State University of New York, 2007); Sabrina Mervin, ed., *Les mondes chiites et l'Iran* (Paris: Karthala, 2007); and Alessandro Monsutti, Silvia Naef and Farian Sabahi, eds., *The Other Shiites: From the Mediterranean to Central Asia* (Bern: Peter Lang, 2007).

19. Rogan, "Sectarianism and Social Conflict in Damascus," 510.

20. Mahdi 'Amil, *Fi al-dawla al-ta'ifiyya* (Beirut: Dar al-Farabi, 1989), 18.

21. Khalaf, *Civil and Uncivil Violence in Lebanon*, 27.

22. Roshanack Shaery-Eisenlohr, "Constructing Lebanese Shi'ite Nationalism: Transnationalism, Shi'ism, and the Lebanese State" (PhD diss., University of Chicago, 2005), 36–37. See also Shaery-Eisenlohr, *Shi'ite Lebanon: Transnational Religion and the Making of National Identities* (New York: Columbia University Press, 2008); and Axel Havemann, "Historiography in 20th-Century Lebanon: Between Confessional Identity and National Coalescence," *Bulletin of the Royal Institute for Inter-Faith Studies* 4(2) (2002): 49–69. S. V. R. Nasr makes an analogous claim for understanding sectarianism in Pakistan, arguing that, "at its core, sectarianism is a form of religio-political nationalism, and as such, our examination of its root causes are [sic] directly related to discussions of identity mobilization and ethnic conflict." Nasr, "Islam, the State and the Rise of Sectarian Militancy in Pakistan," in Christophe Jaffrelot, ed., *Pakistan: Nationalism Without a Nation?* (New Delhi and Manohar: Centre de Sciences Humaines; London and New York: Zed Books; New York: Distributed in the USA exclusively by Palgrave, 2002), 87.

23. Rogers Brubaker and Frederick Cooper, "Beyond 'Identity'," *Theory and Society* Vol. 29, No. 1 (Feb., 2000): 1–47.

24. Clyde G. Hess, Jr. and Herbert L. Bodman, Jr. "Confessionalism and Feudality in Lebanese Politics," *Middle East Journal* Vol. 8, No. 1 (1954), 22, 25.

25. Michael Hudson, *The Precarious Republic: Political Modernization in Lebanon* (New York: Random House, 1968), 25.

26. Jamal R. Nassar, "Sectarian Political Cultures: The Case of Lebanon," *The Muslim World* Vol. 85, No. 3–4 (1995), 247.

27. Ibid., 246.

28. C. A. Bayly, "The Pre-History of 'Communalism'? Religious Conflict in India, 1700–1860," *Modern Asian Studies* Vol. 19, No. 2 (1985): 177–203; Juan R. I. Cole, *Roots of North Indian Shi'ism in Iran and Iraq: Religion and State in Awadh, 1722–1859* (Berkeley and Los Angeles: University of California Press, 1989); Gyanendra Pandey, *The Construction of Communalism in Colonial North India* (Delhi and New York: Oxford University Press, 1990); Ayesha Jalal, "Exploding Communalism: The Politics of Muslim Identity in South Asia," in Sugata Bose and Ayesha Jalal, eds., *Nationalism, Democracy and Development: State and Politics in India* (Delhi: Oxford University Press, 1997), 76–103; Mushirul Hasan, "Traditional Rites and Contested Meanings: Sectarian Strife in Colonial Lucknow," in Mushirul Hasan, ed., *Islam, Communities and the Nation: Muslim Identities in South Asia and Beyond* (New Delhi: Manohar, 1998), 341–366; Zaman, "Sectarianism in Pakistan"; and Mariam Abou Zahab, "Sectarianism as a Substitute Identity: Sunnis and Shias in Central and South Punjab," in Soofia Mumtaz, Jean-Luc Racine and Imran Anwar Ali, eds., *Pakistan: The Contours of State and Society* (Oxford: Oxford University Press, 2002), 77–95.

29. 'Amil, *Fi al-dawla al-ta'ifiyya*, 17; Ussama Makdisi, "Revisiting Sectarianism," in Thomas Scheffler, ed., *Religion Between Violence and Reconciliation* (Beirut: Orient-Institut, 2002), 180; and the quotation is from John L. Gillin, "A Contribution

to the Sociology of Sects," *The American Journal of Sociology* Vol. 16, No. 2 (1910), 236. See also Fayez A. Sayigh, *al-Ta'ifiyya: bahth fi asbabiha wa-akhtariha wa-'ilajiha* (Beirut: Manshurat Maktabat al-Wajib, 1947); Anis Sayigh, *Lubnan al-ta'ifi* (Beirut: Dar al-Sira' al-Fikri, 1955); and Mas'ud Dahir, *al-Judhur al-tarikhiyya li-l-mas'ala al-ta'ifiyya al-lubnaniyya, 1697–1861* (Beirut: Ma'had al-Inma' al-'Arabi, 1981).

30. Makdisi, *The Culture of Sectarianism*, 6.

31. Ibid., 77.

32. Timothy Mitchell, "Preface," in Mitchell, ed., *Questions of Modernity* (Minneapolis: University of Minnesota Press, 2000), xi–xii.

33. David Martin, *The Religious and the Secular: Studies in Secularization* (New York: Schocken Books, 1969); Talal Asad, *Genealogies of Religion: Discipline and Reason in Medieval Christianity and Islam* (Baltimore: Johns Hopkins University Press, 1993); Aamir R. Mufti, "Secularism and Minority: Elements of a Critique," *Social Text* No. 45 (1995): 75–96; Gauri Viswanathan, *Outside the Fold: Conversion, Modernity, and Belief* (Princeton, N.J.: Princeton University Press, 1998); Derek R. Peterson and Darren R. Walhof, eds., *The Invention of Religion: Rethinking Belief in Politics and History* (New Brunswick, NJ: Rutgers University Press, 2002); Asad, *Formations of the Secular: Christianity, Islam, Modernity* (Stanford: Stanford University Press, 2003); Saba Mahmood, *Politics of Piety: The Islamic Movement and the Feminist Subject* (Princeton, N.J.: Princeton University Press, 2004); Tomoko Masuzawa, *The Invention of World Religions: Or, How European Universalism Was Preserved in the Language of Pluralism* (Chicago: University of Chicago Press, 2005); Charles Hirschkind and David Scott, eds., *Powers of the Secular Modern: Talal Asad and His Interlocutors* (Stanford, CA: Stanford University Press, 2006); and Anthony J. Carroll, S. J., *Protestant Modernity: Weber, Secularisation, and Protestantism* (Scranton: University of Scranton Press, 2007).

34. Jalal, "Exploding Communalism," 79.

35. The quote is from Pierre Rondot, *Les institutions politiques du Liban: des communautés traditionelles à l'état moderne* (Paris: Institut d'études de L'Orient contemporain, 1947), 21. See also Meir Zamir, *The Formation of Modern Lebanon* (Ithaca, NY: Cornell University Press, 1988); Zamir, *Lebanon's Quest: The Road to Independence* (London: I. B. Tauris, 2000); Kais M. Firro, *Inventing Lebanon: Nationalism and the State under the Mandate* (London: I. B. Tauris, 2003); and Asher Kaufman, *Reviving Phoenicia: The Search for Identity in Lebanon* (London: I. B. Tauris, 2004).

36. Kamal Salibi, *A House of Many Mansions: The History of Lebanon Reconsidered* (Berkeley and Los Angeles: University of California Press, 1988), 232.

37. Farid El-Khazen, *The Breakdown of the State in Lebanon, 1967–1976* (London: I. B. Tauris, 2002), 69.

38. Salibi, *A House of Many Mansions*, 206.

39. Ahmad Beydoun, *Identité confessionnelle et temps social chez les historiens libanaises contemporains* (Beirut: L'Université Libanaise, 1984), 582.

40. Mounzer Jaber, "al-Shi'a fi Jabal 'Amil bayna al-mabda'iyya wa-l-hifaz 'ala al-dhat," *al-Muntalaq* 105 (1993), 63. I am using the term "lachrymose" experimentally here, and in a way that is indebted to, but strays somewhat beyond, the original argument made in Mark R. Cohen, "The Neo-Lachrymose Conception of Jewish-Arab History," *Tikkun* Vol 6. No. 3 (May–June 1991): 55–60.

41. 'Ali al-Zayn, *Li-l-bahth 'an tarikhina fi Lubnan* (Beirut, 1973); al-Zayn, *Fusul min tarikh al-shi'a fi Lubnan* (Beirut: Dar al-Kalima li-l-Nashr, 1979); Beydoun, ed., *Safahat min tarikh Jabal 'Amil;* 'Ali 'Abd al-Mun'im Shu'ayb, *Matalib Jabal 'Amil: al-wahda, al-musawa fi Lubnan al-Kabir, 1900–1936* (Beirut: al-Mu'assasa al-Jam'iyya, 1987); and Nawal Fayyad, *Safahat min tarikh Jabal 'Amil fi al-'ahdayn al-'uthmani wa-l-faransi* (Beirut: Dar al-Jadid, 1998).

42. Talal Jaber, "Chiites et pouvoir politique au Liban 1967–1974: contribution à une approche socio-religieuse" (Thèse de 3ᵉ cycle, Université de Paris VII, 1980); 'Ali 'Abed Fattuni, "Tatawwur al-ta'lim fi madaris al-jam'iyya al-khayriyya al-islamiyya al-'amiliyya fi Bayrut min khilal watha'iqiha al-asliyya, 1923–1943" (PhD diss., Lebanese University, 1986); Hala Soubra, "La théorie de l'état dans la pensée chiite libanaise contemporaine" (DEA, Université de Paris I, Sorbonne, 1990); Muhammad Fattuni, "Tatawwur al-tarbiyya wa-l-ta'lim fi madaris al-jam'iyya al-khayriyya al-islamiyya al-'amiliyya min khilal watha'iqiha al-asliyya (1943–1975)" (PhD diss., Lebanese University, 1992); Hicham Jaber, "Les chiites dans la vie politique du Liban avant et après l'indépendance" (DEA, Université de Paris IV, 1993); Mustafa Muhammad Bazzi, *Jabal 'Amil fi muhitihi al-'arabi, 1864–1948* (Beirut: al-Majlis al-Islami al-Shi'i al-A'la, 1993); Bazzi, *al-Takamul al-iqtisadi bayna Jabal 'Amil wa muhitihi al-'arabi, 1850–1950* (Beirut: Dar al-Mawasim li-l-Tiba'a wa-l-Nashr wa-l-Tawzi', 2002); and Bazzi, *Jabal 'Amil wa tawabi'hu fi shamal Filastin (bahth fi tatawwur al-milkiyya al-'aqariyya)* (Beirut: Dar al-Mawasim, 2002).

43. Sulayman Taqi al-Din, "al-Janub al-lubnani bi-ri'ayat al-istiqlal," in Beydoun, ed., *Safahat min tarikh Jabal 'Amil,* 149, my emphasis.

44. Jean Lapierre, *Le mandat français en Syrie; origines, doctrine, exécution* (Paris: Librairie du Recueil Sirey, 1936), 69. See also Stephen Hemsley Longrigg, *Syria and Lebanon under French Mandate* (London: Oxford University Press, 1958); Khoury, *Syria and the French Mandate;* Marwan Buheiry, *Beirut's Role in the Political Economy of the French Mandate, 1919–1939* (Oxford: Centre for Lebanese Studies, 1992); Thompson, *Colonial Citizens;* Nadine Méouchy, ed., *France, Syrie et Liban 1918–1946;* Firro, *Inventing Lebanon;* Nadine Méouchy and Peter Sluglett, eds., *The French and British Mandates in Comparative Perspective;* and Keith David Watenpaugh, *Being Modern in the Middle East: Revolution, Nationalism, Colonialism, and the Arab Middle Class* (Princeton, N.J.: Princeton University Press, 2006). On Shi'ism in French Mandate Lebanon in particular, see Sabrina Mervin, *Un réformisme chiite: ulémas et lettrés du Ğabal 'Āmil (actuel Liban-Sud) de la fin de l'empire ottoman à l'indépendance du Liban*

(Paris: Éditions Karthala, CERMOC and IFEAD, 2000); Tamara Chalabi, *The Shi'is of Jabal 'Amil and the New Lebanon: Community and Nation-State, 1918–1943* (London: Palgrave Macmillan, 2006); Kais Firro, "The Shi'is in Lebanon: Between Communal *'Asabiyya* and Arab Nationalism, 1908–21," *Middle Eastern Studies* Vol. 42, No. 4 (July 2006): 535–550; and Firro, "Ethnicizing the Shi'is in Mandatory Lebanon," *Middle Eastern Studies* Vol. 42, No. 5 (September 2006): 741–759.

45. *Al-'Irfan* Vol. 26, No. 6 (October 1935), 465. For more on *al-'Irfan*, see Tarif Khalidi, "Shaykh Ahmad 'Arif al-Zayn and *al-'Irfan*," in Marwan R. Buheiry, ed., *Intellectual Life in the Arab East, 1890–1939* (Beirut: American University of Beirut, Center for Arab and Middle East Studies, 1981), 110–124; and Silvia Naef, "La presse en tant que moteur du renouveau culturel et litteraire: la revue chiite libanaise al-'Irfan," *Etudes asiatiques, revue de la societé Suisse-Asie* (1996): 385–397.

46. MAE-Nantes, Carton N° 1206, "Etat d'Esprit dans la Zone Frontière," Sûreté aux Armées, January 8, 1946.

47. Lewis, *The Assassins,* 139.

48. Makdisi, "Reconstructing the Nation-State: The Modernity of Sectarianism in Lebanon," *Middle East Report* no. 200 (Jul. –Sep., 1996), 25; and Fuad I. Khuri, *From Village to Suburb: Order and Change in Greater Beirut* (Chicago: University of Illinois Press, 1975), 201.

49. Hasan al-'Alawi, *al-Shi'a wa-l-dawla al-qawmiyya fi al-'Iraq 1914–1990* (Qum: Dar al-Thaqafa, 1991), 167. See also Pierre-Jean Luizard, *La formation de L'Irak contemporaine* (Paris: CNRS Editions, 1991); Chibli Mallat, *The Renewal of Islamic Law: Muhammad Baqer as-Sadr, Najaf and the Shi'i International* (Cambridge: Cambridge University Press, 1993); Nakash, *The Shi'is of Iraq;* Meir Litvak, *Shi'i Scholars of Nineteenth-Century Iraq: The 'Ulama' of Najaf and Karbala'* (Cambridge: Cambridge University Press, 1998); Nakash, "The Nature of Shi'ism in Iraq," in Faleh Abdul-Jabar, ed., *Ayatollahs, Sufis and Ideologues: State, Religion and Social Movements in Iraq* (London: Saqi Books, 2002), 23–35; and, on the diversity of Iraqi sectarian and non-sectarian identities, Orit Bashkin, *The Other Iraq: Pluralism and Culture in Hashemite Iraq* (Stanford, Calif: Stanford University Press, 2009).

50. Roger Owen, "The Political Economy of Grand Liban, 1920–1970," in Roger Owen, ed., *Essays on the Crisis in Lebanon* (London: Ithaca Press, 1976), 24. See also Ghassan Salamé, "'Strong' and 'Weak' States: A Qualified Return to the Muqaddimah," in Luciani Giacomo, ed., *The Arab State* (Berkeley and Los Angeles: University of California Press, 1990), 29–64; and Nazih Ayubi, *Over-stating the Arab State: Politics and Society in the Middle East* (London: I. B. Tauris, 1995).

51. Albert Hourani, "Ideologies of the Mountain and the City," in Owen, ed., *Essays on the Crisis in Lebanon,* 33–41; and Michael Johnson, *Class and Client in*

Beirut: The Sunni Muslim Community and the Lebanese State, 1840–1985 (London: Ithaca Press, 1986).

52. Paul Kingston, "Review of Kais Firro, *Inventing Lebanon: Nation and State under the Mandate,*" *MIT-Electronic Journal of Middle East Studies* (*MIT-EJMES*), December 2004 (http://web.mit.edu/cis/www/mitejmes/intro.htm; accessed 12/11/06).

53. George Steinmetz, "Introduction," in George Steinmetz, ed., *State/Culture: State-Formation After the Cultural Turn* (Ithaca, NY: Cornell University Press, 1999), 9.

54. See, for example, Michael Anderson, "Islamic Law and the Colonial Encounter in British India," in Chibli Mallat and Jane Connors, eds., *Islamic Family Law* (London: Graham and Trotman, 1993), 205–23; Nasser Hussain, *The Jurisprudence of Emergency: Colonialism and the Rule of Law* (Ann Arbor: University of Michigan Press, 2003); Tamara Loos, *Subject Siam: Family, Law, and Colonial Modernity in Thailand* (Ithaca, NY: Cornell University Press, 2006); Sally Engle Merry, *Colonizing Hawaii: The Cultural Power of Law* (Princeton, N.J.: Princeton University Press, 2000); David Murray, *Colonial Justice: Justice, Morality, and Crime in the Niagara District, 1791–1849* (Toronto: Published for the Osgoode Society for Canadian Legal History by University of Toronto Press, 2002); and Jeanne Maddox Toungara, "Inventing the African Family: Gender and Family Law Reform in Cote d'Ivoire," *Journal of Social History* 28, no. 1 (1994): 37–61.

55. Martin Chanock, *Law, Custom and Social Order: The Colonial Experience in Malawi and Zambia* (Cambridge: Cambridge University Press, 1985), 222.

56. Allan Christelow, *Muslim Law Courts and the French Colonial State in Algeria* (Princeton, N.J.: Princeton University Press, 1985), 14.

57. Dominique Sarr and Richard Roberts, "The Jurisdiction of Muslim Tribunals in Colonial Senegal, 1857–1932," in Kristin Mann and Richard Roberts, eds., *Law in Colonial Africa* (Portsmouth, NH: Heinemann, 1991), 141.

58. Emmanuelle Saada, "The Empire of Law: Dignity, Prestige, and Domination in the Colonial Situation," *French Politics, Culture and Society* Vol. 20, No. 2 (Summer 2002), 105.

59. Oussama Arabi, *Studies in Modern Islamic Law and Jurisprudence* (The Hague: Kluwer Law International, 2001), esp. 121–146.

60. Thompson, *Colonial Citizens,* 149.

61. J. N. D. Anderson, "Law as a Social Force in Islamic Culture and History," *BSOAS* 20 (1957), 40.

62. J. G. Assaf, *La compétence des tribunaux du statut personnel au Liban et en Syrie* (Beirut: Imprimerie Khalifé, 1935), 99.

63. Iris Agmon, *Family and Court: Legal Culture and Modernity in Late Ottoman Palestine* (Syracuse, NY: Syracuse University Press, 2006), 236.

64. Asad, *Formations of the Secular,* 227. See also Ziba Mir-Hosseini, *Marriage on Trial: A Study in Comparative Islamic Family Law* (London: I. B. Tauris, 1999);

and Arzoo Osanloo, "Islamico-civil "Rights Talk": Women, Subjectivity, and Law in Iranian Family Court," *American Ethnologist* Vol. 33, No, 2 (May 2006): 191–209.

65. The only two published exceptions I am aware of are: Mu'tamar li-tarikh madinat Sur, *Watha'iq al-mu'tamar al-awwal li-tarikh madinat Sur: min al-'ahd al-finiqi hatta al-qarn al-'ishrin* (15–16 Haziran 1996) (Tyre: Muntada Sur al-Thaqafi, 1996); and *Watha'iq al-mu'tamar al-thani li-tarikh madinat Sur: al-tarikh al-ijtima'i wa-l-iqtisadi fi mukhtalif al-hiqab al-tarikhiyya* (24–25 Ayyar 1997) (Tyre: Muntada Sur al-Thaqafi, 1998). See also Haydar Muhammad Karaki. "al-Khasa'is al-dimughrafiyya wa-l-ijtima'iyya li-zahiratay al-zawaj wa-l-talaq 'ind al-shi'a min khilal al-mahkama al-ja'fariyya fi Bayrut 1978–1982" (Master's thesis, Lebanese University, 1983).

66. A partial list of this literature that shapes my approach would have to include: Christelow, *Muslim Law Courts and the French Colonial State in Algeria;* Beshara Doumani, "Palestinian Islamic Court Records: A Source for Socioeconomic History," *MESA Bulletin* (1985): 155–172; Ron Shaham, *Family and the Courts in Modern Egypt: A Study Based on Decisions by the Shari'a Courts 1900–1955* (Leiden: Brill, 1997); Judith E. Tucker, *In the House of the Law: Gender and Islamic Law in Ottoman Syria and Palestine* (Berkeley and Los Angeles: University of California Press, 1998); Arabi, *Studies in Modern Islamic Law and Jurisprudence;* Najwa al-Qattan, "Litigants and Neighbors: The Communal Topography of Ottoman Damascus," *CSSH* Vol. 44, No. 3 (Jul., 2002): 511–533; Leslie P. Peirce, *Morality Tales: Law and Gender in the Ottoman Court of Aintab* (Berkeley and Los Angeles: University of California Press, 2003); Agmon, *Family and Court;* and Elyse Semerdjian, *"Off the Straight Path": Illicit Sex, Law, and Community in Ottoman Aleppo* (Syracuse, NY: Syracuse University Press, 2008). Muhammad 'Adnan al-Bakhit, *Kashshaf ihsa'i zamani li-sijillat al-mahakim al-shar'iyya wa-l-awqaf al-islamiyya fi bilad al-sham* (Amman: al-Jami'a al-Urduniyya, Markaz al-Watha'iq wa-l-Makhtutat, 1984), an important inventory of *sijill* collections found in Greater Syria, doesn't mention the existence of Shi'i *shari'a* courts at all.

1. The Incomplete Nationalization of Jabal 'Amil

1. Mounzer Jaber, "Pouvoir et société au Jabal 'Amil de 1749 à 1920 dans la conscience des chroniques chiites et dans un essai d'interpretation" (Thèse de 3e Cycle, Université de Paris IV, 1978); Andrew J. Newman, "The Myth of the Clerical Migration to Safawid Iran: Arab Shiite Opposition to 'Ali al-Karaki and Safawid Shiism," *Die Welt des Islams* Vol. 33, No. 1 (Apr. 1993): 66–112; Stefan Winter, "Shiite Emirs and Ottoman Authorities: The Campaign against the Hamadas of Mt Lebanon, 1693–1694," *Archivum Ottomanicum* Vol. 18 (2000): 209–245; Rula Jurdi Abisaab, *Converting Persia: Religion and Power in the Safavid Empire* (London: I. B. Tauris, 2004); Winter, "'Un lys dans des épines': Maronites et Chiites

au Mont Liban, 1698–1763," *Arabica: Revue d'études arabes* Vol. 51, No. 4 (2004): 478–492; Ja'far Muhajir, *Jabal 'Amil bayna al-shahidayn: al-haraka al-fikriyya fi Jabal 'Amil fi qarnayn (min awasit al-qarn al-thamin li-l-hijra/al-rab' 'ashr li-l-milad hatta awasit al-qarn al-'ashr/al-sadis 'ashr)* (Damascus: IFPO, 2005); and H. E. Chehabi, ed., *Distant Relations: Iran and Lebanon in the Last 500 Years* (London: Centre for Lebanese Studies in association with I. B. Tauris Publishers, 2006).

2. Muhammad Taqi al-Faqih, *Jabal 'Amil fi al-tarikh* (Beirut: Dar al-Adwa', 1986); Abdul-Rahim Abu Husayn, "The Shiites in Lebanon and the Ottomans in the 16th and 17th Centuries," in *Convegno sul tema* (15 April 1991, Roma), *La Shi'a nell'impero ottomano* (Rome: Accademia nazionale dei Lincei; Fondazione Leone Caetani, 1993), 107–119; C. Edmund Bosworth, "Baha' al-Din al-'Amili in the Two Worlds of the Ottomans and the Safavids," in *La Shi'a nell'impero ottomano*, 85–105; Marco Salati, "Toleration, Persecution and Local Realities: Observations on Shiism in the Holy Places and *Bilad Al-Sham* (16th–17th Centuries)," in *La Shi'a nell'impero ottomano*, 121–148; Rula Abisaab, "Shi'ite Beginnings and Scholastic Tradition in Jabal 'Amil," *The Muslim World* Vol. 89, No. 1 (1999): 1–21; Muhajir, *Jabal 'Amil bayna al-shahidayn;* and Haydar Rida al-Rakini, *Jabal 'Amil fi qarn (1163–1247 H/1749–1832 M)* (Beirut: Dar al-Fikr al-Lubnani, 1997).

3. Fouad Ajami, *The Vanished Imam: Musa Al-Sadr and the Shi'a of Lebanon* (Ithaca, NY: Cornell University Press, 1986), 155.

4. Ahmad Rida, "al-Matawila aw al-Shi'a fi Jabal 'Amil," *al-'Irfan* May 11, 1910; June 9, 1910; July 8, 1910; October 5, 1910; and November 3, 1910.

5. Muhsin al-Amin, *Khitat Jabal 'Amil* (Beirut: Matba'at al-Insaf, 1961), 52.

6. Mounzer Jaber, "al-Kiyan al-siyasi li-Jabal 'Amil qabla 1920," in Ibrahim Beydoun, ed., *Safahat min tarikh Jabal 'Amil* (Beirut: al-Majlis al-Thaqafi li-Lubnan al-Janubi, 1979), 83–106.

7. Muhammad 'Ali Makki, *Tarikh al-shi'a fi Lubnan* (manuscript, n.d.). Library, 'Amiliyya School and Society (*al-kuliyya al-'amiliyya*).

8. Majed Halawi, *A Lebanon Defied: Musa al-Sadr and the Shi'a Community* (Boulder: Westview Press, 1992), 7. For a vivid discussion of the term Mutawali in contemporary Beirut as a pejorative cultural identifier of Shi'i taste and culture through jokes and anecdotes, see Roshanack Shaery-Eisenlohr, *Shi'ite Lebanon: Transnational Religion and the Making of National Identities* (New York: Columbia University Press, 2008), 40–49.

9. Volney, C.-F., *Voyage en Égypte et en Syrie*, ed. Jean Gaulmier (Paris: Mouton, 1959 [1787]), 245–246.

10. Louis Lortet, *La Syrie d'aujourd'hui: voyages dans la Phénicie, le Liban et la Judée, 1875–1880* (Paris: Librairie Hachette, 1884), 115–116.

11. Henri Lammens, *Sur la frontière nord de la terre promise* (Paris: Imprimerie de D. Dumoulin et Co., 18—?), 5.

12. Wortabet, *Researches into the Religions of Syria; or, Sketches, Historical and Doctrinal, of its Religious Sects* (London: James Nisbet and Co, 1860), 282. Bernard

H. Springett lifted entire passages from Wortabet without attribution in his mish-mash of writings on esoteric sectarian communities in Greater Syria. Springett, *Secret Sects of Syria and the Lebanon* (London: Kegan Paul, 2007 [1922]).

13. Richard Robert Madden, *The Turkish Empire: In Its Relations with Christianity and Civilization* (London: T. C. Newby, 1862), 238. The work Madden refers to without attribution is William MacClure Thomson, *The Land and the Book; Or, Biblical Illustrations Drawn From the Manners and Customs, the Scenes and Scenery, of the Holy Land* (New York: Harper & brothers, 1859).

14. Raymond O'Zoux, *Les états du Levant sous mandat français* (Paris: Larose, 1931), 43.

15. Eugen Weber, *Peasants into Frenchman: The Modernization of Rural France, 1870–1914* (Stanford, CA: Stanford University Press, 1976), 49.

16. 'Abdallah al-Sbaiti, *Abu Dharr al-Ghifari* (Tyre: Matba'at Sur al-Haditha, 1945); Muhammad al-Shahid, *Li-madha sumiya Jabal 'Amil bi-ard Abi Dharr al-Ghifari: 'ard tahqiqi tarikhi wa-musawwar 'an maji' wa-iqamat Abi Dharr fi bilad al-sham wa-taswir maydani li-maqami Abi Dharr fi Mays al-Jabal wa-Sarafand* (Beirut: Maktabat Sayyid al-Shuhada', 1998); and Sabrina Mervin, *Un réformisme chiite: ulémas et lettrés du Ǧabal 'Amil (actuel Liban-Sud) de la fin de l'empire otto-man à l'indépendance du Liban* (Paris: Éditions Karthala, CERMOC and IFEAD, 2000), 386–389.

17. Louis Lortet, *La Syrie d'aujourd'hui,* 116.

18. Ernest Chantre, "Observations anthropologiques sur les Métoualis," *Bulletin de la Société d'Anthropologie de Lyon* Vol. 14 (1895): 58–61.

19. Frederick Jones Bliss, *The Religions of Modern Syria and Palestine* (New York: Charles Scribner's Sons, 1912), 295, 296.

20. Madden, *The Turkish Empire,* 239–240.

21. Yusuf Sufayr, *Jughrafiyat Lubnan al-kabir wa-hukumat Suriya wa-Filastin* (Beirut: 1924), 149.

22. Henri Lammens, *La Syrie, précis historique* (Beyrouth: Imprimerie Catholique, 1921).

23. Asher Kaufman, *Reviving Phoenicia: The Search for Identity in Lebanon* (London: I. B. Tauris, 2004).

24. Henri Lammens, "Les "Perses" du Liban et l'origine des Métoualis," *Mélanges de l'Université Saint-Joseph* Vol. 14 (1929): 21–39. Further citations to this work are given in the text.

25. Kais Firro, *Inventing Lebanon: Nationalism and the State under the Mandate* (London: I. B. Tauris, 2003), 160, citing 'Ali 'Abd al-Mun'im Shu'ayb, *Matalib Jabal 'Amil: al-wahda, al-musawa fi Lubnan al-Kabir, 1900–1936* (Beirut: al-Mu'assasa al-Jam'iyya, 1987), 100–104.

26. Madden, *The Turkish Empire,* 237.

27. David Urquhart, *The Lebanon (Mount Souria)* (London: T. C. Newby, 1860), 230–231. Further citations to this work are given in the text.

28. Lammens, *Sur la frontière nord de La Terre Promise,* 6–7, 20.

29. Wortabet, *Researches into the Religions of Syria,* 281.

30. Bliss, *The Religions of Modern Syria and Palestine,* 305–306.

31. J. Darché, *Les chiites du Liban,* Rapport N° 108 du CHEAM, (1937), 14–15.

32. Lortet, *La Syrie d'aujourdhui,* 115.

33. Lammens, *Sur la frontière nord de La Terre Promise,* 20.

34. J. Delore, S.J., "Missions in Far-Off Lands Today," *The Pilgrim of Our Lady of Martyrs,* Vol. 20, No. 3 (July 1904), 137.

35. On evangelical Protestant encounters with the Levant in general, and Mount Lebanon in particular, see Ussama Makdisi, "Reclaiming the Land of the Bible: Missionaries, Secularism, and Evangelical Modernity," *American Historical Review* Vol. 102, No. 3 (Jun., 1997), 680–713; and Makdisi, *Artillery of Heaven: American Missionaries and the Failed Conversion of the Middle East* (Ithaca, NY: Cornell University Press, 2007).

36. Muhammad Rafiq al-Tamimi and Muhammad Bahjat, *Wilayat Bayrut: Vol. 1: al-qism al-janubi: alwiyat Bayrut wa-'Akka wa-Nablus* (Beirut: Dar Lahd Khatir, 1987 [1917–18]), 320. On Muhammad Rafiq al-Tamimi and Muhammad Bahjat, see Wajih Kawtharani, "al-Hayat al-iqtisadiyya fi wilayat Bayrut 'ashiyata al-harb al-'alamiyya al-ula min khilal kitab "Wilayat Bayrut" li-Rafiq al-Tamimi wa-Muhammad Bahjat," *Revue d'Histoire Maghrebine* 12 (39–40) (1985): 375–390; and Jens Hanssen, *Fin-de-Siècle Beirut: The Making of an Ottoman Provincial Capital* (Oxford: Oxford University Press, 2005), 80–81.

37. Isma'il Haqqi, *Lubnan: mabahith 'ilmiyya wa-ijtima'iyya,* Part Two (Beirut: al-Jami'a al-Lubnaniyya, al-Matba'a al-Adabiyya, 1970 [1918]), 667.

38. Palestine Exploration Fund, *Questions on the Metawileh* (London: 18—?), 15, 20, 37. See also Alexander Blei, "Ha-Edah Hamitualit Be'levanon Ve-Yikhhudah," *Hamizrah He'hadash* Vol. 23, No. 2 (1973): 194–201.

39. Jacques Seguin, *Le Liban-Sud: espace périphérique, espace convoité* (Paris: L'Harmattan, 1989), 59.

40. Aron Rodrigue, "Difference and Tolerance in the Ottoman Empire: Interview by Nancy Reynolds," *Stanford Humanities Review* Vol. 5, No. 1 (1995): 81–90; and Maurus Reinkowski, *Ottoman 'Multiculturalism'? The Example of the Confessional System in Lebanon* (Beirut: 1999). On land issues, see Michael Gilsenan, "A Modern Feudality? Land and Labour in North Lebanon, 1858–1950," in Tarif Khalidi, ed., *Land Tenure and Social Transformation in the Middle East* (Beirut: American University of Beirut, 1984), 449–463; Peter Sluglett and Marion Farouk-Sluglett, "The Application of the 1858 Land Code in Greater Syria: Some Preliminary Observations," in Khalidi, ed., *Land Tenure and Social Transformation in the Middle East,* 409–424; and Alexander Schölch, "Was There a Feudal System in Ottoman Lebanon and Palestine?" in David Kushner, ed., *Palestine in the Late Ottoman Period: Political, Social and Economic Transformation* (Jerusalem: Yad Izhak Ben-Zvi, 1986), 130–145. See also Dina Rizk Khoury, *State and Provincial*

Society in the Ottoman Empire: Mosul, 1540–1834 (Cambridge: Cambridge University Press, 1997); and Ariel Salzmann, "Citizens in Search of a State: The Limits of Political Participation in the Late Ottoman Empire," in Michael Hanagan and Charles Tilly, eds., *Extending Citizenship, Reconfiguring States* (Lanham: Rowman & Littlefield Publishers Inc, 1999), 37–66.

41. Leila Fawaz, *Merchants and Migrants in Nineteenth-Century Beirut* (Cambridge, Mass.: Harvard University Press, 1983); Engin Akarlı, *The Long Peace: Ottoman Lebanon, 1861–1920* (Berkeley and Los Angeles: University of California Press, 1993); Fawaz, *An Occasion for War: Civil Conflict in Lebanon and Damascus in 1860* (London: Centre for Lebanese Studies and I. B. Tauris Publishers, 1994); Carol Hakim-Dowek, "The Origins of the Lebanese National Idea, 1840–1914" (D. Phil., University of Oxford, 1997); Ussama Makdisi, *The Culture of Sectarianism: Community, History and Violence in Nineteenth-century Ottoman Lebanon* (Berkeley and Los Angeles: University of California Press, 2000); and Hanssen, *Fin-de-Siècle Beirut*.

42. Roger Lescot, *Les chiites du Liban-Sud,* Rapport N° 3 du CHEAM (1936), 7, 12.

43. Darché, *Les chiites du Liban,* 24.

44. Khalil Ahmad Khalil, "al-Janub: qadiyyat watan wa-umma," in Farhan Salih, ed., *Janub Lubnan: waqi'uhu wa-qadayahu* (Beirut: Dar al-Tali'a, 1973), 14. This fourfold categorization of 'Amili class structure can be found even earlier. Cf. Muhammad Jawad Mughniyya, *al-Wad' al-hadir fi Jabal 'Amil fi matla' al-istiqlal: bidayat al-qahr wa-l-hirman* (Beirut: Dar al-Tayyar al-Jadid, 1990 [1947]); for more on Mughniyya, see chapter six.

45. Ahmad Ba'albeki, "al-Janub: qadiyyat mintaqa fi al-watan am qadiyyat watan fi al-mintaqa," in al-Majlis al-Thaqafi li-Lubnan al-Janubi, ed., *Dirasat hawla Janub Lubnan* (Beirut: al-Majlis al-Thaqafi li-Lubnan al-Janubi, 1981), 64–65.

46. Waddah Shararah, *al-Umma al-qalqa: al-'amiliyyun wa-l-'asabiyya al-'amiliyya 'ala 'atabat al-dawla al-lubnaniyya* (Beirut: Dar al-Nahar, 1996); Elizabeth Thompson, *Colonial Citizens: Republican Rights, Paternal Privilege and Gender in French Syria and Lebanon* (New York: Columbia University Press, 2000); Tamara Chalabi, *The Shi'is of Jabal 'Amil and the New Lebanon: Community and Nation-State, 1918–1943* (London: Palgrave Macmillan, 2006); and Kais Firro, "The Shi'is in Lebanon: Between Communal 'Asabiyya and Arab Nationalism, 1908–21," *Middle Eastern Studies* Vol. 42, No. 4 (July 2006): 535–550. On *al-'Irfan,* see, for example, Tarif Khalidi, "Shaykh Ahmad 'Arif Al-Zayn and *Al-'Irfan*," in Marwan R. Buheiry, eds., *Intellectual Life in the Arab East, 1890–1939* (Beirut: American University of Beirut, Center for Arab and Middle East Studies, 1981), 110–124; Silvia Naef, "La presse en tant que moteur du renouveau culturel et litteraire: la revue chiite libanaise al-'Irfan," *Etudes asiatiques, revue de la societé Suisse-Asie* (1996): 385–397; and Naef, "Les chiites du Liban et le mandat français: la position de la revue *Al-'Irfan,*" in Christoph Herzog, Raoul Motika, and Michael Ursinus, eds., *Querelles privées et*

contestations publiques: le rôle de la presse dans la formation de l'opinion publique au Proche Orient (Istanbul: Les Éditions Isis, 2002), 233–245.

47. *Al-'Irfan,* Vol. 7, No. 7 (April 1922), 437–438. Al Sulayman cites 1924 figures placing the Shiʻi population at 103,068 out of a total of 544,944, a very low estimate. Ibrahim Al Sulayman, *Buldan Jabal ʻAmil: qilaʻhu wa-madarisuhu wa-jusuruhu wa-murujuhu wa-matahinuhu wa-jibaluhu wa-mashahiduhu* (Beirut: Mu'assasat al-Da'ira, 1995), 46–47; on population counts in Lebanon, also see Rania Maktabi, "The Lebanese Census of 1932 Revisited: Who Are the Lebanese?" *British Journal of Middle Eastern Studies* Vol. 26, No. 2 (1999): 219–241. For more on Jabal ʻAmil during this period, see Mustafa Bazzi, "Hukumat Faysal fi zill al-atmaʻ wa-l-tanafus al-duwwaliayn," *al-Muntalaq* 105 (1993): 75–114; and Ahmad Rida, *Mudhakkirat li-l-tarikh, hawadith Jabal ʻAmil 1914–1922* (Beirut: Dar al-Nahar li-l-Nashr, 2009). On the early years of the French Mandate, see Nadine Méouchy, ed., *France, Syrie et Liban 1918–1946: les ambiguités et les dynamiques de la relation mandataire* (Damascus: IFEAD, 2002); Jean-David Mizrahi, *Genèse de l'état mandataire: service des renseignements et bandes armées en Syrie et au Liban dans les années 1920* (Paris: Publications de la Sorbonne, 2003); Nadine Méouchy and Peter Sluglett, eds., *The British and French Mandates in Comparative Perspectives* (Leiden: Brill, 2004); and Michael Provence, *The Great Syrian Revolt and the Rise of Arab Nationalism* (Austin: University of Texas Press, 2005).

48. Mounzer Jaber, "al-Janub amam al-sigha . . . sahal la waʻr (1943–1975)," *al-Safir,* April 7, 2006.

49. Chalabi, *The Shiʻis of Jabal ʻAmil;* Shuʻayb, *Matalib Jabal ʻAmil.* For a different argument, see Kais M. Firro, "Ethnicizing the Shiʻis in Mandatory Lebanon," *Middle Eastern Studies* Vol. 42, No. 5 (September 2006): 741–759.

50. Lebanon, Majlis al-Wuzara'. *al-Bayanat al-wizariyya al-lubnaniyya,* 10–11, my emphasis.

2. The Modernity of Shiʻi Tradition

1. Fouad Ajami, *The Vanished Imam: Musa al-Sadr and the Shiʻa of Lebanon* (Ithaca, NY: Cornell University Press, 1986); and Majed Halawi, *A Lebanon Defied: Musa al-Sadr and the Shiʻa Community* (Boulder: Westview Press, 1992).

2. Marshall G. S. Hodgson, "How Did the Early Shiʻa Become Sectarian?" *Journal of the American Oriental Society* 75(1) (1955): 1–13.

3. Devin J. Stewart, *Islamic Legal Orthodoxy: Twelver Shiite Responses to the Sunni Legal System* (Salt Lake City: University of Utah Press, 1998); Liyakat N. Takim, *The Heirs of the Prophet: Charisma and Religious Authority in Shiʻite Islam* (Albany, NY: State University of New York Press, 2006); and Maria Massi Dakake, *The Charismatic Community: Shiʻite Identity in Early Islam* (Albany, NY: State University of New York, 2007). See also Christopher Melchert, *The Formation of the Sunni Schools of Law, 9th–10th centuries C.E* (Leiden: Brill, 1997).

4. Sabrina Mervin, *Un réformisme chiite: ulémas et lettrés du Ǧabal ʿAmil (actuel Liban-Sud) de la fin de l'empire ottoman à l'indépendance du Liban* (Paris: Éditions Karthala, CERMOC and IFEAD, 2000), 237.

5. This point is exemplified by the popular slogan: "Would that we had been with you to prevail in great victory" (*ya laytna kunna maʿka li-nafuz fawzan ʿaziman*).

6. Juan Cole, *Sacred Space and Holy War: The Politics, Culture and History of Shi'ite Islam* (London: I. B. Tauris, 2002), 173–188.

7. On the Karbala paradigm, see Michael Fischer, *Iran: From Religious Dispute to Revolution* (Cambridge, Mass.: Harvard University Press, 1980). On Karbala in various historical contexts, see Mahmoud Ayoub, *Redemptive Suffering in Islam: A Study of the Devotional Aspects of ʿAshura" in Twelver Shi'ism* (The Hague: Mouton Publishers, 1978); Margaret Kartomi, "Tabut—A Shi'a Ritual Transplanted From India to Sumatra," in David P. Chandler and M. C. Ricklefs, eds., *Nineteenth and Twentieth Century Indonesia: Essays in Honour of Professor J. D. Legge* (Clayton: Centre of Southeast Studies, Monash University, 1986), 141–162; Keith Hjortshoj, "Shi'i Identity and the Significance of Muharram in Lucknow, India," in Martin Kramer, ed., *Shi'ism, Resistance and Revolution* (Boulder, CO: Westview Press, 1987), 289–309; Mushirul Hasan, "Traditional Rites and Contested Meanings: Sectarian Strife in Colonial Lucknow," in Mushirul Hasan, ed., *Islam, Communities and the Nation: Muslim Identities in South Asia and Beyond* (New Delhi: Manohar, 1998), 341–366; Ibrahim Haydari, *Trajidiya Karbalaʾ: susiyulujiya al-khitab al-shiʿi* (Beirut: Dar al-Saqi, 1999); David Pinault, *Horse of Karbala: Muslim Devotional Life in India* (London: Palgrave, 2001); Janet Afary, "Shiʿi Narratives of Karbala and Christian Rites of Penance: Michel Foucault and the Culture of the Iranian Revolution, 1978–1979," *Radical History Review* 86 (Spring 2003): 7–35; Frank J. Korom, *Hosay Trinidad: Muharram Performances in an Indo-Caribbean Diaspora* (Philadelphia: University of Pennsylvania Press, 2003); Kamran Aghaie, *The Martyrs of Karbala: Shiʿi Symbols and Rituals in Modern Iran* (Seattle and London: University of Washington Press, 2004); Kamran Scot Aghaie, ed., *The Women of Karbala: Ritual Performance and Symbolic Discourses in Modern Shiʿi Islam* (Austin: University of Texas Press, 2005); Toby M. Howarth, *The Twelver Shiʿa as a Muslim Minority in India: Pulpit of Tears* (London and New York: Routledge, 2005); Syed Akbar Hyder, *Reliving Karbala: Martyrdom in South Asian Memory* (Oxford: Oxford University Press, 2006); and Zulkifli, "The Struggle of the Shi'is in Indonesia" (PhD diss., University of Leiden, 2009), esp. 118–122.

8. Ali J. Hussain cites Ibn Kathir's *al-Bidaya wa-l-nihaya*, in an entry from 963 A.D. Hussain, "The Mourning of History and the History of Mourning: The Evolution of Ritual Commemoration of the Battle of Karbala," *CSSAAME* Vol. 25, No. 1 (2005), 84. Yitzhak Nakash cites Ibn al-Athir's *al-Kamil fi al-tarikh*. Nakash, "An Attempt to Trace the Origin of the Rituals of ʿAshuraʾ," *Die Welt des Islams* Vol. 33, No. 2 (November 1993), 169.

9. Kamran Aghaie, "The Karbala Narrative: Shi'i Political Discourse in Modern Iran in the 1960s and 1970s," *Journal of Islamic Studies* Vol. 12 (2001), 175.

10. Albert Hourani, "From Jabal 'Amil to Persia," *BSOAS* Vol. 49, No. 1 (1986): 133–140; Ja'far Muhajir, *al-Hijra al-'amiliyya ila Iran fi al-'asr al-safawi: asbabuha al-tarikhiyya wa-nata'ijuha al-thaqafiyya wa-l-siyasiyya* (Beirut: Dar al-Rawda, 1989); Rula Jurdi Abisaab, *Converting Persia: Religion and Power in the Safavid Empire* (London: I. B. Tauris, 2004); and Muhajir, *Jabal 'Amil bayna al-shahidayn: al-haraka al-fikriyya fi Jabal 'Amil fi qarnayn (min awasit al-qarn al-thamin li-l-hijra/al-rab' 'ashr li-l-milad hatta awasit al-qarn al-'ashr/al-sadis 'ashr)* (Damascus: IFPO, 2005).

11. Jean Calmard, "Shi'i Rituals and Power II. The Consolidation of Safavid Shi'ism: Folklore and Popular Religion," in Charles Melville, ed., *Safavid Persia: The History and Politics of an Islamic Society* (London: I. B. Tauris & Co. Ltd. with the Centre of Middle Eastern Studies, University of Cambridge, 1996), 141. See also Abisaab, "The Ulama of Jabal 'Amil in Safavid Iran, 1501–1736: Marginality, Migration and Social Change," *Iranian Studies* Vol. 27 (1–4) (1994): 103–122.

12. Karen M. Kern, "The Prohibition of Sunni-Shi'i Marriages in the Ottoman Empire: A Study of Ideologies" (PhD diss., Columbia University, 1999), 105, 108.

13. Ilber Ortayli, "Les groupes hétérodoxes et l'administration ottomane," in Krisztina Kehl-Bodrogi, Barbara Kellner-Heinkele, and Anke Otteer-Beaujean, eds., *Syncretistic Religious Communities in the Near East* (Leiden: Brill, 1997), 211. On heterodox Muslim communities in Ottoman *bilad al-sham*, see Dick Douwes and Norman N. Lewis, "The Trials of Syrian Ismailis in the First Decade of the 20th Century," *IJMES* Vol. 21 (1989): 215–232; and Stefan Winter, "The Nusayris Before the Tanzimat in the Eyes of Ottoman Provincial Administrators, 1804–1834," in Thomas Philipp and Christoph Schumann, eds., *From the Syrian Land to the States of Syria and Lebanon* (Würzburg: Ergon in Kommission, 2004), 97–112. I would like to thank Peter Sluglett for these two references.

14. Marco Salati, "Toleration, Persecution and Local Realities: Observations on Shiism in the Holy Places and the *Bilad Al-Sham* (16th–17th Centuries)," in *La Shi'a nell'impero ottomano* (Rome: Academia nazionale Dei Lincei; Fondazione Leone Caetani, 1993), 144–145. The same argument is made in Abdul-Rahim Abu Husayn, "The Shiites in Lebanon and the Ottomans in the 16th and 17th Centuries," in *La Shi'a nell'impero ottomano*, 107–119.

15. John Wortabet, *Researches into the Religions of Syria; or, Sketches, Historical and Doctrinal, of its Religious Sects* (London: James Nisbet and Co, 1860), 272ff.

16. Bliss, *The Religions of Modern Syria and Palestine*, 298–299.

17. Frederic Maatouk, *La représentation de la mort de l'Imam Hussein à Nabatieh (Liban-Sud)* (Beirut: 1974); and Maatouk, "'Ashura' (lubnaniyya) wa-nass 1936," *Abwab* 6 (Fall 1995): 148–158.

18. Maatouk, "'Ashura' (lubnaniyya)," 150. The records from the Ja'fari *shari'a* courts in Beirut and elsewhere, particularly Nabatiyya, indicate the presence of a number of Iranians in Lebanon during the Mandate period. Thierry Zarcone, "La communauté iranienne d'Istanbul à la fin du XIXᵉ et au début du XXᵉ siècle," in *La Shi'a nell'Impero ottomano,* 57–83; and Zarcone, "La situation du chi'isme à Istanbul au XIXᵉ et au début du XXᵉ siècle," in Thierry Zarcone and F. Zarinebaf-Shahr, eds., *Les iraniens d'Istanbul* (Istanbul-Tehran: IFEA/IFRI, 1993), 97–111. Talal Jaber cites 1895 as the first year in which Iranian students in Nabatiyya acquired Ottoman approval to observe 'Ashura' publicly. "Chiites et pouvoir politique au Liban 1967–1974: contribution à une approche socio-religieuse" (Thèse de 3ᵉ cycle, Université de Paris VII, 1980). Nakash argued that the introduction of flagellation into Iraq "was probably facilitated by the Ottoman reversal in 1831 of the Mamluk ban prohibiting the observance of 'Ashura'" in public after they had resumed direct control of the country." Nakash, "An Attempt to Trace the Origin," 176–177. Meir Litvak concurred: "The reassertion of direct Ottoman control over Iraq removed various restrictions on Shi'i devotional rites." Litvak, *Shi'i Scholars of Nineteenth-Century Iraq: The 'Ulama' of Najaf and Karbala'* (Cambridge: Cambridge University Press, 1998), 184.

19. On Rashid Baydoun and the 'Amiliyya society, see E. A. Early, "The 'Amiliyya Society of Beirut: A Case Study of an Emerging Urban Za'im" (M.A. Thesis, American University of Beirut, 1971); Ali Abed Fattuni, "Tatawwur al-ta'lim fi madaris al-jam'iyya al-khayriyya al-islamiyya al-'amiliyya fi Bayrut min khilal watha'iqiha al-asliyya 1923–1943" (PhD diss., Lebanese University, 1986); Fatima Mahmoud Jaffal, "Rashid Yusuf Baydoun 1889–1971" (Master's thesis, Lebanese University, 1990); and Muhammad Fattuni, "Tatawwur al-tar-biyya wa-l-ta'lim fi madaris al-jam'iyya al-khayriyya al-islamiyya al-'amiliyya min khilal watha'iqiha al-asliyya (1943–1975)" (PhD diss., Lebanese University, 1992).

20. *Al-'Irfan* Vol. 20, No. 2 (July 1930), 170.

21. Early, "The 'Amiliyya Society of Beirut," 63–64.

22. Fuad I. Khuri *From Village to Suburb: Order and Change in Greater Beirut* (Chicago: University of Illinois Press, 1975), 185.

23. Muhsin al-Amin *Khitat Jabal 'Amil* (Beirut: Matba'at al-Insaf, 1961), 149.

24. *Al-'Irfan* Vol. 7, No. 1 (October 1921), 62. Although the practice of cutting is likely to have spread to the Arab world from the Caucasus by way of Iran, it was often referred to as an "Iranian" practice among Lebanese Shi'is, probably because of those Iranian immigrants who first brought it to Jabal 'Amil. See Nakash, "An Attempt to Trace the Origin"; and Volker Adam, "Why Do They Cry? Criticisms of Muharram Celebrations in Tsarist and Socialist Azerbaijan," in Rainer Brunner and Werner Ende, eds., *The Twelver Shia in Modern Times: Religious Culture and Political History* (Leiden: Brill, 2002), 114–34.

25. Joseph Olmert, "Shi'is and the Lebanese State," in Martin Kramer, ed., *Shi'ism, Resistance and Revolution* (Boulder, CO: Westview Press, 1987), 189–201; Maatouk, *La représentation de la mort*.

26. 'Ali 'Abd al-Mun'im Shu'ayb, *Matalib Jabal 'Amil: al-wahda, al-musawa fi Lubnan al-Kabir, 1900–1936* (Beirut: al-Mu'assasa al-Jam'iyya, 1987); Mustafa Muhammad Bazzi, *Jabal 'Amil fi muhitihi al-'arabi, 1864–1948* (Beirut: al-Majlis al-Islami al-Shi'i al-A'la, 1993); and Nawal Fayyad, *Safahat min tarikh Jabal 'Amil fi al-'ahdayn al-'uthmani wa-l-faransi* (Beirut: Dar al-Jadid, 1998).

27. See, for example, Sabrina Mervin, "L'«entité alaouite», une création française," in Pierre-Jean Luizard, ed., *Le choc colonial et l'islam: les politiques religieuses des puissances coloniales en terres d'islam* (Paris: La Découverte, 2006), 343–58.

28. MAE-Nantes, Carton N° 1664, BIH, Caza de Tyr, No. 20, "A/s de la cérémonie religieuse chiite," 11–18 May 1932. For more on Sharaf al-Din, see his autobiography, *Bughyat al-raghibin fi silsilat Al Sharaf al-Din: tarikh ajyal fi tarikh rijal: kitab nasab wa tarikh wa tarajim* (2 vols.). (Beirut: al-Dar al-Islamiyya, 1991).

29. MAE-Nantes, Carton N° 1662, BIH de Merdjayoun N° 46, 9 June 1930, my emphasis.

30. MAE-Nantes, Carton N° 1663, BIH, Caza de Tyr, No. 19, Divers, 3–9 May 1933.

31. J. Darché, *Les chiites du Liban,* Rapport N° 108 du CHEAM, (1937), 18.

32. MAE-Nantes, Carton N° 607, Cérémonie à la Mosquée Chiite de Tyr, March 25, 1935. Also see the poetry of Habib Al Ibrahim, *al-Mawlid wa-l-ghadir* (Sidon: Matba'at al-'Irfan, 1947), 9–15.

33. Sebastian Günther points out that after Abu'l Faraj al-Isfahani, "the maqatil disappeared as a relatively independent genre of historico-biographical literature in Arabic" and the *maqtal* became "almost exclusively concerned with the martyrdom of al-Husayn and his companions." Günther, "Maqâtil Literature in Medieval Islam," *Journal of Arabic Literature* Vol. 25, No. 3 (1994), 207–208.

34. Muhsin al-Amin, *Sirat al-Sayyid Muhsin al-Amin al-'Amili,* ed. Haitham el-Amin and Sabrina Mervin (Beirut: Riyad el-Rayyes, 2000), 58–59, 61–63. The autobiography was originally published as one volume of his biographical dictionary and magnum opus, Muhsin al-Amin, *A'yan al-shi'a* (Damascus: Ibn Zaydun, 1944).

35. According to Talal Jaber, the text (which he appends to his thesis) was still in use in the 1970s and had been edited by Sadiq's son, Shaykh Muhammad Taqi al-Sadiq. Jaber, "Chiites et pouvoir politique au Liban 1967–1974," 144. According to Sabrina Mervin, the Imami Shi'i community in Damascus, while under the leadership of Sayyid Muhsin al-Amin, relied on *maqatil* by Abu Mikhnaf and Ibn Tawwus. Mervin "'Ashura': A comparative study of the ritual practices in different Shiite communities (Lebanon and Syria)," unpublished paper; now published as

"Les larmes et le sang des chiites: corps et pratiques rituelles lors des célébrations de 'ashûrâ' (Liban, Syrie)," *Revue des mondes musulmans et de la Méditerranée, N° 113–114, Le corps et le sacré dans l'Orient musulman,* (November 2006): 153–166.

36. Maatouk, "'Ashura' (lubnaniyya)," 155–157.

37. *Al-'Irfan* Vol. 13, No. 10 (June 1927), 1195. Hibat al-Din al-Shahrastani, *Nahdat al-Husayn* (Baghdad: Matba'at al-Jazira, 2nd ed. 1937 [1344]). Al-Shahrastani went on to become the first president of the Ja'fari *shari'a* court in Baghdad. For more on al-Shahrastani, see chapter three; and Muhammad Baqir Ahmad al-Bahadili, *al-Sayyid Hibat al-Din al-Shahrastani: atharuhu al-fikriyya wa-mawaqifuhu al-siyasiyya (1301–1386/1884–1967)* (Beirut: Mu'assasat al-Fikr al-Islami, 2002).

38. Lata Mani, *Contentious Traditions: The Debate on Sati in Colonial India* (Berkeley and Los Angeles: University of California Press, 1998), 77.

39. Muhsin al-Amin, *al-Majalis al-saniyya fi manaqib wa-masa'ib al-'itra al-nabawiyya (5 vols.)* (Damascus: Matba'at Karam, 1951–1954); and al-Amin, *Lawa'ij al-ashjan fi maqtal al-imam Abi 'Abd Allah al-Husayn Ibn 'Ali Ibn Abi Talib 'alayhim al-salam* (Sidon: Matba'at al-'Irfan, 1934 [1911]). Muhammad al-Qasim claims that the influence of *al-Majalis al-saniyya* "was in elite sectors (*al-awsat al-khassa*) that read books, without having an influence on the general population (*al-awsat al-'amma*)." Al-Qasim, *Thawrat al-tanzih: "Risalat al-tanzih" taliha mawaqif minha wa-ara' fi al-Sayyid Muhsin al-Amin* (Beirut: Dar al-Jadid, 1996), 14. Erika Glassen identifies Azerbaijan-born Iranian cleric, Shaykh Asadallah Mamaqani, a Shi'i reformist who lived in Istanbul around the turn-of-the-century, as the author of a tract critical of the nature of Muharram practices among Iranians in Istanbul, entitled *Din va Shu'an,* which was first published in 1918. Glassen, "Muharram-Ceremonies (Azadari) in Istanbul at the End of the XIXth and the Beginning of the XXth Century," in Zarcone and Zarinebaf-Shahr, eds., *Les iraniens d'Istanbul,* 128–29. Rainer Brunner notes that *al-Din wal-shu'un* was published in Istanbul in 1334/1915–1916 and then roundly criticized by Agha Buzurg al-Tihrani. Brunner, *Islamic Ecumenism in the 20th Century: The Azhar and Shiism Between Rapprochement and Restraint* (Leiden: Brill, 2004), 48, ff. 17. Volker Adam discusses an even earlier dispute that broke out in 1877 when a Baku newspaper printed criticism by Muhammad Sadiq of Muharram flagellations on grounds quite similar to those of al-Amin. Adam, "Why Do They Cry?" 119–121.

40. Muhammad al-Husayn Al Kashif al-Ghita', *al-Ayyat al-bayyinat fi qam' al-bid' wa-l-dalalat* (Najaf: al-Matba'a al-'Alawiyya, 1345 [1926]).

41. 'Abd al-Husayn Sadiq, *Sima' al-sulaha'* (Sidon: Matba'at al-'Irfan, 1345 [1927]), 5. Further citations to this work are given in the text.

42. Al Kashif al-Ghita', *al-Ayyat al-bayyinat,* 17–19.

43. This notion of *inkar al-munkar* indexes the theme of "commanding right and forbidding evil" (*al-amr bi-l-ma'ruf wa-l-nahy 'an al-munkar*), which is present throughout the array of texts criticizing al-Amin. See Michael Cook,

Commanding Right and Forbidding Wrong in Islamic Thought (Cambridge: Cambridge University Press, 2000).

44. For more on the life of 'Abd al-Husayn Sadiq, see Hasan Sadiq, "al-Shaykh 'Abd al-Husayn Sadiq," *al-'Irfan* Vol. 31, No. 9–10 (August-September 1945): 485–490.

45. Muhsin al-Amin, *Risalat al-tanzih li-a'mal al-shabih* (Sidon: Matba'at al-'Irfan, 1347). Further citations to this work are given in the text.

46. Muhsin al-Amin, *al-Majalis al-saniyya: manaqib wa-masa'ib al-'itra al-nabawiyya*, Vol. 1 (Najaf: Matba'at al-Nu'man, 1342); and al-Amin, *Iqna' al-la'im 'ala iqamat al-ma'atim* (Qum: Mu'assasat al-Ma'arif al-Islamiyya, 1998). For two quite different uses of the term "authenticated," see Ahmad Dallal, "Appropriating the Past: Twentieth-Century Reconstruction of Pre-Modern Islamic Thought," *Islamic Law and Society* Vol. 7, No. 3 (October 2000): 325–358; and Lara Deeb, *An Enchanted Modern: Gender and Public Piety in Shi'i Lebanon* (Princeton, N.J.: Princeton University Press, 2006), esp. 131–133 and 154–158. On al-Amin's approach to education, see Mervin, *Un réformisme chiite*, 162–177.

47. Talal Asad, *Genealogies of Religion: Discipline and Reason in Medieval Christianity and Islam* (Baltimore: Johns Hopkins Press, 1993).

48. 'Abd al-Amir al-Basri, another critic of al-Amin's work, also wrote that the "concept of no-harm is foreign." 'Abd al-Amir al-Basri, *Lahjat al-sidq wa-lisan al-haqq* (Najaf: al-Matba'a al-Haydariyya, 1348), 26. Al-Basri saw al-Amin's work as an "affront" to all Iraqi Shi'a, specifically speaking in the name of that community, comparing it at times to Jabal 'Amil.

49. Al-Amin included the quotation in Persian, which says something about his intended audience: educated, multilingual, elite *'ulama'*.

50. I would like to thank Cyrus Schayegh for early help with translation from Persian.

51. Mary Douglas, *Purity and Danger: An Analysis of Concepts of Pollution and Taboo* (London: Routledge & Kegan Paul, 1966), 4.

52. Iranian scholars and religious intellectuals appear to have been notably absent from this debate. Although Jalal Al-e Ahmad read *Risalat al-tanzih* and translated it into Persian, this was not until 1943, and the text, translated as "Illegitimate Mourning" (*Azadariha-ye namashru'*) remained out of print until 1992. Also, although Ali Shariati gave a lecture on Muhsin al-Amin in 1972, there is no indication that any Iranians directly participated in the 'Ashura' debates. H. E. Chehabi and Hassan I. Mneimneh, "Five Centuries of Lebanese-Iranian Encounters," in H. E. Chehabi, ed., *Distant Relations: Iran and Lebanon in the Last 500 Years* (London: Centre for Lebanese Studies in association with I. B. Tauris Publishers, 2006), 1–47.

53. 'Abdallah al-Sbaiti, *Rannat al-asa, aw, nazra fi risalat al-tanzih li-a'mal al-shabih* (Najaf: Matba'at al-Najah, 1347 [1928–29]). Further citations to this work are given in the text. Intriguingly, the copy of this text that I consulted at the

American University of Beirut had the following message scrawled on the cover page and the first page of text: "This was written by Sayyid 'Abd al-Husayn Sharaf al-Din and attributed to his brother-in-law 'Abdallah al-Sbaiti." For more on 'Abdallah al-Sbaiti, see 'Abd al-Amir al-Sbaiti, "al-'Allama al-munadil al-Shaykh 'Aballah al-Sbaiti," *al-'Irfan* Vol. 80, No. 5–6 (July/August 1996): 58–65.

54. Hasan Muzaffar, *Nusrat al-mazlum* (Najaf: al-Matba'a al-'Alawiyya, 1345). Further citations to this work are given in the text.

55. On some of the often graphic dimensions of 'Ashura' iconography, see Peter J. Chelkowski, "Iconography of the Women of Karbala: Tiles, Murals, Stamps, and Posters," in Aghaie, ed., *The Women of Karbala,* 119–38.

56. 'Ali Naqi al-Lakhnawi, *Iqalat al-'athir fi iqamat al-sha'a'ir* (Najaf: al-Matba'a al-Haydariyya, 1348 [1930]), 57–58.

57. Muhsin al-Khorrazi argues that the essential problem with such cross-dressing, or any other potentially gender-bending behavior, is "intended or desired effect" (*qasd*). If there is no intention for a man to "become like a woman" (*ta'annuth*) or for a woman "to become like a man" (*tadhakkur*), then anything goes. This reasoning is buttressed by the philological insistence that some notion of intention is precisely what distinguishes "resemblance" (*shabh*) from "imitation" (*tashabbuh*). Al-Khorrazi, "Tashabbuh al-rajul bi-l-mar'a wa bi-l-'aks," *Fiqh Ahl al-Bayt* Vol. 3, No. 9 (1998): 163–174.

58. 'Abd al-Husayn al-Hilli, *al-Naqd al-nazih li-risalat al-tanzih* (Najaf: al-Matba'a al-Haydariyya, 1347 [1929]). Further citations to this work are given in the text. The text was edited more recently by Nizar al-Ha'iri and renamed, *al-Sha'a'ir al-husayniyya fi al-mizan al-fiqhi* (Damascus: Maktabat al-Taff, 1995 [2nd ed.]).

59. See also 'Abd al-Rida Al Kashif al-Ghita', *al-Anwar al-husayniyya wa-l-sha'a'ir al-islamiyya* (Bombay, 1927).

60. Al-Amin, *A'yan al-shi'a,* vol. 40.

61. Reprinted as an appendix in Jaber, "Chiites et pouvoir politique au Liban 1967–1974." A slightly different version can be found in Hasan Nur al-Din, *'Ashura' fi al-adab al-'amili al-mu'asir* (Beirut: al-Dar al-Islamiyya, 1988), 263–287.

62. Muhammad al-Ganji, *Kashf al-tamwih 'an risalat al-tanzih li-a'mal al-shabih* (Najaf: al-Matba'a al-'Alawiyya, 1347 [1929]).

63. *Al-'Irfan* Vol. 21, No. 1 (January 1931), 54–57.

64. "Ma'atim al-Husayn," *al-'Irfan* Vol. 21, No. 3 (March 1931): 362–368. The works cited, several of which we have already discussed above, were: 'Abd al-Husayn Sharaf al-Din, *al-Majalis al-fakhira;* Murtada al-Kadhimi, *al-Nazra al-dami'a* (which Sabrina Mervin argues was actually written by Murtada Al Yasin, although she was also unable to consult the source); 'Abd al-Husayn al-Hilli, *al-Naqd al-nazih;* Muhammad 'Ali Sharaf al-Din, *Taht rayat al-Husayn* (originally published in the diasporic journal *al-Huda*); 'Abdallah al-Sbaiti, *Rannat al-asa;* and Muhammad Husayn Muzaffar, *al-Shi'ar al-husayni.*

65. Habib bin Muzahir, "Kalima hawla ma'atim al-Husayn," *al-'Irfan* Vol. 21, No. 4–5 (April 1931): 581–584; "Hawla al-ma'atim al-husayniyya," *al-'Irfan* Vol. 21, No. 4–5 (April 1931): 599–600.

66. "Yawm 'Ashura', yawm al-tadhiyya wa-l-aba'," *al-'Irfan* Vol. 25, No. 1 (April 1934), 115.

67. Muhammad Rashid Rida, *al-Sunna wa-l-shi'a, aw al-wahhabiyya wa-l-rafida: haqa'iq diniyya tarikhiyya ijtima'iyya islahiyya* (Cairo: Matba'at al-Manar, 1929), 31. For a very different discussion of "moderate" versus "extremist" Shi'i sects in the early Islamic milieu, see Bernard Lewis, *The Assassins: A Radical Sect in Islam* (London: Weidenfeld and Nicolson, 1972 [1967]), esp. 22–26.

68. "'Ashura'," *al-'Irfan* Vol. 29, No. 2 (April 1939), 230. Al-Shahrastani, *Nahdat al-Husayn.*

69. *Al-'Irfan* Vol. 30, No. 1–2 (Feb–Mar 1940), 156.

70. "'Ashura'," *al-'Irfan* Vol. 29, No. 2 (April 1939), 230.

71. "'Ashura' wa-Karbala," *al-'Irfan* Vol. 33, No. 1 (December 1946), 13.

72. On Shi'is as national minorities, see Cole, *Sacred Space and Holy War.* My use of the term "cultural intimacy" is inspired by Michael Herzfeld, *Cultural Intimacy: Social Poetics of the Nation State* (New York: Routledge, 1997).

73. Werner Ende, "The Flagellations of Muharram and the Shi'ite 'ulama'," *Der Islam* (1978), 31, 36.

74. Yitzhak Nakash, *The Shi'is of Iraq* (Princeton, N.J.: Princeton University Press, 1994), 154–55.

75. Hussain, "The Mourning of History," 87.

76. Mervin, *Un réformisme chiite,* 267–74.

77. Roger Lescot, *Les chiites du Liban-Sud,* Rapport N° 3 du CHEAM, (1936), 21.

78. Nizar al-Zayn, "Bayni wa-bayn al-qari'," *al-'Irfan* Vol. 57, No. 1–2 (May/June 1969), 22–23.

79. Michael Hudson, *The Precarious Republic: Political Modernization in Lebanon* (New York: Random House, 1968), 25.

80. Marilyn Robinson Waldman, "Tradition as a Modality of Change: Islamic Examples," *History of Religions* Vol. 25, No. 4 (1986), 339.

81. See 'Abbas Sabbagh, "'Ashura' bayna al-nahda al-diniyya wa-l-bu'd al-siyasi: al-tatbir lam yakhtafi tamaman raghm al-fatawa bi-tahrimihi," *al-Nahar,* February 9, 2006. Lara Deeb explores the radicalization of 'Ashura' rhetoric and practice in the wake of the Israeli invasion. Deeb, "Living Ashura in Lebanon: Mourning Transformed to Sacrifice," *CSSAAME* Vol. 25, No. 1 (2005), esp. 131–135. Sayyid Muhammad Husayn Fadlallah is perceived as the renewer of al-Amin's critical position vis-à-vis politicized versions of 'Ashura' in Zvika Krieger, "Blood Feud: Hezbollah's politicization of Ashura," *The New Republic,* February 14, 2007 (Available at http://zvikakrieger.wordpress.com/contact/recent-articles/blood-feud/; accessed 3/19/10).

3. Institutionalizing Personal Status

1. The phrase I overheard, in colloquial Lebanese, was *khalas, lamma fatat al-khilafa, fat al-khilaf.* Sayyid Muhsin al-Amin offered a similar interpretation of pan-Islamic amity in the face of colonial assault: "We differed on who our *khalifa* was until the French High Commissioner became our *khalifa.*" Cited in Wajih Kawtharani, "Jabal 'Amil wa-l-tarikh al-ta'ifi al-lubnani," *al-'Irfan* Vol. 74, No. 7–8 (1986), 79. Despite the hopefulness of al-Amin's sentiment, in some ways the problem of the Caliphate remains at the heart of matters of both Shi'i identity and difference. See Muhammad Jawad al-Chirri, *al-Khilafa fi al-dustur al-islami* (Beirut: Matba'at al-Ittihad, 1946).

2. Christopher Melchert, *The Formation of the Sunni Schools of Law, 9th–10th Centuries C.E.* (Leiden: Brill, 1997); Devin J. Stewart, *Islamic Legal Orthodoxy: Twelver Shiite Responses to the Sunni Legal System* (Salt Lake City: University of Utah Press, 1998); Arzina R. Lalani, *Early Shi'i Thought: The Teachings of Imam Muhammad al-Baqir* (London: I. B. Tauris in association with the Institute of Ismaili Studies, 2000); Liyakat N. Takim, *The Heirs of the Prophet: Charisma and Religious Authority in Shi'ite Islam* (Albany, NY: State University of New York Press, 2006); and Maria Massi Dakake, *The Charismatic Community: Shi'ite Identity in Early Islam* (Albany, NY: State University of New York, 2007).

3. Robert Gleave argues that Shi'i *mujtahids* accept something like "restricted analogy"; contrary to certain understandings of Shi'i Islam, they don't restrict *qiyas* outright. Gleave, "Imami Shi'i Refutations of Qiyas," in Bernard Weiss, ed., *Studies in Islamic Legal Theory* (Leiden: Brill, 2002), 267–291. Gleave has also written a fascinating study of those Imami Shi'is opposed to the juristic exercise of *ijtihad*—Akhbaris—and suggestively refers to the Akhbariyya as a "scripturalist" tradition. Gleave, *Scripturalist Islam: The History and Doctrines of the Akhbari Shi'i School* (Leiden: Brill, 2007). Wael B. Hallaq argues that *ijtihad* was not restricted to the Shi'a. See Hallaq, "Was the Gate of Ijtihad Closed?" *IJMES* Vol. 16, No. 1 (Mar. 1984): 3–41; and Hallaq, "On the Origins of the Controversy about the Existence of Mujtahids and the Gate of Ijtihad," *Studia Islamica* No. 63 (1986): 129–141.

4. Talal Jaber, "Le discours shiite sur le pouvoir," *Peuples Mediterranéens* (July–Sep 1982), 77.

5. Norman Calder, "Judicial Authority in Imami Shi'i Jurisprudence," *Bulletin (British Society for Middle Eastern Studies)* (1979): 104–108; and Abdulaziz Abdulhussein Sachedina, *The Just Ruler (al-sultān al-'ādil) in Shī'ite Islam: The Comprehensive Authority of the Jurist in Imamite Jurisprudence* (New York: Oxford University Press, 1988).

6. T. M. Aziz schematically distinguishes between the "Statist" school—represented by Khomeini—which advocates for a kind of clerical monopoly over state affairs, on the one hand, and the "Populist" school—epitomized by Lebanese

mujtahid Muhammad Jawad Mughniyya—who identify the source of authority in Shiʿi society to rest with some notion of the "people." Aziz, "Popular Sovereignty in Contemporary Shiʿi Political Thought," *The Muslim World* Vol. 86, No. 3–4 (July-October 1996): 273–293.

7. Robert Gleave, "The Qadi and the Mufti in Akhbari Shiʿi Jurisprudence," in Peri Bearman, Wolfhart Heinrichs, and Bernard G. Weiss, eds., *The Law Applied: Contextualizing the Islamic Shariʿa: A Volume in Honor of Frank E. Vogel* (London: I. B. Tauris, 2008), 250.

8. Wilferd Madelung, "A Treatise of the Sharif al-Murtada on the Legality of Working for the Government," *BSOAS* Vol. 40, No. 3 (1980): 18–31.

9. Albert Hourani, "From Jabal ʿAmil to Persia," *BSOAS* Vol. 49, No. 1 (1986): 133–140; Rula Abisaab, "The Ulama of Jabal ʿAmil in Safavid Iran, 1501–1736: Marginality, Migration and Social Change," *Iranian Studies* 27(1–4) (1994): 103–122; Rula Jurdi Abisaab, *Converting Persia: Religion and Power in the Safavid Empire* (London: I. B. Tauris, 2004); and Irene Schneider, "Religious and State Jurisdiction During Nasir al-Din Shah's Reign," in Robert Gleave, ed., *Religion and Society in Qajar Iran* (London and New York: RoutledgeCurzon, 2005), 84–110.

10. Roger Savory, *Iran under the Safavids* (Cambridge: Cambridge University Press, 1980), 93.

11. Said Amir Arjomand, "Conceptions of Authority and the Transition of Shiʿism from Sectarian to National Religion in Iran," in Farhad Daftary and Josef W. Meri, eds., *Culture and memory in Medieval Islam: Essays in honour of Wilferd Madelung* (London: I. B. Tauris Publishers in association with the Institute of Ismaili Studies, 2003), 405.

12. Abbas Amanat, "In Between the Madrasa and the Marketplace: The Designation of Clerical Leadership in Modern Shiʿism," in Said Arjomand, ed., *Authority and Political Culture in Shiʿism* (Albany, NY: State University of New York, 1988), 111.

13. Hamid Algar, *Religion and State in Iran, 1785–1906: The Role of the Ulama in the Qajar Period* (Berkeley and Los Angeles: University of California Press, 1969).

14. Linda Walbridge, ed. *The Most Learned of the Shiʿa: The Institution of the Marjaʿ Taqlid* (New York: Oxford University Press, 2001).

15. Ahmad Kazemi Moussavi, "The Institutionalization of Marjaʿ-i Taqlid in the Nineteenth Century Shiʿite Community," *The Muslim World* Vol. 84, No. 3–4 (July–October 1994), 286.

16. Abbas Amanat, "From *Ijtihad* to *Wilayat-i Faqih*: The Evolution of the Shiite Legal Authority to Political Power," in Abbas Amanat and Frank Griffel, eds., *Shariʿa: Islamic Law in the Contemporary Context* (Stanford, CA: Stanford University Press, 2007), 122.

17. The growing centrality of *al-hawza al-'ilmiyya* in late nineteenth- and early twentieth-century Iraq is discussed in Sabrina Mervin, "La quête du savoir à Nağaf. Les études religieuses chez les chi'ites imâmites de la fin du XIXe siècle à 1960," *Studia Islamica* 81 (1995): 165–185. On the growing scholarly and institutional competition between Najaf and Qom from the mid-twentieth century, see Devin J. Stewart, "The Portrayal of an Academic Rivalry: Najaf and Qum in the Writings and Speeches of Khomeini, 1964–78," in Linda Walbridge, ed., *The Most Learned of the Shi'a: The Institution of the Marja' Taqlid* (New York: Oxford University Press, 2001), 216–229.

18. John Spagnolo, *France and Ottoman Lebanon: 1861–1914* (London: Ithaca Press, 1977); Leila Fawaz, *Merchants and Migrants in Nineteenth-Century Beirut* (Cambridge, Mass.: Harvard University Press, 1983); Engin Akarlı, *The Long Peace: Ottoman Lebanon, 1861–1920* (Berkeley and Los Angeles: University of California Press, 1993); and Bruce Masters, *Christians and Jews in the Ottoman Arab World: The Roots of Sectarianism* (Cambridge: Cambridge University Press, 2001).

19. Masters, *Christians and Jews in the Ottoman Empire*, 2.

20. Juan Cole, *Sacred Space and Holy War: The Politics, Culture and History of Shi'ite Islam* (London: I. B. Tauris, 2002), 16–30.

21. Allen Christelow, *Muslim Law Courts and the French Colonial State in Algeria* (Princeton, N.J.: Princeton University Press, 1985), 4. See also Michael Anderson, "Islamic Law and the Colonial Encounter in British India," in Chibli Mallat and Jane Connors, eds., *Islamic Family Law* (London: Graham and Trotman, 1993), 205–223.

22. Martin Chanock, *Law, Custom and Social Order: The Colonial Experience in Malawi and Zambia* (Cambridge: Cambridge University Press, 1985); Bernard S. Cohn, "Law and the Colonial State in India," in June Starr and Jane F. Collier, eds., *History and Power in the Study of Law: New Directions in Legal Anthropology* (Ithaca, NY: Cornell University Press, 1989), 131–152; Kristin Mann and Richard Roberts, eds., *Law in Colonial Africa* (Portsmouth, NH: Heinemann, 1991); Jeanne Maddox Toungara, "Inventing the African Family: Gender and Family Law Reform in Cote d'Ivoire," *Journal of Social History* Vol. 28, no. 1 (1994): 37–61; Sally Engle Merry, *Colonizing Hawai'i: The Cultural Power of Law* (Princeton, N.J.: Princeton University Press, 2000); Lauren A. Benton, *Law and Colonial Cultures: Legal Regimes in World History, 1400–1900* (New York: Cambridge University Press, 2002); and Tamara Loos, *Subject Siam: Family, Law, and Colonial Modernity in Thailand* (Ithaca, NY: Cornell University Press, 2006).

23. Pierre Rondot, *Les institutions politiques du Liban: des communautés traditionelles à l'état moderne* (Paris: Institut d'études de L'Orient contemporain, 1947). See also Raymond F. Betts, *Assimilation and Association in French Colonial Theory 1890–1914* (New York: Columbia University Press, 1960; reprint, Lincoln: University of Nebraska Press, 2005).

24. Stephen Hemsley Longrigg, *Syria and Lebanon under French Mandate* (London: Oxford University Press, 1958), 263.

25. Rondot, *Les institutions politiques du Liban,* 56.

26. Sulayman Taqi al-Din, *al-Qada' fi Lubnan* (Beirut: Dar al-Jadid, 1996), 421.

27. Herbert J. Liebesny, "Comparative Legal History: Its Role in the Analysis of Islamic and Modern Near Eastern Legal Institutions," *The American Journal of Comparative Law* Vol. 20, No. 1 (1972), 41.

28. Thompson, *Colonial Citizens,* 152. See also Sabrina Mervin, *Un réformisme chiite: ulémas et lettrés du Ğabal 'Amil (actuel Liban-Sud) de la fin de l'empire ottoman à l'indépendance du Liban* (Paris: Éditions Karthala, CERMOC and IFEAD, 2000), 394–398.

29. Muhsin al-Amin, *Khitat Jabal 'Amil* (Beirut: Matba'at al-Insaf, 1961), 111–112.

30. Marco Salati, "Presence and Role of the *Sadat* in and from Ğabal 'Amil (14th–18th Centuries)," *Oriente Moderno* Vol. 79, No. 2 (1999): 610.

31. John Wortabet, *Researches into the Religions of Syria; or, Sketches, Historical and Doctrinal, of its Relgious Sects* (London: James Nisbet and Co, 1860), 281.

32. Malek Abisaab, "Shiite Peasants and a New Nation in Colonial Lebanon: The Intifada of Bint Jubayl, 1936," *CSSAAME* Vol. 29, No. 3 (2009), 496. What makes this tendentious claim even more problematic is the fact that Abisaab fails to cite even a single source here.

33. Ibrahim Al Sulayman, *Buldan Jabal 'Amil: qila'hu wa-madarisuhu wa-jusuruhu wa-murujuhu wa-matahinuhu wa-jibaluhu wa-mashahiduhu* (Beirut: Mu'assasat al-Da'ira, 1995), 39–40.

34. Salati, "Presence and Role of the *Sadat,*" 604 ff. 31.

35. When I asked members of the current administration at the Sidon court what conditions Munir 'Usayran would have been working under as a practicing judge before 1926, I was told that it was not uncommon for multiple judges— say, one judge employing Hanafi standards and one Ja'fari judge—to work in the same court.

36. 'Ali 'Abd al-Mun'im Shu'ayb, *Matalib Jabal 'Amil: al-wahda, al-musawa fi Lubnan al-Kabir, 1900–1936* (Beirut: al-Mu'assasa al-Jam'iyya, 1987); Kais Firro, *Inventing Lebanon: Nationalism and the State Under the Mandate* (London: I. B. Tauris, 2003); and Tamara Chalabi, *The Shi'is of Jabal 'Amil and the New Lebanon: Community and Nation-State, 1918–1943* (London: Palgrave Macmillan, 2006).

37. *Al-'Irfan* Vol. 9, No. 4 (January 1924), 363.

38. MJS, "Continuation of the case of Rida Bek al-Tamir," September 5, 1923.

39. Muhammad Taqi al-Faqih, *Hajar wa-tin, Vol. 4* (Beirut: Dar al-Adwa', 1990), 68.

40. MAE-Nantes, Carton N° 607, Information no. 101, "Déclaration du Cheikh Mounir Asseyran sur l'autonomie des juridictions chiites," May 17, 1934. This same note can also be found in MAE-Nantes, Carton N° 456.

41. MAE-Nantes, Carton N° 1541, "S. G. Cabinet," April 8, 1925.

42. Sabrina Mervin, "L'«entité alaouite», une création française," in Pierre-Jean Luizard, ed., *Le choc colonial et l'islam: les politiques religieuses des puissances coloniales en terres d'islam* (Paris: La Découverte, 2006), 343–358.

43. MAE-Nantes, Carton N° 1541, "A/s Juridictions religieuses," May 11, 1925.

44. MAE-Nantes, Carton N° 1541, "Note," April 29, 1925.

45. "The Ja'fari *madhhab*," *al-'Irfan* Vol. 11, No. 5 (January 1926), 559.

46. The governor of Beirut, Léon Cayla, signed the *arrêté* on January 27, 1926, and Henri de Jouvenel signed it into law on January 30, 1926; the government record (*al-jarida al-rasmiyya*) published the law two weeks later, on February 12, 1926. "With Respect to the Ja'fari *Madhhab*," *al-Jarida al-Lubnaniyya al-rasmiyya*, February 12, 1926. Compare this to the formation of colonial courts in West Africa at the turn of the twentieth century, which was structurally based in the French civil law tradition as well. Richard Roberts, *Litigants and Households: African Disputes and Colonial Courts in the French Soudan, 1895–1912* (Portsmouth, NH: Heinemann, 2005).

47. Samir Kassir, *La guerre du Liban: de la dissension nationale au conflit régional (1975–1982)* (Beirut: Karthala; CERMOC, 1994), 30.

48. Wajih Kawtharani argued that Muhsin al-Amin remained the "conscience of the umma" for not "collaborating" with the French, expressing the "word of truth" in the face of an unrelenting colonialism; al-Amin "refused to enter the *institution of the colonizer* even if *their* institutions were dressed in Islamic garb." On another occasion, al-Amin is quoted as saying, "Whosoever is a servant of God is not content to become a servant of the High Commissioner." Kawtharani, "Jabal 'Amil," 79, my emphasis. Hani Fahs also briefly discusses the implications of 'Abd al-Husayn Sharaf al-Din's refusal. See Fahs, *al-Shi'a wa-l-dawla fi Lubnan: malamih fi al-ru'ya wa-l-dhakira* (Beirut: Dar al-Andalus, 1996), 93.

49. al-Faqih, *Hajar wa-tin*, Vol. 4, 70.

50. *al-Bashir*, February 1, 1926, 2. 'Abd al-Husayn Sharaf al-Din was accompanied by three MPs from South Lebanon during this meeting: Yusuf al-Zayn, Fadl al-Fadl and 'Abd al-Latif al-As'ad. The newspaper *Lisan al-hal* incorrectly identified Shaykh Husayn Sadiq as head of the delegation. *Lisan al-hal*, January 17, 1926, 2. This and other encounters between French colonial officials and Shi'i religious figures acquired greater importance in the wake of the death of al-Amin and Sharaf al-Din, as their descendants took potshots at one another over whose father (or grandfather!) was the most independent, the most hostile toward colonial interference. Author interviews with various employees of the Ja'fariyya School, Tyre, October 17, 2005.

51. Al Sulayman, *Buldan Jabal 'Amil*, 41. See also Muhammad Jawad Mughniyya, "Dalil al-'aql." In *al-Wad' al-hadir fi Jabal 'Amil fi matla' al-istiqlal: bidayat al-qahr wa-l-hirman* (Beirut: Dar al-Tayyar al-Jadid; Dar al-Jawad, 1990 [1947]), 527–532.

52. *Al-'Irfan* Vol. 11, No. 6 (February 1926), 669. His salary was initially set at 60 liras but would subsequently be put up on a par with salaries for a comparable Sunni position. *Al-'Irfan* Vol. 11, No. 7 (March 1926), 783.

53. Mervin, *Un réformisme chiite,* 433, 396.

54. Muhsin al-Amin, *Sirat al-Sayyid Muhsin al-Amin al-'Amili* ed., Haitham al-Amin and Sabrina Mervin (Beirut: Riyad el-Rayyes, 2000), 194.

55. MAE-Nantes, Cabinet Politique, Carton N° 2940, "Le Conseiller Administratif du Liban-Sud à Monsieur le Gouverneur des Colonies, Conseiller auprès du Secrétaire d'État du Gouvernement Libanais," Beirut, March 1940.

56. Ahmad 'Arif al-Zayn, *Tarikh Sayda* (Sidon: Matba'at al-'Irfan, 1913), 163. A personal file on 'Usayran compiled by the Conseiller General in South Lebanon in 1942 also claims that he "completed [his religious studies] in Najaf." MAE-Nantes, Carton N° 1112, "Reseignement (Fiche Individuelle): Cheikh Munir Osseyran."

57. When Muhammad Rashid Rida wrote disparagingly of the mores and habits of the Shi'i community in Iraq, 'Usayran (and others) responded with a series of articles in *al-'Irfan.* See Munir 'Usayran, "Kashf al-sitar 'an shubuhat 'alam kutiba 'an ahwal al-'Iraq fi al-Manar," *al-'Irfan* Vol. 1, No. 7 (July 1909): 350–355; *al-'Irfan* Vol. 1, No. 8 (August 1909), 193–195; and *al-'Irfan* Vol. 1, No. 10 (October 1909): 492–494. Among the responses to Jamal al-Din al-Qasimi's *Mizan al-jarh wa-l-ta'dil* was a piece by Muhammad al-Husayn Al Kashif al-Ghita' ("'Ayn al-Mizan," *al-'Irfan* Vol. 4, No. 9–10 [December 1912/Dhu al-Hijja 1330]: 377–388), and a work by Munir 'Usayran entitled *Ta'dil al-mizan,* which was published in Sidon in 1332, but which I have been unable to track down. See Muhammad Muhsin Agha Buzurg al-Tihrani, *al-Dhari'a ila tasanif al-shi'a* (Beirut: Dar al-Adwa', 1983), 4: 211. Agha Buzurg al-Tihrani also cites another work by 'Usayran, "Kashifat al-litham hilyat al-mu'a fi al-islam," which I have also been unable to find. Agha Buzurg al-Tihrani, *al-Dhari'a ila tasanif al-shi'a,* 17: 243.

58. *Al-'Irfan* Vol. 12, No. 2 (October 1926), 239.

59. Fahs, *al-Shi'a wa-l-dawla fi Lubnan,* esp. 92–95.

60. Julia Clancy-Smith, "Collaboration and Empire in the Middle East and North Africa: Introduction and Response," *CSSAAME* Vol. 24, No. 1 (2004), 126.

61. Author interview with Ja'fari court judge, Beirut, March 9, 2005; and Beydoun, "A Note on Confessionalism," in Theodor Hanf and Nawaf Salam, eds., *Lebanon in Limbo* (Baden-Baden: Nomos Verlagsgesellschaft, 2003), 75.

62. Sami Zubaida, *Law and Power in the Islamic World* (London: I. B. Tauris, 2003), 73.

63. Rondot, *Les institutions politiques du Liban,* Annexe no. 1, 130–133; as well as *Recueil des Arrêtés et Décisions du Grand Liban: Section II—Tome II et dernier (1er Janvier 1926—23 Mai 1926)* (Beirut: Imprimerie des Lettres, 1927).

64. MAE-Nantes, Carton N° 2940, "Lettre du Chef des Ulémas Chiites (Muhsin al-Amin) relative au statut personnel des communautés," Damascus, March 21, 1939.

65. MAE-Nantes, Carton N° 2940, Letter from Abdallah al-Hurr, Muhammad 'Ali Miqdad, Muhammad 'Izz al-Din, et al. à Son Excellence Monsieur le Haut-Commissaire de la République Française, November 28, 1939.

66. Hilmi al-Hajjar "Mahakim al-ahwal al-shakhsiyya min haythu al-qanun," in Lebanese Center for Policy Studies, ed., *al-Qada' al-lubnani: bina' al-sulta wa tatwir al-mu'assasat* (Beirut: al-Markaz al-Lubnani li-l-Dirasat, 1999), 270.

67. MAE-Nantes, Carton N° 607, Information no. 101, "Déclaration du Cheikh Mounir Asseyran sur l'autonomie des juridictions chiites," May 17, 1934.

68. Waddah Shararah presents evidence of the growing estrangement from religious tradition among young men in Jabal 'Amil. By Shararah's count the declining number of "turbaned" men had reached a new low of 42 individuals in the 1940s. Shararah, *Dawlat Hizb Allah: Lubnan mujtama'an islamiyyan* (Beirut: Dar al-Nahar, 1996), 25. On *matlabiyya*, see Shu'ayb, *Matalib Jabal 'Amil;* and Chalabi, *The Shi'is of Jabal 'Amil and the New Lebanon.* On the participation of the new generation from notable religious families in cultural and political organizations, see 'Abbas Bazzi, "Bint Jubayl sanat 1936, al-intifada wa-l-iqta'," *Dirasat 'arabiyya* 5, no. 11 (1969), 78; Qaysar Mustafa, *al-Shi'r al-'amili al-hadith fi Janub Lubnan, 1900–1978* (Beirut: Dar al-Andalus, 1981), 119; and Mervin, *Un réformisme chiite,* 209–212.

69. MAE-Nantes, Fonds Syrie-Liban, Mandat, Carton N° 1663, "A/s la répartition des subsides et le traitement des chiites par l'État Libanais," BIH Merdjayoun et Tyr N° 31, 27 July—3 August 1932. Many more *hawzas* would be established throughout Shi'i Lebanon later in the twentieth century. See Rula Jurdi Abisaab, "The Cleric as Organic Intellectual: Revolutionary Shi'ism in the Lebanese *Hawzas*," in H. E. Chehabi, ed., *Distant Relations: Iran and Lebanon in the Last 500 years* (London: Centre for Lebanese Studies in association with I. B. Tauris Publishers, 2006), 231–258.

70. Brinkley Messick notes how state salaries for *shari'a* court judges were relatively recent innovations in Islamic legal practice in highland Yemen. "Salaries replaced a much-abused practice of court fees, collected by judges directly from those who appeared before them. The theoretical reorientation of the source of judicial income, away from individuals and to the state, is an important measure of an intended shift in the definition of state control and responsibility." Messick, *The Calligraphic State: Textual Domination and History in a Muslim Society* (Berkeley and Los Angeles: University of California Press, 1993), 188.

71. MAE-Nantes, Carton N° 456, "Le Directeur de la Justice à Monsieur le Délégué du Haut-Commissaire auprès de la République Libanaise," Beirut, January 27, 1936.

72. MAE-Nantes, Carton N° 456, "Note: Démarche du Cheikh Munir Osseyran au sujet des traitements des magistrats des juridictions chiites de statut personnel," Beirut, March 4, 1937; MAE-Nantes, Cabinet Politique, Carton N° 456, L'Ambassadeur de France, Haut-Commissaire de la République en Syrie et au Liban à Monsieur le Délégué de Haut-Commissaire auprès de la République Libanaise, Beirut, March 8, 1937; MAE-Nantes, Syrie-Liban, Carton N° 456, Le Délégué du Haut-Commissaire auprès de la République Libanaise to Comte D.

de Martel, Ambassadeur, Haut-Commissaire de la République Française, Cabinet Politique N° 1497, "Magistrats religieux chiites," Beirut, April 20, 1937; MAE-Nantes, Syrie-Liban, Carton N° 456, Cabinet Politique, "Note: Augmentation des traitements des magistrats chiites des tribunaux chérié," Beirut, May 20, 1937; "Tahdid al-rawatib fi al-mahakim al-ja'fariyya," *al-Bashir*, no. 5389, 1937, p. 5, cited in Mervin, *Un réformisme chiite*; and MAE-Nantes, Carton N° 456, Decrets N° 1565 and 1566, signed into law by Emile Eddé, December 10, 1937.

73. MAE-Nantes, Carton N° 456, L'Ambassadeur de France, Haut-Commissaire de la République en Syrie et au Liban à Monsieur le Délégué du Haut-Commissaire auprès de la République Libanaise, December 7, 1936; MAE-Nantes, Syrie-Liban, Cabinet Politique, Beyrouth, Carton N° 456, Cheikh Hassan Sadek, Mufti Chiite de Saida à Monsieur l'Ambassadeur de France, Haut-Commissaire de la République Française, Sidon, December 8, 1936; MAE-Nantes, Carton N° 456, Damien de Martel, "Cabinet Politique N° 10290," Beirut, December 11, 1936.

74. An *arrêté* from December 22 formally created that commission, which was composed of both Sunni and Shi'i figures, including Shaykh Muhammad Tawfiq Khaled, 'Abd al-Husayn Sharaf al-Din, Ahmad al-Husayni, Sami Solh, Wafiq Qassar and Rida Tamir. MAE-Nantes, Carton N° 2960, Abdallah Beyhum, Le Chef du Cabinet du Secrétariat d'Etat, Arrêté No. 531, December 22, 1939. Also see the translated telegrams of support from January 24, 26, and 27, 1940, MAE-Nantes, Carton N° 2960.

75. *Al-'Irfan* Vol. 29, No. 8–9 (December 1939-January 1940), 885.

76. MAE-Nantes, Carton N° 2960, Aref Zein, Abbas Hor, Hassan Maroua, Nadim Jaouhar, Khalil Assairan, Nagib Chaib à Son Excellence le Secrétaire d'État, Beirut, n.d. (possibly January 26, 1940).

77. MAE-Nantes, Syrie-Liban, Carton N° 383, "Note a/s tribunaux chériés," Sidon, November 19, 1940; MAE-Nantes, Syrie-Liban, Carton N° 383, Mémoire relatif aux Tribunaux Jaafari adressée à Son Excellence, Monsieur Gabriel Puaux, Haut-Commissaire de la République Française, received November 20, 1940, translated November 21, 1940.

78. MAE-Nantes, Carton N° 2960, Hussein Moughannié à Son Excellence le Haut-Commissaire de la République française, "Objet: a/s de la fusion des tribunaux Jaafari avec les tribunaux sunnites," Sidon, December 28, 1939.

79. MAE-Nantes, Carton N° 2960, Chiekh [*sic*] Hussein Moughnye, Le President de l'Association des Ulemas à Son Excellence Monsieur le Haut-Commissaire de la République Française en Syrie et au Liban c/o de Monsieur le Conseiller Administratif du Liban Sud, March 5, 1940.

80. Allan Christelow, "The Transformation of the Muslim Court System in Colonial Algeria: Reflections on the Concept of Autonomy," in Aziz al-Azmeh, ed., *Islamic Law: Social and Historical Contexts* (London and New York: Routledge, 1988), 220.

81. Oussama Arabi, *Studies in Modern Islamic Law and Jurisprudence* (The Hague: Kluwer Law International, 2001), esp. 121–146.

82. Meir Zamir, *Lebanon's Quest: The Road to Independence* (London: I. B. Tauris, 2000), 244.

83. Leonard Binder, ed., *Politics in Lebanon* (New York: John Wiley and Sons, 1966); Iliya F. Harik, *Politics and Change in a Traditional Society: Lebanon, 1711–1845* (Princeton, N.J.: Princeton University Press, 1968); Michael Hudson, *The Precarious Republic: Political Modernization in Lebanon* (New York: Random House, 1968); and William Polk, *The Opening of South Lebanon, 1788–1840: A Study of the Impact of the West on the Middle East* (Cambridge, Mass.: Harvard University Press, 1963).

84. Nadine Méouchy, "L'État et espaces communautaires dans le Liban sous Mandat français," *Maghreb, Machrek* 123 (1989), 88–90. The same point is reiterated in Méouchy, "Le Pacte National 1943–1946: les ambiguïtés d'un temps politique d'exception," in Gérard D. Khoury, ed., *Sélim Takla 1895–1945: une contribution à l'indépendance du Liban* (Paris, Beyrouth: Karthala, Dar al-Nahar, 2004), 463.

85. Zubaida, *Law and Power in the Islamic World,* 151.

86. Jamal J. Nasir, *The Islamic Law of Personal Status* (The Hague: Kluwer Law International, 2002), 34

87. Sofia Saadeh, "Basic Issues Concerning the Personal Status Laws in Lebanon," in Thomas Scheffler, ed., *Religion between Violence and Reconciliation* (Beirut: Orient-Institut, 2002), 450.

88. Chibli Mallat, *Shi'i Thought from the South of Lebanon* (Oxford: Centre for Lebanese Studies, 1988), 16.

89. Beydoun, "A Note on Confessionalism," 76.

90. For the text of the law, see "Qanun al-mahakim al-shar'iyya," in 'Arif Zayn al-Zayn, ed., *Qawanin wa-nusus wa-ahkam al-ahwal al-shakhsiyya wa-tanzim al-tawa'if al-islamiyya fi Lubnan* (Beirut: Manshurat al-Halabi al-Huquqiyya, 2003), 409–410. See, too, 'Ali Hubb Allah, *Sharh qanun al-mahakim al-shar'iyya al-Lubnani li-l-ta'ifatayn al-ja'fariyya wa-l-sunniyya al-sadir bi-tarikh 16/7/1962 ma'a ta'dilatihi hatta 'am 2002 M: dirasat wa-buhuth fiqhiyya wa-qanuniyya muqarana* (Beirut: Dar al-Mahajja al-Bayda', 2003).

91. Al-Hajjar, "Mahakim al-ahwal al-shakhsiyya min haythu al-qanun," 269.

92. On the distinction between French colonial policy and practice, see David Robinson, "French 'Islamic' policy and practice in late nineteenth-century Senegal," *Journal of African History* Vol. 29, No. 3 (1988): 415–435.

4. Practicing Sectarianism

1. MAE-Nantes, Carton N° 2958, Le Délégué du Haut-Commissaire pour le Contrôle Général des Wakfs, "Note Pour Monsieur le Secrétaire Général: Requête des musulmans Djafarites de Macheguera," Beirut, July 24, 1928; and MAE-Nantes, Carton N° 2958, Le Haut-Commissariat P. I. de la République Française

(Privat Aubouard) à Monsieur le Délégué du Haut-Commissaire, N° 5479 "Gestion des Wakfs de la communauté chiite," Beirut, October 19, 1929.

2. Lauren Benton, "Colonial Law and Cultural Difference: Jurisdictional Politics and the Formation of the Colonial State," *CSSH* Vol. 41, No. 3 (Jul., 1999): 563–588; and Simon Harrison, "Cultural Difference as Denied Resemblance: Reconsidering Nationalism and Ethnicity," *CSSH* Vol. 45, No. 2 (Apr., 2003): 343–361.

3. Ayesha Jalal, "Negotiating Colonial Modernity and Cultural Difference: Indian Muslim Conceptions of Community and Nation, 1878–1914," in Leila Tarazi Fawaz and C. A. Bayly, eds., *Modernity and Culture: From the Mediterranean to the Indian Ocean* (New York: Columbia University Press, 2002), 241.

4. See Gyanendra Pandey, *The Construction of Communalism in Colonial North India* (Delhi and New York: Oxford University Press, 1990); and Ussama Makdisi, *The Culture of Sectarianism: Community, History and Violence in Nineteenth-century Ottoman Lebanon* (Berkeley and Los Angeles: University of California Press, 2000). Such an instrumental reading of sectarianism in Pakistan can also be found more recently in Tahir Kamran, "Contextualizing Sectarian Militancy in Pakistan: A Case Study of Jhang," *Journal of Islamic Studies* Vol. 20, No. 1 (2009): 55–85.

5. Roger Lescot, *Les chiites du Liban-Sud,* Rapport N° 3 du CHEAM, (1936), 13–14.

6. Louis Cardon, *Le régime de la propriété foncière en Syrie et au Liban* (Paris: Recueil Sirey, 1932), 110–111.

7. Louis Rolland and Pierre Lampué, *Précis de legislation coloniale* (Paris: Librarie Dalloz, 1931), 7, 100.

8. D. I. Murr and Ed. Bourbousson, "Du statut personnel en Syrie et au Liban," *Bulletin de l'Institut Intermediaire International de la Haye* Vol. 26 , No. 2 (1932), 264.

9. Pierre Rondot, *Les institutions politiques du Liban: des communautés traditionelles à l'état moderne* (Paris: Institut d'études de L'Orient contemporain, 1947), 69.

10. Bilani and Decocq, "Preface," in Maher Mahmassani and Ibtissam Messarra, eds., *Statut Personnel: textes en vigeur au Liban* (Beirut: Faculté de droit et des sciences économiques, 1970), v, my emphasis.

11. On the history of *waqf* administration in other colonial contexts, see Gregory C. Kozlowski, *Muslim Endowments and Society in British India* (Cambridge: Cambridge University Press, 1985); Tim Carmichael, "British 'Practice' towards Islam in the East Africa Protectorate: Muslim Officials, *Waqf* Administration and Secular Education in Mombasa and Environs, 1895–1920," *Journal of Muslim Minority Affairs* Vol. 17, No.2 (Oct. 1997): 293–310; and Khoo Salma Nasution, "Colonial Intervention and Transformation of Muslim *Waqf* Settlements in Urban Penang: The Role of the Endowments Board," *Journal of Muslim Minority Affairs* Vol. 22, No. 2 (Oct. 2002): 299–315.

12. MJN, Sijill al-watha'iq al-shar'iyya, (Case 31: dabt 3, safha 2, asas 81 or 86, writing illegible), January 11 1930—September 7, 1936. The case was also sent to the President of the Higher Court (*mahkamat al-tamyiz*) on July 27, from whom it was then returned with the summons to Nabatiyya on July 31 requesting that the local court adjudicate the case.

13. MAE-Nantes, Carton N° 2958, Letter N° 5 adressée à Monsieur le Délégué du Haut-Commissaire pour le Contrôle Général des Wakfs, July 26, 1930. The same letter can also be found in the folder labeled Correspondences (*murasalat*), 1929–1932, in the Sidon Ja'fari court.

14. MAE-Nantes, Carton N° 2958, Letter N° 181 adressée à Monsieur le Président de la Cour de Cassation Chéréi Jaafari, July 28, 1930. Although the French translation refers to the author as, "Le Cadi de Saida," signature "illegible," the original Arabic letter, which was attached, clearly bears the signature of Asadallah Safa. Neematallah Hamdar was a Shi'i notable from the village of Bashtilida-Jubayl. See 'Ali Raghib Haydar Ahmad, *al-Muslimun al-shi'a fi Kisirwan wa-Jubayl: siyasi-yyan—tarikhiyyan—ijtima'iyyan bi-l-watha'iq wa-l-suwwar 1842–2006* (Beirut: Dar al-Hadi, 2007), 616.

15. MJS, "Correspondences" Folder, "Letter from Qa'immaqam of Jezzine to the Saida Judge," August 27, 1930.

16. MJS, "Correspondences" Folder, Na'im Nu'man Rizq, Ilyas Musa Kawtharani, Ilyas Tannus Aoun and Khalil al-Nashif to the Qa'immaqam," August 27, 1930.

17. MJS, "Correspondences" Folder, Munir 'Usayran to Saida Judge, September 25, 1930.

18. Aharon Layish, "The Muslim *Waqf* in Jerusalem after 1967: Beneficiaries and Management," in Faruk Bilici, ed., *Le waqf dans le monde musulman contem-porain (XIXᵉ–XXᵉ Siècles): fonctions sociales, économiques et politiques: actes de la Table ronde d'Istanbul, 13–14 Novembre 1992* (Istanbul: Institut français d'études anatoliennes, 1994), 162.

19. MJN, 'adad 17: (dabt 17, safha 119, asas 69), May 12, 1931.

20. MJS, Letter from residents of 'Aqrun to the President of the Ja'fari Court, November 1934.

21. MAE-Nantes, Carton N° 2958, Le Délégué Du H. C. Pour le Contrôle Général Des Wakfs à Son Excellence le President de la Cour de Cassation Cherieh Jaafari, N° 564, Beirut, August 6, 1930; MAE-Nantes, Carton N° 2958, "DROGMANAT: Cour de Cassation Chéréi, N° 8, Monsieur le Délégué du Haut-Commissaire pour le Contrôle Général des Wakfs," November 22, 1930.

22. Daftar al-waridat al-mahfuza 'ayanan li-l-awqaf wa-tawliyyatiha (hereafter DA), MJB, No. 5, April 4, 1931.

23. DA, No. 4, no date. "There is no specific study on the Murtadà family to date," Marco Salati correctly notes. Yet as late as the turn of the twenty-first cen-tury, "the Murtadàs are the administrators of the *mazar* [of Nabi Nuh] and, more

importantly, of the Shi'i shrine of Sayyidah (Sitt) Zaynab, just outside Damascus." Salati, "Presence and Role of the *Sadat* in and from Ğabal 'Amil (14th–18th Centuries)," *Oriente Moderno* Vol. 79, No. 2 (1999), 599 ff. 9.

24. DA, No. 12, November 12, 1935.

25. MAE-Nantes, Carton N° 944, Pechkoff, "Note: Situation Politique au Liban-Sud et son evolution, N° 179," Sidon, April 6, 1936.

26. Mervin, *Un réformisme chiite*, 273.

27. MJT, Waqf folder, January 12, 1932; "al-Madrasa al-ja'fariyya wa-l-awqaf fi Sur," *al-'Irfan* Vol. 30, No. 8–9 (November–December 1940): 383–387.

28. MAE-Nantes, Carton N° 2958, Kazem Khalil, Lettre adressée à Monsieur Conseiller du Haut-Commissariat pour les Wakfs Musulmans, August 2, 1933.

29. MAE-Nantes, Carton N° 2958, L'Inspecteur Général du Contrôle des Wakfs et de l'Immatriculation Foncière à Son Excellence le President de la Cour de Cassation, Objet: a.s. Constitution d'un Conseil Supérieur des Wakfs Chiites, August 18, 1933.

30. Although Munir 'Usayran never used the term, this categorical dilemma might have been resolved by considering Shi'i *waqf*s in the pre-Mandate period as "exceptional" (*mustathna*), that is, those which have no formal registration and, therefore, are administered under the auspices of the Ja'fari *shari'a* courts. Salim Hariz, *al-Waqf: dirasat wa-abhath* (Beirut: al-Jami'a al-Lubnaniyya, 1994), 26. See also Muhammad Ja'far Shams al-Din, *al-Waqf wa-ahkamuhu fi al-fiqh al-islami wa-l-qawanin al-lubnaniyya: dirasa muqarana* (Beirut: Dar al-Hadi, 2005), 69–72.

31. MAE-Nantes, Carton N° 2958, Munir Osseiran à Monsieur Inspecteur-Général du Contrôle des Wakfs et de l'Immatriculation Foncière, Beirut, November 28, 1933.

32. MAE-Nantes, Carton N° 2957, Le Directeur de la Justice à Monsieur Délégué du Haut-Commissaire auprès de la République Libanaise, Beirut, September 23, 1933.

33. DA, No. 18, July 11, 1936, 16.

34. Allan Christelow, "The Transformation of the Muslim Court System in Colonial Algeria: Reflections on the Concept of Autonomy," in Aziz al-Azmeh, ed., *Islamic Law: Social and Historical Context* (London and New York: Routledge, 1988), 226.

35. Mushirul Hasan, "Traditional Rites and Contested Meanings: Sectarian Strife in Colonial Lucknow," in Mushirul Hasan, ed., *Islam, Communities and the Nation: Muslim Identities in South Asia and Beyond* (New Delhi: Manohar, 1998), 361.

36. MJB, 356/1929, August 22, 1929.

37. MJB, 356/1929, September 11, 1929.

38. MJB, 356/1929, October 30, 1929.

39. MAE-Nantes, Carton N° 2958, Mounir Osseiran à Monsieur L'Inspecteur General du Contrôle des Wakfs et de l'Immatriculation Foncière, Beirut, November 19, 1932.

40. MAE-Nantes, Carton N° 2958, Le Délégué Genéral du Haut-Commissaire à Monsieur le Délégué du Haut-Commissaire auprès du Gouvernement de la République Libanaise, Beirut, November 25, 1932; MAE-Nantes, Carton N° 2958, Comte D. de Martel, Ambassadeur, Haut-Commissaire de la République Française en Syrie et au Liban à Monsieur le Conseiller du Haut-Commissariat, Délégué du Haut-Commissaire auprès du Gouvernement de la République Libanaise, Beirut, December 19, 1933.

41. MAE-Nantes, Carton N° 2958, Letter from Ahmad Sa'id Ahmad to Munir 'Usayran, February 28, 1931.

42. Sidon Ja'fari judge Asadallah Safa to President of Ja'fari Court, DA, No. 2, March 11, 1931; MAE-Nantes, Carton N° 2958, N° 58, Letter from Asadallah Safa to Mounir 'Usayran, March 11, 1931.

43. DA, March 14, 1931.

44. MJS, "Letter from "abna' al-ta'ifa al-islamiyya in Joun" to the President of the Higher Ja'fari *shari'a* court (w/ 33 signatures)," January 10, 1934.

45. MAE-Nantes, Carton N° 2958, Le President de la Cour de Cassation Cherieh Djafaarite, Djoun, June 25, 1936.

46. MAE-Nantes, Carton N° 607, Telegram no. 2085 from Nabatiyya to Beirut, June 23–24, 1936.

47. MJS, Daftar Sadirat 1929, "Copy of a petition from the people of Joun, by way of the governor of the Shuf, to the President of the Ja'fari Court," February 12, 1929.

48. MAE-Nantes, Carton N° 2958, Le Cadi Djafarite de Saida à Monsieur le Conservateur Foncier du Liban-Sud, Sidon, November 13, 1933.

49. MAE-Nantes, Carton N° 2958, Mounir Osseiran à Monsieur L'Inspecteur General Du Contrôle des Wakfs et de L'Immatriculation Foncière, Beirut, November 22, 1933.

50. MAE-Nantes, Carton N° 2958, Le Délégué du Haut-Commissaire auprès de la République Libanaise à Monsieur le Comte D. de Martel, Ambassadeur, Haut-Commissaire de la République Française (Contrôle des Wakfs et de l'Immatriculation Foncière), Beirut, July 17, 1934.

51. MAE-Nantes, Carton N° 2958, Contrôle des Wakfs et de Immatriculation Foncière, No. 298, L'Inspecteur General du Contrôle des Wakfs et de l'Immatriculation Foncière à Son Excellence le President de la Cour De Cassation Cherieh Jaafarie. Objet: a.s. du cimetière "El Ansar" sis à Saida, Beirut, July 28, 1934.

52. MAE-Nantes, Carton N° 2958, Adel Abdallah Osseiran, Ahmad Nassif El Assaad, Nazar El Zein, Hussein Khalil, Ali Jawad, Hussein Ali Nasser, Hassan El Fadel et al. à le Cadi Chérri Djafarite of Saida, Ali Mouhssein El Husseini, Sidon, January 18, 1938.

53. MAE-Nantes, Carton N° 2958, Mounir Osseiran à Monsieur L'Inspecteur General Du Contrôle des Wakfs et de L'Immatriculation Foncière, Beirut, November 22, 1933.

54. Ayesha Jalal, "Exploding Communalism: The Politics of Muslim Identity in South Asia," in Sugata Bose and Ayesha Jalal, eds., *Nationalism, Democracy and Development: State and Politics in India* (Delhi: Oxford University Press, 1997), 79.

55. Mounzer Jaber, "al-Kiyan al-siyasi li-Jabal 'Amil qabla 1920," in Ibrahim Beydoun, ed., *Safahat min tarikh Jabal 'Amil* (Beirut: al-Majlis al-Thaqafi li-Lubnan al-Janubi, 1979), 97.

56. C. A. Bayly, "The Pre-History of 'Communalism'? Religious Conflict in India, 1700–1860," *Modern Asian Studies* Vol. 19, No. 2 (1985), 189.

57. For another riff on the double entendre of "practice," see Gary Wilder, "Practicing Citizenship in Imperial Paris," in John L. Comaroff and Jean Comaroff, eds., *Civil Society and the Political Imagination in Africa* (Chicago: The University of Chicago Press, 2000), 51; and Wilder, *The French Imperial Nation-State: Negritude and Colonial Humanism Between the Two World Wars* (Chicago: The University of Chicago Press, 2005).

58. Tamara Chalabi, *The Shi'is of Jabal 'Amil and the New Lebanon: Community and Nation-State, 1918–1943* (London: Palgrave Macmillan, 2006); and 'Ali 'Abd al-Mun'im Shu'ayb, *Matalib Jabal 'Amil: al-wahda, al-musawa fi Lubnan al-Kabir, 1900–1936* (Beirut: al-Mu'assasa al-Jam'iyya, 1987).

59. Stephen Hemsley Longrigg, *Syria and Lebanon under French Mandate* (London: Oxford University Press, 1958), 264.

60. Nadine Méouchy, "La réforme des juridictions religieuses en Syrie et au Liban (1921–1939): raisons de la puissance mandataire et raisons des communautés," in Pierre-Jean Luizard, ed., *Le choc colonial et l'islam: les politiques religieuses des puissances coloniales en terres d'islam* (Paris: La Découverte, 2006), 362.

5. Adjudicating Society at the Ja'fari Court

1. Fouad Ajami, *The Vanished Imam: Musa Al-Sadr and the Shi'a of Lebanon* (Ithaca, NY: Cornell University Press, 1986), 11. See also As'ad Abukhalil's review of Ajami, *MERIP* (Jan–Feb 1987), 46.

2. I use the term advisedly because there are no dedicated archives to speak of, but rooms that may contain metal file cabinets that hold incomplete collections of folders, files and notebooks. These were inside functioning courts, sources for ongoing, current cases and not spaces devoted to historical research.

3. Lawrence Rosen, "Islamic 'Case Law' and the Logic of Consequence," in June Starr and Jane F. Collier, eds., *History and Power in the Study of Law: New Directions in Legal Anthropology* (Ithaca, NY: Cornell University Press, 1989), 318.

4. My access to these sources was graciously facilitated by the hospitality of the leadership of the Ja'fari Court in Lebanon, particularly President Hassan

'Awwad—but also many others, who shall remain nameless—under the condition that all those who appear in those records would remain anonymous. I have honored those requests, therefore, by using pseudonyms where appropriate. It would be worthwhile for a historian of Islamic law to provide a quantitative analysis of cases brought before the Ja'fari *shari'a* courts during this period. Such a project would face substantial obstacles, not least of which are due to physical damage to the records, which would render any statistical analysis partial and incomplete. In addition, it would be useful to seek the requisite permissions in order to make such documents publicly available for other researchers.

5. Muhsin al-Amin, *Khitat Jabal 'Amil* (Beirut: Matba'at al-Insaf, 1961), 111.

6. Elizabeth Thompson, *Colonial Citizens: Republican Rights, Paternal Privilege and Gender in French Syria and Lebanon* (New York: Columbia University Press, 2000).

7. On colonial courts in the French Soudan that were similar to those instituted in French Mandate Lebanon, see Richard Roberts, *Litigants and Households: African Disputes and Colonial Courts in the French Soudan, 1895–1912* (Portsmouth, NH: Heinemann, 2005).

8. MAE-Nantes, Carton N° 456, Le Directeur de la Justice à Monsieur le Délégué du Haut-Commissaire auprès de la République Libanaise, Beirut, January 27, 1936.

9. For a brief note on Asadallah Safa, see Hasan Muhammad Salih, *Antulujiyat al-adab al-'amili: al-adab al-'amili min al-taqalid ila al-tajdid* (Beirut: Dar al-Juman, 1997), Vol. 2, 623. The passing of Sayyid Muhammad Yahya Safi al-Din was noted in *al-'Irfan* Vol. 36, No. 3 (March 1949), 334; Sayyid 'Ali Fahs was mourned in *al-'Irfan* Vol. 37, No. 5 (May 1950), 596.

10. Michael G. Peletz, *Islamic Modern: Religious Courts and Cultural Politics in Malaysia* (Princeton, N.J.: Princeton University Press, 2002), 48, 277. For another critique of such reductive interpretations of the practice of authority in Islamic jurisprudence, see David S. Powers, "Kadijustiz or Qadi-Justice? A Paternity Dispute from Fourteenth-Century Morocco," *Islamic Law and Society* Vol. 1, No. 3 (1994): 332–366. As the Ja'fari court records are quite fragmentary, what Powers calls "the art of judicial narrative" must be found through the process of historical reconstruction.

11. MJB, 370/1931, October 15,1931.

12. MJB, 370/1931, January 9, 1932.

13. MJB, 370/1931, November 4, 1931.

14. Legally establishing one's marital status was required in order to raise any other cases (relating to divorce, inheritance, or custody) before the judge.

15. MJB, 164/1938, September 20, 1937.

16. Sabrina Mervin, *Un réformisme chiite: ulémas et lettrés du Ğabal 'Amil (actuel Liban-Sud) de la fin de l'empire ottoman à l'indépendance du Liban* (Paris: Éditions Karthala, CERMOC and IFEAD, 2000), esp. 275–329 (Ch. 7, "Le rapprochement entre les branches de l'Islam (*taqrib*)"); and Rainer Brunner, *Islamic Ecumenism in the 20th Century: The Azhar and Shiism between Rapprochement and Restraint* (Leiden: Brill, 2004).

17. Linda Walbridge, ed., *The Most Learned of the Shi'a: The Institution of the Marja' Taqlid* (New York: Oxford University Press, 2001).

18. MT, 563/1941.

19. MT, 563/1941, November 10, 1942.

20. Lokman Slim, Private Papers, Beirut, Letter from 'Abd al-Latif al-As'ad to 'Abd al-Husayn Muruwwa, May 23, 1935. I am grateful to Lokman Slim for granting me access to part of his rich archival collection.

21. MAE-Nantes, Carton N° 1111, Information N° 132, Conseiller Administratif du Liban-Sud (E. Pruneaud), January 28, 1943.

22. MJB, 27/1939, August 26, 1939.

23. Felicitas Opwis, "*Maslaha* in Contemporary Islamic Legal Theory," *Islamic Law and Society* Vol. 12, No. 2 (2005), 223.

24. *Al-'Irfan* reported that 'Ali Nusret Bek al-As'ad was appointed a consulting member of the Beirut *mahkamat al-isti'naf* to replace Yusuf Bey Mukhaybir Haydar. *Al-'Irfan* Vol. 9, No. 1 (October 1923), 102.

25. MJS, Sijill al-da'awa (Safha 18, Jalsa 5, Sijill 24), December 28, 1929. If the witness was "known" to the court, his testimony (and it was always a he) was deemed trustworthy, whereas Shi'i jurisprudence technically demands four male witnesses for verification. But as Allan Christelow points out, "The term 'witnesses' poorly conveys the meaning of 'shuhud' here, for these were not people who offered evidence in the case, but rather legists who lent their moral reputation and political weight to the judgment." Christelow, *Muslim Law Courts and the French Colonial State in Algeria* (Princeton, N.J.: Princeton University Press, 1985), 58. In the case of purported *zina* below we will also see that witnesses were drawn from a range of class backgrounds.

26. MJS, dabt 4, safha 98, sijill 4, March 1, 1932.

27. MJB, 98/1932, April 30, 1932.

28. MJB, 98/1932, May 10, 1932.

29. MJB, 98/1932, May 18, 1932.

30. As Oussama Arabi points out, "there is no direct or obvious connection between *safah* and unreasonable spending. And yet it was this sense of the word that came to prevail in mainstream classical Sunni jurisprudence, where a semantic equivalence was established between the *safih* and the *mubadhdhir*, the spendthrift." Arabi, "The Interdiction of the Spendthrift (*Al-Safih*): A Human Rights Debate in Classical *Fiqh*," *Islamic Law and Society* Vol. 7, No. 3 (2000), 301.

31. MJB, 98/1932, May 25, 1932.

32. Annelies Moors, *Women, Property, and Islam: Palestinian Experiences, 1920–1990* (New York: Cambridge University Press, 1995); Beshara Doumani, "Endowing Family: Waqf, Property and Gender in Tripoli and Nablus, 1800–1860," *CSSH* Vol. 40, No. 1 (Jan., 1998): 3–41; and Margaret Meriwether, *The Kin Who Count: Family and Society in Ottoman Aleppo, 1770–1840* (Austin: University of Texas Press, 1999).

33. Shala Haeri, *Law of Desire: Temporary Marriage in Islam* (Syracuse, NY: Syracuse University Press, 1989); and Arthur Gribetz, *Strange Bedfellows: Mut'at al-nisa' and Mut'at al-hajj: A Study Based on Sunni and Shi'i Sources of Tafsir, Hadith and Fiqh* (Berlin: Klaus Schwarz Verlag, 1994); but also 'Abd al-Husayn Sharaf al-Din, "Nikah al-mut'a," *al-'Irfan* Vol. 36, No. 10 (October 1949): 1014–1021.

34. MJB, 48/1934–35, November 5, 1934.

35. MJB, 48/1934–35, November 8, 1934.

36. MJB, 48/1934–35, February 14, 1935.

37. MJB, 11/1935, February 21, 1935.

38. MJB, 11/1935, February 27, 1935. The higher court (*mahkamat al-tamyiz*) upheld the ruling several months later. MT 301/1935, December 18, 1935. Reproduced with MJB 11/1935, February 27, 1935.

39. J. Darché, *Les chiites du Liban,* Rapport N° 108 du CHEAM, (1937), 21.

40. MJB, 176/1932, August 30, 1932.

41. MJB, 176/1932, August 16, 1932.

42. MJB, 176/1932, September 19, 1932. I was unable to find the final outcome of this case.

43. Translation from Abdullah Yusuf Ali, *The Holy Qur-an: Text, Translation and Commentary* (Lahore: Shaykh Muhammad Ashraf, 1938), 897–898.

44. Ibid., 902.

45. MJB, 176/1932, September 22, 1932. Shahla Haeri explains how the *raj'i* divorce "is a semi-final divorce in which the bonds of marriage are not completely severed. Although the husband and wife are separated from each other, the wife cannot marry within the next three months following her divorce, and the husband has the right to return to his wife during this period and to resume his marital duties. Just as he has the right to return, she has the right to be supported. On the other hand the husband's right to return is unilateral, meaning that legally the wife's consent is not sought." Haeri, "Divorce in Contemporary Iran: A Male Prerogative in Self-Will," in Chibli Mallat and Jane Connors, eds., *Islamic Family Law* (London: Graham and Trotman, 1993), 64. By contrast, in the case of *khul'*, "not only must a wife forego her brideprice, she must even pay something in order to buy her freedom. . . . Not only must the demand for divorce be litigated, but her husband has to agree to it. A woman may initiate divorce and buy back, as it were, her freedom." Ibid., 66.

46. "*Al-walad li-l-firash wa li-l-'ahir al-hajar.*" Uri Rubin points out that *hajar* has also been interpreted in the figurative sense of "nothing." Rubin, ""Al-Walad Li-l-Firāsh": On the Islamic Campaign against «Zinā»," *Studia Islamica* No. 78 (1993), 5. See also Etan Kohlberg, "The Position of the Walad Zinā in Imāmī Shī'ism," *BSOAS* Vol. 48, No. 2 (1985): 237–266.

47. Reem's lawyer cited the following *hadith: "al-Ilhaq bihi yakun ma' isal ma'ihi ilayha wa-law lam yatahaqqaq dakhulahu 'alayha."*

48. MJB, 176/1932, October 4, 1932.

49. MJB, 231/1932–33, November 12, 1932. Evidence of the divorce transaction was requested from the Higher Court (*mahkamat al-tamyiz al-shar'iyya*) and when the proof was delivered the divorce was confirmed.

50. MJB, 231/1932–33, December 22, 1932.

51. Ottoman law manuals confirm this method of dealing with cases of *zina*. See Colin Imber, "Zinā in Ottoman Law," in Imber, ed., *Studies in Ottoman History and Law* (Istanbul: Isis Press, 1996), 175–206. For a brilliant analysis of a sixteenth-century case of *zina* from a provincial town in the Ottoman Empire, see Leslie Peirce, *Morality Tales: Law and Gender in the Ottoman Court of Aintab* (Berkeley and Los Angeles: University of California Press, 2003), 351–374. For an extensive discussion of *zina* and public morality in the context of Islamic and Ottoman law in eighteenth-century Aleppo, see Elyse Semerdjian, *"Off the Straight Path": Illicit Sex, Law, and Community in Ottoman Aleppo* (Syracuse, NY: Syracuse University Press, 2008), esp. 3–28 (Ch. 1, "*Zina* in Islamic Legal Discourse") and 29–58 (Ch. 2, "*Zina* in Ottoman Law").

52. MJB, 231/1932–33, February 9, 1933.

53. MJB, 231/1932–33, February 20, 1933.

54. For the sake of argument, it might be considered that Reem was coerced into appearing and making her admission just to get Jawad off the hook. On the other hand, one could also imagine that Reem knew the law, namely that such a claim of *zina* needed to be made four times in court and that she wouldn't have to stand behind her claim for long, and that she could remain under the protection of Jawad no matter what she might have said on that first occasion.

55. Fuad I. Khuri, "Secularization and 'Ulama' Networks Among Sunni and Shi'i Religious Officials," in Halim Barakat, ed., *Toward a Viable Lebanon* (London, Washington: Croom Helm; Center for Contemporary Arab Studies, Georgetown University, 1988), 89.

56. Muhammad Qasim Zaman, *The Ulama in Contemporary Islam: Custodians of Change* (Princeton, N.J.: Princeton University Press, 2002), 23.

57. Iris Agmon, *Family and Court: Legal Culture and Modernity in Late Ottoman Palestine* (Syracuse, NY: Syracuse University Press, 2006); Beshara Doumani, "Palestinian Islamic Court Records: A Source for Socioeconomic History," *MESA Bulletin* (1985): 155–172; Peirce, *Morality Tales;* and Yvonne J. Seng, "Standing at the Gates of Justice: Women in the Law Courts of Early Sixteenth-Century Üsküdar, Istanbul," in Mindie Lazarus-Black and Susan F. Hirsch, eds., *Contested States: Law, Hegemony and Resistance* (New York: Routledge, 1993), 207–230.

58. Sally Engle Merry, *Colonizing Hawai'i: The Cultural Power of Law* (Princeton, N.J.: Princeton University Press, 2000), 9.

59. Daisy Hilse Dwyer, "Outside the Courts: Extra-Legal Strategies for the Subordination of Women," in Margaret Jean Hay and Marcia Wright, eds., *African*

Women & the Law: Historical Perspectives (Boston: Boston University African Studies Center, 1982), 90.

60. Matthew H. Sommer, *Sex, Law, and Society in Late Imperial China* (Stanford: Stanford University Press, 2000), 30.

61. Susan F. Hirsch, *Pronouncing and Persevering: Gender and the Discourses of Disputing in an African Islamic Court* (Chicago: The University of Chicago Press, 1998), 245.

62. Martin Chanock, *Law, Custom and Social Order: The Colonial Experience in Malawi and Zambia* (Cambridge: Cambridge University Press, 1985).

6. ʿAmili Shiʿis into Shiʿi Lebanese?

1. Augustus Richard Norton, *Amal and the Shiʿa: Struggle for the Soul of Lebanon* (Austin: University of Texas Press, 1987), 25.

2. Mustafa Muhammad Bazzi, *Jabal ʿAmil wa-tawabiʿhu fi shamal Filastin (bahth fi tatawwur al-milkiyya al-ʿaqariyya)* (Beirut: Dar al-Mawasim, 2002), 42.

3. Masʿud Dahir, *al-Judhur al-tarikhiyya li-l-masʾala al-ziraʿiyya al-lubnaniyya 1900–1950* (Beirut: Manshurat al-Jamiʿa al-Lubnaniyya, 1983), 14.

4. Roger Owen, "The political economy of Grand Liban, 1920–1970," in Owen, ed., *Essays on the Crisis in Lebanon* (London: Ithaca Press, 1976), 23–32; Leila Fawaz, *Merchants and Migrants in Nineteenth-Century Beirut* (Cambridge, Mass.: Harvard University Press, 1983); Owen, "The Study of Middle Eastern Industrial History: Notes on the Interrelationship between Factories and Small-scale Manufacturing with Special References to Lebanese Silk and Egyptian Sugar, 1900–1930," *IJMES* Vol. 16, No. 4. (Nov. 1984): 475–487; Akram Khater, ""House" to "Goddess of the House": Gender, Class, and Silk in 19th-Century Mount Lebanon," *IJMES* Vol. 28, No. 3 (Aug. 1996): 325–348; and Carolyn L. Gates, *The Merchant Republic of Lebanon: Rise of an Open Economy* (London: The Centre for Lebanese Studies in association with I. B. Tauris, 1998).

5. Mustafa Muhammad Bazzi, *Jabal ʿAmil fi muhitihi al-ʿarabi, 1864–1948* (Beirut: al-Majlis al-Islami al-Shiʿi al-Aʿla, 1993); and Bazzi, *al-Takamul al-iqtisadi bayna Jabal ʿAmil wa-muhitihi al-ʿarabi, 1850–1950* (Beirut: Dar al-Mawasim li-l-Tibaʿa wa-l-Nashr wa-l-Tawziʿ, 2002). See also Malek Abisaab, "A History of Women Tobacco Workers: Labor, Community and Social Transformation in Lebanon, 1895–1997" (PhD diss., State University of New York-Binghamton, 2001); and Abisaab, "Shiite Peasants and a New Nation in Colonial Lebanon: The Intifada of Bint Jubayl, 1936." *CSSAAME* Vol. 29, No. 3 (2009): 483–501.

6. Osama Alexander Doumani, "The Tobacco Growers of Southern Lebanon: Politics and Economics of "Change" (PhD diss., University of California, Berkeley, 1974), 55–56. See also Mounzer Jaber, "al-Kiyan al-siyasi li-Jabal ʿAmil qabla 1920," in Ibrahim Beydoun, ed., *Safahat min tarikh Jabal ʿAmil* (Beirut: al-Majlis al-Thaqafi

li-Lubnan al-Janubi, 1979), 91; and 'Ali 'Abd al-Mun'im Shu'ayb, *Matalib Jabal 'Amil: al-wahda, al-musawa fi Lubnan al-Kabir, 1900–1936* (Beirut: al-Mu'assasa al-Jam'iyya, 1987), 12. Majed Halawi claims that some 90% of the workforce in South Lebanon was employed in agriculture as late as the 1950s. Halawi, *A Lebanon Defied: Musa al-Sadr and the Shi'a Community* (Boulder: Westview Press, 1992), 52.

7. Lebanon, Majlis al-Wuzara', *al-Bayanat al-wizariyya al-lubnaniyya wa-munaqashatuha fi majlis al-nuwwab, 1926–1984: al-mujallad al-awwal 1926–1966* (Beirut: Mu'assasat al-Dirasat al-Lubnaniyya, 1986), 26.

8. *Al-'Irfan* Vol. 19, No. 3 (March 1930), 391.

9. Meir Zamir, *Lebanon's Quest: The Road to Independence* (London: I. B. Tauris, 2000), 164.

10. Waddah Shararah, *Transformations d'une manifestation religieuse dans un village du Liban-Sud (Ashura)* (Beirut: Université Libanaise, 1968), 13.

11. Dahir, *al-Judhur al-tarikhiyya*, 188.

12. Haut-Commissaire de la République Française en Syrie et au Liban, *Monopole des Tabacs et Tombacs (Arrêté N° 16/L.R. du 30 Janvier 1935)* (Beirut: Imprimerie de l'Orient).

13. MAE-Nantes, Carton N° 1910, Consellier Administratif, Liban-Sud, BIH N° 5: 29 January to 4 February 1936, 8.

14. 'Abbas Bazzi, "Bint Jubayl sanat 1936, al-intifada wa-l-iqta'," *Dirasat 'arabi-yya* 5(11) (1969), 79–80.

15. The colonial sources refer to seventeen detainees while 'Abbas Bazzi mentions thirty-three. See MAE-Nantes, Carton N° 411, Information N° 1177, Sûreté Beyrouth (Source gendarmerie libanaise), Conseiller administratif du Liban-sud (Pechkoff) to Sûreté Générale, Lt. Douaihy, La Directeur de la Sûreté Générale, Inspecteur-Général des Polices, Beirut, April 1, 1936; MAE-Nantes, Carton N° 411, Le Chef de Bataillon Pechkoff, Conseiller Administratif du Liban Sud, "Note: Manifestations hostiles a Beint Jbail et attaque des locaux municipaux et caracol de cette localité," Sidon, April 2, 1936; and 'Abbas Bazzi, "Bint Jubayl sanat 1936."

16. MAE-Nantes, Carton N° 411, Information N° 1200, Sûreté Générale, Gendarmerie Libanaise, Communiqués de Bent Djebail par Captain Picard à 8 hrs, April 2, 1936; MAE-Nantes, Carton N° 411, Information N° 1187, Le Directeur de la Sûreté Générale, Sûreté Beyrouth, Beirut, April 2, 1936; and 'Abbas Bazzi, "Bint Jubayl sanat 1936," 81.

17. MAE-Nantes, Carton N° 411, "La Vérité Sur Les Évènements de Bint-Jbail," (No author [Pechkoff?]), received April 6, 1936.

18. MAE-Nantes, Carton N° 411, Télégramme No. 1294, Délégué Général à Paris Diplomatie, "Pour M. de Martel," April 7, 1936.

19. Iskandar Riyashi, *Qabl wa-ba'd 1918 ila 1941: tadhakkurat Iskandar al-Ri-yashi* (Beirut: Maktabat al-'Irfan, 1955 [1940]), 210, 214.

20. MAE-Nantes, Carton N° 944, Pechkoff, "Note: Situation Politique au Liban-Sud et son evolution," N° 179, Sidon, April 6, 1936.

21. "La Juridiction Mixte est Saisie des Incidents de Bint-Jebail," *L'Orient,* April 7, 1936, 2; MAE-Nantes, Carton N° 411, Le Chef de Bataillon Pechkoff, Conseiller Administratif du Liban Sud, "Note: Manifestations hostiles a Beint Jbail et attaque des locaux municipaux et caracol de cette localité," Sidon, April 2, 1936; and MAE-Nantes, Carton N° 411, Conseiller Administratif du Liban-Sud N° 190, "Note: Repercussion des évènements de Beint Jbail; Cérémonie de huitaine," Sidon, April 9, 1936.

22. Zamir, *Lebanon's Quest,* 163.

23. Roger Lescot, *Les chiites du Liban-Sud,* Rapport N° 3 du CHEAM, (1936), 15–16, 18, 21.

24. Bazzi, "Bint Jubayl sanat 1936," 85–86; and Mustafa Bazzi, "Intifadat Bint Jubayl wa-Jabal 'Amil 1936 fi al-awwal min Nisan 1936," *Dirasat 'arabiyya* Vol. 28, No. 10–11–12 (1992), 65–66. See also Wajih Kawtharani, "Jabal 'Amil wa-l-tarikh al-ta'ifi al-lubnani," *al-'Irfan* Vol. 74, No. 7–8 (1986): 65–83; and Bazzi, "Intifadat Bint Jubayl wa-Jabal 'Amil fi 1 Nisan 1936 (2)," *Dirasat 'arabiyya* Vol. 29, No. 1–2 (1992): 61–82.

25. Abisaab, "Shiite Peasants and a New Nation in Colonial Lebanon," 484. Also consider the various semantic ramifications in English of using the term *intifada* rather than rebellion, uprising, or revolt to describe "the events" in Bint Jubayl of 1936.

26. Tamara Chalabi, *The Shi'is of Jabal 'Amil and the New Lebanon: Community and Nation-State, 1918–1943.* (London: Palgrave Macmillan, 2006), 135.

27. Interview with the author, March 2, 2005.

28. Of course, these petitions were subject to challenge and contestation. Nizar al-Zayn, for example, criticized some 33 unnamed figures for signing a petition (*mazbata*) that supported the rights of the Monopoly, "as if the Regie is a company headed by the Mahdi, peace be upon him." al-Zayn, *Jabal 'Amil fi rub' qarn, 1913–1938* (Sidon: Matba'at al-'Irfan, 1938), 34.

29. MAE-Nantes, Syrie-Liban, Carton N° 592, Télégramme, Ali Hussein Bezzi and Ali Chamseddine (Bint-Jebeil) to Monsieur le Haut-Commissaire (Beirut), March 24, 1939.

30. MAE-Nantes, Carton N° 2940. Letter from Abdallah al-Hurr, Muhammad 'Ali Miqdad, Muhammad 'Izz al-Din, et al. à Son Excellence Monsieur le Haut-Commissaire de la République Française, November 28, 1939.

31. MAE-Nantes, Carton N° 2940, Note: Relative au statut personnel (Contrôle des Wakfs et de l'Immatricultion Foncière), Beirut, March 16, 1939, 4.

32. al-Zayn, *Jabal 'Amil fi rub' qarn,* 37.

33. MAE-Nantes, Archives Rapatriées de l'Ambassade de France à Beyrouth, série B (1920–1972), Carton no. 11, Dossier no. 189, Allocution prononcée au nom de la communauté chiite par Son Excellence le Cheikh Munir Osseiran, Président de la Cour de Cassation chérié chiite, Beirut, October 24, 1941.

34. MAE-Nantes, Carton N° 784. Information N° 676, Conseiller Administratif du Liban Sud (Pruneaud), Sidon, December 16, 1941; and MAE-Nantes, Carton N°

1112, Reseignement (Fiche Individuelle): Cheikh Munir Osseyran, Observations Nouvelles (Prunaud), November 15, 1942.

35. MAE-Nantes, Carton N° 1095, Ahmad el Assad et al. à Monsieur le Ministre de l'Interieur de la République Libanaise, March 10, 1942; MAE-Nantes, Carton N° 1095, Statuts du Conseil Supérieur "Amili" Musulman, March 10, 1942; and MAE-Nantes, Carton N° 1095, Direction Sûreté Générale aux Armées, Bulletin d'Information Special N° 502: Conseil Supérieur Chiite, Beirut, June 4, 1942.

36. MAE-Nantes, Carton N° 2940, "Note"; and MAE-Nantes, Carton N° 2940, Le Conseiller Administratif du Liban-Sud à Monsieur le Gouverneur des Colonies, Conseiller auprès du Secrétaire d'État du Gouvernement Libanais, Beirut, March 1940.

37. Muhammad Jawad Mughniyya, "Fi al-qada' al-shar'i," *al-'Irfan* Vol. 46, No. 3 (November 1958), 224–226.

38. MAE-Nantes, Carton N° 2940, Affaires Religieuses, Sidon, February 1, 1940.

39. MAE-Nantes, Carton N° 1095, Cabinet politique, N° 1.975, Note Succincte sur Les Moujtaheddin, Sidon, November 17, 1942; and MAE-Nantes, Carton N° 1095, Cabinet politique, Information: Reforme des Tribunaux Cherieh (Suite)—Nomination des Magistrats, N° 1.987, Sidon, November 19, 1942; MAE-Nantes, Carton N° 383, Abdel Hussein Charafeddine El-Moussaoui, Le serviteur de la Loi Musulmane, December 19, 1940.

40. MAE-Nantes, Carton N° 1095, Délégation Générale de la France Combattante au Levant, Conseiller Administratif du Liban-Sud, Information N° 1.968: A/S Reforme des Tribunaux Cheries, Sidon, November 17, 1942; and MAE-Nantes, Carton N° 1095, Le Conseiller Administratif de la France Combattante au Liban-Sud Information, N° 1.987, November 19 1942.

41. *Al-'Irfan* Vol. 37, No. 5 (May 1950), 596.

42. *Al-'Irfan* Vol. 37, No. 7 (June 1950), 835.

43. *Al-'Irfan* Vol. 35, No. 7 (June 1948), 1118.

44. Daftar al-sadirat, MJB, "Min ra'is majlis al-wuzara'," September 9, 1948.

45. "Ri'asat al-mahkama al-ja'fariyya al-'ulya," *al-'Irfan* Vol. 38, No. 10 (September 1951), 1199.

46. Much more has been written by and about the successors to Munir 'Usayran. See Yusuf al-Faqih, *al-Ahwal al-shakhsiyya fi fiqh ahl al-bayt* (Beirut: Dar al-Adwa', 1989 [1951]); but also Muhammd Taqi al-Faqih, *Hajar wa-tin, Vol. 4* (Beirut: Dar al-Adwa', 1990). Mughniyya published very widely; see, for example, *Fiqh al-Imam Ja'far al-Sadiq: 'ard wa-istidlal (6 vols.)* (Qum: Intisharat Quds Muhammadi, 1980). For more about Mughniyya, see Hadi Fadlallah, *Muhammad Jawad Mughniyya: fikr wa-islah* (Beirut: Dar al-Hadi, 1993); 'Ali al-Mahraqi, *Muhammad Jawad Mughniyya: siratuhu wa-'ata'uhu* (al-Manama, Bahrain: Maktabat al-Fahzawi, 1997); T. M. Aziz, "Popular Sovereignty in

Contemporary Shiʻi Political Thought," *The Muslim World* Vol. 86, No. 3–4 (July-October 1996): 273–293; and Chibli Mallat, *Shiʻi Thought from the South of Lebanon* (Oxford: Centre for Lebanese Studies, 1988). Mughniyya was replaced by ʻAbdallah Niʻmeh; see Niʻmeh, *Dalil al-qada' al-jaʻfari* (Beirut: Dar al-Fikr al-Lubnani, 1982).

47. See Hashim Maʻrouf, "al-Qadi ʻind aʼimat al-shiʻa," *al-ʻIrfan* Vol. 39, No. 3 (February 1952): 360–361; and Maʻrouf, "al-Qadi ʻind aʼimat al-shiʻa," *al-ʻIrfan* Vol. 39, No. 4 (March 1952): 387–389.

48. Author interview with Jaʻfari *shariʻa* court judge, Beirut, February 23, 2005.

49. al-Mahraqi, *Muhammad Jawad Mughniyya*, 57.

50. Nadine Méouchy, "Le Pacte National 1943–1946: les ambiguïtés d'un temps politique d'exception," in Gérard D. Khoury, ed., *Sélim Takla 1895–1945: une contribution à l'indépendance du Liban* (Paris, Beyrouth: Karthala, Dar al-Nahar, 2004), 461–500.

51. MAE-Nantes, Carton N° 1095, Sûreté Générale, Information du 23 December 1942, Beirut; Albert H. Hourani, *Syria and Lebanon* (London: Oxford University Press, 1946), 121, cited in Joseph Chamie, "Religious Groups in Lebanon: A Descriptive Investigation," *IJMES* Vol. 11, No. 2 (Apr., 1980), 177; MAE-Nantes, Carton N° 784, Census as of December 31, 1944; and Rania Maktabi, "The Lebanese Census of 1932 Revisited: Who Are the Lebanese?" *British Journal of Middle Eastern Studies* Vol. 26, No. 2 (Nov. 1999): 219–41.

52. Al-Zayn, *Jabal ʻAmil fi rubʻ qarn*, 29.

53. "Nahnu ʻala ʻahdina al-qadim," *al-ʻIrfan* Vol. 31, No. 5–6 (April and May 1945), 202–203.

54. Musa al-Sbaiti, "Hatafat bi-l-umma al-ʻamiliyya," *al-ʻIrfan* Vol. 33, No. 10 (September 1947), 1125.

55. Michelle Hartman and Alessandro Olsaretti, "'The First Boat and the First Oar": Inventions of Lebanon in the Writings of Michel Chiha," *Radical History Review* Vol. 86 (2003): 37–65. See also Fawwaz Traboulsi, *Silat bi-la wasl: Mishal Chiha wa-l-aydiyulujiya al-lubnaniyya* (Beirut: Riad el-Rayyes Books, 1999).

56. Michel Chiha, "Liban-Sud," *L'Orient* (1944), reprinted in Chiha, *Politique interieure* (Beirut: Éditions du Trident, 1964), 49–51.

57. Pierre Rondot, *Les institutions politiques du Liban: des communautés traditionelles à l'état moderne* (Paris: Institut d'études de L'Orient contemporain, 1947), 40.

58. Muhammad Husayn Nasrallah, "al-Hayat fi Jabal ʻAmil," *al-ʻIrfan* Vol. 37, No. 5 (May 1950), 579–580.

59. ʻAbdallah Niʻmeh, "'Ulama' al-din al-yawm," *al-ʻIrfan* Vol. 38, No. 2 (January 1951): 185–186.

60. Muhammd Jawad al-Chirri, *al-Shiʻa fi qafas al-ittiham* (Detroit: al-Markaz al-Islami fi Amrika, 1985), 7.

61. "Jabal 'Amil al-ijtima'i," *al-'Irfan* Vol. 32, No. 8 (July 1946): 721–722.

62. See, for example, Muhammad Jawad al-Chirri, "al-Mabadi' al-islamiyya al-ijtima'iyya al-'amma ki-'ilaj li-amradina," *al-'Irfan* Vol. 33, No. 1 (December 1946): 54–59; "Muhawalatuna li-ithbat al-haja ila ba'th al-anbiya': masa'il ma-ba'd al-tabi'a tahall bi-ghayr al-wahi," *al-'Irfan* Vol. 33, No. 4 (February 1947): 398–404; "Imkan al-mu'jiza," *al-'Irfan* Vol. 33, No. 7 (May 1947): 773–776; and "Imkan al-mu'jiza," *al-'Irfan* Vol. 33, No. 8 (June 1947): 892–895.

63. Muhammad Jawad al-Chirri, *al-Khilafa fi al-dustur al-islami* (Beirut: Dar al-Murtada, 2000 [1946]), 192.

64. Muhammad Jawad al-Chirri, "Din al-huriyya," *al-'Irfan* Vol. 32, No. 8 (July 1946), 745.

65. Al-Chirri, *al-Khilafa fi al-dustur al-islami*, 5. For more on al-Chirri and the Islamic Center of America in Dearborn, see Linda Walbridge, *Without Forgetting the Imam: Lebanese Shi'ism in an American Community* (Detroit: Wayne State University Press, 1997). For a satirical look at the Lebanese Shi'i community in Detroit, see Ahmad Beydoun, *Bint Jubayl Mishighan* (Beirut, 1989).

66. MJB, 96/1937, May 11, 1937.

67. MT, 410/1937, October 27, 1937.

68. Muhammad Jawad Mughniyya, *Tajarib Muhammad Jawad Mughniyya: bi-qalamihi . . . wa-aqlam al-akhirin* (Beirut: Dar al-Jawad, 1980).

69. Muhammad Jawad Mughniyya, *al-Wad' al-hadir fi Jabal 'Amil fi matla' al-istiqlal: bidayat al-qahr wa-l-hirman* (Beirut: Dar al-Tayyar al-Jadid; Dar al-Jawad, 1990 [1947]), 20. Further citations to this work are given in the text.

70. In the early 1930s, Shaykh 'Abd al-Husayn Sadiq had equated the development of Mount Lebanon at the expense of Jabal 'Amil to a "mountain eating a mountain." Cited in Jaber, "al-Kiyan al-siyasi li-Jabal 'Amil qabla 1920," 94.

71. Mallat, *Shi'i Thought from the South of Lebanon*, 19.

72. Muhammad Jawad Mughniyya, *al-Shi'a wa-l-hakimun* (Beirut: al-Maktaba al-Ahliyya, 1961), 21.

73. Aziz, "Popular Sovereignty in Contemporary Shi'i Political Thought," 290.

74. Muhammad Jawad Mughniyya, *al-Khumayni wa-l-dawla al-islamiyya* (Beirut, 1979), 65.

75. Halawi, *A Lebanon Defied*. Further citations to this work are given in the text.

76. Leonard Binder, ed., *Politics in Lebanon* (New York: John Wiley and Sons, 1966); Michael Hudson, *The Precarious Republic: Political Modernization in Lebanon* (New York: Random House, 1968); Thom Sicking and Shereen Khairallah, *The Shi'a Awakening in Lebanon: a Search for Radical Change in a Traditional Way (Cemam Reports, 2: Vision and Revision in Arab Society)* (Beirut: 1974); Norton, *Amal and the Shi'a;* Mahmud A. Faksh, "The Shi'a Community of Lebanon: A New Assertive Political Force," *Journal of South Asian and Middle Eastern Studies*

14, no. 3 (1991): 33–56; and Amal Saad-Ghorayeb, "Factors Conducive to the Politicization of the Lebanese Shi'a and the Emergence of Hizbu'llah," *Journal of Islamic Studies* Vol. 14, No. 3 (2003): 273–307.

77. Khalil Arzuni, "al-Lu'ba al-ta'ifiyya al-lubnaniyya fi tarikh al-shi'a wa-l-mawarina," *al-'Irfan* Vol. 72, No. 6 (June 1984), 32–33.

78. Ibid., 39.

79. Keith D. Watenpaugh, "Towards a New Category of Colonial Theory: Colonial Cooperation and the *Survivors' Bargain*—The Case of the Post-Genocide Armenian Community of Syria under French Mandate," in Nadine Méouchy and Peter Sluglett, eds., *The British and French Mandates in Comparative Perspectives* (Leiden: Brill, 2004), 599.

80. Lara Deeb, *An Enchanted Modern: Gender and Public Piety in Shi'i Lebanon* (Princeton, N.J.: Princeton University Press, 2006), 73.

Epilogue

1. *Al-Safir,* December 21, 2005.

2. *Al-Hayat,* January 22, 2006.

3. Jihad Bannut, *Harakat al-nidal fi Jabal 'Amil* (Beirut: Dar al-Mizan, 1993); Muhammad Kurani, *al-Judhur al-tarikhiyya li-l-muqawama al-islamiyya fi Jabal 'Amil* (Beirut: Dar al-Wasila, 1993); and Najib Nur al-Din, *Aydiyulujiya al-rafd wa-l-muqawama: bahth ijtima'i siyasi fi zahirat al-la'iyya al-shi'iyya* (Beirut: Dar al-Hadi, 2004).

4. Mona Fayyad, "To Be a Shi'i Now . . ." *al-Nahar.* August 7, 2006. See also some of the responses to this article: Nayla Nasir, *al-Nahar,* August 15, 2006; Bashar al-Amin, *al-Nahar,* August 16, 2006; Nayif Karim, *al-Nahar,* August 22, 2006; and Amin Taheri, *al-Nahar,* August 31, 2006.

5. Mona Harb El-Kak, *Politiques urbaines dans la banlieue-sud de Beyrouth* (Beirut: CERMOC, 1996); Judith Palmer Harik, "Between Islam and the System: Sources and Implications of Popular Support for Lebanon's Hizballah," *The Journal of Conflict Resolution* Vol. 40, No. 1 (1996): 41–67; Waddah Shararah, *Dawlat Hizb Allah: Lubnan mujtama'an islamiyyan* (Beirut: Dar al-Nahar, 1996); Hala Jaber, *Hezbollah: Born with a Vengeance* (New York: Columbia University Press, 1997); Magnus Ranstorp, *Hizb'allah in Lebanon: The Politics of the Western Hostage Crisis* (New York: St. Martin's Press, 1997); Amal Saad-Ghorayeb, "Factors Conducive to the Politicization of the Lebanese Shi'a and the Emergence of Hizbu'llah," *Journal of Islamic Studies* Vol. 14, No. 3 (2003): 273–307; Joseph Elie Alagha, *The Shifts in Hizbullah's Ideology: Religious Ideology, Political Ideology and Political Program* (Leiden: ISIM, Amsterdam University Press, 2006); Lara Deeb, *An Enchanted Modern: Gender and Public Piety in Shi'i Lebanon* (Princeton, N.J.: Princeton University Press, 2006); Augustus Richard Norton, *Hezbollah: A Short History* (Princeton, N.J.: Princeton University Press, 2007); and Sabrina Mervin, ed., *Le*

Hezbollah: état des lieux (Paris: Sindbad, 2008). For a less sanguine assessment of the Shi'i Islamization of the southern suburbs of Beirut, see Fadi Toufiq, *Bilad Allah al-dayyiqa: "al-dahiyya" ahlan wa-hizban* (Beirut: Dar al-Jadid, 2005).

6. See for example Wafa' 'Awwad, "'The Civil Center': A National Initiative Draws the Outlines of Lebanon as a 'Civil State'," *al-Akhbar,* 11 July 2007.

7. Augustus Richard Norton, *Amal and the Shi'a: Struggle for the Soul of Lebanon* (Austin: University of Texas Press, 1987), 126.

8. Cf. "The Sunni-Shiite conflict is relatively new in Lebanon, where the long civil war that ended in 1990 revolved mostly around tensions between Christians and Muslims, and their differences over the Palestinian presence in the country. But after Iran helped establish Hezbollah in the early 1980s, Lebanon's long-marginalized Shiites steadily gained power and stature. They have also grown in numbers." Robert F. Worth and Nada Bakri, "Hezbollah Ignites a Sectarian Fuse in Lebanon," *The New York Times,* May 18, 2008.

9. Pierre Rondot, *Les institutions politiques du Liban: des communautés traditionelles à l'état moderne* (Paris: Institut d'études de L'Orient contemporain, 1947), 40.

10. Eugenie Elie Abouchdid, *30 Years of Lebanon & Syria (1917–1947)* (Beirut: The Sader Rihani Printing Co., 1948), 69.

11. Susan Pedersen, "The Meaning of the Mandates System: An Argument," *Geschichte und Gesellschaft* Vol. 32 (2006), 581.

12. Author interview with Ja'fari *shari'a* court judge, Beirut, February 23, 2005.

13. Hani Fahs, "Al-Shi'a al-lubnaniyyun wa-l-dawla," *al-'Irfan* Vol. 80, No, 5–6 (July and August 1996), 68–69.

14. "Al-Majlis al-islami al-shi'i al-a'la," *al-'Irfan* Vol. 57, No. 3 (July 1969), 271.

15. See, for example, Ra'uf Shhuri, "Kitab maftuh ila samahat al-Sayyid Musa al-Sadr," *al-'Irfan* Vol. 57, No. 3 (July 1969): 380–383.

16. "Helou Announces in Congratulating al-Allama al-Sadr and the Shi'i Council: 'This homeland is united by its faith in spiritual values which are the best foundation in this critical period'; al-Sadr: 'We are prepared to meet with every sect in the service of religion and morality'," *al-'Irfan* Vol. 57, No. 3 (July 1969), 412–413.

17. Ibid., 414.

18. Mounzer Jaber, "Al-Janub amam al-sigha . . . sahal la wa'r (1943–1975)," *al-Safir,* April 7, 2006.

19. Yitzhak Nakash, *Reaching for Power: The Shi'a in the Modern Arab World* (Princeton, N.J.: Princeton University Press, 2006), 14.

Bibliography

Archival Collections

France

Fontainebleau: Archives Nationales
Nantes: Ministère des Affaires Étrangères, Centre des Archives Diplomatiques

Lebanon

'Amiliyya Society and School Library (*al-kuliyya al-'amiliyya*), Beirut
Jafet Library, American University of Beirut
Al-Mahkama al-shar'iyya al-ja'fariyya fi Bayrut (Ja'fari *shari'a* court, Beirut)
Al-Mahkama al-shar'iyya al-ja'fariyya fi Nabatiyya (Ja'fari Court, Nabatiyya)
Al-Mahkama al-shar'iyya al-ja'fariyya fi Sayda (Ja'fari Court, Sidon)
Al-Mahkama al-shar'iyya al-ja'fariyya fi Sur (Ja'fari Court, Tyre)
Al-Majlis al-thaqafi li-Lubnan al-janubi (Cultural Center for South Lebanon)
Lokman Slim, Private Papers
Supreme Islamic Shi'i Council

Published Primary Sources

Abouchdid, Eugenie Elie. *30 Years of Lebanon & Syria (1917–1947)*. Beirut: The Sader Rihani Printing Co, 1948.

Abu Mikhnaf. *Maqtal al-imam al-Husayn bin 'Ali*. Beirut: Dar al-Mahajja al-Bayda' and Dar al-Rasul al-Akram, 2000.

Agha Buzurg al-Tihrani, Muhammad Muhsin. *Al-Dhari'a ila tasanif al-shi'a*. Beirut: Dar al-Adwa', 1983.

Al Ibrahim, Habib. *Dhikra al-Husayn*. Sidon: Matba'at al-'Irfan, 1935.

———. *Al-Mawlid wa-l-ghadir*. Sidon: Matba'at al-'Irfan, 1947.

Al Kashif al-Ghita', Abd al-Rida. *Al-Anwar al-husayniyya wa-l-sha'a'ir al-islami-yya*. Bombay: 1927.

Al Kashif al-Ghita', Muhammad al-Husayn. *Al-Ayyat al-bayyinat fi qam' al-bid' wa-l-dalalat.* Najaf: al-Matba'a al-'Alawiyya, 1345 [1926].

———. *Maqtal al-Husayn.* Najaf: al-Maktaba al-Haydariyya, 1964.

Ali, Abdullah Yusuf. *The Holy Qur-an: Text, Translation and Commentary.* Lahore: Shaykh Muhammad Ashraf, 1938.

al-Amin, Muhsin. *Khitat Jabal 'Amil.* Beirut: Matba'at al-Insaf, 1961.

———. *Lawa'ij al-ashjan fi maqtal al-imam Abi 'Abd Allah al-Husayn Ibn 'Ali Ibn Abi Talib 'alayhim al-salam.* Sidon: Matba'at al-'Irfan, 1934 [1911].

———. *Al-Majalis al-saniyya fi manaqib wa-masa'ib al-'itra al-nabawiyya (5 vols.).* Damascus: Matba'at Karam, 1951–1954.

———. *Risalat al-tanzih li-a'mal al-shabih.* Sidon: Matba'at al-'Irfan, 1347.

———. *Sirat al-Sayyid Muhsin al-Amin al-'Amili,* ed. Haitham al-Amin and Sabrina Mervin. Beirut: Riyad el-Rayyes, 2000.

al-Amin, Hasan. *Hill wa-tarhal: dhikrayat.* Beirut: Riyad el-Rayyes, 1999.

———. *Jabal 'Amil: al-sayf wa-l-qalam.* Beirut: Dar al-Amir, 2003.

al-As'ad, Shabib ibn 'Ali. *Al-'Aqd al-munaddad: fi diwan ash'ar al-raji fi al-darayn latafa rabbuhu al-wahid al-ahad.* Istanbul: al-Matba'a al-'Amara, 1309.

Assaf, J. G. *La compétence des tribunaux du statut personnel au Liban et en Syrie.* Beirut: Imprimerie Khalifé, 1935.

Ayoub, Charles. *Les mandats orientaux.* Paris: Librairie de la Société du Recueil Sirey, 1924.

al-Basri, 'Abd al-Amir. *Lahjat al-sidq wa-lisan al-haqq.* Najaf: al-Matba'a al-Haydariyya, 1348.

Bayhum, Muhammad Jamil. *Al-Intidaban fi al-'Iraq wa-Suriya, Inkiltira-Faransa.* Sidon: Matba'at al-'Irfan, 1931.

Beydoun, Ibrahim. *Qara'tu aswatahum fi al-dawwi: awraq janubiyya.* Beirut: Dar al-Mu'arrakh al-'Arabi, 2000.

Bliss, Frederick Jones. *The Religions of Modern Syria and Palestine.* New York: Charles Scribner's Sons, 1912.

Cardon, Louis. *Le régime de la propriété foncière en Syrie et au Liban.* Paris: Recueil Sirey, 1932.

Chantre, Ernest. "Observations anthropologiques sur les Métoualis." *Bulletin de la Société d'Anthropologie de Lyon* Vol. 14 (1895): 58–61.

Chiha, Michel. *Politique intérieure.* Beirut: Éditions du Trident, 1964.

al-Chirri, Muhammad Jawad. *Al-Khilafa fi al-dustur al-islami.* Beirut: Dar al-Murtada, 2000 [1946].

———. *Al-Shi'a fi qafas al-ittiham.* Detroit: al-Markaz al-Islami fi Amrika, 1985.

Dahir, Ya'qub. *Masirat al-Imam al-Sayyid Musa Al-Sadr (12 vols.).* Beirut: Harakat Amal, Hay'at al-Ri'asa, 2000.

Darché, J. *Les chiites du Liban.* Rapport n° 108 du CHEAM, 1937.

Fahs, Hani. *Awraq min daftar al-walad al-'amili*. Beirut: Dar al-Kalima li-l-Nashr, 1979.

al-Ganji, Muhammad. *Kashf al-tamwih 'an risalat al-tanzih li-a'mal al-shabih*. Najaf: al-Matba'a al-'Alawiyya, 1347.

Haqqi, Isma'il. *Lubnan: mabahith 'ilmiyya wa-ijtima'iyya, Part Two*. Beirut: al-Jami'a al-Lubnaniyya, al-Matba'a al-Adabiyya, 1970 [1918].

Haut-Commissaire de la République Française en Syrie et au Liban. *Monopole des Tabacs et Tombacs (Arrêté N° 16/L.R. du 30 Janvier 1935)*. Beirut: Imprimerie de l'Orient.

al-Hilli, Abd al-Husayn. *Al-Naqd al-nazih li-risalat al-tanzih*. Najaf: al-Matba'a al-Haydariyya, 1347.

al-Lakhnawi, 'Ali Naqi. *Iqalat al-'athir fi iqamat al-sha'a'ir*. Najaf: al-Matba'a al-Haydariyya, 1348 [1930].

Lammens, Henri. "Les 'Perses' du Liban et l'origine des Métoualis." *Mélanges de l'Université Saint-Joseph* 14 (1929): 21–39.

———. *Sur la frontière nord de la terre promise*. Paris: Imprimerie de D. Dumoulin et Co., 18—?,

———. *La Syrie, précis historique*. Beirut: Imprimerie Catholique, 1921.

Lapierre, Jean. *Le mandat français en Syrie; origines, doctrine, exécution*. Paris: Librairie du Recueil Sirey, 1936.

Lebanon. Majlis al-Wuzara'. *Al-Bayanat al-wizariyya al-lubnaniyya wa-mu-naqashataha fi majlis al-nuwwab, 1926–1984: al-mujallad al-awwal 1926–1966*. Beirut: Mu'assasat al-Dirasat al-Lubnaniyya, 1986.

Lescot, Roger. *Les chiites du Liban-Sud*. Rapport N° 3 du CHEAM, 1936.

Lortet, Louis. *La Syrie d'aujourd'hui: voyages dans la Phénicie, le Liban et la Judée, 1875–1880*. Paris: Librairie Hachette, 1884.

Madden, Richard Robert. *The Turkish Empire: In its Relations with Christianity and Civilization*. London: T. C. Newby, 1862.

al-Majlis al-Thaqafi li-Lubnan al-Janubi. *Min daftar al-dhikrayat al-janubiyya, Vol. 1*. Beirut: al-Majlis al-Thaqafi li-Lubnan al-Janubi and Dar al-Kuttab al-Lubnani, 1981.

———. *Min daftar al-dhikrayat al-janubiyya, Vol. 2*. Beirut: al-Majlis al-Thaqafi li-Lubnan al-Janubi and Dar al-Kuttab al-Lubnani, 1984.

Mahmassani, Maher and Ibtissam Messarra, eds. *Statut personnel: textes en vigueur au Liban*. Beirut: Faculté de droit et des sciences économiques, 1970.

Mughniyya, Muhammad Jawad. *Fiqh al-Imam Ja'far al-Sadiq: 'ard wa-istidlal* (6 vols.). Beirut: Dar al-'Ilm li-l-Malayyin, 1965–1966.

———. *Al-Husayn wa-batalat Karbala'*. Beirut: Dar Maktabat al-Tarbiyya, 1973.

———. *Tajarib Muhammad Jawad Mughniyya: bi-qalamihi . . . wa-aqlam al-akhirin*. Beirut: Dar al-Jawad, 1980.

———. *Al-Wad' al-hadir fi Jabal 'Amil fi matla' al-istiqlal: bidayat al-qahr wa-l-hir-man*. Beirut: Dar al-Tayyar al-Jadid; Dar al-Jawad, 1990 [1947].

Murr, D. I. and Ed. Bourbousson. "Du statut personnel en Syrie et au Liban." *Bulletin de l'Institut Intermediaire International de la Haye* Vol. 26, No. 2 (1932): 261-270.

Musawbi', Sulayman. *Qamus al-qada' al-'uthmani.* Sidon: Matba'at al-'Irfan, 1330.

Muzaffar, Hasan. *Nusrat al-mazlum.* Najaf: al-Matba'a al-'Alawiyya, 1345.

Ni'meh, 'Abdallah. *Dalil al-qada' al-ja'fari.* Beirut: Dar al-Fikr al-Lubnani, 1982.

O'Zoux, Raymond. *Les états du Levant sous mandat français.* Paris: Larose, 1931.

Palestine Exploration Fund. *Questions on the Metawileh.* London: 18–[?].

al-Ra'i, Raji. *Majmu'at al-qararat al-tamyiziyya li-mahkamatay al-tamyiz al-lubnaniyya wa-l-suriyya min sanat 1919 ila sanat 1929.* Beirut: Matba'at al-Huda, 1928.

Recueil des Arrêtés et Décisions du Grand Liban: Section II—Tome II et dernier (1er Janvier 1926–23 Mai 1926). Beirut: Imprimerie des Lettres, 1927.

Rida, Ahmad. *Mudhakkirat li-l-tarikh, hawadith Jabal 'Amil 1914–1922.* Beirut: Dar al-Nahar li-l-Nashr, 2009.

Rida, Muhammad Rashid. *Al-Sunna wa-l-shi'a aw al-wahhabiyya wa-l-rafida: haqa'iq diniyya tarikhiyya ijtima'iyya islahiyya.* Cairo: Matba'at al-Manar, 1929.

Riyashi, Iskandar. *Qabl wa-ba'd 1918 ila 1941: tadhakkurat Iskandar al-Riyashi.* Beirut: Maktabat al-'Irfan, 1955.

Rolland, Louis and Pierre Lampué. *Précis de législation coloniale.* Paris: Librarie Dalloz, 1931.

Sadiq, 'Abd al-Husayn. *Sima' al-sulaha'.* Sidon: Matba'at al-'Irfan, 1345.

Sayigh, Anis. *Lubnan al-ta'ifi.* Beirut: Dar al-Sira' al-Fikri, 1955.

Sayigh, Fayez A. *Al-Ta'ifiyya: bahth fi asbabiha wa-akhtariha wa-'ilajiha.* Beirut: Manshurat Maktabat al-Wajib, 1947.

al-Sbaiti, 'Abdallah. *Abu Dharr al-Ghifari.* Tyre: Matba'at Sur al-Haditha, 1945.

———. *Rannat al-asa, aw, nazra fi risalat al-tanzih li-a'mal al-shabih.* Najaf: Matba'at al-Najah, 1347.

al-Shahrastani, Hibat al-Din. *Nahdat al-Husayn.* Baghdad: Matba'at al-Jazira, 2nd ed. 1937 [1344].

Sharaf al-Din, 'Abd al-Husayn. *Al-Majalis al-fakhira* (5 vols.). Najaf: Matba'at al-Nu'man, 1967.

———. *Bughyat al-raghibin fi silsilat Al Sharaf Al-Din: tarikh ajyal fi tarikh rijal: kitab nasab wa-tarikh wa-tarajim* (2 vols.). Beirut: Al-Dar al-Islamiyya, 1991.

Sharaf al-Din, Ja'far. "Al-Sayyid Ja'far Sharaf Al-Din." In *Min daftar al-dhikrayat al-janubiyya, Vol. 2,* ed. al-Majlis al-Thaqafi li-Lubnan al-Janubi (Beirut: Dar al-Kitab al-Lubnani, 1984), 11–80.

Sorel, Jean-Albert. *Le mandat français et l'expansion economique de la Syrie et du Liban.* Paris: M. Giard, 1929.

Sufayr, Yusuf. *Jughrafiyat Lubnan al-kabir wa-hukumat Suriya wa-Filastin*. Beirut, 1924.

al-Tamimi, Muhammad Rafiq and Muhammad Bahjat. *Wilayat Bayrut: Vol. 1: al-qism al-janubi: alwiyat Bayrut wa-'Akka wa-Nablus*. Beirut: Dar Lahd Khatir, 1987 [1917–18].

al-Tamir, Rida. *Dhikrayat Rida al-Tamir*. Beirut: Dar al-Nahar, 1997.

Thomson, William MacClure. *The Land and the Book; Or, Biblical Illustrations Drawn From the Manners and Customs, the Scenes and Scenery, of the Holy Land*. New York: Harper & Brothers, 1859.

Urquhart, David. *The Lebanon (Mount Souria)*. London: T. C. Newby, 1860.

Volney, C.-F. *Voyage en Égypte et en Syrie*, ed. Jean Gaulmier. Paris: Mouton, 1959 [1787].

Wortabet, John. *Researches into the Religions of Syria; or, Sketches, Historical and Doctrinal, of Its Religious Sects*. London: James Nisbet and Co, 1860.

Zahir, Sulayman. *Jabal 'Amil fi al-harb al-kawniyya*. Beirut: Dar al-Matbu'at al-Sharqiyya, 1986.

al-Zayn, Ahmad 'Arif. *Tarikh Sayda*. Sidon: Matba'at al-'Irfan, 1913.

al-Zayn, 'Arif Zayn, ed. *Qawanin wa-nusus wa-ahkam al-ahwal al-shakhsiyya wa–tanzim al-tawa'if al-islamiyya fi Lubnan*. Beirut: Manshurat al-Halabi al-Huquqiyya, 2003.

al-Zayn, Nizar. *Jabal 'Amil fi rub' qarn 1913–1938*. Sidon: Matba'at al-'Irfan, 1938.

Secondary Sources

Abisaab, Malek. "Shiite Peasants and a New Nation in Colonial Lebanon: The Intifada of Bint Jubayl, 1936." *CSSAAME* Vol. 29, No. 3 (2009): 483–501.

———. "'Unruly' Factory Women in Lebanon: Contesting French Colonialism and the National State, 1940–1946." *Journal of Women's History* Vol. 16, No. 3 (2004): 55–82.

Abisaab, Rula Jurdi. *Converting Persia: Religion and Power in the Safavid Empire*. London: I. B. Tauris, 2004.

———. "Shi'ite Beginnings and Scholastic Tradition in Jabal 'Amil." *The Muslim World* Vol. 89, No. 1 (1999): 1–21.

———. "The Ulama of Jabal 'Amil in Safavid Iran, 1501–1736: Marginality, Migration and Social Change." *Iranian Studies* Vol. 27, No. 1–4 (1994): 103–122.

Abu Husayn, Abdul-Rahim. "The Shiites in Lebanon and the Ottomans in the 16th and 17th Centuries." In *Convegno sul tema (15 April 1991, Roma), La Shi'a nell'impero ottomano* (Rome: Accademia nazionale dei Lincei; Fondazione Leone Caetani, 1993), 107–119.

———. *The View from Istanbul: Lebanon in the 16th and 17th Centuries*. London: I. B. Tauris, 2003.

Adam, Volker. "Why Do They Cry? Criticisms of Muharram Celebrations in Tsarist and Socialist Azerbaijan." In *The Twelver Shia in Modern Times: Religious Culture and Political History,* eds. Rainer Brunner and Werner Ende (Leiden: Brill, 2002), 114–134.

Afary, Janet. "Shi'i Narratives of Karbala and Christian Rites of Penance: Michel Foucault and the Culture of the Iranian Revolution, 1978–1979." *Radical History Review* 86 (2003): 7–35.

Aghaie, Kamran. "The Karbala Narrative: Shi'i Political Discourse in Modern Iran in the 1960s and 1970s." *Journal of Islamic Studies* 12 (2001): 151–176.

———. *The Martyrs of Karbala: Shi'i Symbols and Rituals in Modern Iran.* Seattle and London: University of Washington Press, 2004.

Aghaie, Kamran Scot. "Introduction: Gendered Aspects of the Emergence and Historical Development of Shi'i Symbols and Rituals." In *The Women of Karbala: Ritual Performance and Symbolic Discourses in Modern Shi'i Islam,* ed. Kamran Scot Aghaie. (Austin: University of Texas Press, 2005), 1–21.

Agmon, Iris. *Family and Court: Legal Culture and Modernity in Late Ottoman Palestine.* Syracuse, NY: Syracuse University Press, 2006.

———. "Recording Procedures and Legal Culture in the Late Ottoman Shari'a Court of Jaffa, 1865–1890." *Islamic Law and Society* Vol. 11, No. 3 (2004): 333–337.

———. "Text, Court, and Family in Late-Nineteenth-Century Palestine." In *Family History in the Middle East: Household, Property, and Gender,* ed. Beshara Doumani (Albany, NY: State University of New York Press, 2003), 201–228.

Ajami, Fouad. *The Vanished Imam: Musa Al-Sadr and the Shi'a of Lebanon.* Ithaca, NY: Cornell University Press, 1986.

Akarlı, Engin. *The Long Peace: Ottoman Lebanon, 1861–1920.* Berkeley and Los Angeles: University of California Press, 1993.

Al Safa, Muhammad Jaber. *Tarikh Jabal 'Amil.* Beirut: Dar al-Nahar, 1998.

Al Sulayman, Ibrahim. *Buldan Jabal 'Amil: qila'hu wa-madarisuhu wa-jusuruhu wa-murujuhu wa-matahinuhu wa-jibaluhu wa-mashahiduhu.* Beirut: Mu'assasat al-Da'ira, 1995.

Alagha, Joseph Elie. *The Shifts in Hizbullah's Ideology: Religious Ideology, Political Ideology and Political Program.* Leiden: ISIM, Amsterdam University Press, 2006.

al-'Alawi, Hasan. *Al-Shi'a wa-l-dawla al-qawmiyya fi al-'Iraq 1914–1990.* Qum: Dar al-Thaqafa, 1991.

Algar, Hamid. *Religion and State in Iran, 1785–1906: The Role of the Ulama in the Qajar Period.* Berkeley and Los Angeles: University of California Press, 1969.

'Ali, Ghassan Shaykh. "Al-Sulta al-siyasiyya fi Jabal 'Amil ba'd sanat 1920 wa-hazimat al-atrak fi al-harb al-kubra al-ula." *Al-Baheth* Vol. 4, No. 2–3 (1981): 101–108.

Amanat, Abbas. "From *Ijtihad* to *Wilayat-i Faqih:* The Evolution of the Shiite Legal Authority to Political Power." In *Shari'a: Islamic Law in the Contemporary Context,* eds. Abbas Amanat and Frank Griffel (Stanford, CA: Stanford University Press, 2007), 120–136.

———. "In Between the Madrasa and the Marketplace: The Designation of Clerical Leadership in Modern Shi'ism." In *Authority and Political Culture in Shi'ism,* ed. Said Arjomand (Albany, NY: State University of New York, 1988), 98–132.

'Amil, Mahdi. *Fi al-dawla al-ta'ifiyya.* Beirut: Dar al-Farabi, 1989.

'Amru, Yusuf Muhammad. *Al-Madkhal ila usul al-fiqh al-ja'fari.* Beirut: Dar al-Zahra', 1981.

———. *Al-Tadhkira, aw, mudhakkirat qadi.* Beirut: al-Mu'assasa al-Lubnaniyya li-l-I'lan, Mu'assasat al-Fikr al-Islami, 2004.

Anderson, J. N. D. "Law as a Social Force in Islamic Culture and History." *BSOAS* 20 (1957): 13–40.

———. "The Role of Personal Statutes in Social Development in Islamic Countries." *CSSH* Vol. 13, No. 1 (Jan., 1971): 16–31.

Anderson, Michael. "Islamic Law and the Colonial Encounter in British India." In *Islamic Family Law,* eds. Chibli Mallat and Jane Connors (London: Graham and Trotman, 1993), 205–223.

Arabi, Oussama. "The Interdiction of the Spendthrift (*Al-Safih*): A Human Rights Debate in Classical *Fiqh*." *Islamic Law and Society* Vol. 7, No. 3 (2000): 300–324.

———. *Studies in Modern Islamic Law and Jurisprudence.* The Hague: Kluwer Law International, 2001.

Arjomand, Said. *Authority and Political Culture in Shi'ism.* Albany, NY: State University of New York, 1988.

———. "Conceptions of Authority and the Transition of Shi'ism from Sectarian to National Religion in Iran." In *Culture and Memory in Medieval Islam: Essays in Honour of Wilferd Madelung,* eds. Farhad Daftary and Josef W. Meri (London: I. B. Tauris Publishers in association with The Institute of Ismaili Studies, 2003), 388–409.

Asad, Talal. *Formations of the Secular: Christianity, Islam, Modernity.* Stanford, CA: Stanford University Press, 2003.

———. *Genealogies of Religion: Discipline and Reason in Medieval Christianity and Islam.* Baltimore: Johns Hopkins Press, 1993.

———. *The Idea of an Anthropology of Islam.* Washington, D.C.: Center for Contemporary Arab Studies, Georgetown University, 1986.

'Awad, 'Abd al-'Aziz Muhammad. *Al-Idara al-'uthmaniyya fi wilayat Suriya, 1864–1914.* Cairo: Dar al-Ma'arif, 1969.

Ayoub, Mahmoud. *Redemptive Suffering in Islam: A Study of the Devotional Aspects of 'Ashura' in Twelver Shi'ism.* The Hague: Mouton Publishers, 1978.

Ayubi, Nazih. *Over-Stating the Arab State: Politics and Society in the Middle East.* London: I. B. Tauris, 1995.

Aziz, T. M. "Popular Sovereignty in Contemporary Shi'i Political Thought." *The Muslim World* Vol. 86, No. 3–4 (1996): 273–293.

Ba'albeki, Ahmad. "Al-Janub: qadiyyat mintaqa fi al-watan am qadiyyat watan fi al-mintaqa." In *Dirasat hawla janub Lubnan,* ed. al-Majlis al-Thaqafi li-Lubnan al-Janubi (Beirut: 1981), 59–67.

al-Bahadili, Muhammad Baqir Ahmad. *Al-Sayyid Hibat al-Din al-Shahrastani: atharuhu al-fikriyya wa-mawaqifuhu al-siyasiyya (1301–1386/1884–1967).* Beirut: Mu'assasat al-Fikr al-Islami, 2002.

al-Bakhit, Muhammad 'Adnan. *Kashshaf ihsa'i zamani li-sijillat al-mahakim al-shar'iyya wa-l-awqaf al-islamiyya fi bilad al-sham.* Amman: al-Jami'a al-Urduniyya, Markaz al-Watha'iq wa-l-Makhtutat, 1984.

Bakić-Hayden, Milica. "Nesting Orientalisms: The Case of Former Yugoslavia." *Slavic Review* Vol. 54, No. 4 (Winter 1995): 917–931.

Bannut, Jihad. *Harakat al-nidal fi Jabal 'Amil.* Beirut: Dar al-Mizan, 1993.

Bashkin, Orit. *The Other Iraq: Pluralism and Culture in Hashemite Iraq.* Stanford, CA: Stanford University Press, 2009.

Basile, Basile P. *Statut personnel et compètence judiciare des communautés confessionnelles au Liban.* Kaslik: Université Saint-Esprit, 1993.

Bayat, Mangol. *Mysticism and Dissent: Socioreligious Thought in Qajar Iran.* Syracuse, NY: Syracuse University Press, 1982.

Bayly, C. A. "The Pre-History of 'Communalism'? Religious Conflict in India, 1700–1860." *Modern Asian Studies* Vol. 19, No. 2 (1985): 177–203.

Bazzi, 'Abbas. "Bint Jubayl sanat 1936, al-intifada wa-l-iqta'." *Dirasat 'arabiyya* Vol. 5, No. 11 (1969): 72–88.

Bazzi, Mustafa Muhammad. "Hukumat Faysal fi zill al-atma' wa-l-tanafus al-duwaliayn." *Al-Muntalaq* 105 (September 1993): 75–114.

———. "Intifadat Bint Jubayl wa-Jabal 'Amil 1936 fi al-awwal min Nisan 1936." *Dirasat 'arabiyya* Vol. 28, No. 10–11–12 (1992): 65–92.

———. "Intifadat Bint Jubayl wa-Jabal 'Amil fi 1 Nisan 1936 (2)." *Dirasat 'arabiyya* Vol. 29, No. 1–2 (1992): 61–82

———. *Jabal 'Amil fi muhitihi al-'arabi, 1864–1948.* Beirut: al-Majlis al-Islami al-Shi'i al-A'la, 1993.

———. *Jabal 'Amil wa-tawabi'uhu fi shamal Filastin (bahth fi tatawwur al-milkiyya al-'aqariyya).* Beirut: Dar al-Mawasim, 2002.

———. *Al-Takamul al-iqtisadi bayna Jabal 'Amil wa-muhitihi al-'arabi, 1850–1950.* Beirut: Dar al-Mawasim li-l-Tiba'a wa-l-Nashr wa-l-Tawzi', 2002.

Bearman, Peri, Rudolph Peters, and Frank E. Vogel, eds. *The Islamic School of Law: Evolution, Devolution, and Progress.* Cambridge, Mass.: Islamic Legal Studies Program, Harvard Law School: Distributed by Harvard University Press, 2005.

Benton, Lauren. "Colonial Law and Cultural Difference: Jurisdictional Politics and the Formation of the Colonial State." *CSSH* Vol. 41, No. 3 (Jul., 1999): 563–588.

———. *Law and Colonial Cultures: Legal Regimes in World History, 1400–1900.* New York: Cambridge University Press, 2002.

Betts, Raymond F. *Assimilation and Association in French Colonial Theory 1890–1914.* Lincoln: University of Nebraska Press, 2005 [1960].

Beydoun, Ahmad. *Bint Jubayl Mishighan.* Beirut, 1989.

———. *Identité confessionnelle et temps social chez les historiens libanaises contemporains.* Beirut: L'Université Libanaise, 1984.

———. "A Note on Confessionalism." In *Lebanon in Limbo,* eds. Theodor Hanf and Nawaf Salam (Baden-Baden: Nomos Verlagsgesellschaft, 2003), 75–86.

———. "Al-Tawa'if—al-manatiq fi Lubnan." *Al-Waq'* Vol. 1, No. 2 (1981): 81–90.

Beydoun, Ibrahim, ed. *Safahat min tarikh Jabal 'Amil.* Beirut: Dar al-Farabi, 1979.

Binder, Leonard, ed. *Politics in Lebanon.* New York: John Wiley and Sons, 1966.

Blei, Alexander. "Ha-Edah Hamitualit Be'levanon Ve-Yikhhudah." *Hamizrah He'hadash* Vol. 23, No. 2 (1973): 194–201.

Bosworth, C. Edmund. "Baha' al-Din al-'Amili in the Two Worlds of the Ottomans and the Safavids." In *Convegno sul tema (15 April 1991, Roma), La Shi'a nell'impero ottomano* (Rome: Academia nazionale Dei Lincei; Fondazione Leone Caetani, 1993), 85–105.

Bourdieu, Pierre. *Outline of a Theory of Practice.* Cambridge: Cambridge University Press, 1977.

Braude, Benjamin. "Founding Myths of the Millet System." In *Christians and Jews in the Ottoman Empire: The Functioning of a Plural Society,* eds. Benjamin Braude and Bernard Lewis (New York: Holmes & Meier Publishers, 1982), 69–88.

Brown, Nathan J. "Sharia and State in the Modern Muslim Middle East." *IJMES* Vol. 29, No. 3 (1997): 359–376.

Brubaker, Rogers and Frederick Cooper. "Beyond 'Identity'." *Theory and Society* Vol. 29, No. 1 (2000): 1–47.

Brunner, Rainer. *Islamic Ecumenism in the 20th Century: The Azhar and Shiism between Rapprochement and Restraint.* Leiden: Brill, 2004.

Brunner, Rainer and Werner Ende. "Preface." In *The Twelver Shia in Modern Times: Religious Culture and Political History,* eds. Rainer Brunner and Werner Ende (Leiden: Brill, 2002), ix–xx.

Buckley, Ron P. "On the Origins of Shi'i Hadith." *The Muslim World* Vol. 88, No. 2 (1998): 165–84.

Buheiry, Marwan. *Beirut's Role in the Political Economy of the French Mandate, 1919–1939.* Oxford: Centre for Lebanese Studies, 1992.

Cahiers de l'École Supérieure des Lettres. *Colloque 'Ashura'.* Beirut: 1974.

Cairns, David. "The Object of Sectarianism: The Material Reality of Sectarianism in Ulster Loyalism." *The Journal of the Royal Anthropological Institute* Vol. 6, No. 3 (2000): 437–452.

Calder, Norman. "Judicial Authority in Imami Shi'i Jurisprudence." *Bulletin (British Society for Middle Eastern Studies)* (1979): 104–108.

Calmard, Jean. "Les rituels shiites et le pouvoir. L'imposition du shiisme Safavide: eulogies et malédictions canoniques." In *Etudes Safavides*, ed. Jean Calmard (Paris-Téhéran: Institut Français de Recherche en Iran, 1993), 109–150.

———. "Shi'i Rituals and Power II. The Consolidation of Safavid Shi'ism: Folklore and Popular Religion." In *Safavid Persia: The History and Politics of an Islamic Society*, ed. Charles Melville (London: I. B. Tauris & Co. Ltd. with the Centre of Middle Eastern Studies, University of Cambridge, 1996), 139-190.

Carmichael, Tim. "British 'Practice' towards Islam in the East Africa Protectorate: Muslim Officials, *Waqf* Administration and Secular Education in Mombasa and Environs, 1895–1920." *Journal of Muslim Minority Affairs* Vol. 17, No.2 (Oct. 1997): 293–310.

Carroll S. J., Anthony J. *Protestant Modernity: Weber, Secularisation, and Protestantism*. Scranton: University of Scranton Press, 2007.

Chalabi, Tamara. *The Shi'is of Jabal 'Amil and the New Lebanon: Community and Nation-State, 1918–1943*. London: Palgrave Macmillan, 2006.

Chamie, Joseph. "Religious Groups in Lebanon: A Descriptive Investigation." *IJMES* Vol. 11, No. 2 (1980): 175–187.

Chanock, Martin. *Law, Custom and Social Order: The Colonial Experience in Malawi and Zambia*. Cambridge: Cambridge University Press, 1985.

Chehabi, H. E., ed. *Distant Relations: Iran and Lebanon in the Last 500 Years*. London: Centre for Lebanese Studies in association with I. B. Tauris Publishers, 2006.

Chelkowski, Peter J. "Iconography of the Women of Karbala: Tiles, Murals, Stamps, and Posters." In *The Women of Karbala: Ritual Performance and Symbolic Discourses in Modern Shi'i Islam*, ed. Kamran Scot Aghaie (Austin: University of Texas Press, 2005), 119–38

Christelow, Allan. *Muslim Law Courts and the French Colonial State in Algeria*. Princeton, N.J.: Princeton University Press, 1985.

———. "The Transformation of the Muslim Court System in Colonial Algeria: Reflections on the Concept of Autonomy." In *Islamic Law: Social and Historical Contexts*, ed. Aziz al-Azmeh (London and New York: Routledge, 1988), 215–230.

Clancy-Smith, Julia. "Collaboration and Empire in the Middle East and North Africa: Introduction and Response." *CSSAAME* Vol. 24, No. 1 (2004): 123–127.

Clarke, L. "The Shi'i Construction of Taqlid." *Journal of Islamic Studies* Vol. 12, No. 1 (2001): 40–64.

Cobban, Helena. "Shi'ism in the Arab World." In *Expectation of the Millenium: Shi'ism in History*, eds. Hamid Dabashi, Seyyed Hossein Nasr and Seyyed Vali Reza Nasr (Albany, NY: State University of New York, 1989), 255–260.

Cohen, Mark R. "The Neo-Lachrymose Conception of Jewish-Arab History." *Tikkun* Vol. 6. No. 3 (May–June 1991): 55–60.

Cohn, Bernard S. "Law and the Colonial State in India." In *History and Power in the Study of Law: New Directions in Legal Anthropology*, eds. June Starr and Jane F. Collier (Ithaca, NY: Cornell University Press, 1989), 131–152.

Cole, Juan R. I. *Roots of North Indian Shi'ism in Iran and Iraq: Religion and State in Awadh, 1722–1859*. Berkeley and Los Angeles: University of California Press, 1989.

———. *Sacred Space and Holy War: The Politics, Culture and History of Shi'ite Islam*. London: I. B. Tauris, 2002.

Commins, David Dean. *Islamic Reform: Politics and Social Change in Late Ottoman Syria*. New York: Oxford University Press, 1990.

Cook, Michael. *Commanding Right and Forbidding Wrong in Islamic Thought*. Cambridge: Cambridge University Press, 2000.

Coulson, N. J. *Succession in the Muslim Family*. Cambridge: Cambridge University Press, 1971.

Crews, Robert D. "Empire and the Confessional State: Islam and Religious Politics in Nineteenth-Century Russia." *American Historical Review* Vol. 108, No. 1 (2003): 50–83.

———. *For Prophet and Tsar: Islam and Empire in Russia and Central Asia*. Cambridge, Mass.: Harvard University Press, 2006.

Crow, Ralph E. "Religious Sectarianism in the Lebanese Political System." *The Journal of Politics* Vol. 24, No. 3 (1962): 489–520.

Dahir, Mas'ud. "Jabal 'Amil fi itar al-tajzi'a al-isti'mariyya li-l-mashriq al-'arabi." In *Safahat min tarikh Jabal 'Amil*, ed. Ibrahim Beydoun (Beirut: al-Majlis al-Thaqafi li-Lubnan al-Janubi, 1979), 107–130.

———. *Al-Judhur al-tarikhiyya li-l-mas'ala al-ta'ifiyya al-lubnaniyya, 1697–1861*. Beirut: Ma'had al-Inma' al-'Arabi, 1981.

———. *Lubnan: al-istiqlal, al-mithaq wa-l-sigha*. Beirut: Ma'ahad al-Inma' al-'Arabi, 1977.

Dakake, Maria Massi. *The Charismatic Community: Shi'ite Identity in Early Islam*. Albany, NY: State University of New York, 2007.

———. "Hiding in Plain Sight: The Practical and Doctrinal Significance of Secrecy in Shi'ite Islam." *Journal of the American Academy of Religion* Vol. 74, No. 2 (2006): 324–355.

Dallal, Ahmad. "Appropriating the Past: Twentieth-Century Reconstruction of Pre-Modern Islamic Thought." *Islamic Law and Society* Vol. 7, No. 3 (October 2000): 325–358.

Darwish, 'Ali Ibrahim. *Jabal 'Amil bayna 1516–1697: al-hayat al-siyasiyya wa-l-thaqafiyya*. Beirut: Dar al-Hadi, 1993.

Deeb, Lara. *An Enchanted Modern: Gender and Public Piety in Shi'i Lebanon* Princeton, N.J.: Princeton University Press, 2006.

————. "Living Ashura in Lebanon: Mourning Transformed to Sacrifice." *CSSAAME* Vol. 25, No. 1 (2005): 122–137.

Deguilhem, Randi and Abdelhamid Hénia, eds. *Les Fondations pieuses (waqf) en Méditerranée: enjeux de société, enjeux de pouvoir.* Koweït: Fondation publique des awqaf du Koweït, 2004.

al-Dhahabi, Muhammad Husayn. *Al-Ahwal al-shakhsiyya bayna madhhab ahl al-sunna wa-madhhab al-ja'fariyya.* Baghdad: Sharikat al-Tab'a wa-l-Nashr, 1958.

Dib, Yusuf. *Fihrist Jabal 'Amil: 1909–1986.* Beirut: al-Markaz al-Lubnani li-l-Buhuth wa-l-Tawthiq wa-l-'Ilam, 1989.

Diyab, Hasan. *Tarikh Sur al-ijtima'i 1920–1943.* Beirut: Dar al-Farabi, 1988.

Douglas, Mary. *How Institutions Think.* Syracuse, N.Y: Syracuse University Press, 1986.

————. *Purity and Danger: An Analysis of Concepts of Pollution and Taboo.* London: Routledge & Kegan Paul, 1966.

Doumani, Beshara. "Endowing Family: Waqf, Property and Gender in Tripoli and Nablus, 1800–1860." *CSSH* Vol. 40, No. 1 (Jan., 1998): 3–41.

————. "Palestinian Islamic Court Records: A Source for Socioeconomic History." *MESA Bulletin* (1985): 155–172.

Douwes, Dick and Norman N. Lewis. "The Trials of Syrian Ismailis in the First Decade of the 20th Century." *IJMES* Vol. 21 (1989): 215–232.

Dubar, Claude and Salim Nasr. *Les classes sociales au Liban.* Paris: Presses de la Fondation nationale des sciences politiques, 1976.

Dwyer, Daisy Hilse. "Outside the Courts: Extra-Legal Strategies for the Subordination of Women." In *African Women & the Law: Historical Perspectives*, ed. Margaret Jean Hay and Marcia Wright (Boston: Boston University African Studies Center, 1982), 90-109.

Ebersole, Gary L. "The Function of Ritual Weeping Revisited: Affective Expression and Moral Discourse." *History of Religions* Vol. 39, No. 3 (2000): 211–246.

Eickelman, Dale F. and Armando Salvatore. "Muslim Publics." In *Public Islam and the Common Good*, eds. Armando Salvatore and Dale F. Eickelman (Leiden: Brill, 2004), 3–27.

Eisenman, Robert H. *Islamic Law in Palestine and Israel: A History of the Survival of Tanzimat and Shari'a in the British Mandate and the Jewish State.* Leiden: Brill, 1978.

Eliash, Joseph. "The Ithna'ashari-Shi'i Juristic Theory of Political and Legal Authority." *Studia Islamica* No. 29 (1969): 17–30.

El-Kak, Mona Harb. *Politiques urbaines dans la banlieue-sud de Beyrouth.* Beirut: CERMOC, 1996.

El-Khazen, Farid. *The Breakdown of the State in Lebanon, 1967–1976.* London: I. B. Tauris, 2002.

Ende, Werner. "The Flagellations of Muharram and the Shiʿite ʿulamaʾ." *Der Islam* (1978): 19–36.

Fadlallah, Hadi. *Muhammad Jawad Mughniyya: fikr wa-islah.* Beirut: Dar al-Hadi, 1993.

Faghfoory, Mohammad H. "The Ulama-State Relations in Iran: 1921–1941." *IJMES* Vol. 19, No. 4 (1987): 413–432.

Fahs, Hani, *Al-Shiʿa wa-l-dawla fi Lubnan: malamih fi al-ruʾya wa-l-dhakira.* Beirut: Dar al-Andalus, 1996.

Faksh, Mahmud A. "The Shiʿa Community of Lebanon: A New Assertive Political Force." *Journal of South Asian and Middle Eastern Studies* Vol. 14, No. 3 (1991): 33–56.

al-Faqih, Muhammad Taqi. *Hajar wa-tin.* Beirut: Dar al-Adwaʾ, 1990.

———. *Jabal ʿAmil fi al-tarikh.* Beirut: Dar al-Adwaʾ, 1986.

al-Faqih, Yusuf. *Al-Ahwal al-shakhsiyya fi fiqh ahl al-bayt.* Beirut: Dar al-Adwaʾ, 1989.

Farhan, Adnan. *Harakat al-ijtihad ʿind al-shiʿa al-imamiyya.* Beirut: Dar al-Hadi, 2004.

Faʿur, ʿAli. "Al-Ihsaʾat al-sukaniyya waʿ-ʿawaʾiq al-tanmiyya fi janub Lubnan maʿa taqdirat awwaliyya li-l-sukkan fi al-mudn wa-l-quraʾ al-janubiyya." *Al-Baheth* Vol. 4, No. 2–3 (1981): 21–51.

———. *Janub Lubnan: takwinuhu al-tabiʿi, manakhuhu, miyahu, turbatuhu wa-nabatatuhu (al-juzʾ al-awwal).* Beirut: Dar al-Baheth, 1985.

Fawaz, Leila. *Merchants and Migrants in Nineteenth-Century Beirut.* Cambridge, Mass.: Harvard University Press, 1983.

———. *An Occasion for War: Civil Conflict in Lebanon and Damascus in 1860.* London: Centre for Lebanese Studies and I. B. Tauris Publishers, 1994.

Fayyad, Nawal. *Safahat min tarikh Jabal ʿAmil fi al-ʿahdayn al-ʿuthmani wa-l-faransi.* Beirut: Dar al-Jadid, 1998.

Firro, Kais M. "Ethnicizing the Shiʿis in Mandatory Lebanon." *Middle Eastern Studies* Vol. 42, No. 5 (September 2006): 741–759.

———. *Inventing Lebanon: Nationalism and the State under the Mandate.* London: I. B. Tauris, 2003.

———. "The Shiʿis in Lebanon: Between Communal ʿAsabiyya and Arab Nationalism, 1908–21." *Middle Eastern Studies* Vol. 42, No. 4 (July 2006): 535–550.

Fischer, Michael. *Iran: From Religious Dispute to Revolution.* Cambridge, Mass.: Harvard University Press, 1980.

Friedlaender, Israel. *The Heterodoxies of the Shiites in the Presentation of Ibn Hazm.* New Haven, CT: [s.n.], 1909.

———. "Jewish-Arabic Studies I. Shiitic Elements in Jewish Sectarianism." *The Jewish Quarterly Review* Vol. 1, No. 2 (1910): 183–215.

Gates, Carolyn L. *The Merchant Republic of Lebanon: Rise of an Open Economy.* London: The Centre for Lebanese Studies in association with I. B. Tauris, 1998.

Ghalyun, Burhan. *Nizam al-ta'ifiyya min al-dawla ila al-qabila.* Beirut: al-Markaz al-Thaqafi al-'Arabi, 1990.

Ghandour, Zeina. "Religious Law in a Secular State: The Jurisdiction of the Shari'a Courts of Palestine and Israel." *Arab Law Quarterly* Vol. 5, No. 1 (1990): 25–48.

Gharib, Hasan Khalil. *Nahwa tarikh fikri-siyasi li-shi'at Lubnan (awda' wa-itti-jahat)* (2 vols.). Beirut: Dar al-Kunuz al-Adabiyya, 2000.

Ghazzal, Zouhair. "Review: Waddah Sharara, *Al-Umma Al-Qaliqa* and Muham-mad Husayn Fadlallah, *Al-Masa'il Al-Fiqhiyya.*" *Islamic Law and Society* Vol. 5, No. 3 (1998): 448–456.

Gillin, John L. "A Contribution to the Sociology of Sects." *The American Journal of Sociology* Vol. 16, No. 2 (1910): 236–252.

Gilsenan, Michael. "A Modern Feudality? Land and Labour in North Lebanon, 1858–1950." In *Land Tenure and Social Transformation in the Middle East,* ed. Tarif Khalidi (Beirut: American University of Beirut, 1984), 449–463.

Glassen, Erika. "Muharram-Ceremonies (Azadari) in Istanbul At the End of the XIXth and the Beginning of the XXth Century." In *Les iraniens d'Istanbul,* ed. Thierry Zarcone and F. Zarinebaf-Shahr (Istanbul-Tehran: IFEA/IFRI, 1993), 113–129.

Gleave, Robert. "Imami Shi'i Refutations of Qiyas." In *Studies in Islamic Legal Theory,* ed. Bernard Weiss. (Leiden: Brill, 2002), 267–291.

———. *Inevitable Doubt: Two Theories of Shi'i Jurisprudence.* Leiden: Brill, 2000.

———. "Marrying Fatimid Women: Legal Theory and Substantive Law in Shi'i Jurisprudence." *Islamic Law and Society* Vol. 6, No. 1 (1999): 38–68.

———. "Political Aspects of Modern Shi'i Legal Discussions: Khumayni and Khu'i on Ijtihad and Qada'." In *Shaping the Islamic Reformation,* ed. B. A. Roberson (London: Frank Cass, 2003), 96–116.

———. "The Qadi and the Mufti in Akhbari Shi'i Jurisprudence." In *The Law Applied: Contextualizing the Islamic Shari'a: A Volume in Honor of Frank E. Vogel,* eds. Peri Bearman, Wolfhart Heinrichs, and Bernard G. Weiss (London: I. B. Tauris, 2008), 235–258.

Gonzalez-Quijano, Yves. "Les interpretations d'un rite: celebrations de la 'Achoura au Liban." *Maghreb, Machrek* 115 (1987): 5–27.

Gottschalk, Peter. "A Categorical Difference: Communal Identity in British Epis-temologies." In *Religion and Violence in South Asia: Theory and Practice,* eds. John R. Hinnells and Richard King (London: Routledge, 2007), 195–210.

Gregory, Brad S. "The Other Confessional History: On Secular Bias in the Study of Religion." *History and Theory* 45 (2006): 132–149.

Gribetz, Arthur. *Strange Bedfellows: Mut'at Al-Nisa' and Mut'at Al-Hajj: A Study Based on Sunni and Shi'i Sources of Tafsir, Hadith and Fiqh.* Berlin: Klaus Schwarz Verlag, 1994.

Günther, Sebastian. "Maqâtil Literature in Medieval Islam." *Journal of Arabic Literature* Vol. 25, No. 3 (1994): 192–212.

Haeri, Shala. "Divorce in Contemporary Iran: A Male Prerogative in Self-Will." In *Islamic Family Law*, eds. Chibli Mallat and Jane Connors (London: Graham and Trotman, 1993), 55-69.

⸻. *Law of Desire: Temporary Marriage in Islam*. Syracuse, NY: Syracuse University Press, 1989.

⸻. "Temporary Marriage and the State in Iran: An Islamic Discourse on Female Sexuality." *Social Research* Vol. 59, No. 1 (1992): 201-223.

Hajj, Kamal Yusuf. *Al-Ta'ifiyya al-banna'a aw falsafat al-mithaq al-watani*. Beirut: Matba'at al-Rahbaniyya, 1961.

al-Hajjar, Hilmi. "Mahakim al-ahwal al-shakhsiyya min haythu al-qanun." In *al-Qada' al-lubnani: bina' al-sulta wa-tatwir al-mu'assasat*, ed. Lebanese Center for Policy Studies (Beirut: al-Markaz al-Lubnani li-l-Dirasat , 1999), 269-296.

Halawi, Majed. *A Lebanon Defied: Musa al-Sadr and the Shi'a Community*. Boulder: Westview Press, 1992.

Hallaq, Hassan. *Dirasat fi tarikh Lubnan al-mu'asir 1913-1943: min jam'iyyat Bayrut al-islahiyya ila al-mithaq al-watani al-lubnani*. Beirut: Dar al-Nahda al-'Arabiyya, 1985.

Hallaq, Wael B. "On the Origins of the Controversy about the Existence of Mujtahids and the Gate of Ijtihad." *Studia Islamica* No. 63 (1986): 129-141.

⸻. "Was the Gate of Ijtihad Closed?" *IJMES* Vol. 16, No. 1 (1984): 3-41.

Hamdan, Kamal. "About the Confessional State in Lebanon." In *State and Society in Lebanon*, ed. Leila Fawaz in cooperation with Fida Nasrallah and Nadim Shehadi (Oxford: Tufts University and the Centre for Lebanese Studies, 1991), 93-99.

Hammoud, Zaynab. "Shihadat janubiyya." *Al-Baheth* Vol. 4, No. 2-3 (1981): 299-323.

Hammud, Muhammad Jamil. *Radd al-hujum 'an sha'a'ir al-Imam al-Husayn al-mazlum: al-buka' wa-l-tatbir: bahth fiqhi istidlali yatanawal mawdu' al-tatbir wa-l-ishkalat 'alayh*. Beirut: Markaz al-'Itra li-l-Dirasat wa-l-Buhuth, 2004.

Hanf, Theodor. "The Sacred Marker: Religion, Communalism, and Nationalism." In *Dealing with Difference: Religion, Ethnicity, and Politics: Comparing Cases and Concepts*, ed. Theodor Hanf (Baden-Baden: Nomos Verlagsgesellschaft, 1999), 385-397.

Hanssen, Jens. *Fin-de-Siècle Beirut: The Making of an Ottoman Provincial Capital*. Oxford: Oxford University Press, 2005.

Harik, Iliya F. *Politics and Change in a Traditional Society; Lebanon, 1711-1845*. Princeton, N.J.: Princeton University Press, 1968.

Harik, Judith Palmer. "Between Islam and the System: Sources and Implications of Popular Support for Lebanon's Hizballah." *The Journal of Conflict Resolution* Vol. 40, No. 1 (1996): 41-67.

Hariz, Salim. *Al-Waqf: dirasat wa-abhath*. Beirut: al-Jami'a al-Lubnaniyya, 1994.

Harrison, Simon. "Cultural Difference as Denied Resemblance: Reconsidering Nationalism and Ethnicity." *CSSH* Vol. 45, No. 2 (Apr., 2003): 343–361.

Hasan, Mushirul. "Traditional Rites and Contested Meanings: Sectarian Strife in Colonial Lucknow." In *Islam, Communities and the Nation: Muslim Identities in South Asia and Beyond*, ed. Mushirul Hasan (New Delhi: Manohar, 1998), 341–366.

Hassun, Muhammad. *Qira'a fi risalat al-tanzih li-l-Sayyid Muhsin al-Amin*. Qom: Sa'id Ibn Jubayr, 1423.

Havemann, Axel. "Historiography in 20th-Century Lebanon: Between Confessional Identity and National Coalescence." *Bulletin of the Royal Institute for Inter-Faith Studies* Vol. 4, No. 2 (2002): 49–69.

Haydari, Ibrahim. "The Rituals of 'Ashura': Genealogy, Functions, Actors and Structures." In *Ayatollahs, Sufis and Ideologues: State, Religion and Social Movements in Iraq*, ed. Faleh Abdul-Jabar (London: Saqi Books, 2002), 101–113.

———. *Trajidiya Karbala': susiyulujiya al-khitab al-shi'i*. Beirut: Dar al-Saqi, 1999.

Herzfeld, Michael. *Cultural Intimacy: Social Poetics of the Nation State*. New York: Routledge, 1997.

———. "Intimating Culture: Local Contexts and International Power." In *Off Stage/On Display: Cultural Intimacy in an Age of Public Culture*, ed. Andrew Shyrock (Stanford, CA: Stanford University Press, 2004), 317–335.

———. "Localism and the Logic of Nationalistic Folklore: Cretan Reflections." *CSSH* Vol. 45, No. 2 (Apr., 2003): 281–310.

Hess, Jr., Clyde G. and Herbert L. Bodman, Jr. "Confessionalism and Feudality in Lebanese Politics." *Middle East Journal* Vol. 8, No. 1 (1954): 10–26.

Hirsch, Susan F. "Kadhi's Courts as Complex Sites of Resistance: The State, Islam, and Gender in Postcolonial Kenya." In *Contested States: Law, Hegemony and Resistance*, eds. Mindie Lazarus-Black and Susan F. Hirsch (New York: Routledge, 1994), 207–230.

———. *Pronouncing and Persevering: Gender and the Discourses of Disputing in an African Islamic Court*. Chicago: The University of Chicago Press, 1998.

Hirschkind, Charles and David Scott, eds. *Powers of the Secular Modern: Talal Asad and His Interlocutors*. Stanford, CA: Stanford University Press, 2006.

Hitti, Philip. *Lebanon in History: From the Earliest Times to the Present*. London: MacMillan, 1967.

———. *A Short History of Lebanon*. London: MacMillan, 1965.

Hjortshoj, Keith. "Shi'i Identity and the Significance of Muharram in Lucknow, India." In *Shi'ism, Resistance and Revolution*, ed. Martin Kramer (Boulder, CO: Westview Press, 1987), 289–309.

Hodgson, Marshall G. S. "How Did the Early Shi'a Become Sectarian?" *Journal of the American Oriental Society* Vol. 75, No. 1 (1955): 1–13.

———. *The Order of Assassins: The Struggle of the Early Nizârî Ismâ'îlîs against the Islamic World.* The Hague: Mouton, 1955.

Hourani, Albert. "From Jabal 'Amil to Persia." *BSOAS* Vol. 49, No. 1 (1986): 133–140.

———. "Ideologies of the Mountain and the City." In *Essays on the Crisis in Lebanon*, ed. Roger Owen (London: Ithaca Press, 1976), 33–41.

Howarth, Toby M. *The Twelver Shi'a as a Muslim Minority in India: Pulpit of Tears.* London and New York: Routledge, 2005.

Hubb Allah, 'Ali. *Sharh qanun al-mahakim al-shar'iyya al-lubnani li-l-ta'ifatayn al-ja'fariyya wa-l-sunniyya al-sadir bi-tarikh 16/7/1962 ma'a ta'dilatihi hatta 'am 2002 M: dirasat wa-buhuth fiqhiyya wa-qanuniyya muqarana.* Beirut: Dar al-Mahajja al-Bayda', 2003.

Hubb Allah, Haydar, ed. *Jadal wa-mawaqif fi al-sha'a'ir al-husayniyya.* Beirut: Dar al-Hadi li-l-Tiba'a wa-l-Nashr wa-l-Tawzi', 2009.

Hudson, Michael. *The Precarious Republic: Political Modernization in Lebanon.* New York: Random House, 1968.

Hussain, Ali J. "The Mourning of History and the History of Mourning: The Evolution of Ritual Commemoration of the Battle of Karbala." *CSSAAME* Vol. 25, No. 1 (2005): 78–88.

Hussain, Nasser. *The Jurisprudence of Emergency: Colonialism and the Rule of Law.* Ann Arbor: University of Michigan Press, 2003.

Hyder, Syed Akbar. *Reliving Karbala: Martyrdom in South Asian Memory.* Oxford: Oxford University Press, 2006.

Ibrahim, Fu'ad. *Al-Faqih wa-l-dawla: al-fikr al-siyasi al-shi'i.* Beirut: Dar al-Kunuz al-Adabiyya, 1998.

Imber, Colin. "Zinā in Ottoman Law." In *Studies in Ottoman History and Law*, ed. Colin Imber (Istanbul: Isis Press, 1996), 175–206.

Jaber, Hala. *Hezbollah: Born with a Vengeance.* New York: Columbia University Press, 1997.

Jaber, Mounzer. "Al-Kiyan al-siyasi li-Jabal 'Amil qabla 1920." In *Safahat min tarikh Jabal 'Amil*, ed. Ibrahim Beydoun (Beirut: al-Majlis al-Thaqafi li-Lubnan al-Janubi, 1979), 83–106.

———. *Al-Sharit al-lubnani al-muhtall: masalik al-ihtilal, masarat al-muwajaha, masir al-ahali.* Beirut: Institute for Palestine Studies, 1999.

———. "Al-Shi'a fi Jabal 'Amil bayna al-mabda'iyya wa-l-hifaz 'ala al-dhat." *Al-Muntalaq* Vol. 105 (September 1993), 61–74.

Jaber, Talal. "Le discours shi'ite sur le pouvoir." *Peuples Méditerranéens* (1982): 75–92.

Jafri, S. Husain M. *Origins and Early Development of Shi'a Islam.* London: Longman, 1979.

Jalal, Ayesha. "Exploding Communalism: The Politics of Muslim Identity in South Asia." In *Nationalism, Democracy and Development: State and Politics in India*, eds. Sugata Bose and Ayesha Jalal (Delhi: Oxford University Press, 1997), 76–103.

———. "Negotiating Colonial Modernity and Cultural Difference: Indian Muslim Conceptions of Community and Nation, 1878–1914." In *Modernity and Culture: From the Mediterranean to the Indian Ocean*, eds. Leila Tarazi Fawaz and C. A. Bayly (New York: Columbia University Press, 2002), 230–260.

Johnson, Michael. *Class and Client in Beirut: The Sunni Muslim Community and the Lebanese State, 1840–1985*. London: Ithaca Press, 1986.

al-Jumayli, 'Abbas. *Al-Murshid ila al-ahkam al-ja'fariyya fi al-ahwal al-shakhsiyya*. Najaf: Matba'at al-Nu'man, 1958.

Kanazi, George J. "The Massacre of Al-Husayn B. 'Ali: Between History and Folklore." In *Studies in Canonical and Popular Arabic Literature*, eds. Shimon Ballas and Reuven Snir (Toronto: York Press, 1998), 23–36.

Khashan, Hilal. *Inside the Lebanese Confessional Mind*. Lanham, Md: University Press of America, 1992.

Kamran, Tahir. "Contextualizing Sectarian Militancy in Pakistan: A Case Study of Jhang." *Journal of Islamic Studies* Vol. 20, No. 1 (2009): 55–85.

Kaplan, Benjamin J. *Divided by Faith: Religious Conflict and the Practice of Toleration in Early Modern Europe*. Cambridge, Mass.: Belknap Press of Harvard University Press, 2007.

Kartomi, Margaret. "Tabut—A Shi'a Ritual Transplanted from India to Sumatra." In *Nineteenth and Twentieth Century Indonesia: Essays in Honour of Professor J. D. Legge*, eds. David P. Chandler and M. C. Ricklefs (Clayton: Centre of Southeast Studies, Monash University, 1986), 141–162

Kassir, Samir. *La guerre du Liban: de la dissension nationale au conflit régional, 1975–1982*. Beirut: Karthala; CERMOC, 1994.

al-Katib, Ahmad. *Tatawwur al-fikr al-siyasi al-shi'i min al-shura ila wilayat al-faqih*. Beirut: Dar al-Jadid, 1998.

Kaufman, Asher. *Reviving Phoenicia: The Search for Identity in Lebanon*. London: I. B. Tauris, 2004.

Kawtharani, Wajih. "Al-Hayat al-iqtisadiyya fi wilayat Bayrut 'ashiyata al-harb al-'alamiyya al-ula min khilal kitab "Wilayat Bayrut" li-Rafiq al-Tamimi wa-Muhammad Bahjat." *Revue d'Histoire Maghrebine* Vol. 12, No. 39–40 (1985): 375–390.

———. *Bayna fiqh al-islah al-shi'i wa-wilayat al-faqih: al-dawla wa-l-muwatin*. Beirut: Dar al-Nahar, 2007.

Keddie, Nikki R. and Juan R. I. Cole, eds. *Shi'ism and Social Protest*. New Haven, CT: Yale University Press, 1986.

Khalaf, Samir. *Civil and Uncivil Violence in Lebanon: A History of the Internationalization of Communal Conflict*. New York: Columbia University Press, 2002.

Khalidi, Tarif. "Shaykh Ahmad 'Arif Al-Zayn and *al-'Irfan*." In *Intellectual Life in the Arab East, 1890–1939*, ed. Marwan R. Buheiry (Beirut: American University of Beirut, Center for Arab and Middle East Studies, 1981), 110–124.

Khalifeh, Nabil. *Al-Shi'a fi Lubnan: thawrat al-dimughrafiya wa-l-hirman*. Beirut: 1984.

El-Khalil, Ali. "The Role of the South in Lebanese Politics." In *Lebanon: A History of Conflict and Consensus*, eds. Nadim Shehadi and Dana Haffar Mills (London: The Centre for Lebanese Studies in association with I. B. Tauris, 1988), 305–314.

Khalil, Khalil Ahmad. "Janub Lubnan bayna al-dawla wa-l-thawra." *Dirasat 'arabiyya* (1975): 22–33.

Khater, Akram Fouad. ""House" to "Goddess of the House": Gender, Class, and Silk in 19th-Century Mount Lebanon." *IJMES* Vol. 28, No. 3 (Aug. 1996): 325–348.

———. *Inventing Home: Emigration, Gender, and the Middle Class in Lebanon, 1870–1920*. Berkeley and Los Angeles: University of California Press, 2001.

al-Khorrazi, Muhsin. "Tashabbuh al-rajul bi-l-mar'a wa bi-l-'aks." *Fiqh Ahl al-Bayt* Vol. 3, No. 9 (1998): 163–174.

Khoury, Dina Rizk. *State and Provincial Society in the Ottoman Empire: Mosul, 1540–1834*. Cambridge: Cambridge University Press, 1997.

Khoury, Philip S. *Syria and the French Mandate: The Politics of Arab Nationalism, 1920–1945*. Princeton, N.J.: Princeton University Press, 1987.

Khuri, Fuad I. *From Village to Suburb: Order and Change in Greater Beirut*. Chicago: University of Illinois Press, 1975.

———. "Secularization and 'Ulama' Networks among Sunni and Shi'i Religious Officials." In *Toward a Viable Lebanon*, ed. Halim Barakat (London, Washington: Croom Helm; Center for Contemporary Arab Studies, Georgetown University, 1988), 68–98.

Kingston, Paul. "Review of Kais Firro, *Inventing Lebanon: Nation and State under the Mandate*," *MIT-Electronic Journal of Middle East Studies (MIT-EJMES)*, December 2004 (http://web.mit.edu/cis/www/mitejmes/intro.htm; accessed 12/11/06).

Kohlberg, Etan. *Belief and Law in Imami Shi'ism*. Aldershot, UK: Variorum, 1991.

———. "The Position of the Walad Zinā in Imāmī Shī'īsm." *BSOAS* Vol. 48, No. 2 (1985): 237–66.

———. "Some Imami Views of Taqiyya." *Journal of the American Oriental Society* 90 (1975): 395–402.

Kozlowski, Gregory C. *Muslim Endowments and Society in British India*. Cambridge: Cambridge University Press, 1985.

Kurani, Muhammad. *Al-Judhur al-tarikhiyya li-l-muqawama al-islamiyya fi Jabal 'Amil*. Beirut: Dar al-Wasila, 1993.

Lalani, Arzina R. *Early Shi'i Thought: The Teachings of Imam Muhammad al-Baqir.* London: I. B. Tauris in association with the Institute of Ismaili Studies, 2000.

Launay, Robert and Benjamin F. Soares. "The Formation of an 'Islamic Sphere' in French Colonial West Africa." *Economy and Society* Vol. 28, No. 4 (1999): 497–519.

Layish, Aharon. "The Muslim Waqf in Jerusalem After 1967: Beneficiaries and Management." In *Le waqf dans le monde musulman contemporain (XIXe–XXe Siècles): fonctions sociales, économiques et politiques: actes de la Table ronde d'Istanbul, 13–14 Novembre 1992,* ed. Faruk Bilici (Istanbul: Institut français d'études anatoliennes, 1994), 145–167.

Lebanese Center for Policy Studies, ed. *Al-Qada' al-lubnani: bina' al-sulta wa-tatwir al-mu'assasat.* Beirut: LCPS, 1999.

Lewis, Bernard. *The Assassins: A Radical Sect in Islam.* London: Weidenfeld and Nicolson, 1972 [1967].

Liebesny, Herbert J. "Comparative Legal History: Its Role in the Analysis of Islamic and Modern Near Eastern Legal Institutions." *The American Journal of Comparative Law* Vol. 20, No. 1 (1972): 38–52.

Litvak, Meir. *Shi'i Scholars of Nineteenth-Century Iraq: The 'Ulama' of Najaf and Karbala'.* Cambridge: Cambridge University Press, 1998.

Longrigg, Stephen Hemsley. *Syria and Lebanon under French Mandate.* London: Oxford University Press, 1958.

Loos, Tamara. *Subject Siam: Family, Law, and Colonial Modernity in Thailand.* Ithaca, NY: Cornell University Press, 2006.

Luizard, Pierre-Jean. *La formation de l'Irak contemporaine: le rôle politique des ulémas chiites à la fin de la domination ottomane et au moment de la construction de l'État irakien.* Paris: CNRS Editions, 1991.

Maatouk, Frederic. "'Ashura' (lubnaniyya) wa-nass 1936." *Abwab* 6 (1995): 148–158.

———. *La représentation de la mort de l'imam Hussein à Nabatieh (Liban-Sud).* Beirut: 1974.

Madelung, Wilferd. "Shi'i Attitudes Toward Women as Reflected in Fiqh." In *Society and the Sexes in Medieval Islam,* ed. Afaf Lutfi al-Sayyid Marsot (Malibu, CA: Undena Publications, 1979), 69–79.

———. "A Treatise of the Sharif Al-Murtada on the Legality of Working for the Government." *BSOAS* Vol. 40, No. 3 (1980): 18–31.

Mahdavi, Shireen. "The Position of Women in Shi'a Iran: Views of the 'Ulama'." In *Women and the Family in the Middle East: New Voices of Change,* ed. Elizabeth Warnock Fernea (Austin: University of Texas Press, 1985), 255–268.

Mahmood, Saba. *Politics of Piety: The Islamic Movement and the Feminist Subject.* Princeton, N.J.: Princeton University Press, 2004.

al-Mahraqi, 'Ali. *Muhammad Jawad Mughniyya: siratuhu wa-'ata'uhu.* al-Manama, Bahrain: Maktabat al-Fahzawi, 1997.

Majdhub, Talal. *Tarikh Sayda al-ijtima'i.* Beirut, 1983.

Makdisi, Ussama. *Artillery of Heaven: American Missionaries and the Failed Conversion of the Middle East.* Ithaca, NY: Cornell University Press, 2007.

———. *The Culture of Sectarianism: Community, History and Violence in Nineteenth-Century Ottoman Lebanon.* Berkeley and Los Angeles: University of California Press, 2000.

———. "Ottoman Orientalism." *American Historical Review* Vol. 107, No. 3 (2002): 768–96.

———. "Reclaiming the Land of the Bible: Missionaries, Secularism, and Evangelical Modernity." *American Historical Review* Vol. 102, No. 3 (Jun., 1997): 680–713.

———. "Reconstructing the Nation-State: The Modernity of Sectarianism in Lebanon." *Middle East Report* No. 200 (Jul. –Sep., 1996): 23–26, 30.

———. "Revisiting Sectarianism." In *Religion between Violence and Reconciliation,* ed. Thomas Scheffler (Beirut: Orient-Institut, 2002), 179–191.

Makki, Muhammad Kazim. *Al-Haraka al-fikriyya wa-l-adabiyya fi Jabal 'Amil.* Beirut: Dar al-Andalus, 1963.

Maktabi, Rania. "The Lebanese Census of 1932 Revisited: Who Are the Lebanese?" *British Journal of Middle Eastern Studies* Vol. 26, No. 2 (1999): 219–241.

Mallat, Chibli. "Introduction—Islamic Family Law: Variations on State Identity and Community Rights." In *Islamic Family Law,* eds. Chibli Mallat and Jane Connors (London: Graham and Trotman, 1993), 1–10.

———. *The Renewal of Islamic Law: Muhammad Baqer as-Sadr, Najaf and the Shi'i International.* Cambridge: Cambridge University Press, 1993.

———. *Shi'i Thought from the South of Lebanon.* Oxford: Centre for Lebanese Studies, 1988.

———. "Shi'ism and Sunnism in Iraq: Revisiting the Codes." In *Islamic Family Law,* eds. Chibli Mallat and Jane Connors (London: Graham and Trotman, 1993), 71–91.

Mani, Lata. *Contentious Traditions: The Debate on Sati in Colonial India.* Berkeley and Los Angeles: University of California Press, 1998.

Mann, Kristin and Richard Roberts. "Law in Colonial Africa." In *Law in Colonial Africa,* eds. Kristin Mann and Richard Roberts (Portsmouth, NH: Heinemann, 1991), 3–58.

Martin, David. *The Religious and the Secular: Studies in Secularization.* New York: Schocken Books, 1969.

Masters, Bruce. *Christians and Jews in the Ottoman Arab World: The Roots of Sectarianism.* Cambridge: Cambridge University Press, 2001.

Masud, Muhammad Khalid, Rudolph Peters and David S. Powers, eds. *Dispensing Justice in Islam: Qadis and Their Judgements.* Leiden: Brill, 2006.

Masuzawa, Tomoko. *The Invention of World Religions: Or, How European Univer-salism Was Preserved in the Language of Pluralism*. Chicago: University of Chicago Press, 2005.

Mazzaoui, Michael M. "Shi'ism and Ashura in South Lebanon." In *Ta'zieh and Ritual Drama in Iran*, ed. Peter Chelkowski (New York: New York University Press, 1979), 228–237.

McEoin, Denis. "Aspects of Militancy and Quietism in Imami Shi'ism." *Bulletin (British Society for Middle Eastern Studies)* (1984): 18–27.

Melchert, Christopher. *The Formation of the Sunni Schools of Law, 9th–10th Centuries C.E.* Leiden: Brill, 1997.

Méouchy, Nadine. "État et espaces communautaires dans le Liban sous Mandat français." *Maghreb, Machrek* 23 (1989): 88–95.

———— ed. *France, Syrie et Liban 1918–1946: les ambiguités et les dynamiques de la relation mandataire*. Damascus: IFEAD, 2002.

————. "Le Pacte National 1943–1946: les ambiguïtés d'un temps politique d'exception." In *Sélim Takla 1895–1945: une contribution à l'indépendance du Liban*, ed. Gérard D. Khoury (Paris, Beyrouth: Karthala, Dar An-Nahar, 2004), 461–500.

————. "La réforme des juridictions religieuses en Syrie et au Liban (1921–1939): raisons de la puissance mandataire et raisons des communautés." In *Le choc colonial et l'islam: les politiques religieuses des puissances coloniales en terres d'islam*, ed. Pierre-Jean Luizard (Paris: La Découverte, 2006), 359–382.

Méouchy, Nadine, and Peter Sluglett, eds. *The British and French Mandates in Comparative Perspective*. Leiden: Brill, 2004.

Meriwether, Margaret. *The Kin Who Count: Family and Society in Ottoman Aleppo, 1770–1840*. Austin: University of Texas Press, 1999.

Merry, Sally Engle. *Colonizing Hawai'i: The Cultural Power of Law*. Princeton, N.J.: Princeton University Press, 2000.

Mervin, Sabrina. "Les autorités religieuses dans le chiisme duodécimain contem-porain." *Archive de science sociale des religion* 125 (2004): 63–78.

————. "The Clerics of Jabal 'Amil and the Reform of Religious Teaching in Najaf Since the Beginning of the 20th Century." In *The Twelver Shia in Modern Times: Religious Culture and Political History*, eds. Rainer Brunner and Werner Ende (Leiden: Brill, 2001), 79–86.

————. "L'«entité alaouite», une création française." In *Le choc colonial et l'islam: les politiques religieuses des puissances coloniales en terres d'islam*, ed. Pierre-Jean Luizard (Paris: La Découverte, 2006), 343–58.

————. ed. *Le Hezbollah: état des lieux*. Paris: Sindbad, 2008.

————. "Les larmes et le sang des chiites: corps et pratiques rituelles lors des célébrations de 'ashûrâ' (Liban, Syrie)." *Revue des mondes musulmans et de la Méditerranée, N° 113–114, Le corps et le sacré dans l'Orient musulman* (November 2006): 153–166.

————. "Le Liban-Sud entre deux générations de réformistes." *Revue des Mondes Musulmans et la Méditerranée (Débats intellectuels au Moyen-Orient dans l'entre-deux-guerres)* 95–98 (2003): 257–266.

————. ed. *Les mondes chiites et l'Iran.* Paris: Karthala, 2007.

————. "La quête du savoir à naǧaf. Les études religieuses chez les chi'ites imâmites de la fin du XIXᵉ siècle à 1960." *Studia Islamica* 81 (1995): 165–185.

————. *Un réformisme chiite: Ulémas et lettrés du Ǧabal 'Amil (actuel Liban-Sud) de la fin de l'Empire ottoman à l'indépendance du Liban.* Paris: Éditions Karthala, CERMOC and IFEAD, 2000.

Messick, Brinkley. *The Calligraphic State: Textual Domination and History in a Muslim Society.* Berkeley and Los Angeles: University of California Press, 1993.

Millward, William G. "Aspects of Modernism in Shi'a Islam." *Studia Islamica* No. 37 (1973): 111–128.

Mir-Hosseini, Ziba. *Marriage on Trial: A Study in Comparative Islamic Family Law.* London: I. B. Tauris, 1999.

Mitchell, Timothy, ed. *Questions of Modernity.* Minneapolis: University of Minnesota Press, 2000.

Mizrahi, Jean-David. *Genèse de l'état mandataire: service des renseignements et bandes armées en Syrie et au Liban dans les années 1920.* Paris: Publications de la Sorbonne, 2003.

Modarressi, Hossein. *An Introduction To Shi'i Law.* London: Ithaca Press, 1984.

Momen, Moojan. *An Introduction to Shi'i Islam.* New Haven: Yale University Press, 1986.

Monsutti, Alessandro, Silvia Naef, and Farian Sabahi, eds. *The Other Shiites: From the Mediterranean to Central Asia.* Bern, New York: Peter Lang, 2007.

Moors, Annelies. *Women, Property, and Islam: Palestinian Experiences, 1920–1990.* New York: Cambridge University Press, 1995.

Moussavi, Ahmad Kazemi. "The Institutionalization of Marja'-i Taqlid in the Nineteenth Century Shi'ite Community." *The Muslim World* Vol. 84, No. 3–4 (1994): 279–299.

Muhajir, Ja'far. *Al-Hijra al-'amiliyya ila Iran fi al-'asr al-safawi: asbabuha al-tarikhiyya wa-nata'ijuha al-thaqafiyya wa-l-siyasiyya.* Beirut: Dar al-Rawda, 1989.

————. *Jabal 'Amil bayna al-shahidayn: al-haraka al-fikriyya fi Jabal 'Amil fi qarnayn (min awasit al-qarn al-thamin li-l-hijra/al-rab' 'ashr li-l-milad hatta awasit al-qarn al-'ashr/al-sadis 'ashr).* Damascus: IFPO, 2005.

Mufti, Aamir R. "Secularism and Minority: Elements of a Critique." *Social Text* No. 45 (1995): 75–96.

Mumtaz, Soofia, Jean-Luc Racine and Imran Anwar Ali, eds. *Pakistan: The Contours of State and Society.* Oxford: Oxford University Press, 2002.

Murray, David. *Colonial Justice: Justice, Morality, and Crime in the Niagara District, 1791–1849.* Toronto: Published for the Osgoode Society for Canadian Legal History by University of Toronto Press, 2002.

Mustafa, Qaysar. *Al-Shi'r al-'amili al-hadith fi janub Lubnan, 1900–1978*. Beirut: Dar al-Andalus, 1981.

Mu'tamar li-tarikh madinat Sur. *Watha'iq al-mu'tamar al-awwal li-tarikh madinat Sur: min al-'ahd al-finiqi hatta al-qarn al-'ishrin (15–16 Haziran 1996)*. Tyre: Muntada Sur al-Thaqafi, 1996.

———. *Watha'iq al-mu'tamar al-thani li-tarikh madinat Sur: al-tarikh al-ijtima'i wa-l-iqtisadi fi mukhtalif al-hiqab al-tarikhiyya (24–25 Ayyar 1997)*. Tyre: Muntada Sur al-Thaqafi, 1998.

Naef, Silvia. "Les chiites du Liban et le Mandat français: la position de la revue Al-'Irfan." In *Querelles privées et contestations publiques: le rôle de la presse dans la formation de l'opinion publique au Proche Orient*, eds. Christoph Herzog, Raoul Motika, and Michael Ursinus (Istanbul: Les Éditions Isis, 2002), 233–245.

———. "La presse en tant que moteur du renouveau culturel et litteraire: la revue chiite libanaise al-'Irfan." *Etudes asiatiques, revue de la societé Suisse-Asie* (1996): 385–397.

———. "Shi'i-Shiyu'i: Or, How to Become a Communist in a Holy City." In *The Twelver Shia in Modern Times: Religious Culture and Political History*, eds. Rainer Brunner and Werner Ende (Leiden: Brill, 2002), 255–267.

Nakash, Yitzhak. "An Attempt to Trace the Origin of the Rituals of 'Ashura'." *Die Welt des Islams* Vol. 33, No. 2 (1993): 161–181.

———. "The Conversion of Iraq's Tribes to Shi'ism." *IJMES* Vol. 26, No. 3 (1994): 443–463.

———. "The Nature of Shi'ism in Iraq." In *Ayatollahs, Sufis and Ideologues: State, Religion and Social Movements in Iraq*, ed. Faleh Abdul-Jabar (London: Saqi Books, 2002), 23–35.

———. *Reaching for Power: The Shi'a in the Modern Arab World*. Princeton, N.J.: Princeton University Press, 2006.

———. *The Shi'is of Iraq*. Princeton, N.J.: Princeton University Press, 1994.

Nasir, Jamal J. *The Islamic Law of Personal Status*. The Hague: Kluwer Law International, 2002.

Nasr, S. V. R. "Islam, the State and the Rise of Sectarian Militancy in Pakistan." In *Pakistan: Nationalism Without a Nation?* ed. Christophe Jaffrelot (New Delhi and Manohar: Centre de Sciences Humaines; London and New York: Zed Books; New York: Distributed in the USA exclusively by Palgrave, 2002), 85–114.

Nasr, Vali. *The Shia Revival: How Conflicts within Islam Will Shape the Future*. New York: Norton, 2006.

Nassar, Jamal R. "Sectarian Political Cultures: The Case of Lebanon." *The Muslim World* Vol. 85, No. 3–4 (1995): 246–265.

Nasution, Khoo Salma. "Colonial Intervention and Transformation of Muslim *Waqf* Settlements in Urban Penang: The Role of the Endowments Board." *Journal of Muslim Minority Affairs* Vol. 22, No. 2 (Oct. 2002): 299–315.

Newman, Andrew J. "The Myth of the Clerical Migration to Safawid Iran: Arab Shiite Opposition to 'Ali Al-Karaki and Safawid Shiism." *Die Welt des Islams* Vol. 33, No. 1 (1993): 66–112.

Norton, Augustus Richard. *Amal and the Shi'a: Struggle for the Soul of Lebanon.* Austin: University of Texas Press, 1987.

———. *Hezbollah: A Short History.* Princeton, N.J.: Princeton University Press, 2007.

———. "Ritual, Blood, and Shiite Identity: Ashura in Nabatiyya, Lebanon." *The Drama Review* Vol. 49, No. 4 (2005): 140–155.

Nur al-Din, Hasan. *'Ashura' fi al-adab al-'amili al-mu'asir.* Beirut: al-Dar al-Islamiyya, 1988.

Nur al-Din, Najib. *Aydiyulujiya al-rafd wa-l-muqawama: bahth ijtima'i siyasi fi zahirat al-la'iyya al-shi'iyya.* Beirut: Dar al-Hadi, 2004.

Oberoi, Harjot. *The Construction of Religious Boundaries: Culture, Identity, and Diversity in the Sikh World.* Chicago: University of Chicago Press, 1994.

Olmert, Joseph. "Shi'is and the Lebanese State." In *Shi'ism, Resistance and Revolution,* ed. Martin Kramer (Boulder, CO: Westview Press, 1987), 189–201.

Opwis, Felicitas. "*Maslaha* in Contemporary Islamic Legal Theory." *Islamic Law and Society* Vol. 12, No. 2 (2005): 182–223.

Ortayli, Ilber. "Les groupes hétérodoxes et l'administration ottomane." In *Syncretistic Religious Communities in the Near East,* eds. Krisztina Kehl-Bodrogi, Barbara Kellner-Heinkele, and Anke Otteer-Beaujean (Leiden: Brill, 1997), 205–211.

Osanloo, Arzoo. "Islamico-civil 'Rights Talk': Women, Subjectivity, and Law in Iranian Family Court." *American Ethnologist* Vol. 33, No. 2 (2006): 191–209.

Owen, Roger. "The Political Economy of Grand Liban, 1920–1970." In *Essays on the Crisis in Lebanon,* ed. Roger Owen (London: Ithaca Press, 1976), 23–32.

———. "The Study of Middle Eastern Industrial History: Notes on the Interrelationship between Factories and Small-Scale Manufacturing with Special References to Lebanese Silk and Egyptian Sugar, 1900–1930." *IJMES* Vol. 16, No. 4. (Nov., 1984): 475–487.

Pandey, Gyanendra. *The Construction of Communalism in Colonial North India.* Delhi and New York: Oxford University Press, 1990.

———. "Can a Muslim be an Indian?" *CSSH* Vol. 41, No. 4 (Oct., 1999): 608–629.

Pedersen, Susan. "The Meaning of the Mandates System: An Argument." *Geschichte und Gesellschaft* 32 (2006): 560–582.

Peirce, Leslie P. *Morality Tales: Law and Gender in the Ottoman Court of Aintab.* Berkeley and Los Angeles: University of California Press, 2003.

Peletz, Michael G. *Islamic Modern: Religious Courts and Cultural Politics in Malaysia.* Princeton, N.J.: Princeton University Press, 2002.

Peters, Rudolph. "What Does It Mean to Be an Offical Madhhab? Hanafism and the Ottoman Empire." In *The Islamic School of Law: Evolution, Devolution, and Progress*, eds. Peri Bearman, Rudolph Peters, and Frank E. Vogel (Cambridge, Mass.: Islamic Legal Studies Program, Harvard Law School: Distributed by Harvard University Press, 2005), 147–158.

Peterson, Derek R. and Darren R. Walhof, eds. *The Invention of Religion: Rethinking Belief in Politics and History*. New Brunswick, N.J.: Rutgers University Press, 2002.

Pinault, David. *Horse of Karbala: Muslim Devotional Life in India* London: Palgrave, 2001.

———. "Shia Lamentation Rituals and Reinterpretations of the Doctrine of Intercession: Two Cases from Modern India." *History of Religions* Vol. 38, No. 3 (1999): 285–305.

Polk, William. *The Opening of South Lebanon, 1788–1840: A Study of the Impact of the West on the Middle East*. Cambridge, Mass.: Harvard University Press, 1963.

Powers, David S., "Kadijustiz or Qadi-Justice? A Paternity Dispute from Fourteenth-Century Morocco." *Islamic Law and Society* Vol. 1, No. 3 (1994): 332–366.

———. *Law, Society, and Culture in the Maghrib, 1300–1500*. Cambridge: Cambridge University Press, 2002.

———. "Orientalism, Colonialism, and Legal History: The Attack on Family Endowments in Algeria and India." *CSSH* Vol. 31, No. 3 (Jul., 1989): 535–571.

Provence, Michael. *The Great Syrian Revolt and the Rise of Arab Nationalism*. Austin: University of Texas Press, 2005.

al-Qasim, Muhammad. *Thawrat al-tanzih: "Risalat al-tanzih" taliha mawaqif minha wa-ara' fi al-Sayyid Muhsin al-Amin*. Beirut: Dar al-Jadid, 1996.

al-Qattan, Najwa. "Litigants and Neighbors: The Communal Topography of Ottoman Damascus." *CSSH* Vol. 44, No. 3 (Jul., 2002): 511–533.

Rabbath, Edmond. *La formation historique du Liban politique et constitutionnel: essai de synthèse*. Beirut: Université Libanaise, 1973.

al-Rakini, Haydar Rida. *Jabal 'Amil fi qarn (1163–1247 H/1749–1832 M)*. Beirut: Dar al-Fikr al-Lubnani, 1997.

Ranstorp, Magnus. *Hizb'allah in Lebanon: The Politics of the Western Hostage Crisis*. New York: St. Martin's Press, 1997.

al-Rasheed, Madawi. "The Shia of Saudi Arabia: A Minority in Search of Cultural Authenticity." *British Journal of Middle Eastern Studies* 25, No. 1 (1998): 121–138.

Redissi, Hamadi. *Le pacte de nadjd, ou Comment l'islam sectaire est devenue l'islam*. Paris: Seuil, 2007.

Reinkowski, Maurus. *Ottoman 'Multiculturalism'? The Example of the Confessional System in Lebanon*. Beirut: 1999.

Roberts, Richard. *Litigants and Households: African Disputes and Colonial Courts in the French Soudan, 1895–1912*. Portsmouth, NH: Heinemann, 2005.

Robinson, David. "French 'Islamic' Policy and Practice in Late Nineteenth-Century Senegal." *Journal of African History* Vol. 29, No. 3 (1988): 415–435.

———. *Paths of Accommodation: Muslim Societies and French Colonial Authorities in Senegal and Mauritania, 1880–1920.* Athens and Oxford: Ohio University Press and James Currey, 2000.

Rodrigue, Aron. "Difference and Tolerance in the Ottoman Empire: Interview by Nancy Reynolds." *Stanford Humanities Review* Vol. 5, No. 1 (1995): 81–90

———. "From *Millet* to Minority: Turkish Jewry." In *Paths of Emancipation: Jews, States, and Citizenship*, eds. Pierre Birnbaum and Ira Katznelson (Princeton, N.J.: Princeton University Press, 1995), 238–261.

Rogan, Eugene L. "Sectarianism and Social Conflict in Damascus: The 1860 Events Reconsidered." *Arabica: Revue d'Etudes Arabes* Vol. 51, No. 4 (2004): 493–511.

Rondot, Pierre. *Les institutions politiques du Liban: des communautés traditionelles à l'état moderne.* Paris: Institut d'études de L'Orient contemporain, 1947.

Rosen, Lawrence. *The Anthropology of Justice: Law as Culture in Islamic Society.* Cambridge: Cambridge University Press, 1989.

———. "Islamic 'Case Law' and the Logic of Consequence." In *History and Power in the Study of Law: New Directions in Legal Anthropology*, eds. June Starr and Jane F. Collier (Ithaca, NY: Cornell University Press, 1989), 302–319.

Rubin, Uri. "'Al-Walad Li-L-Firāsh': On the Islamic Campaign Against «Zinā»." *Studia Islamica* No. 78 (1993): 5–26.

Saad-Ghorayeb, Amal. "Factors Conducive to the Politicization of the Lebanese Shi'a and the Emergence of Hizbu'llah." *Journal of Islamic Studies* Vol. 14, No. 3 (2003): 273–307.

Saada, Emmanuelle. "The Empire of Law: Dignity, Prestige, and Domination in the Colonial Situation." *French Politics, Culture and Society* Vol. 20, No. 2 (2002): 98–120.

Saadeh, Sofia. "Basic Issues Concerning the Personal Status Laws in Lebanon." In *Religion between Violence and Reconciliation*, ed. Thomas Scheffler (Beirut: Orient-Institut, 2002), 449–456.

Sachedina, Abdulaziz Abdulhussein. *Islamic Messianism: The Idea of Mahdi in Twelver Shi'ism.* Albany, NY: State University of New York Press, 1981.

———. *The Just Ruler (al-sultān al-'ādil) in Shī'ite Islam: The Comprehensive Authority of the Jurist in Imamite Jurisprudence.* New York: Oxford University Press, 1988.

Sa'd, Hasan Muhammad. *Jabal 'Amil bayna al-atrak wa-l-faransiyyin, 1914–1920.* Beirut: Dar al-Katib, 1980.

Salamé, Ghassan. "'Strong' and 'Weak' States: A Qualified Return to the Muqaddimah." In *The Arab State*, ed. Luciani Giacomo (Berkeley and Los Angeles: University of California Press, 1990), 29–64.

Salati, Marco. "Presence and Role of the *Sadat* in and from Ǧabal 'Amil (14th–18th Centuries)." *Oriente Moderno* Vol. 79, No. 2 (September 1999): 597–627.

———. "Toleration, Persecution and Local Realities: Observations on Shiism in the Holy Places and the *Bilad Al-Sham* (16th–17th Centuries)." In *Convegno sul tema (15 April 1991, Roma), La Shi'a nell'impero ottomano.* (Rome: Academia nazionale Dei Lincei; Fondazione Leone Caetani, 1993), 121–148.

Salibi, Kamal. *A House of Many Mansions: The History of Lebanon Reconsidered.* Berkeley and Los Angeles: University of California Press, 1988.

———. *The Modern History of Lebanon.* London: Weidenfeld and Nicolson, 1965.

Salih, Farhan. *Janub Lubnan: waq'uhu wa-qadayah.* Beirut: Dar al-Tali'a, 1973.

Salih, Hasan Muhammad. *Antulujiyat al-adab al-'amili: al-adab al-'amili min al-taqalid ila al-tajdid* (3 vols.). Beirut: Dar al-Juman, 1997.

Salzmann, Ariel. "Citizens in Search of a State: The Limits of Political Participation in the Late Ottoman Empire." In *Extending Citizenship, Reconfiguring States,* eds. Michael Hanagan and Charles Tilly (Lanham: Rowman & Littlefield Publishers Inc, 1999), 37–66.

Sarr, Dominique and Richard Roberts. "The Jurisdiction of Muslim Tribunals in Colonial Senegal, 1857–1932." In *Law in Colonial Africa,* eds. Kristin Mann and Richard Roberts (Portsmouth, NH: Heinemann, 1991), 131–145.

Savory, Roger, *Iran under the Safavids.* Cambridge: Cambridge University Press, 1980.

———. "The Problem of Sovereignty in an Ithna Ashari ("Twelver") Shi'i State." In *Religion and Politics in the Middle East,* ed. Michael Curtis (Boulder, CO: Westview Press, 1981), 129–138.

al-Sayf, Tawfiq. *Nazariyyat al-sulta fi al-fiqh al-shi'i.* Casablanca: al-Markaz al-Thaqafi al-'Arabi, 2002.

Schneider, Irene. "Religious and State Jurisdiction during Nasir Al-Din Shah's Reign." In *Religion and Society in Qajar Iran,* ed. Robert Gleave (London and New York: RoutledgeCurzon, 2005), 84–110.

Schölch, Alexander. "Was There a Feudal System in Ottoman Lebanon and Palestine?" In *Palestine in the Late Ottoman Period: Political, Social and Economic Transformation,* ed. David Kushner (Jerusalem: Yad Izhak Ben-Zvi, 1986), 130–145.

Seguin, Jacques. *Le Liban-Sud: espace périphérique, espace convoité.* Paris: L'Harmattan, 1989.

Semerdjian, Elyse. *"Off the Straight Path": Illicit Sex, Law, and Community in Ottoman Aleppo.* Syracuse, NY: Syracuse University Press, 2008.

Seng, Yvonne J. "Standing at the Gates of Justice: Women in the Law Courts of Early Sixteenth-Century Üsküdar, Istanbul." In *Contested States: Law,*

Hegemony and Resistance, ed. Mindie Lazarus-Black and Susan F. Hirsch (New York: Routledge, 1993), 207–230.

Shaery-Eisenlohr, Roshanack. *Shi'ite Lebanon: Transnational Religion and the Making of National Identities.* New York: Columbia University Press, 2008.

———. "Territorializing Piety: Genealogy, Transnationalism, and Shi'ite Politics in Modern Lebanon." *CSSH* Vol. 51, No. 3 (Jul., 2009): 533–562.

Shaham, Ron. *Family and the Courts in Modern Egypt: A Study Based on Decisions by the Shari'a Courts 1900–1955.* Leiden: Brill, 1997.

al-Shahid, Muhammad. *Li-madha sumiya Jabal 'Amil bi-ard Abi Dharr al-Ghifari: 'ard tahqiqi tarikhi wa-musawwar 'an maji' wa-iqamat Abi Dharr fi bilad al-sham wa-taswir maydani li-maqami Abi Dharr fi Mays al-Jabal wa-Sarafand.* Beirut: Maktabat Sayyid al-Shuhada', 1998.

Shams al-Din, Muhammad Ja'far. *Al-Waqf wa-ahkamuhu fi al-fiqh al-islami wa-l-qawanin al-lubnaniyya: dirasa muqarana.* Beirut: Dar al-Hadi, 2005.

Shanahan, Rodger. *The Shi'a of Lebanon: Clans, Parties and Clerics.* London: Tauris Academic Studies, 2005.

Shararah, Waddah. *Dawlat Hizb Allah: Lubnan mujtama'an islamiyyan.* Beirut: Dar al-Nahar, 1996.

———. *Transformations d'une manifestation religieuse dans un village du Liban-Sud (Ashura).* Beirut: Université Libanaise, 1968.

———. *Al-Umma al-qalqa: al-'amiliyyun wa-l-'asabiyya al-'amiliyya 'ala 'atabat al-dawla al-lubnaniyya.* Beirut: Dar al-Nahar, 1996.

Shehadeh, Lamia Rustum. "The Legal Status of Married Women in Lebanon." *IJMES* Vol. 30, No. 4 (1998): 501–519.

Shehadi, Nadim. *The Idea of Lebanon: Economy and State in the Cénacle Libanais, 1946–54.* Oxford: Centre for Lebanese Studies, 1987.

Shu'ayb, 'Ali 'Abd al-Mun'im. *Matalib Jabal 'Amil: al-wahda, al-musawa fi Lubnan al-Kabir, 1900–1936.* Beirut: al-Mu'assasa al-Jam'iyya, 1987.

Sindawi, Khalid. "Visit to the Tomb of Al-Husayn B. 'Ali in Shiite Poetry: First to Fifth Centuries A.H. (8th–11th Centuries C.E.)." *Journal of Arabic Literature* Vol. 37, No. 2 (2006): 230–258.

Skovgaard-Petersen, Jacob. "Levantine State Muftis: An Ottoman Legacy?" In *Late Ottoman Society: The Intellectual Legacy*, ed. Elisabeth Özdalga (London: RoutledgeCurzon, 2005), 274–288.

Sluglett, Peter and Marion Farouk-Sluglett. "The Application of the 1858 Land Code in Greater Syria: Some Preliminary Observations." In *Land Tenure and Social Transformation in the Middle East*, ed. Tarif Khalidi, (Beirut: American University of Beirut, 1984), 409–424.

———. "Some Reflections on the Sunni/Shi'i Question in Iraq." *Bulletin (British Society for Middle Eastern Studies)* Vol. 5, No. 2 (1978): 79–87.

Sommer, Matthew H. *Sex, Law, and Society in Late Imperial China.* Stanford, CA: Stanford University Press, 2000.

Soueid, Mohammad. "Omar Amiralay, the Circassian, Syrian, Lebanese." In *Insights into Syrian Cinema: Essays and Conversations with Contemporary Filmmakers,* ed. Rasha Salti (New York: Rattapallax Press, 2006), 99–111.

Spagnolo, John. *France and Ottoman Lebanon: 1861–1914.* London: Ithaca Press, 1977.

Springett, Bernard H. *Secret Sects of Syria and the Lebanon.* London: Kegan Paul, 2007 [1922?].

Starr, June and Jane F. Collier, eds. *History and Power in the Study of Law: New Directions in Legal Anthropology.* Ithaca, NY: Cornell University Press, 1994.

Stein, Jeff. "Can You Tell A Sunni from a Shiite?" *The New York Times,* October 17, 2006.

Steinmetz, George, ed. *State/Culture: State-Formation After the Cultural Turn.* Ithaca, NY: Cornell University Press, 1999.

Stewart, Devin J. *Islamic Legal Orthodoxy: Twelver Shiite Responses to the Sunni Legal System.* Salt Lake City: University of Utah Press, 1998.

———. "The Portrayal of an Academic Rivalry: Najaf and Qum in the Writings and Speeches of Khomeini, 1964–78." In *The Most Learned of the Shi'a: The Institution of the Marja' Taqlid,* ed. Linda Walbridge (New York: Oxford University Press, 2001), 216–229.

Stoten, D., ed. *A State Without a Nation.* Durham: University of Durham, Centre for Middle Eastern and Islamic Studies, 1992.

Suny, Ronald Grigor. "Constructing Primordialism: Old Histories for New Nations." *Journal of Modern History* 73 (2001): 862–896.

Tabataba'i, Hossein Modarressi. *An Introduction to Shi'i Law: A Bibliographical Study.* London: Ithaca Press, 1984.

Takim, Liyakat N. *The Heirs of the Prophet: Charisma and Religious Authority in Shi'ite Islam.* Albany, NY: State University of New York Press, 2006.

Taqi al-Din, Sulayman. "Al-Janub al-lubnani bi-ri'ayat al-istiqlal." In *Safahat min tarikh Jabal 'Amil,* ed. Ibrahim Beydoun (Beirut: al-Majlis al-Thaqafi li-Lubnan al-Janubi; Dar al-Farabi, 1979), 131–57.

———. *Al-Qada' fi Lubnan.* Beirut: Dar al-Jadid, 1996.

Thompson, Elizabeth. *Colonial Citizens: Republican Rights, Paternal Privilege and Gender in French Syria and Lebanon.* New York: Columbia University Press, 2000.

Toufiq, Fadi. *Bilad Allah al-dayyiqa: "al-dahiyya" ahlan wa-hizban.* Beirut: Dar al-Jadid, 2005.

Toungara, Jeanne Maddox. "Inventing the African Family: Gender and Family Law Reform in Cote d'Ivoire." *Journal of Social History* 28, no. 1 (1994): 37–61.

Traboulsi, Fawwaz. *Silat bi-la wasl: Mishal Chiha wa-l-aydiyulujiya al-lubnaniyya.* Beirut: Riad el-Rayyes Books, 1999.

Tucker, Ernest. "Nadir Shah and the Ja'fari *Madhhab* Reconsidered." *Iranian Studies* 27 (1994): 163–179.

Tucker, Judith E. *In the House of the Law: Gender and Islamic Law in Ottoman Syria and Palestine.* Berkeley and Los Angeles: University of California Press, 1998.

Van Leeuwen, Richard. *Notables and Clergy in Mount Lebanon: The Khazin Sheikhs and the Maronite Church (1736–1840).* Leiden: E. J. Brill, 1994.

Viswanathan, Gauri. *Outside the Fold: Conversion, Modernity, and Belief.* Princeton, N.J.: Princeton University Press, 1998.

Walbridge, Linda, ed. *The Most Learned of the Shi'a: The Institution of the Marja' Taqlid.* New York: Oxford University Press, 2001.

Waldman, Marilyn Robinson. "Tradition as a Modality of Change: Islamic Examples." *History of Religions* Vol. 25, No. 4 (1986): 318–340.

Wansbrough, John E. *The Sectarian Milieu: Content and Composition of Islamic Salvation History.* New York: Oxford University Press, 1978.

Watenpaugh, Keith David, *Being Modern in the Middle East: Revolution, Nationalism, Colonialism, and the Arab Middle Class.* Princeton, N.J.: Princeton University Press, 2006.

———. "Towards a New Category of Colonial Theory: Colonial Cooperation and the *Survivors' Bargain*—The Case of the Post-Genocide Armenian Community of Syria under French Mandate." In *The British and French Mandates in Comparative Perspectives*, eds. Nadine Méouchy, and Peter Sluglett (Leiden: Brill, 2004), 597–622.

Weber, Eugen. *Peasants into Frenchman: The Modernization of Rural France, 1870–1914.* Stanford, CA: Stanford University Press, 1976.

Wilder, Gary. *The French Imperial Nation-State: Negritude and Colonial Humanism between the Two World Wars.* Chicago: The University of Chicago Press, 2005.

———. "Practicing Citizenship in Imperial Paris." In *Civil Society and the Political Imagination in Africa*, eds. John L. Comaroff and Jean Comaroff (Chicago: The University of Chicago Press, 2000), 44–71.

Winter, Stefan. ""Un lys dans des épines": Maronites et Chiites au Mont Liban, 1698–1763." *Arabica: Revue d'études arabes* Vol. 51, No. 4 (2004): 478–492.

———. "The Nusayris Before the Tanzimat in the Eyes of Ottoman Provincial Administrators, 1804–1834." In *From the Syrian Land to the States of Syria and Lebanon*, eds. Thomas Philipp and Christoph Schumann (Würzburg: Ergon in Kommission, 2004), 97–112.

———. "Shiite Emirs and Ottoman Authorities: The Campaign Against the Hamadas of Mt Lebanon, 1693–1694." *Archivum Ottomanicum* 18 (2000): 209–245.

Zaman, Muhammad Qasim. "Sectarianism in Pakistan: The Radicalization of Shi'i and Sunni Identities." *Modern Asian Studies* Vol. 32, No. 3 (1998): 689–716.

———. *The Ulama in Contemporary Islam: Custodians of Change.* Princeton, N.J.: Princeton University Press, 2002.

Zamir, Meir. *The Formation of Modern Lebanon.* Ithaca, NY: Cornell University Press, 1988.

———. *Lebanon's Quest: The Road to Independence.* London: I. B. Tauris, 2000.

———. "Politics and Violence in Lebanon." *The Jerusalem Quarterly* No. 25 (1982): 3–26.

Zarcone, Thierry. "La communauté iranienne d'Istanbul à la fin du XIXe et au début du XXe siècle." In *Convegno sul tema (15 April 1991, Roma), La Shi'a nell'impero ottomano* (Rome: Accademia nazionale dei Lincei; Fondazione Leone Caetani, 1993), 57–83.

———. "La situation du chi'isme à Istanbul au XIXe et au début du XXe siècle." In *Les iraniens D'Istanbul,* eds. Thierry Zarcone and F. Zarinebaf-Shahr (Istanbul-Tehran: IFEA/IFRI, 1993), 97–111.

al-Zayn, 'Ali. *Fusul min tarikh al-shi'a fi Lubnan.* Beirut: Dar al-Kalima li-l-Nashr, 1979.

———. *Li-l-bahth 'an tarikhina fi Lubnan.* Beirut: 1973.

Zayn al-Din, 'Aida. *Al-Tatawwur al-iqtisadi wa-l-ijtima'i wa-l-siyasi li-madinat Ba'labakk fi 'ahd al-intidab al-faransi 1920–1943.* Beirut: Dar al-Farabi, 2005.

Zisser, Eyal. *Lebanon: The Challenge of Independence.* London: I. B. Tauris, 2000.

Zubaida, Sami. *Law and Power in the Islamic World.* London: I. B. Tauris, 2003.

Unpublished Theses and Dissertations

Abisaab, Malek. "A History of Women Tobacco Workers: Labor, Community and Social Transformation in Lebanon, 1895–1997." PhD diss., State University of New York—Binghamton, 2001.

Chalabi, Tamara Ahmad. "Community and Nation-State: The Shi'is of Jabal 'Amil and the New Lebanon, 1918–1943." PhD diss., Harvard University, 2003.

Doumani, Osama Alexander. "The Tobacco Growers of Southern Lebanon: Politics and Economics of Change." PhD diss., University of California, Berkeley, 1974.

Early, E. A. "The 'Amiliyya Society of Beirut: A Case Study of an Emerging Urban Za'im." Master's thesis, American University of Beirut, 1971.

Fattuni, 'Ali 'Abed. "Tatawwur al-ta'lim fi madaris al-jam'iyya al-khayriyya al-is-lamiyya al-'amiliyya fi Bayrut min khilal watha'iqiha al-asliyya 1923–1943." PhD diss., Lebanese University, 1986.

Fattuni, Muhammad. "Tatawwur al-tarbiyya wa-l-ta'lim fi madaris al-jam'iyya al-khayriyya al-islamiyya al-'amiliyya min khilal watha'iqiha al-asliyya (1943–1975)." PhD diss., Lebanese University, 1992.

Hakim-Dowek, Carol. "The Origins of the Lebanese National Idea, 1840–1914." D. Phil., University of Oxford, 1997.

Jaber, Hicham. "Les chiites dans la vie politique du Liban avant et après l'indépendance." DEA, Université de Paris IV, 1993

Jaber, Mounzer, "Pouvoir et société au Jabal Amil de 1749 à 1920 dans la conscience des chroniques chiites et dans un essai d'Interpretation." Thèse de 3e cycle, Université de Paris IV, 1978.

Jaber, Talal, "Chiites et pouvoir politique au Liban 1967–1974: contribution à une approche socio-religieuse." Thèse de 3e cycle, Université de Paris VII, 1980.

Jaffal, Fatima Mahmoud, "Rashid Yusuf Baydoun 1889–1971." Master's thesis, Lebanese University, 1990.

Karaki, Haydar Muhammad. "Al-Khasa'is al-dimughrafiyya wa-l-ijtima'iyya li-zahiratay al-zawaj wa-l-talaq 'ind al-shi'a min khilal al-mahkama al-ja'fariyya fi Bayrut 1978–1982." Master's thesis, Lebanese University, 1983.

Kern, Karen M. "The Prohibition of Sunni-Shi'i Marriages in the Ottoman Empire: A Study of Ideologies." PhD diss., Columbia University, 1999.

Ménager, Marianne. "L'intégration politique des communautés chiites du Djebel Amel et de la Biqa' au Liban sous le Mandat Français 1920–1943." Mémoire de maîtrise, Université d'Angers, 2002.

San Geroteo, Lucie. "La construction identitaire d'une communauté religieuse au Liban: les chiites (1920–1964)." Mémoire de maîtrise, Université de Paris I, 2001.

Shaery-Eisenlohr, Roshanack. "Constructing Lebanese Shi'ite Nationalism: Transnationalism, Shi'ism, and the Lebanese State." PhD diss., University of Chicago, 2005.

Soubra, Hala. "La théorie de l'état dans la pensée chiite libaniase contemporaine." DEA, Université de Paris I (Sorbonne), 1990.

Zulkifli. "The Struggle of the Shi'is in Indonesia." PhD diss., University of Leiden, 2009.

Acknowledgments

This book evolved out of a research agenda now over five years old and is indebted to the material support of more than a few institutions. I would like to thank the Stanford History Department and its staff as well as the Graduate School of Humanities and Sciences for providing financial and administrative assistance throughout my tenure as a graduate student. I am grateful to both the Arabic School at Middlebury College and the Center for Arabic Study Abroad at the American University in Cairo for providing me with the financial aid, institutional support, and invaluable time necessary for the acquisition of language skills that allowed me to carry out the research for this project. I was granted generous funding for archival research carried out in Lebanon and France over the course of several years by the Fulbright-Hays Dissertation Research Program, the Social Science Research Council-American Council of Learned Societies International Dissertation Research Fellowship (funded by the Andrew W. Mellon Foundation), the Stanford History Department, the Department of Near Eastern Studies at Princeton University, and the William F. Milton Fund of Harvard University.

Portions of chapter two appeared in different forms in "The Cultural Politics of Shi'i Modernism: Morality and Gender in Early 20th-Century Lebanon." *IJMES* Vol. 39, No. 2 (May 2007): 249–270; an earlier version of chapter four appeared as "Institutionalizing Sectarianism: The Lebanese Ja'fari Court and Shi'i Society Under the French Mandate." *Islamic Law and Society* Vol. 15, No. 3 (2008): 371–407; and an earlier version of chapter five appeared as "Practicing Sectarianism in Mandate Lebanon: Shi'i Cemeteries, Religious Patrimony, and the Everyday Politics of Difference." *Journal of Social History* Vol. 43, No. 3 (March 2010): 707–733.

In Lebanon, from the spring of 2005 until the summer of 2006, I was a research affiliate at the Center for Arab and Middle Eastern Studies (CAMES) at the American University of Beirut (AUB). The enjoyable period I spent at CAMES was made much more so thanks to the hospitality and kindness of Professor John Meloy, then the Director of the Center, as well as the warmth and assistance of the staff, especially Mrs. Nina Ghattas; in addition, the librarians at the AUB Jafet

Library were helpful with my many requests. At the Institut Français du Proche-Orient (IFPO) in Beirut, Sabrina Mervin provided regular professional and emotional support throughout the tumultuous period of overseas field research. I would like to sincerely thank the President of the Lebanese Ja'fari Court, Shaykh Hassan 'Awwad for approving my request to do research in the courts. The staff of the Ja'fari courts in Beirut and South Lebanon was especially adept at making me feel particularly welcome; Abu Ahmad and Abu Rabi' helped to make my research rewarding, both professionally and personally. A unique assortment of people living in Beirut at the same time made my period of fieldwork into a rich experience. For friendship and guidance I thank 'Abbas Beydoun, Mounzer Jaber, Fadi Toufiq, Iman Humaydan Younes, and Lokman Slim; I am also grateful for Mark Ajluni, Lee Fredrix, 'Abir, Lulu, and Umm Adham, Ghassan and his entire family, especially Hajj 'Ali, Ellen Fleischmann, Michael Provence, Cyrus Schayegh, and Mary Wilson. In France, the staff of the Centre des Archives Diplomatiques at the Ministère des Affaires Étrangères in Nantes was extremely organized, cheerful, and unusually supportive throughout the pleasant time I spent doing research there. Paris would not be the same without Keith, Stephanie, and, now, Zoe.

Throughout my relatively short academic career, I have had the exceptional good fortune of working with skillful and selfless advisers. Joel Beinin has indefatigably provided unabashed criticism, insight, and inspiration. Ahmad Dallal has been an incomparable mentor whose scholarly erudition is rivaled only by his kindness. Aron Rodrigue helped to keep me grounded and offered important advice at key moments. Beshara Doumani has been unflappably supportive from the start. All of this unmitigated encouragement is exactly as it should be but seems, somehow, unusual and all too rare.

My editor at Harvard University Press, Kathleen McDermott, employed just the right mix of subtle pressure and supportive encouragement. Marianna Vertullo was tireless and consistently positive as she shepherded me through the grueling stages of copyediting and proofreading. I would like to thank the anonymous readers for the press for helping to make this a better and hopefully more important book. I am grateful to Carol Hakim, Jens Hanssen, Sabrina Mervin, and Peter Sluglett for sharing exceedingly useful comments with me at a very late stage in the game. More than one eleventh-hour reading by Siobhan Phillips saved my life. I would like to thank Scott Walker for designing lovely maps for my book; thanks also to Joseph Garver and the Harvard Map Collection for their cheerful assistance. Michael Cook and the Department of Near Eastern Studies graciously provided me with the wonderful opportunity of spending the 2007–08 academic year in Princeton through a postdoctoral fellowship; that year was made even more enjoyable because of Cemil Aydin, Julianne Hammer, Mirjam Kunkler, Michael Laffan and the entire Laffan clan, Melani McAlister, and Lauren Scott. The privilege of joining the Society of Fellows at Harvard has afforded me more time to work on this book, the opportunity to let other interests run wild and flourish, and the happy occasion to live in Cambridge. The staff at Widener Library has been tireless in my requests for materials. I would like to extend a special thanks to Diana Morse and Kelly Katz, the lifeblood of the Society, and Wally Gilbert, its chairman. I am grateful to my fellow fellows for helping me enjoy this extended "time off": Diana Allan, Tania Rinaldi Barkat, Hadi Barkat, Siobhan Phillips, Manu Prakash, David Smyth, and Rob Pringle. Over these peripatetic years, I would not have survived without the support of friends who I thank here, in no particular order: Kirk Johnson, Ian Read, Nirvana Tanoukhi, Brendan and Hilary Neagle, Marcy Brink-Danan, Zaki Haider, Adam Weintraub, Toby Jones, Steve Chesney, Shira Robinson, Crystal Li and Andrew Cohen, David Pardes, and Chris, Martina, and Landon Heppner.

I could not have written this book without my family. The Feldmans and Yowells have been welcoming me for what seems like a lifetime already and I thank them for that. My parents and my sisters have always been a source of unconditional love. My East Bay family—Wendy, Allen, Micayla, and Harrison, and Diane, David, and Alexander—continue to endow me with homes away from home. That being said, I'm so glad to live in a world where I can call Shirley Feldman home. For her abundant generosity, her extraordinary care, and her steady devotion, I can only continue to beg for forgiveness. This book is dedicated to her, my wife, with immeasurable love and abiding gratitude.

Index